Liverpool

JOSEPH SHARPLES

with contributions by
RICHARD POLLARD

PEVSNER ARCHITECTURAL GUIDES
YALE UNIVERSITY PRESS
NEW HAVEN & LONDON

For my mother, and in memory of my father

YALE UNIVERSITY PRESS
NEW HAVEN AND LONDON
302 Temple Street, New Haven CT06511
47 Bedford Square, London WC1B 3DP

www.pevsner.co.uk
www.lookingatbuildings.org
www.yalebooks.co.uk
www.yalebooks.com

Published 2004
10 9 8 7 6 5 4

Set in Adobe Minion by SNP Best-set Typesetter Ltd., Hong Kong
Printed in Singapore by CS Graphics

Library of Congress Cataloging-in-Publication Data

Sharples, Joseph, 1961–
Liverpool / Joseph Sharples ; with contributions by Richard Pollard Pevsner.
    p. cm. – (Pevsner architectural guides (New Haven, Conn.))
    Includes bibliographical references and index.
    ISBN 0-300-10258-5 (pbk. : alk. paper)
    1. Architecture – England – Liverpool – Guidebooks. 2. Architecture – England – Liverpool Region – Guidebooks. 3. Liverpool (England) – Buildings, structures, etc. – Guidebooks. 4. Liverpool (England) – Guidebooks. I. Pevsner, Richard Pollard. II. Title. III. Series.
    NA971.L5 S48 2004
    720´.9427´53 – dc22
                                    2003024154

Liverpool

PEVSNER ARCHITECTURAL GUIDES

Founding Editor: Nikolaus Pevsner

PEVSNER ARCHITECTURAL GUIDES

The Buildings of England series was created and largly written
by Sir Nikolaus Pevsner (1902–83). First editions of the county
volumes were published by Penguin Books between 1951 and 1974.
The continuing programme of revisions and new volumes has
been supported by research financed through the Buildings Books
Trust since 1994.

The Buildings Books Trust gratefully acknowledges a major grant
from English Heritage towards the cost of research, writing and
illustrations for this volume, as well as assistance with photography.

Contents

How to use this book

This book is designed as a practical guide for exploring the buildings of Liverpool and its inner suburbs. The divisions between the centre, the docks and the inner city sections are shown on the map on p. xii. Six Major Buildings or groups of buildings have entries of their own. The docks are treated in a separate section, with an introduction and two Walks. The rest of the inner city is covered by eight further Walks, each of which has its own street map showing the area covered. The last section suggests three excursions to areas of outstanding interest nearby, two of which are on the Cheshire side. Outer Liverpool will be treated in more detail in the forthcoming *Buildings of England* hardback volume, *Lancashire: Liverpool and the South West*.

In addition, certain topics are singled out for special attention and presented in separate boxes:

History and Planning: Seven Ancient Streets p. 6, Population p. 10, Pier Head Expansion p. 70, Water Supply p. 266

Lost Buildings: Liverpool Castle p. 4, Lost C18 Churches p. 179

Domestic Building: Court Housing and Cellar Dwellings p. 8, Terraced Houses p. 243, Housing Co-Operatives and Community Architecture p. 272

St George's Hall: Relief Sculptures p. 52, Heating and Ventilation p. 58

Patrons and Architects: Charles Reilly and the Liverpool School of Architecture p. 218, The Fosters p. 232, The Horsfalls: Liverpool Church Builders p. 247

Cathedrals: Sculpture by Edward Carter Preston (Anglican Cathedral) p. 77, Metropolitan Cathedral Repairs p. 90

Building Techniques: Ferro-Concrete (Royal Liver Building) p. 68, Fireproofing p. 167

The Docks: Dock and River Wall Design p. 96, Redeveloping Albert, Canning and Salthouse Docks, 1960–80 p. 106, Albert Dock: Repair and Reuse p. 109, Hydraulic Power p. 115, Getting from River to Dock: an Engineering Challenge p. 117, Construction and Safety p. 127

Transport and Movement: The Liverpool Overhead Railway p. 100, Elevated Walkways p. 160, The Liverpool & Manchester Railway p. 188

Trade and Industry: Rope Walks p. 196, C18 and Early C19 Warehouses p. 205

1. Memorial to the Heroes of the Marine Engine Room, St Nicholas Place, Pier Head, by William Goscombe John (unveiled 1916), detail

Acknowledgements

This book is based on the Liverpool section of Nikolaus Pevsner's *South Lancashire*, published in 1969. Our greatest debt is therefore owed to him. We also reused the research notes prepared for that book by the late Edward Hubbard, and can only repeat Sir Nikolaus's praise for their thoroughness and precision.

Liverpool would not have been possible without a major grant from English Heritage to cover the costs of research and writing. Most of the photographs were also supplied by English Heritage, and we are grateful to its photographers, especially Tony Perry and Bob Skingle. While this book was in preparation, English Heritage was undertaking its own work on aspects of Liverpool's historic environment. Its investigators Sarah Brown, John Cattell, Colum Giles and Ian Goodall generously shared their findings, and Peter de Figueiredo made available his research on the Pier Head before publication.

A book such as this depends to a great extent on the cooperation of librarians and archivists. All the staff of Liverpool Record Office and Liverpool Central Library were extremely helpful, and uncomplainingly produced the heaviest, bulkiest and dustiest material from their very rich holdings. At the University of Liverpool library, Maureen Watry and the Special Collections and Archives staff were generous with their time, as was the University Archivist, Adrian Allan, who also read the University section of the typescript and made many useful suggestions. Thanks are due to John Moore, Dawn Littler, Anne Gleave, Karen Howard and Sarah Starkey of the Maritime Archives and Library at the Merseyside Maritime Museum; the staff of the Walker Art Gallery; and Meg Whittle of the Liverpool Archdiocesan Archives. Beyond Liverpool, help came from Michael Powell of Chetham's Library; the Lancashire Record Office; the British Architectural Library; the V&A Print Room; Br James Hodkinson SJ of the Jesuit archives; Sally North and Neil Bingham of the RIBA Drawings Collection; Mike Chrimes of the Institute of Civil Engineers; Ian Leith of the National Monuments Record; Jessie Campbell and Nicholas Webb of Barclays Group Records; Tina Staples of HSBC Midland Group archives; Laura Taylor of Lloyds TSB Group archives, and Sarah Millard of the Bank of England.

Miles Broughton and Quentin Hughes shared their wide knowledge of Liverpool architecture. So did Janet Gnosspelius, Adrian Jarvis and John Vaughan, and along with Frank Salmon and Gavin Stamp they read parts of the typescript and made many useful comments. Unpublished research carried out by former students at the Liverpool School of Architecture (John W. Totterdill, R.E. Fleetwood, J.M.G. Cox, A.B. Eves, J.G. Pickard, R.S. Clarke, Rodney W. Hanson, Foon Tai Chow and Frank Newberry) was a valuable source, as was Gillian Moore's work on Peter Ellis, Douglas Wall's on Thomas Shelmerdine's libraries and John Baily's on Thomas Rickman. Jane Longmore's thesis on the Corporation Estate only came to hand at a late stage, but was very useful. Alyson Pollard and Dave Moffat gave access to their work on the Audsleys, and supplied information on stained glass. Lynn Pearson shared her findings on the Mersey Brewery, and she and Penny Beckett helped with tiles and architectural ceramics. James Darwin provided information on the former Royal Institution and other buildings, Sharman Kadish on synagogues, Colin Cunningham on Waterhouse and Rory O'Donnell on the Pugins. Pamela Russell helped on the subject of Sarah Clayton, and Andrew Richardson on Robert Threadgold. Bill Halsall answered questions on community architecture and housing co-ops.

The following supplied information about individual buildings: Robbie Bell (St George); Geoffrey Brandwood (Our Lady, Eldon St); Neil Burton (St James); Peter Cahill and Neville King (reservoirs); Monsignor Peter Cookson (Metropolitan Cathedral); Mike Davies, Max Pugh and Robin Wolley (St Margaret); Alan Frost and Michael Shippobottom (Town Hall); Alan Matthews and Geoff Ingham (St Michael-in-the-Hamlet); Alan Turner and Dave Molyneux (Lewis's); Dr Cecil Moss (Princes Road Synagogue); Richard Myring (Liverpool Medical Institution); Ann J. Thomas (Cunard Building); Br Ken Vance SJ (St Francis Xavier); Jim Wainwright (John Lewis Partnership); Hong Wan (Chinese Arch); Philip Ward-Jackson (Indian Mutiny memorial); Dick Webster (Liverpool Women's Hospital).

We are grateful for the co-operation of Liverpool City Council staff, especially John Hinchliffe and Glynn Marsden, and John Flynn, who checked planning records. At the University of Liverpool, Geoffrey Boswell, Matthew Clough, Bob Dawson and John Hardie were particularly helpful. At National Museums Liverpool, Pete Betts, Xanthe Brooke, David Crombie, John Edmondson, Robin Emmerson, Jessica Feather, Alex Kidson, Norman Killon, Moira Lindsay, Sandra Penketh, Paul Rees, Sam Sportun and Julian Treuherz all gave assistance.

This book would not have been possible without the advice and guidance of Simon Bradley at Yale University Press, who offered ideas and insights at every stage. Emily Lees and Emily Rawlinson co-ordinated the illustrations, Emily Winter did the page layouts, and Sally Salvesen oversaw the whole project. Stephany Ungless copyedited the text with great attention to detail, Touchmedia drew the maps and Alan Fagan the architectural plans, and Christine Shuttleworth compiled the indexes. Gavin Watson and everyone at the Buildings Books Trust were supportive throughout.

We would also like to thank David Angluin, Mark Bell, Mary Bennett, Paul Bennett, Ian Bradbury, Tony Bradshaw, David Brazendale, Jonathan Brittain, Norman Bush, Annette Butler, Scott Carlin, Peter Cormack, John K. Davies, Definitive, John Dewsnap, Mark Dring, Ian Dungavell, Alex Elam, Karen Evans, Sarah-Jane Farr, the Rev Dr Mark Fisher, Michael Forsyth, Andy Foster, Andy Foyle, Susan Freeman, the Rev Robert Gallagher, Florence Gersten, Carol Hardie, Richard Hare, Ruth Harman, Marion Harney, Bob Harrington, Clare Hartwell, Chris Hennessey, Billy Hodge, Peter Howell, Roger Hull, Matthew Hyde, Steve Lambert, Jennifer Lewis, Liverpool Community College Estates Management, Brian Lukacher, Fr Chris McCoy, Robin McGhie, John Minnis, Edward Morris, Maggie Mullan and Dominic Wilkinson, Robert Orledge and Charles McFeeters, Simon Osborne and the staff of Speke Hall, Julia Carter Preston and Mike Pugh Thomas, the Rev Dr Ben Rees, Robin Riley, Liz Robinson and Robert Thorne, Nancy Scerbo, Richard Sharples, Sally Sheard, Ken Smith, Colin Stansfield, the Rev Simon Starkey, Alan Swerdlow, Adrian Thompson, John Tiernan, Mark Travis, David Walker, Sharon Walker, June Wharton, Colin Wilkinson, Sue Wrathmell and the late Fritz Spiegl.

Finally, we owe a great debt to Tom Wesley, who acted as Pevsner's driver in Manchester during the writing of *South Lancashire*, over thirty-five years ago. He tested our text by walking the streets of Liverpool with it, and his comments led to many valuable improvements. Any remaining shortcomings in the directions are due to us, but there would have been more without his energetic help.

JS, RP

2. Detail of Policeman's Lodge, Wapping Dock, by Jesse Hartley (*c.* 1856)

Walk 1 – The South Docks – p. 102

Walk 2 – The North Docks – p. 120

Walk 3 – Between Church Street and
Lime Street – p. 174

Walk 4 – Bold Street – Duke Street Area –

Walk 5 – University of Liverpool
via Mount Pleasant – p. 210

Walk 6 – Georgian Residential Area – p. 22

Walk 7 – North of the Centre – p. 251

Walk 8 – Via London Road to Everton – p. 2

Walk 9 – South of the Centre – p. 269

Walk 10 – Prince's Park and Sefton Park –

City Centre – p. 131

0   500   1000 metres

0   1000 2000 3000 feet

A565

DERBY ROAD

REGENT ROAD

A59
A580

VAUXHALL ROAD

SCOTLAND ROAD

WEST DERBY ROAD

PRESCOT ROA

KINGSWAY
ROAD TUNNEL

A5047

PIER HEAD

EDGE LANE

QUEENSWAY
ROAD TUNNEL

RAILWAY TUNNEL

Lime Street Station

Central Station

SMITHDOWN ROAD

UPPER PARLIAMENT ST

RIVER MERSEY

ULLET ROAD

PARK ROAD

Sefton
Park

N

AIGBURTH ROAD A561

Airport

3. Liverpool, showing areas covered by walks

Introduction

Introduction

Liverpool has the most splendid setting of any English city. It lies on the E bank of the broad River Mersey, which rises gently to a ridge crowned by the two cathedrals. Its shape is roughly a semicircle, the straight side formed by the waterfront, with the Pier Head at its centre. The combination of hills and water shows many buildings to advantage, and the higher ground to the E gives spectacular views across the city to the river, the open sea, and the distant mountains of North Wales. This setting has been radically transformed by human intervention: the long line of docks is built on land reclaimed from the river, and the creek or Pool that was the original harbour has vanished completely, filled in and built over. Sandstone lies just below the surface – the impressive railway cutting leading to Lime Street Station goes through solid rock – and quarries close to the centre provided building stone in the C18 and early C19. Later, stone was imported from Storeton on the Wirral, from Runcorn and Woolton, and from further away for certain major buildings. Brick has been the commonest material since the C18.

Unlike some comparable cities – Glasgow, Newcastle, even Manchester – Liverpool inherited virtually nothing from its medieval past, and is essentially a creation of the C18 onwards. Moreover, for two hundred years it was a boom town, driven by commerce, so that older buildings were regularly swept away regardless of historical interest. In the centre, just one survives from before the mid C18. Redevelopment in the second half of the C20 added little of value, so that late Georgian, Victorian and Edwardian buildings still predominate. Controlling the mighty river with its huge tidal range required walls and quays of colossal size and strength, and the same heroic scale characterized much of the C19 and early C20 city, from the most utilitarian warehouses to the richest public buildings. Despite widespread decay and destruction since the Second World War, a combination of rugged solidity and sublime grandeur is still one of the defining qualities of Liverpool's architecture.

This guide concentrates on the city centre, corresponding roughly with the municipal borough as it existed until 1835, plus most of the Dock

4. Liverpool from the Mersey, the Pier Head in the foreground, the Anglican Cathedral in the distance

5. Liverpool Castle, reconstruction by E.W. Cox, 1892

The castle stood on the site of Derby Square, overlooking the Pool to the s. Since it was removed the ground level has been lowered; originally it occupied the highest and most defensible point of the medieval town. Built early in the c13, it was partly dismantled after the Civil War, and the remains above ground were demolished in the 1720s. It was roughly square in plan, with round towers at three corners and a gatehouse with projecting semicircular towers at the NE angle, facing N along Castle Street. A rock-cut moat was possibly a later addition. A tunnel running W under what is now James Street led from the castle to the river. Long after the castle had been demolished, the deep basements of two c19 bank buildings on the N side of Derby Square, between Castle Street and Fenwick Street, were constructed within its former moat.

In 1912 a full-size replica was begun by William Hesketh Lever, the future Lord Leverhulme, beside one of Liverpool Corporation's reservoirs at Rivington, Lancs.

Estate. It also covers parts of two neighbouring townships absorbed subsequently: Everton, to the E, which developed from a select residential area in the late c18 to a densely built-up quarter in the c19; and Toxteth Park, to the s, where public parks were laid out in the 1840s and 1860s, becoming a focus for affluent suburban housing.

From the Thirteenth to the Seventeenth Century

Before the later C17 Liverpool was a very modest settlement. The town grew on the peninsula between the river and the tidal creek known as the Pool – now obliterated, but following the course of Canning Place, Paradise Street, Whitechapel and Old Haymarket [6]. It is first mentioned *c.* 1192, and in 1207 it was made a borough by King John, a convenient harbour for communication with Ireland. The **medieval borough** consisted of seven streets, the pattern of which is still clearly visible (*see* topic box, p. 6). A castle was built in the early C13 on a site now partly occupied by the Queen Victoria monument (*see* topic box, facing). The small chapel of St Mary del Key near the water's edge, first mentioned in 1257, gave its name to Chapel Street. Its remains were pulled down in the early C19. Close to it, the church of Our Lady and St Nicholas was built *c.* 1360. Medieval Liverpool was not a parish, and the church was only a chapel of ease of the parish church at Walton, 3 m. (4.8 km.) to the N. The present building dates largely from the 1940s.*
In 1406 Sir John Stanley obtained permission to fortify his house at the foot of what is now Water Street. Known as the Tower, this survived until the early C19; its site is covered by Tower Buildings.

The **development** of Liverpool as a great commercial port began properly in the mid C17, when trade with the colonies in America and the West Indies was added to established European, Irish and coastal trade. The Civil War was a setback to growth, but after the Restoration economic progress was rapid. Liverpool's position was ideal for transatlantic trade, importing tobacco and sugar from the New World and exporting goods from the nascent industries of the Midlands and the North. The first recorded American cargo – thirty tons of tobacco – arrived in 1648, and the refining of sugar from the West Indies began *c.* 1667, in the vicinity of Dale Street. The trading community was boosted after the mid 1660s by London merchants, displaced by the Plague and Great Fire. At this time the 3rd Lord Molyneux (whose ancestor had bought the lordship of Liverpool earlier in the century) brought about a key event in the expansion of the town. In 1668 he laid out Lord Street, running E from the castle, with the intention of bridging the Pool and opening up the waste ground beyond. The Burgesses, however, held that waste and Pool were rightfully theirs. The dispute was settled in 1672 when the Corporation took a thousand-year lease of the lordship in return for an annual rent, and in 1776 they bought out the lease and acquired permanent possession. Thus from the late C17 the Corporation controlled the development of a very large area immediately E of the medieval core, roughly from what is now London Road in the N to Parliament Street in the s, and as far E as Crown Street (more or less the area covered by Walks 3–6 in this book).

*In the present municipal area there is only one medieval church, at Childwall (*see* the forthcoming *Buildings of England: Lancashire: Liverpool and the South West*).

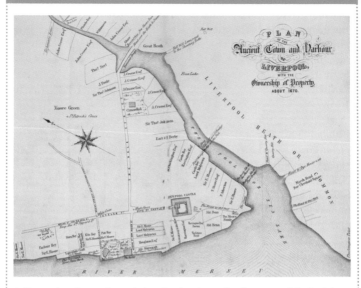

6. Liverpool c. 1670, conjectural plan showing the medieval streets and the Pool, from Thomas Baines, *History of the Commerce and Town of Liverpool . . .* (1852)

The streets which made up early c13 Liverpool formed an H-plan with the crossbar extended N and S. Their names, as given in later records, were: Mill Street, Juggler Street and Castle Street (together forming the extended crossbar, parallel with the river along the ridge), Chapel Street and Bank Street (running down to the river), and Moor Street and Dale Street (running inland). Juggler Street was later renamed High Street, and part was subsequently absorbed into Exchange Flags. In the c16, Mill Street, Bank Street and Moor Street were renamed Old Hall Street, Water Street and Tithebarn Street respectively.

Nothing survives above ground to illustrate the **architecture of the c17 town**, and in our area only the Ancient Chapel of Toxteth in Park Road is of c17 origin, though reconstructed [165]. (Speke Hall is earlier, but was built some miles out in the country.) Celia Fiennes described Liverpool in 1698 as having twenty-four streets, with 'mostly new built houses of brick and stone after the London fashion . . . built high and even'. The chief new public building was the Town Hall of 1673, replacing an earlier thatched structure. The new Hall was raised on stone pillars that formed an arcade, serving as an exchange.

The Eighteenth Century

Spectacular growth began with the C18. In 1715 Liverpool opened the first commercial enclosed wet **dock** in the world [58]. Designed by *Thomas Steers*, it was constructed within the wide mouth of the Pool (the higher reaches were subsequently covered over to create Paradise Street, Whitechapel etc.). The Old Dock, as it came to be called, was the focus for rapid development E of the historic centre. New **streets** radiated from it, including Duke Street and Hanover Street, with merchants' dwellings and associated warehouses and counting houses. Daniel Defoe, who had visited *c.* 1680 and 1690, returned soon after 1715 and marvelled at the transformation. 'Liverpoole is one of the wonders of Britain', he wrote, 'What it may grow to in time, I know not.' As for architecture, 'there is no town in England, London excepted, that can equal Liverpoole for the fineness of the streets, and the beauty of the buildings; many of the houses are all of free stone and completely finished; and all the rest (of the new part I mean) of brick, as handsomely built as London it self.'

Of this prosperous early C18 town the only survival is the former Blue Coat School (now Bluecoat Chambers), 1716–18 [106]. It is large for an early Georgian school, of brick with stone dressings, in a vigorous but provincial style derived from Wren. It stood originally beside the new stone parish church of St Peter, but this, along with every other C18 Anglican church in the centre, has vanished (*see* topic box, p. 179). Also gone is the Infirmary of 1745–9, a handsome brick and stone hospital on the edge of town, on the site now occupied by St George's Hall. But the most splendid mid-C18 **public building** was the new Town Hall and Exchange of 1749–54, by *John Wood* of Bath [28]. Significantly, Wood had recently designed the new Exchange at Bristol, the rival west coast port that Liverpool was rapidly overtaking. Wood's façades survive, somewhat altered. Ornately Palladian and with lavish sculptural decoration [9], they brought a new standard of refinement and display to the town.

Wood's Town Hall was originally hemmed in by narrow medieval streets, but in the newly developing area E of the former Pool, more spacious **planning** was possible. Around the middle of the C18 Clayton Square and Williamson Square were laid out, along with the smaller Wolstenholme Square and Cleveland Square near the Old Dock. Only fragments of these developments remain, and the most ambitious, Clayton Square, has been completely erased. It was symmetrical and had houses in uniform terraces. The initiative for such schemes came from lessees acting as property developers in isolation. Despite the Corporation having control of the entire area E of the Pool, no systematic plan was imposed, and streets tended to follow the lines of existing lanes and fields. The first attempt at a formally planned suburb in fact lay just outside the Corporation estate, on land to the S owned by the Earl of Sefton. Here from 1771 the builder *Cuthbert Bisbrown* laid out an extensive street grid intended to form the new high-class residential area of Harrington, for 'gentlemen not obliged by business to reside in the centre and bustle of the town.' But the scheme failed, perhaps from its very isolation, and the streets were built up with inferior housing in the early C19. The only significant building to come out of the Harrington venture was the church of St James, 1774–5, notable for its Gothic cast-iron gallery columns.

In the 1780s–90s, houses spread steadily SE along streets such as Duke Street, Seel Street and Bold Street. The grandest survivor is Thomas

Court Housing and Cellar Dwellings

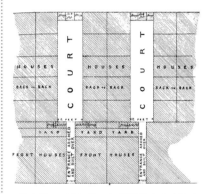

7. Plan of court housing, by W.H. Duncan (1840)

From the late C18 to the mid C19, the rapid increase in population led to the constrution of much high-density, insanitary housing for Liverpool's poor. Houses were built in courts, at the rear of terraced properties fronting the street. Each court was reached by a tunnel-like passage, and consisted of two short terraces facing each other across a narrow space. The houses were back-to-backs, the rear wall shared with the next court, and were generally of three storeys with one room to each floor. Appallingly overcrowded, with minimal ventilation, no running water, and only one or two communal earth closets in each court, they were places of extreme squalor and a fearful source of disease. The Liverpool Building Act of 1842 and Liverpool Sanitary Act of 1846 introduced improvements in design, and in 1864 the construction of narrow, closed courts was banned. By this time, however, there were 3,073 in the borough, consisting of 17,825 houses with an estimated population of 110,000. A thousand courts were still inhabited in 1903 and the last were only cleared in the 1960s. An altered 1840s terrace of back-to-backs survives off Duke Street, but this did not form part of a court. In Pembroke Place two houses of c. 1840 flank a narrow gap that was originally the entrance to a court.

Cellars were used as dwellings from the late C18. In 1789–90 there were 1,728 occupied cellars in Liverpool, housing 6,780 – 12.6 per cent of the population; by 1846, 29,080 people were living in 7,577 cellars. These consisted generally of a single room, reached via steps from outside. Some were still inhabited as late as 1914.

Parr's of *c.* 1799 in Colquitt Street, with its attached office and warehouse [121]. In 1783–4 prestigious Rodney Street was laid out, beginning the more spacious residential development of the high ground to the E. The 1780s also saw the earliest court housing for the numerous poor of the booming port (*see* topic box, facing). These slum courts and their successors blighted Liverpool into the C20.

Liverpool's position on the Mersey was an overwhelming advantage for international trade, but the early C18 town was effectively land-locked by mosses and meres, and growth depended on improving inland **communications**. The turnpike road from Liverpool to Prescot dates from 1726. In the mid C18 it was extended, linking up with other turnpikes. In the 1730s the River Weaver was made navigable into Cheshire, and the Mersey and Irwell Navigation scheme made it possible to convey goods by water to Manchester (the Mersey had already been improved below Warrington in the 1690s). Canals followed: the Sankey Canal from the St Helens coalfield to the Mersey was constructed 1755–7, with Liverpool engineering expertise and money, followed by the Bridgewater Canal, linking the Duke of Bridgewater's collieries at Worsley with the Mersey at Runcorn. In 1770 the great Leeds and Liverpool Canal was begun, eventually connecting the port with the manufacturing towns of NE Lancashire and Yorkshire when completed in 1816. To the N of the town the canal ran parallel with the river to its terminus in Old Hall Street. Coal yards and noxious industries sprang up along its banks, setting the tone for this area in the C19.

In 1786 the Corporation obtained its first **Improvement Act**, giving it powers to widen older streets. The W side of Castle Street was rebuilt on its present line, with uniform classical façades designed by *Samuel*

Hope of Manchester or *John Foster Sen.* Slight remains are still visible amid today's Victorian banks and insurance offices. Even the anonymous author of an otherwise unflattering description wrote of the transformed Castle Street in 1795: 'no town in England can shew anything superior of its height and length'. Parts of Water Street and Dale Street were also widened – the houses at the corner of Trueman Street and Dale Street are of this date [8] – and the buildings abutting the Town Hall demolished. In 1788 *James Wyatt* was engaged to extend Wood's building on the N side, adding the refined Neoclassical ballroom block and designing a dome to cover the courtyard. When the original building was gutted by fire in 1795, Wyatt redesigned its interior, providing a magnificent staircase hall under the dome, and reception rooms of exceptional splendour, completed 1820 [30]. Among English civic buildings of its date, Liverpool Town Hall is probably second only to London's Mansion House in its richness.

By the end of the C18 four new wet **docks** had been built in addition to the Old Dock. Customs revenues rose from £50,000 in 1700 to almost £681,000 by 1785, and in 1792 Liverpool was handling about a sixth of the tonnage from all English ports, whereas in 1716 her share had been one twenty-fourth. A large measure of this prosperity was due to the **slave trade**, for which Liverpool was by 1740 the chief port in Europe. Her ships followed a triangular route: to West Africa, where they exchanged manufactured goods for slaves, on to the West Indies and the Americas, where the slaves were sold, then back to Liverpool laden with sugar, rum, tobacco and cotton. The link between this ignominious source of wealth and Liverpool's expansive architecture was underlined with grim force by the Rev. William Bagshaw Stevens in 1797: 'throughout this large-built Town every Brick is cemented to its fellow Brick by the blood and sweat of Negroes.'

Population

1700	5,715	1821	119,000
1720	11,833	1831	165,000
1742	18,000	1841	286,000*
1766	25,787	1851	376,000
1777	34,107	1871	493,000
1790	55,732	1891	518,000
1801	78,000	1901	685,000*

*Boundary change in previous decade.

Figures for the C18 are estimates by the C19 historian Thomas Baines. Figures from 1801 onwards are from R. Lawton and C.G. Pooley, *The Social Geography of Merseyside in the 19th Century*, final report to the SSRC, Department of Geography, University of Liverpool, 1976.

9. Town Hall frieze detail (mid-c18)

The Early Nineteenth Century

The slave trade was abolished in 1807, but the predicted collapse in Liverpool's fortunes did not follow. More docks were built, and revenue from dock dues rose from £28,365 in 1801 to £130,911 in 1824. Expansion continued, and in architecture and planning a Neoclassical orderliness became widespread. In the centre the most significant work was the new Exchange of 1803–8, just behind the Town Hall. Built by the elder *Foster*, perhaps with the involvement of *Wyatt*, it was a large and dignified block containing a news room, counting houses and warehousing. It was demolished and replaced in the 1860s, and again in the mid c20, but the spacious quadrangle of Exchange Flags which it enclosed survives. In this piazza at the heart of the town, merchants transacted business in the open air, overlooked from 1813 by the Nelson monument of *M.C. Wyatt* and *Richard Westmacott* [10]. Followed in 1822 by *Westmacott*'s equestrian bronze of George III in London Road, this marked the beginning of a taste for ambitious public sculpture which lasted into the c20. More modest than the Exchange is the very early purpose-built bank of Messrs Heywood in Brunswick Street, 1798–1800 [80]. It is combined with the proprietor's dwelling, but the ashlar-faced bank predominates and the house is secondary. This was the first of the showpiece financial buildings that lined Castle Street and its tributaries during the c19.

An anonymous author described Liverpool in 1795 as 'the only town in England of any pre-eminency that has not one single erection or endowment, for the advancement of science, the cultivation of the arts, or promotion of useful knowledge.' Though based on a rather narrow definition of the arts – the Theatre Royal opened in Williamson Square in 1772, the Music Hall in Bold Street in 1786 (both demolished) – this observation is probably fair. However, from *c*. 1800 more serious **cultural interests** found architectural expression. *Thomas Harrison*'s distinguished Lyceum in Bold Street, 1800–2 [116], accommodated not only a news room, but also the Liverpool Library (one of the earliest subscription libraries), and the elder *Foster*'s Athenaeum of 1799 in

Church Street (demolished) and Union News Room of 1800 in Duke Street both housed libraries too. Among the founders of the Athenaeum was William Roscoe (1753–1831), lawyer, poet, MP, anti-slavery campaigner, historian, botanist and art collector. He rose from humble beginnings to acquire an international reputation as a scholar and man of letters. In a town preoccupied with making money, he was active in schemes for promoting more civilized values: the foundation of the Botanic Gardens in 1802, of the Liverpool Academy in 1810, and of the Liverpool Royal Institution, opened 1817. The latter occupied the converted Parr house in Colquitt Street. Following Roscoe's bankruptcy, part of his Old-Master collection was acquired and displayed by the Institution from 1819, a forerunner of the public art galleries established in many towns later in the century.

The conversion of Parr's house was carried out by *Edmund Aikin*, also responsible for the subscription assembly rooms of 1814–16 in Mount Pleasant called the Wellington Rooms [127]. These were later joined by *Clark Rampling*'s elegantly curved Medical Institution, containing library and lecture theatre, and *A.H. Holme*'s imposing Mechanics' Institution in nearby Mount Street [142], both opened 1837. All are products of the **Greek Revival**, which dominated Liverpool architecture *c*. 1815–*c*. 1840. The town at this period was often compared with the maritime cities of Antiquity, and the adoption of Greek architecture can be seen as symbolic, over and above mere fashion. The porch added by *Aikin* to the Liverpool Royal Institution was perhaps the first use of the Greek Doric order in Liverpool, but the leading local figure in the Revival was the Corporation Surveyor, *John Foster Jun.*, most of whose buildings have been demolished (*see* topic box, p. 232).

The greatest monument of the new Liverpool of these years, classically inspired and culturally aspiring, is *Harvey Lonsdale Elmes*'s St George's Hall [31]. It came about through combining separate projects for assize courts and a concert hall. Elmes's winning entries in the 1839 competitions for these were of no great individuality, but his combined design of 1840–1 is exceptionally inventive. The great hall is flanked by the courts, with a smaller round concert room at the N end, these spaces being expressed in the massing and the varied treatment of the façades. St George's Hall is quite unlike the conventional adaptations of temple architecture in the younger Foster's buildings. Pevsner in 1969 called it 'the freest neo-Grecian building in England and one of the finest in the world', though part of Elmes's originality lay in his use of Roman sources as well as Greek. The magnificent interiors were completed after Elmes's death by *C.R. Cockerell*, and belong more properly to the Victorian age.

Of the many classical churches and Nonconformist chapels built in the first four decades of the C19 shockingly few remain. Among the losses are St Michael Upper Pitt Street, St Catherine Abercromby Square and the church of the School for the Blind, all by the younger *Foster*; St Saviour Upper Huskisson Street; the Methodist chapels in Great Homer Street, Moss Street (Brunswick Chapel) and Upper Stanhope Street; Mount Pleasant Presbyterian Church; Renshaw Street Unitarian Chapel; and Pembroke Baptist Chapel. Apart from Foster's St Andrew, Rodney Street [138] and his Oratory for St James's Cemetery, the only survivors are *Samuel Rowland*'s St Bride, Percy Street [144], *Joseph Franklin*'s Great George Street Congregational Church [124], and *John Slater*'s St Patrick (R.C.), Park Place [164]. Externally, St Bride is as pure and temple-like as the Oratory, with a pedimented Ionic portico and no tower. St Patrick is less refined but more individual, with its two squat Greek Doric porches tucked into the angles of the transepts. *Franklin*'s Congregational Church of 1840–1, Corinthian and with a noble domed tower, shows a move away from Greek austerity towards Roman – and indeed Victorian – richness. The excellent collection of Neoclassical funerary **sculpture** in the Oratory includes important monuments by *Chantrey* and *Gott,* as well as works by *John Gibson*, who began his career in Liverpool before settling in Rome, and who owed much to the encouragement of Liverpool patrons.

Early **Gothic Revival** churches have also disappeared, but some extremely interesting ones remain. The tower and delightful openwork spire of Our Lady and St Nicholas, begun 1811, are by the arch-Grecian *Thomas Harrison* [84]. St Luke, facing the top of Bold Street, was built by the Corporation, 1811–31, and nominally designed by the *Fosters* [120]. The prominent chancel seems to anticipate the Ecclesiologists, but the tower has Decorated windows above Perpendicular ones, something that archaeologically minded Goths would not have countenanced. The influential system of classifying medieval architecture under the terms Early English, Decorated, etc., was invented in Liverpool by the Quaker

Thomas Rickman as St Luke was under construction. It was while working here in an insurance broker's office that he began to study old buildings, publishing the results in 1817 as *An Attempt to Discriminate the Styles of English Architecture from the Conquest to the Reformation*. As a designer, Rickman's name is linked with three extraordinary churches built 1812–16 by the wealthy ironmaster *John Cragg*. Only fragments of St Philip, Hardman Street survive, but St George, Everton [159] and St Michael-in-the-Hamlet [177] still stand. Rickman made drawings for Cragg, but to what extent he influenced the appearance of these churches is unclear – he said of Cragg: 'His ironwork is too stiff in his head to bend to any beauty' – and they are chiefly remarkable for their pioneering use of cast-iron prefabricated parts. Rickman's pupil, *John Broadbent*, turned his hand to both Greek and Gothic. His Greek Revival St Augustine, Shaw Street has been demolished, but his St Anthony (R.C.), Scotland Road of 1832–3 stands. It is in a plain lancet style, with a wide, column-free interior [152]. Of secular Gothic in this period there is *Elmes*'s Collegiate Institution in Shaw Street, 1840–3. Among Gothic houses, the few survivors in our area are a pair dated 1835 in the otherwise classical Percy Street, and the picturesque group built by *Cragg* at St Michael's Hamlet.

In **residential architecture and planning** the start of the C19 saw important new developments. It was the Corporation, rather than a private lessee, which took the initiative with Great George Square. Laid out before 1803, it is more generous than any C18 predecessor, with a large enclosed garden like the London squares. Developers who leased the plots were required to conform with an agreed elevation, and though only fragments remain they give some idea of the spacious dignity thus achieved. Contemporary with this was the development of Mosslake Fields, now the centre of the University of Liverpool. Here too the Corporation took the lead. *John Foster Sen.*'s plan for a grid of streets centred on Abercromby Square was approved in 1800, but little progress was made until after 1816. Again, there was an agreed design for terraces round the square, prepared by the elder Foster in 1819, though some variation crept in during execution [130]. Restrictive covenants prevented court housing and cellar dwellings, and industry and warehousing were also excluded. From 1827, the adjoining larger area between Falkner Street and Upper Parliament Street was similarly laid out, with Falkner Square in the middle. In Percy Street [143] and Gambier Terrace [145] in the 1830s stone was used instead of brick, and a more imaginative approach to terrace design was adopted (*see* topic box, p. 243). So by the 1840s almost the whole of the eastern, elevated half of the Corporation estate had been built up with broad, straight streets of predominantly high-class houses.

The historic **centre** was increasingly given over to commerce (and, away from the principal streets, the dwellings of the poor). An Act of 1826 made important civic improvements possible: under *John Foster*

Jun., St George's Crescent was laid out as a formal gateway from Derby
Square into Lord Street; and Lord Street, North and South John Street,
and South Castle Street were all widened and rebuilt with regular, stucco-
fronted blocks. Of these new buildings the only survivors are on the w
side of North John Street [11]. They may be the earliest speculative office
blocks in Liverpool – just a few years later than the earliest in London.
At the same time the Old Dock was filled in to form Canning Place, and
here rose the colossal new Custom House, the younger *Foster*'s greatest
work. Its dome and N portico closed the view s from the Town Hall,
while its w portico commanded the dock road. With its demolition after
Second World War damage, a symbolic focal point for much of the
centre was lost. As remarkable in its way was *Foster*'s earlier St John's
Market, 1820–2, a long rectangular block stretching from Roe Street to
Elliot Street and covering an area the size of St George's Hall. Inside was
a single, undivided space with a timber roof on rows of cast-iron
columns. It was the forerunner of all the great C19 market halls
in the provinces, and anticipated the early train sheds. Of the same
utilitarian stamp were numerous multi-storey warehouses [123]. Once
dominant in the streets closest to the river, they are represented by only
a few survivors (*see* topic box, p. 255). A key event at this time was the
opening of the Liverpool & Manchester Railway in 1830 (*see* topic box,
p. 188). The creation of the Lime Street terminus, opened in 1836, had
far-reaching consequences for the planning of the town. It was fronted
by a monumental Neoclassical screen, designed by the younger *Foster*
(demolished). Three years later the site opposite was chosen for St
George's Hall, and over the next sixty years a succession of grand public
buildings turned the area into a sort of civic forum, elevated above the
old centre.

Liverpool in the early C19 assumed an architectural character very different from Manchester. Dedicated to commerce rather than manufacturing, it was free from utilitarian mill buildings and the smoke and clatter that went with them. Its new residential quarter was well-planned, punctuated by classical churches and public buildings, and in its old, congested centre it was beginning to carve out spacious new thoroughfares. After a visit to noisy, smoky Manchester in 1826 the artist John James Audubon returned with relief 'to bright Liverpool again', where the streets 'looked very wide, very clean, very well lined with very handsome buildings'. A few years later Alexis de Tocqueville made the same comparison, but saw beneath the surface: 'Liverpool is a beautiful town. Poverty is almost as great as it is at Manchester, but it is hidden.'

Victorian Liverpool, 1840s–80s

Mid-C19 Liverpool was overwhelmingly a place of trade. In 1844 the German visitor J.G. Kohl wrote of it: 'Among the great cities of the world . . . there is no other so exclusively devoted to commerce. Every house . . . is either a counting-house, a warehouse, a shop, or a house that in one way or other is either an instrument or the result of trade. The great buildings and institutions of the town are a custom-house, an exchange, a set of docks, a railway station, or something else that is intended, directly or indirectly, to be serviceable to commerce.' Significantly, Liverpool's contribution to the Great Exhibition of 1851 was not a product of manufacturing, but an elaborate self portrait: a detailed model of the dock system and commercial centre, on a scale of 8 ft to 1 m (1:660), supported on pedestals in the form of cast-iron elephants. Nothing, it was said, could have given foreign visitors a better idea of Britain's industrial resources and mercantile influence than 'this happy picture of the flourishing port of Liverpool'.

The growing complexity of the **Dock Estate** in the mid C19 was reflected in the range and scale of its buildings. *Jesse Hartley*'s stand out, superbly crafted in granite and often startlingly original [2, 68]. Pevsner described them as some of the finest examples in Europe of romantic *architecture parlante*, here expressing the strength of resistance to water and the bulk of ships. Hartley began in Grecian style, e.g. his 1830s gatepiers in the dock wall. In the 1840s this gave way to castellated Gothic [76], equally symbolic of the physical and financial security of the docks, e.g. the accumulator towers at Stanley Dock and Wapping Dock; and to high idiosyncrasy, e.g. the Canning Half-Tide Dock Gatemen's Shelters. His masterpiece of utilitarian classicism, Albert Dock, was also erected in the 1840s [64]. Later warehouses were for single commodities e.g. the massive Italianate grain warehouses by *G.F. Lyster*, 1866–8, at Waterloo Dock [72]. (For a full account of the Docks, *see* pp. 93–101.)

12. Detail from a panorama of Liverpool, *Illustrated London News* (1865)

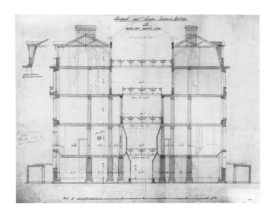

13. Former Liverpool & London Insurance Co. offices, Dale Street, by C.R. Cockerell (1856–8), section

14. Albany Building, Old Hall Street, by J.K. Colling (1856–8). Lithograph from W. Herdman, *Views in Modern Liverpool*, 1864

Like the increasingly ambitious architecture of the Dock Estate, the ever more opulent **office buildings** erected from the 1840s onwards illustrate Liverpool's preoccupation with commerce. Barned's Building in Sweeting Street appears to date from *c.* 1840 and takes the form of a sober, dignified terrace of repetitive bays. A new approach was introduced soon after at Brunswick Buildings, now demolished, just off Castle Street. This was an Italian Renaissance palazzo of considerable ostentation – the architectural press compared it to a Pall Mall club-house – and one of the earliest instances anywhere of a speculative office building treated in so self-important a manner. Inside was a central court, with balustraded access galleries to the upper floors, and a roof of glass and iron.

The need to admit ample light was a factor in the design of all Victorian office buildings, and the glass-roofed central light-well became a standard feature in Liverpool. Such an atrium formed part of *C.R. Cockerell*'s great building for the Liverpool & London Insurance Co., 1856–8 [13, 87]. Though visually a single unit, it was designed as four distinct blocks, all but the front one being let to tenants. The rectangular space in the middle (now filled in) was roofed with glass, lined with galleries, and faced with reflective white-glazed tiles. Its functionalism must have contrasted starkly with the Venetian Renaissance street elevations. Of the same date is the Albany Building, a very large speculative block designed by *J.K. Colling* [14, 96]. The exterior is of polychrome brick with sandstone and polished granite dressings, embellished with carved foliage treated in a flat, non-naturalistic manner. The central court is open to the sky, and the offices are reached from broad internal corridors, pierced by light-wells and lit from above.

The Italian Renaissance provided models for much mid-c19 commercial architecture. Florentine palaces had an obvious symbolic appeal for Liverpool's merchant princes, as did those of Venice, the seat of a maritime trading empire. Italian Gothic elements sometimes

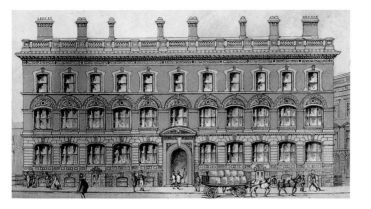

appear – for example in *Henry Sumners*'s Berey's Buildings and *J.A. Picton*'s No. 11 Dale Street – but classicism generally prevails, and the Ruskin-inspired Venetian Gothic so prominent in Manchester is almost absent. Thus *Picton*'s Hargreaves Buildings in Chapel Street, 1859 [84], is Venetian in the classical manner of the late c15 Palazzo Corner-Spinelli. A Gothic block worth singling out is Seel's Building of *c.* 1872, in Church Street. It is a rare commercial work by *E.W. Pugin*, and has a very curiously modelled façade.

Writing about Liverpool office design in 1857, the *Building News* noted that 'the size and frequency of the windows gives very little opportunity for dignified repose.' *Peter Ellis*'s Oriel Chambers in Water Street, 1864, represents perhaps the most extreme solution to the problem of lighting such a building. The exterior stonework is pared down to narrow, buttress-like strips, between which fifty-six identical iron-framed oriel windows project like so many faceted glass bubbles [15]. Desks within these oriels are daylit from front, top and sides. The elevation facing the courtyard is even more extraordinary: continuous bands of glazing pass in front of the stanchions of the iron frame, a very early instance of curtain-wall construction. Critics were outraged by Ellis's rejection of historical styles and his novel use of materials. The local magazine *The Porcupine* called Oriel Chambers 'hard, liney, and meagre', the *Building News* 'a kind of greenhouse architecture run mad.' Ellis remains a frustratingly shadowy figure: before Oriel Chambers and No. 16 Cook Street [86] only a couple of very ordinary designs by him are known, and he may have been more active as a surveyor and valuer than as an architect.

Parallel with the growth of speculative offices runs the development of the prestigious **flagship building** for a single occupant, though more often than not such buildings included lettable space too. Banks led the way here. Joint-stock banking came to Liverpool in 1831, and two early Victorian premises survive, the former North and South Wales Bank in Derby Square, 1838–40, by *Edward Corbett* of Manchester [16], and the

15. Oriel Chambers, Water Street, by Peter Ellis (1864)

former Royal Bank in Dale Street, *c.* 1837–8, by *Samuel Rowland* [88]. Corbett's building is compromised by a narrow, irregular site, but is rich and imposing nonetheless. Rowland's is a much more polished performance in a pure and fastidious Greek Revival style. It forms part of a larger scheme, the bank being situated in the courtyard, though the detail of the street frontage is a good deal richer and less orthodox than that of the bank proper.

Both these banks use architecture to assert commercial status and stability. A few years later, this tendency found still more powerful expression in *Philip Hardwick* and *Jesse Hartley*'s Dock Traffic Office [17], and in the Liverpool branch of the Bank of England, 1845–8 [81], the last and arguably the best of three provincial branches designed by *Cockerell*. The Bank had previously occupied a private house in Hanover Street, and the move contributed significantly to the transformation of Castle Street into Liverpool's premier business thoroughfare. Though not as large as some later neighbours, the individual parts of Cockerell's bank are colossal, giving an impression of unshakeable strength and solidity. *Lucy & Littler*'s former Alliance Bank, 1868, at the corner of Derby Square, illustrates the Victorian trend away from Cockerell's sobriety towards less discriminating display, as do several buildings of the 1870s–80s at the other end of Castle Street by the prolific *George Enoch Grayson*. The former Union Bank in Brunswick Street, by contrast, is a thoroughly correct palazzo from as late as *c.* 1870, probably by the aged *John Cunningham*.

Among the most distinctive structures of Victorian Liverpool are **mixed-use buildings**, combining office accommodation and storage facilities for several businesses. Even the Alliance Bank incorporated vaults intended for 'wine merchants or others', and the basement of the Albany was also designed as warehousing. Mixed-use buildings are particularly numerous in and around Victoria Street, a new thoroughfare cut through in the 1860s. Fowler's Buildings [98], designed by *Picton* in 1865, has a grand front block containing offices, with larger and plainer polychrome brick warehouses behind. Just off Victoria Street (in Stanley Street) is the powerful Granite Buildings of *c.* 1882 by *Grayson*, in a severe and original style which reminded Pevsner of Lethaby. Facing the street, this very large block contains offices, behind an impressive pedimented façade of granite. At the back, by contrast, is a row of gabled fruit warehouses, faced with utilitarian glazed white bricks. The Queen Anne style makes its most impressive appearance in Victoria Street, in Commercial Saleroom Buildings [99], an early work by *James F. Doyle*, opened in 1879.

The wealth generated in Liverpool's offices and warehouses is reflected in **public buildings** of the period. St George's Hall (*see* p. 13 above) was officially opened in 1854. *Cockerell*'s Concert Hall interior [35], with gilded bronze, coloured marbles and a floor of polychrome tiles, has an imperial Roman richness, very different from Elmes's sober

16. Castle Moat House (former North & South Wales bank), Derby Square, by Edward Corbett (1838–40)

17. Dock Traffic Office, Albert Dock, by Philip Hardwick (completed 1848); top floor added by Jesse Hartley (1849)

exterior. His Small Concert Room is just as lavish, but more intimate [36]. In the second half of the C19 St George's Hall became the focal point for a group of grand public buildings dedicated to art, culture, law and learning. First came *John Weightman*'s Museum and Library [38], 1857–60, borrowing Elmes's Graeco-Roman manner. The Walker Art Gallery by *Cornelius Sherlock* and *H.H. Vale*, 1874–7, and the Picton Reading Room [40] by *Sherlock* alone, 1875–9, are still Neoclassical, though *F. & G. Holme*'s County Sessions House [41], 1882–4, opts for a degree of High Renaissance swagger. That the generally restrained classicism of these buildings was a response to St George's Hall seems clear if we compare them with the Municipal Buildings of 1862 etc., a short distance away in Dale Street [89]. This block of administrative offices was begun by *Weightman* and completed under *E.R. Robson*, his successor as Corporation Surveyor. It has French pavilion roofs, foliate capitals, and a tower with an unclassifiable spire. The statues of local worthies in St George's Hall show Victorian Liverpool's enthusiasm for **public sculpture**, evident outside in the Wellington Column, and in *Thomas Thornycroft*'s equestrian monuments to Prince Albert and Queen Victoria.

Wealth was also expressed in the proliferation of **shops**. In 1856 the *Liverpool Albion* reported that 'in the trading streets shop architecture is rivalling, or rather surpassing, in taste the commercial edifices near the 'Change'. Interesting mid-century examples are Messrs Cripps's building at Nos. 14–16 Bold Street [117], with its huge expanses of plate glass, and *Lewis Hornblower*'s premises for Elkington's in Church Street. In a class apart is the magnificent and exceptionally early department store Compton House [104], designed and built by *Thomas Haigh & Co.* in 1866–7, which survives in Church Street as Marks & Spencer. In Castle Street is *Salomons, Wornum & Ely*'s Queen Anne-style art gallery for Agnew's, of 1877.

For **religious buildings**, Gothic is the norm from the 1840s onwards. Roman Catholic churches survive in greater numbers than those of other denominations. Mass immigration from famine-stricken Ireland in the 1840s swelled Liverpool's already large Catholic population, and many churches were built for them from the mid century. St Francis Xavier, Everton, by *J.J. Scoles*, opened in 1848 [158]. The design provides good sight lines and plenty of space, rather than a convincingly medieval interior, but it is truly splendid, not least because of the highly decorated altars and other original furnishings. The spectacular Sodality Chapel is an addition of 1885–7 by *Edmund Kirby*. By contrast *Weightman & Hadfield*'s St Alban in Athol Street, 1849, imitates a medieval parish church in the manner favoured by A.W.N. Pugin. It was built to serve the dense slums beside the N docks, but now stands isolated and converted to secular use. *Hadfield* (with his son) was also responsible for the apsed chapel of the Notre Dame Convent in Mount Pleasant, 1865–7, with its impressive polychrome exterior. A.W.N. Pugin's son *E.W. Pugin* built several churches in Liverpool, where he had an office. St Vincent de Paul in St James Street, 1856–7, has one of the elaborate reredoses at which he excelled. Our Lady of Reconciliation in Eldon Street, 1859–60, is plainer, but more innovative in plan, with broad nave and apse under a continuous roof [153].

In all the area covered by this book, only two notable mid-Victorian Anglican churches survive, both benefactions of the Horsfall family (*see* topic box, p. 247). Christ Church Linnet Lane, 1867–71, by *Culshaw & Sumners*, has prominent fronts in two parallel streets and enjoyably unconventional details [169]. St Margaret Princes Road, 1868–9 by the great *George Edmund Street*, was the centre of the High Church movement in Liverpool, and has an interior rich with mural painting and glass by *Clayton & Bell*. It belongs to an extraordinary cluster of religious buildings in the same street, which illustrate the cultural diversity of C19 Liverpool: *Henry Sumners*'s Greek Orthodox church of St Nicholas [147], opened 1870, is an enlarged copy of a specific Byzantine church; the ruinous Welsh Presbyterian church by the brothers *W. & G. Audsley*, opened 1868, is French Gothic with a magnificent spire; and the synagogue of 1871–4, by the *Audsleys* again, fuses Moorish and Gothic to sumptuous effect, both in its sombre exterior and in its gloriously polychrome interior [149]. The former synagogue of 1856–7 in Hope Place, by *Thomas Wylie*, is much smaller and simpler.

The survival of Nonconformist buildings is so patchy that it is impossible to draw conclusions about the stylistic preferences of different denominations. The former Baptist Chapel of 1847 in Shaw Street is late Greek Revival. In Belvidere Road, Prince's Park, both Methodists and Presbyterians were building in Gothic by the 1850s and early 1860s, but the former Welsh Presbyterian chapel of 1860–1 in Chatham Street, by *Oliver & Lamb*, is debased Italianate. *W.I. Mason*'s Toxteth Tabernacle of 1870–1, for the Baptists, is a bizarre mix of Italianate and Gothic, in which the dominant motif is the classical pediment. St Peter's Methodist Church in nearby High Park Street, 1877–8 by *C.O. Ellison*, is entirely Gothic, but with a very unorthodox turret.

In housing and planning, the outstanding innovation of this period was the creation of **public parks** as the focus of residential suburbs. The earliest was Prince's Park [167], the initiative of the philanthropist Richard Vaughan Yates, who paid for it to be laid out from 1842 by *Joseph Paxton* and *James Pennethorne*. As with Regent's Park in London, the idea was that plots round the edges would be developed with high-class houses, and the rental income from these would pay for the park's upkeep. The earliest houses are classical, stuccoed, and mostly arranged in pairs or short terraces backing on to the curving walks of the park, with its lake and its undulating, wooded landscape [168]. From the 1850s the Council followed Yates's example, aiming to surround the town with a belt of parks. Wavertree Park and Sheil Park (outside our area) opened in 1856 and 1862 respectively. Then, under the Liverpool Improvement Act of 1865, three much bigger projects were launched: Stanley Park to the N, Newsham Park to the E and Sefton Park to the s. Sefton Park was the most ambitious – the largest public park anywhere in the country since Regent's Park in the early C19. The design competition was won in 1867 by the Parisian landscape gardener *Edouard André* and the local architect *Lewis Hornblower*, and the layout follows the naturalistic style of the Paris parks (which in turn derived from Paxton and Loudon in England). The fringes were sold off as building plots, to recoup the costs of making the park. The architecture is a disappointment, mostly very large and rather dull villas. An exception is The Towers in Ullet Road [171], a huge Gothic house of 1874 by *G.A. Audsley*. The wealthiest citizens meanwhile built mansions beyond Prince's Park and Sefton Park in areas such as Allerton and Mossley Hill, outside the scope of this guide.

Sefton Park was too far from the centre to offer the urban poor much benefit. W.S. Trench, Medical Officer of Health, lamented in 1868 that 'while the town council could vote thousands of pounds for parks, in which the working population could have but very moderate enjoyment, it seemed almost impossible . . . to purify and cleanse quarters of the town where fresh air, light and cleanliness were so necessary.' In the 1840s Dr William Henry Duncan had highlighted the link between Liverpool's alarming mortality rate and its insanitary court and cellar dwellings (*see* topic box, p. 8). Largely as a result of his work, the Town Council promoted the Liverpool Sanitary Act of 1846, which resulted in a Health Committee and the appointment of Duncan as Medical Officer of Health – the country's first. The 1842 Liverpool Building Act had introduced elementary controls on the design of new housing, and these were taken further in the 1846 Act, but courts continued to be built, and standards of construction were low: the term 'jerry building' to denote poor-quality bricklaying seems to have originated in Liverpool around this time. Isolated examples of **model housing** for workers were completed in the 1850s, but of these nothing remains. The Council undertook the purchase and demolition of insanitary property, but left redevelopment to speculative builders. In 1867, however, it held a competition for the design of labourers' dwellings, and as a result built St Martin's Cottages (demolished) in Ashfield Street, Vauxhall. These rather bleak four-storey flats, with lavatories on the half-landings of their open staircases, were perhaps the first municipal housing in England outside London.

Architectural evidence remains for some developments in **public health provision** during these years. In the 1850s sanitation was improved by the provision of water from Rivington (*see* topic box, p. 266), and of the reservoirs built in Liverpool in connection with this scheme, those at High Park Street in Toxteth and Margaret Street in Everton survive. They were designed by *Thomas Duncan*, water engineer to the Corporation, whose Everton water tower is one of the most powerful monuments of Victorian Liverpool [160]. Liverpool pioneered public washhouses: the first, established in 1842, has been demolished, and the earliest remaining seems to be the former Steble Street Baths and Washhouse, 1874. Surviving early hospitals are the former Lying-in Hospital, 1861 by *J.D. Jee*, and the Eye and Ear Infirmary, 1878–80 by *C.O. Ellison*, both in Myrtle Street. Of other charitable institutions, *John Cunningham's* exceptional Sailors' Home of 1845 etc., a turreted Jacobean block with a glazed central court, has regrettably been demolished. The School for the Blind was rebuilt in Hardman Street by *A.H. Holme*, 1849–51, with an elegant classical front. The Workshops for the Outdoor Blind in Cornwallis Street, 1870, are Gothic, by *George T. Redmayne* of Manchester. Gothic, too, is the Young Men's Christian Association in Mount Pleasant, 1874–7, by *H.H. Vale*.

In 1880, with a population of over half a million, Liverpool was raised to the status of a city. **Railway expansion** gives some idea of its growth. Lime Street Station, already rebuilt twice, was doubled in size in the 1870s; the new Central Station of the Cheshire Lines Committee opened in 1874; and Exchange Station in Tithebarn Street, the terminus of the Lancashire & Yorkshire Railway (originally opened 1850) was rebuilt on a greatly enlarged scale in the 1880s. In 1886 Liverpool was linked with Birkenhead by the under-river Mersey Railway, and in 1893 the Overhead Railway came into use (*see* topic box, p. 100). This elevated commuter line overlooked the docks, which by the end of the C19 stretched unbroken along the Mersey for 5.5 m. (8.9 km.).

Rebuilding in the **central business streets** continued, with new offices becoming larger, and with Northern Renaissance and subsequently English Baroque styles more in evidence. Much of Castle Street was transformed by the busy practice of *Grayson & Ould*. The polychromy of their British & Foreign Marine Insurance Co., 1888–90, was taken further by *W.D. Caröe* in his fanciful Adelphi Bank, of *c*. 1891–2 [82]. *Henry Tanner*'s General Post Office of 1894–9 – a Loire château, shorn of its towers after bomb damage – and *Charles E. Deacon*'s City Education Offices of 1897–8 in Sir Thomas Street, illustrate the same trends. With the striped marble façade of *Norman Shaw*'s Parr's Bank [18], 1898–1901, Castle Street's C19 transformation was complete, making it one of the most opulent Victorian commercial streets in the country.

Alfred Waterhouse, an architect born in Liverpool but based in London, was particularly active in his native town in the 1880s–90s (his hotel in front of Lime Street Station [112] is an earlier work of 1868–71). As well as two insurance offices in the centre, he designed the Victoria Building [19, 133] for University College (founded 1881), and the former Royal Infirmary [134]. These, along with some lesser university buildings, make up a very extensive group in his familiar brick-and-red-terracotta manner.* The Victoria Building is richly Gothic; the Infirmary plainer and mostly in a round-arched style.

Shaw's 1895–8 building for the White Star Line in James Street [91] was the first of a new generation of giant office blocks, establishing an enlarged scale for the city centre. Its banded brick and stone with angle turrets have an obvious kinship with his New Scotland Yard in London, but its high and narrow proportions also evoke the gabled warehouses that were once a feature of Liverpool's waterfront. The local architect *James F. Doyle*, who supervised construction, also won the competition (judged by Shaw) for the new Royal Insurance Building of 1896–1903 in

---

*They probably gave rise to the term 'red brick university', coined by Bruce Truscot in the 1940s to describe the new municipal universities of the late C19.

18. NatWest Bank (originally Parr's), Castle Street, by Norman Shaw (1898–1901)

North John Street [94]. This extremely impressive Baroque pile has a landmark tower capped by a gilded dome, and the façade incorporates a frieze by *C.J. Allen*. Behind the richly decorated masonry is a virtually self-sufficient steel frame – perhaps the earliest designed for a British building – that carries the upper storeys and leaves the huge ground-floor public office completely free of columns. The Corporation Surveyor *Thomas Shelmerdine* could also handle Baroque when the occasion called for grandeur (e.g. in the Hornby Library of 1906), but the most characteristic works from his office are in a free version of Jacobean, for instance the Everton Library of 1896 [161] and Hatton Garden Fire Station of 1895–8.

19. Entrance Hall of Victoria Building, University of Liverpool, by Alfred Waterhouse (1889–92)

As well as commercial buildings, *Doyle* designed **houses**, including the Old English – and very Norman-Shaw-like – Gledhill of 1881 beside Sefton Park [175]. It was in this affluent suburb that three exceptionally good Gothic Revival **churches** were built in the 1880s–90s by non-Liverpool architects. First came *J.L. Pearson*'s St Agnes, 1883–5 [172]. It is in the style of the c13, red brick on the outside but stone within, and vaulted throughout. It was the gift of Douglas Horsfall (*see* topic box, p. 247), whose house nearby was designed by *Shaw* (demolished). *Shaw* also did the vicarage at St Agnes, 1885–7, in a simplified and very freely composed Gothic. A short distance away is the R.C. church of St Clare, 1889–90, by the young *Leonard Stokes* [173]. Stokes here uses Gothic motifs with great latitude. His pulpit, for instance, with its inward-sloping sides, is highly personal and only loosely related to historical precedent. St Clare has a fine reredos by *George Frampton* and *Robert Anning Bell*, but for Arts-and-Crafts furnishings the nearby Unitarian Church of 1896–9 is altogether richer. Linked with its church hall by a library and cloister, the whole picturesque group is the work of *Thomas Worthington & Son* of Manchester. It has woodcarving by *Allen*, metalwork by *Richard Llewellyn Rathbone*, stained glass by *Morris & Co*, and outstanding murals by *Gerald Moira* in the vestry and library [174].

It is surprising that the **Arts and Crafts** did not flourish more in Liverpool. At University College in the 1890s a School of Architecture and Applied Arts was founded, where architects trained alongside stone carvers, metalworkers and stained-glass artists. Anning Bell, Rathbone and Allen all taught there. Sculpture by *Allen* and copper panels by a student, *H. Bloomfield Bare*, form part of the decoration of *Walter W.*

Thomas's remarkable Philharmonic Hotel [141], *c.* 1898–1900, but apart from this the practical results of Liverpool's experiment in architectural education are not easy to find. More tangible is the wealth of architectural sculpture and public monuments commissioned *c.* 1880–1915 from practitioners of the New Sculpture. These artists revitalized British sculpture from the 1880s onwards, introducing a poetic naturalism influenced by France in place of the worn-out conventions of Neoclassicism. *Hamo Thornycroft*'s statue of Charles Turner and son, in Waterhouse's Turner Memorial Home, dates from 1885. The panels on the E side of St George's Hall, always intended by Elmes for sculpture, were eventually carved between 1882 and 1901 by *Thomas Stirling Lee*, *Allen* and *Conrad Dressler* (*see* topic box, p. 52), and *Lee* also did the exquisite bronze doors for the Adelphi Bank. The last of the great group of public buildings in William Brown Street, *E.W. Mountford*'s Museum Extension and Central Technical School [39], 1896–1901, has much allegorical sculpture by *F.W. Pomeroy*. In St John's Gardens, laid out at the same time, statues of local philanthropists by *Frampton* and *Pomeroy* surround the Gladstone Memorial by *Thomas Brock* and *William Goscombe John*'s King's Liverpool Regiment Memorial. *Allen* did the bronze statuary on the Queen Victoria Monument in Derby Square of 1902–6, designed by *F.M. Simpson* (Professor of Architecture at University College) with *Willink & Thicknesse* [90]. At the Pier Head is *Frampton*'s iconographically unusual Alfred Jones Memorial, along with monuments to Edward VII and the Heroes of the Marine Engine Room by *John*, the latter unveiled in 1916 and notable for its dignified representation of manual workers [1].

Pomeroy's statue of Monsignor Nugent, 1905, and *Frampton*'s of Canon Lester, 1907, commemorate two heroes of the slums. They serve as a reminder that while architecture in the city centre and the wealthier suburbs had reached new levels of splendour, squalid social conditions were still widespread. After St Martin's Cottages in the 1860s, no **improved housing** for the poor was erected by the Corporation until Victoria Square of 1885 and Juvenal Dwellings of 1891 (both demolished). Slum clearance continued, but redevelopment was left to speculative builders, and indeed Victoria Square was intended as 'an example to be followed in the future by private enterprise'. From 1895, however, the Corporation undertook to replace demolished slums with housing for those dispossessed. The only survivals from this period belong to the Bevington Street Area scheme, opened 1912. They consist of terraced houses in a friendly cottage style [154] and three-storey flats in Eldon Grove with bay windows and half-timbering. At the corner of Eldon Street and Vauxhall Road a very interesting experimental block of flats was built in 1904–5 by the City Engineer *J.A. Brodie*. The floor, walls and ceiling of each room consisted of pre-cast reinforced concrete slabs, made with clinker from the City's refuse incinerators. The slabs were cast with door, window and fireplace openings, and were dovetailed into each other and bolted together. This early example of system-building has been demolished.

Walter W. Thomas (d. 1912) of Philharmonic Hotel fame is not to be confused with *Walter Aubrey Thomas* (d. 1934), the most individual Liverpool architect of the early 1900s. Specializing in commercial buildings, he was responsible for the Lord Street Arcade of 1901 [92], State Insurance of 1903–5, and Tower Buildings of 1906 etc. [102]. His work shows notable inventiveness and stylistic variety, as well as ambition matched by technological resourcefulness. Thomas's greatest undertaking was the colossal concrete-framed Royal Liver Building of 1908–11 [42–44], one of the famous early c20 trio at the Pier Head. Its neighbours are the headquarters of the Mersey Docks and Harbour Board [46] by *Briggs & Wolstenholme* with *Hobbs & Thornely*, 1903–7, and the Cunard Building [45] of 1914–16, by *Willink & Thicknesse* with *Arthur J. Davis*. These three signify the high-water mark of Liverpool's prosperity, and together give the city its unique waterfront silhouette. A match for them in scale and ostentation was the Cotton Exchange in Old Hall Street, 1905–6, by *Matear & Simon*. Its tremendous façade has gone, but part of the granite trading-floor colonnade survives, as does the functional but impressive N elevation, largely of cast iron and glass [20].

The Cunard Building, the latest of the Pier Head group, shows a decisive shift away from Baroque exuberance towards a cooler, more restrained **classicism**. The source of this was partly France (Arthur J. Davis had trained at the Ecole des Beaux Arts and practised with a French partner) and partly the classicism of American architects such as McKim, Mead & White. Transatlantic influence found fertile soil in early c20 Liverpool, where from 1904 *Charles Reilly* was Professor of Architecture (*see* topic box, p. 218). Other early examples of this new classicism, large in scale but relatively restrained in detail, include *Frank Atkinson*'s Adelphi Hotel of 1911–14, *Stanley Adshead*'s 1911 interior remodelling of the Playhouse, *Gerald de Courcy Fraser*'s Premier Buildings [108] of 1912–14 and Bon Marché of 1912–18, and *Aubrey Thomas*'s Crane Building of 1913–15. *Reilly* himself built little, but his Guild of Students of 1910–13 is a good illustration of his tastes [132].

Liverpool became an Anglican diocese in 1880, but not until 1904 did work start on building a **cathedral**. Even in a city where classicism was so deeply rooted, there was a prejudice in favour of Gothic as proper for a church, and *Giles Gilbert Scott*'s competition-winning design of 1903 was chosen from an entirely Gothic shortlist. Completely redesigned in 1909–10, and revised a number of times before completion in the 1970s, Scott's cathedral is both a culmination of the c19 Gothic Revival and a highly individual, unhistorical work of imagination [47, 50]. Vast in scale, it carries forward into the c20 that taste for the gigantic and sublime which is so typical of c19 Liverpool. Functionally, the plan is not entirely convincing, but in emotional terms, by generating awe and

20. Cotton Exchange, Old Hall Street, by Matear & Simon (1905–6), N front

wonder through the enclosure of vast spaces, the building is an overwhelming triumph. The control Scott exercised over the furnishings
and fittings gives the interior a remarkably harmonious consistency.

The Interwar Years

In the city centre, the American-influenced classicism of Reilly's students reached its peak in *Herbert J. Rowse*'s India Buildings [101] of
1923–30 (in conjunction with *Arnold Thornely*), and Martins Bank of
1927–32. Rowse, the outstanding Liverpool architect of the interwar
years, had travelled and worked in North America after his Liverpool
training, and these two grandly scaled and immaculately detailed buildings would not be out of place in New York or Montreal. The arcaded
and Travertine-clad banking hall of Martins is one of the sights of
Liverpool [100]. *Harold Dod*'s Athenaeum of 1924 is another sophisticated essay in the style [105]; so too are *Briggs, Wolstenholme &
Thornely*'s West Africa House, and *Thornely*'s 1931–3 remodelling of the
Walker Art Gallery entrance hall.

  During the 1930s, however, classicism seemed to have run its course,
and some architects began to explore alternative approaches. *Rowse*
adopted a streamlined Art Deco style in his ventilating stations
and entrance features for the first Mersey road tunnel [21], while for the
Philharmonic Hall of 1936–9 he was influenced by the blocky brick
architecture of W.M. Dudok. *Minoprio & Spencely*'s 1930–2 extension
to the School for the Blind is severely simplified classical, while
Dod's Harold Cohen Library of 1936–8 is a Jekyll and Hyde design,

21. George's Dock Ventilation and Control Station, Pier Head, by Herbert J. Rowse (designed 1932)

stripped classical in front and functional brick at the rear, with windows in continuous bands. *Reilly* himself, in partnership with *Lionel Budden* and *J.E. Marshall*, designed the Leverhulme Building of the Liverpool School of Architecture with the main windows forming a horizontal strip in the approved Modernist way, though its use of brick defers to the late Georgian terraces of neighbouring Abercromby Square. In commercial architecture, the best of Liverpool's Art Deco picture palaces is *William R. Glen*'s former Forum Cinema in Lime Street, with its curving stone façade, and one of the most 'progressive' buildings is *Robert Threadgold*'s former department store in London Road.

But it was in **public housing** of the 1930s that European Modernism made its boldest appearance in Liverpool, in large blocks of multi-storey flats built under the direction of *Lancelot Keay*, Director of Housing from 1925 and later City Architect. The best, St Andrew's Gardens, survives [135]. It was designed by *John Hughes*, a student of Reilly's, and has sweeping balconies and windows in long bands. Its semicircular form was inspired by Berlin's Horseshoe Estate. Keay built Neo-Georgian council houses too, for example at Speke from 1938, and in other new suburbs that lie outside the scope of this guide. Speke is also the site of Liverpool Airport, where the terminal building [178] and hangars of 1935–40 by *Edward Bloomfield* are a celebration of high-speed travel as eloquent as Rowse's tunnel structures.

In contrast to such Modernist ventures stands the greatest single interwar project, the **Roman Catholic Cathedral** designed by *Lutyens* [53] and begun with amazing confidence in 1933. The crypt – the only part to be carried out – gives a sense of the stupendous scale intended, and also of the style [22]. Lutyens's design drew on ideas from Ancient Rome, Byzantium and Renaissance Italy, but was not a backward-looking piece of historicism. Like Scott's Anglican Cathedral, it was a deeply imaginative development from traditional themes, as unmistakably a C20 work as Keay's nearby blocks of flats.

Liverpool's tradition of high-quality architectural **sculpture** continued. Rowse's tunnel buildings have effective carved decoration by *Edmund C. Thompson* and *George T. Capstick*, and the former also worked on the interior of his Philharmonic Hall [140]. *Minoprio & Spencely*'s Blind School extension has Modernist reliefs by *John Skeaping*. In the Anglican Cathedral, *Edward Carter Preston*'s columnar portal figures [49] and various monuments blend fluidly with Scott's architecture. But the dominant sculptor of these years was *Herbert Tyson Smith*, whose flat, linear style suited both classical and modern architecture, and whose career continued into the 1960s. The bronze doors and other sculptural embellishments of *Rowse*'s Martins Bank are his, and so are the powerful reliefs on the Cenotaph [23], one of the most arresting memorials anywhere to the dead of the First World War. Its emphasis on grief and loss seems all the more extraordinary when compared with the conventional heroics of *Joseph Phillips*'s war memorial for the Exchange News Room and *Derwent Wood*'s for the Cotton Exchange, or with the Neoclassical allegory of *Henry Pegram*'s Cunard memorial (done in conjunction with *Willink & Thicknesse*).

22. Crypt of the Roman Catholic Cathedral, by Edwin Lutyens (begun 1933)

23. Detail of Cenotaph relief, by H. Tyson Smith (unveiled 1930)

The Postwar Years

Its strategic importance made Liverpool a key target in the Second
World War. Bombing reduced to rubble a large part of the business
district s of Lord Street and Derby Square [24], and many other
important buildings were destroyed or severely damaged. Some, such
as the former Blue Coat School and the gutted Museum in William
Brown Street, were rebuilt behind preserved façades; others, damaged
but reparable, were demolished to generate short-term employment
(the fate of Foster's great Custom House).

Reconstruction in the lean 1950s was patchy in quality. The s side of
Lord Street was drearily rebuilt with characterless shops. Elsewhere,
prestigious sites were filled with respectfully traditional buildings,
harking back to the years before the war. *Morter & Dobie*'s Reliance
House in Water Street is pure Neo-Georgian. Spinney House of 1951–5
is a rather coarse echo of Rowse by *Alfred Shennan*, who also did Pearl
Assurance House, following the curve of the younger *Foster*'s bombed
St George's Crescent. *Gerald de Courcy Fraser* designed the stripped
classical rebuilding of his own pre-war Lewis's department store, with
Epstein's colossal statue on the façade representing the scarred city's
resurgence [109]. The freshest early postwar office building is *H.
Hinchliffe Davies*'s lively Corn Exchange of 1953–9, while adjoining
the docks, Tate & Lyle's parabolic Sugar Silo of 1955–7 [78] is the most
exciting continuation of the functional warehouse tradition.

In 1959 there was a decisive break with the past, when *Lutyens*'s
Roman Catholic cathedral scheme was abandoned and the competition

for a new design was announced. *Frederick Gibberd*'s winning proposal, completed in 1967, is Liverpool's most important building from the second half of the c20, and the only one of international significance. The centralized plan is expressed externally in the great conical roof, the radiating buttresses with chapels between, and the circular lantern tower with its crown of pinnacles [52]. Its distinctive shape adds a skyline counterpoint to the tower of Scott's Anglican Cathedral. Leading artists provided the furnishings, notably *John Piper* and *Patrick Reyntiens*, whose abstract stained glass floods the interior with intensely coloured light [55].

The **University of Liverpool** was quick to plan for increased student numbers, commissioning *William Holford* as early as 1946 to draw up expansion proposals. These formed the basis for the takeover and gradual demolition of the Georgian streets around Abercromby Square, and for the decision to employ a variety of architects rather than just one. The earliest buildings are rather timid, except *Basil Spence*'s Chadwick Laboratory of 1957–9. Those put up from the early 1960s onwards, as expansion gathered pace and public funding increased, are more assertive. Most appealing are the Arts and Law buildings of 1961–6 by *Bryan & Norman Westwood, Piet & Partners*, grouped round a pleasantly landscaped space. The aggressive Sports Centre [129] by *Denys Lasdun & Partners*, and *Yorke, Rosenberg & Mardall*'s clinical white-tiled Electrical Engineering and Electronics building, are the most memorable of the rest. Adjoining the university is *Holford Associates*' Royal Liverpool University Hospital, planned 1963–5 but not opened until 1978. Its great size and elevated site make it a landmark, and the towering ward block and highly sculptural boiler house are powerful Brutalist works.

With hindsight, wartime bomb damage was less destructive than the subsequent efforts of architects and planners. Under *Ronald Bradbury* (appointed City Architect and Director of Housing, 1948) and *J.W. Boddy* (who took over responsibility for housing in 1963), **flats** in slab

24. Bomb damage, looking s from the Queen Victoria Monument to the Custom House, 1944

blocks and towers were built in great numbers, notably in Everton. Tower blocks were also intended to replace the C19 villas surrounding Sefton Park, but only a few were carried out. In 1963 prefabricated construction was adopted, when the Council accepted a tender for almost two and a half thousand dwellings in towers built according to the French *Camus* system; other industrialized systems were also used. The failure, in social terms, of much of this high-rise housing led to its demolition in the 1980s–90s, along with most of Keay's inner-city flats. In 1965 construction of *James A. Roberts*'s giant St John's Precinct began. Its introverted bulk not only erased Foster's 1820–2 market hall and the surrounding street pattern, but also injured the setting of St George's Hall. Reconstruction received further encouragement in 1965 when the **Liverpool City Centre Plan** [25] was published. Drawn up under the leadership of planning consultant *Graeme Shankland* and City Planning Officer *Walter Bor*, this headily up-beat document was intended to provide a framework for comprehensive redevelopment. Its authors declared that two-thirds of the centre was obsolete, and that projected rates of growth in population and prosperity made wholesale renewal both necessary and feasible. A mere handful of buildings were earmarked for preservation, plus four conservation areas: the business core around the Town Hall and Castle Street, St George's Hall and William Brown Street, Bold Street, and Rodney Street. New roads were central to the Plan, and demolition on an enormous scale was required to build them. Although this programme was eventually scaled back, the city was nevertheless fragmented by multi-lane highways that cut off the centre from the waterfront and from the inner districts to the N and E. The dual carriageway for buses that ploughs between St George's Hall and Williamson Square is of the same date. To the N, large areas were cleared for the approaches to a second road tunnel under the Mersey, Kingsway, the first stage of which opened in 1971. One successful transport proposal in the Plan was an underground loop line linking the main railway stations, and a tunnel connecting the two principal commuter lines from the N and S, which came into use in 1977.

Shankland and Bor recommended that new high-rise buildings should be grouped in clusters framing the old business centre, a policy that produced several large office blocks in and around Old Hall Street to the N, and later the Queen Elizabeth II Law Courts to the S. Of the former, *Tripe & Wakeham*'s Royal Insurance headquarters of 1972–6 (now Royal & Sun Alliance) is the only notable one [97], a giant stepped pyramid which enriches the city's silhouette from the river. Commercial buildings in the centre are mostly forgettable, except *Bradshaw, Rowse & Harker*'s extraordinary bank of *c.* 1971, with an angular glass façade that screams for attention in sober C19 Dale Street. More appealing is *Hall, O'Donahue & Wilson*'s lively 1968 extension to the Playhouse [113], a welcome reminder amid so much dull 1960s architecture that Liverpool enjoyed a surge of creativity at this time. In music, the Beatles

25.
Rebuilding
proposals,
*Liverpool
City Centre
Plan* (1965)

brought worldwide attention, and were part of a vibrant scene that also included poetry (Penguin's bestselling *Mersey Sound* anthology was published in 1967) and art (the first biennial John Moores exhibition of contemporary art was held at the Walker Art Gallery in 1957–8).

The Late Twentieth Century Onwards

The confidence that gave rise to the City Centre Plan was short-lived. The collapse of British manufacturing in general, and of the Lancashire textile industry in particular, deprived the port of its core business, while the decline of Imperial links and the emergence of Europe as Britain's main trading partner meant Liverpool lost out to the ports of the SE. At the same time containerization reduced the need for man-power. The local economy was so narrowly based on the port that the consequences were disastrous. Unemployment reached appalling levels, and the population fell from 746,000 in 1961 to 510,000 in 1981. In that year racial tensions, on top of dire social conditions, led to rioting in Toxteth in which many buildings were destroyed. Contemplating the seemingly terminal decline of her home city in 1983, the novelist Beryl Bainbridge saw it as the victim of a range of destructive forces, from misguided politicians and planners to the inexorable tide of history and economics: 'Someone's murdered Liverpool and got away with it.'

Central government responded with various initiatives. The **Merseyside Development Corporation** was established in 1981 (before the riots) to bring about regeneration. It was responsible for the Liverpool International Garden Festival of 1984, which left a legacy of reclaimed industrial land s of the centre, the elegant Festival Hall by *Arup Associates* (now disused), and some interesting public sculpture, since relocated to city-centre sites. Around the South Docks, closed to shipping in 1972, housing, small businesses and leisure uses were established. Architecturally, the MDC's greatest achievement was the restoration of the long-derelict Albert Dock warehouses [64], a landmark in the rehabilitation of the city's redundant C19 buildings. The conversion of part of one block by *James Stirling* to house a Liverpool outpost of the Tate Gallery set a very high standard for future reuse schemes. In the inner city, many dilapidated Georgian terraces in the Canning Street–Upper Parliament Street area were saved through a major programme of refurbishment in the 1980s, largely grant-aided by English Heritage.

The preservation of the Albert Dock – threatened with demolition when Pevsner described it in 1969 – was a victory for conservationists, and in the late 1970s and early 80s successful campaigns were also waged to retain the Lyceum and St Francis Xavier's church, with national as well as local support. Like other post-industrial cities, Liverpool has since come to see 'heritage' as the key to a lucrative tourist trade. A sense of nostalgia for the ravaged C19 city, and a loss of confidence in contemporary design, seems to be reflected in the adoption of 'Victorian' polychrome brickwork and other decorative details in some large developments of the 1980s, for instance *David Backhouse*'s Cavern Walks and dockside housing at Mariner's Wharf, and the Clayton Square Shopping Centre by the *Seymour Harris Partnership*. The more fundamental qualities of Liverpool's best Victorian architecture – strength and solidity expressed through resilient materials, and a sense of scale appropriate to the city's topography – have generally not been imitated.

Council housing built in the 1980s, to replace Keay's interwar estates and the postwar slabs and towers, also shows a return to C19 materials and scale. The houses are of brick and generally of two storeys, but instead of terraces they are mostly detached or semi-detached. Disenchantment with failed municipal housing schemes of the past fuelled the rise of housing co-operatives and community architecture in the 1970s and 80s. As a result, large areas of the inner city now have the informal, spacious, low-rise character previously associated with suburbs [155].

It is a measure of the city's lack of prosperity that so few architecturally significant buildings have been erected in the last twenty years, while some deplorable ones have been permitted in prominent locations. That the execrable 1991–3 Customs and Excise building by *PSA Projects*, *Birmingham* [69] should have been built on such a glorious waterfront site is deeply depressing; likewise that *Geoffrey Reid Associates*' feeble Commutation Plaza should now close the grand view up William Brown Street. The most enlightened client of new architecture has been the Liverpool John Moores University, which commissioned the Aldham Robarts Learning Resource Centre of 1992–3 from *Austin-Smith:Lord* [139], followed by the Peter Jost Enterprise Centre and Avril

26. FACT, Wood Street, by Austin-Smith:Lord (completed 2003)

Robarts Learning Resource Centre. By comparison with these earlier successes, the same architects' recent FACT building is disappointing outside, though the interior is spatially intriguing [26]. *David Marks Julia Barfield Architects*' Watersport Centre, 1993–4, is outstanding: an elegant pavilion that appears to float serenely in the Queen's Dock [69].

Much of the best architecture of recent years has involved creative **adaptation and reuse**. In the 1990s the former girls' school, Blackburne House, was sensitively transformed into a women's training centre by *Pickles Martinez Architects*; *Brock Carmichael Associates* adapted and extended the neighbouring former Mechanics' Institution to become the Liverpool Institute of Performing Arts (LIPA) [142]; and *Ken Martin* turned the Midland Railway goods warehouse into the Conservation Centre of National Museums Liverpool [114]. Of the same period are *Dave King* and *Rod McAllister*'s interesting high-tech additions to the 1930s School of Architecture and the 1960s wing of the Guild of Students, both at the University of Liverpool. But the leading exponents of reuse have been the developers Urban Splash, originally with their in-house designers *Design Shed*, latterly with *Shed KM*. Their pioneering Concert Square scheme, completed 1994, included the residential conversion of a former C19 chemical factory, the first such venture in Liverpool (other than the Albert Dock and Wapping warehouses), which initially lagged behind Manchester in this respect. Through the creation of a lively open space fringed by bars, it began the regeneration of this run-down area. In the late 1990s they built apartments within the preserved shell of *Elmes*'s fire-damaged Collegiate Institution, combining new and old with flair and ingenuity [157]. And it is not only historic buildings that have been revived: *Union North*'s Cablehouse is an imaginative residential conversion of a 1960s factory, and *Brock Carmichael Associates*' Beetham Plaza was adapted from a dreary office block of the same period.

Of all British cities, Liverpool rose most spectacularly in the C18 and C19, and collapsed most dramatically in the second half of the C20. It is a story written clearly in the city's streets and buildings. After decades of decline the economic tide may now have turned, but although there is much construction underway or planned in the centre, it remains to be seen whether the results will live up to the best architecture of the past. A far-reaching project that will be of enormous significance is currently in its early stages. It involves extending the shopping area westward from behind the former Blue Coat School to Canning Place, rebuilding a largely derelict part of the city centre. This promises to help reunite the central area with the waterfront and, unlike the monolithic shopping developments of the 1960s, it is planned to consist of separate buildings designed by a range of architects. A second ambitious proposal, for a 'landmark' building beside the Pier Head (*see* topic box, p. 70), has so far come to nothing. Aside from these major projects, a steady stream of new-build and conversion schemes caters to the fashion for city-centre living and the boom in student housing, but the standard of design is often poor. Against this background of change, in 2003 it was announced that Liverpool will hold the title European Capital of Culture in 2008. If it proves a spur to raise architectural standards and recover the creative flair and ambition of the past, it will be an accolade worth having.

Major Buildings

Town Hall

High Street

The Town Hall [27] has a complicated history. Built in the mid C18 by *John Wood*, it was modified, extended and reconstructed in the late C18–early C19 by *John Foster Sen.* under the direction of *James Wyatt*. Further changes in the late C19 and C20 will be noted as we come to them.

History and Exterior

The building stands near the ancient centre of Liverpool, on a commanding site at the junction of High Street, Dale Street, Castle Street and Water Street. Its immediate predecessor of 1673 stood just to the s, 'placed on pillars and arches of hewen stone', with the Public Exchange for merchants below. In 1747 the Council began negotiations to purchase the present site for a new building, and in 1749 a design by *John Wood* of Bath was approved. Six years earlier Wood had completed the Bristol Exchange, publishing the plans and a description in 1745. It is

27. Town Hall, by John Wood (1749–54); dome (completed 1802) and portico (completed 1811) by James Wyatt.

28. *The Exchange* (now Town Hall), engraving by E. Rooker after P. P. Burdett (1773)

hardly surprising that Liverpool, with its considerable wealth and limited architectural talent, should have bought in the services of one of the outstanding architects of the day. The Liverpool businesswoman Sarah Clayton, acting on behalf of the Council in assessing his suitability, reported from Bath on 5 June 1749: 'on all hands he is agreed to be a great genius'. The work was supervised by his son, *John Wood Jun.*

The first stone of **Wood's building** was laid on 14 September 1749, and it opened in 1754. Like its C17 predecessor, it consisted of a ground-floor exchange with a council room and other public offices above. Older buildings abutted the w and N sides, so it had only two elevations, s and E, which survive in altered form. What was presumably their original state is shown in a view published by Enfield in 1773 [28]. Each is nine bays long, with a rusticated ground floor, Corinthian pilasters to the *piano nobile*, and round-arched windows with square Corinthian piers between the pilasters. The middle three bays on the E side break forward slightly under a pediment, and here the pilasters give way to attached Corinthian columns, arranged 2-1-1-2. Originally the middle of the principal, s side was the same, but with sculpture in the pediment; the portico here is a later addition. Between the capitals on both fronts are panels of vigorous **carving** in high relief, mostly illustrating the foreign trade which was the source of Liverpool's wealth. On the E these include, in the words of John Prestwich (probably writing in the 1780s), 'Busts of Blackamoors & Elephants with the Teeth of the Latter, with such like emblematical Figures, representing the African Trade & Commerce' [9]. *Thomas Johnson*, *William Mercer* and *Edward Rigby*, who appear in the accounts as carvers, may have been responsible.*

*The s pediment sculpture – an allegory of Liverpool's maritime commerce – was by *William Stephenson.*

Tripartite central entrances on each side originally gave access to the Exchange courtyard in the middle, Doric colonnades making covered walks on all four sides. According to contemporary descriptions it was dark and confined, and the merchants preferred to transact business in the street outside. Another account says the building had a 'noble cupola', and a large, square, lead-covered dome with a lantern appears above the centre of the s range on John Eyes's map of 1765. Was this inelegant structure part of Wood's design? Inside, Wood's building had a grand stair off the E walk, and principal rooms on all four sides of the first floor, including the Town Hall (s range), Council Room and assembly rooms.

A campaign of **alterations** began in 1785 when the Exchange Committee resolved that adjoining buildings be removed. By 1786 orders were given for the newly exposed w front to be plastered and painted, but it was not until 1792 that *John Foster Sen.* prepared a new design for this façade. It closely follows Wood's s and E fronts, though the first-floor windows are slightly different. (Orders for altering the ground floor of the E elevation were given in 1796, when the square-headed windows shown in Enfield's illustration were presumably replaced with the present round-headed ones.) The carved panels continue the theme of maritime commerce but make no direct reference to the slave trade – a more controversial subject by the end of the C18. The square dome was taken down in 1786, and the ambitious idea of erecting a new dome over the central court was conceived. In 1787 instructions were given to demolish the houses on the N side, with the intention of erecting a large extension for the mayor's office and court, with a new assembly room above.

In connection with these proposals *Foster* surveyed the building and made drawings for minor alterations, but the Exchange Committee did not think he was qualified to carry out the job alone. They instructed him in 1788 to send survey drawings to two London architects, a Mr Leverton (presumably Thomas Leverton) and *Thomas Whetton* (who had already provided designs for a new Council Room ceiling), and the following month he was ordered to show the plans to *James Wyatt* so that he could 'give his opinion upon and make Designs for the intended improvements to the North Side'. Wyatt attended the Committee in October, when his designs for a new dome and N block were adopted. Thereafter, Foster supervised the building under instruction from Wyatt, occasionally suggesting minor modifications.

Wyatt's N addition follows Wood's s front in having a rusticated basement with round-arched windows, but is distinguished by its higher roof and sparer, more refined ornament. The portico with its four pairs of Corinthian columns did not originally project so far. It was rebuilt using the original columns in 1899–1900, in connection with the reconstruction of the Council Chamber (*see* Interior, below). The badly weathered **statues** above were ordered from *Richard Westmacott Sen.*

in 1792. The three-bay end elevations have paired pilasters framing niches, and oval windows under garlands.

On 18 January 1795 the Exchange was devastated by fire. Wyatt and Foster's unfinished N addition escaped unscathed, but Wood's building was gutted. The Council at once decided to rebuild within the external walls. Wyatt's **dome** was completed in 1802. It rests on a high drum with tall pedimented Corinthian aedicules at the angles (perhaps derived from Gandon's Dublin Custom House, and ultimately from Wren at Greenwich), and large tripartite windows between, divided by further pairs of columns. At the cardinal points of the springing of the dome are four clock faces, each supported by a lion and a unicorn, and crowning the whole a *Coade*-stone **statue** of a seated female figure, variously identified as Minerva or Britannia, by *J.C. Rossi*. Today it is overshadowed by taller neighbours, but when built Wyatt's noble dome was a dominant feature of the skyline. The projecting **portico** in the middle of the s front, completed in 1811, replaced Wood's centrepiece; at the same time the attic windows on this side were replaced by panels carved with swags and garlands, probably by *Frederick Legé*. The portico helps bring the dome into a more harmonious relationship with the lower part, and adds interest to the views from Water Street and Dale Street. The space underneath (intended for election hustings) encloses two ramps, ingeniously introduced by *Donald W. Insall & Associates* in the early 1990s to improve access. At both ends are arched openings with luscious wrought ironwork in C18 style by *George Wragge*. These seem to have been introduced in 1913 by *Romaine-Walker & Jenkins*. Sturdy early C19 cast-iron **railings** incorporating Greek Revival lamp standards, made by *William Bennett* of Liverpool, surround the building.

Interior

The main entrance leads into the **Vestibule**, something of a surprise after the Neoclassical exterior. Encaustic tile floor of 1848, incorporating the arms of Liverpool. Sumptuous wooden fireplace, made up from C17 Flemish carvings, presented in 1893; in 1898 the oak panelling was added by *Frederick Moore Simpson* (with door handles and fingerplates by *Richard Llewellyn Rathbone*) and the groin-vaulted ceiling was plastered. The four shallow lunettes above the panelling have poor murals by *J.H. Amschewitz*, completed 1909: King John Creating Liverpool a Free Port (w), Industry and Peace (N), Liverpool the Centre of Commerce (E), and Education and Progress (s). These commemorate the 700th anniversary of Liverpool's first 'charter' in 1207, and the employment of a London artist was loudly resented by local painters.

In the post-1795 reconstruction the ground floor on the E **side** was intended to house the Surveyor, Town Clerk and Treasurer, whose rooms appear to survive in altered form. They have groined vaults (ordered in 1802) and one now contains a good *ex situ* C18 marble fireplace, with a relief representing Navigation. At the back in Wyatt's N

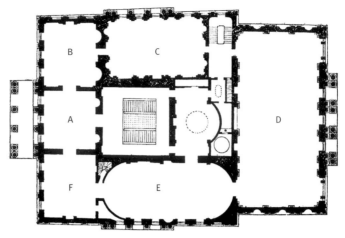

29. Town Hall, first-floor plan from the *Kaleidoscope, c.* 1820 (service areas since altered): A, Central Reception Room; B, West Reception Room; C, Dining Room; D, Large Ballroom; E, Small Ballroom; F, East Reception Room

addition is the **Council Chamber**, enlarged in 1899–1900 to fill the ground floor. The centre was extended out, creating a recess for the Lord Mayor's dais and resulting in the external changes to the N portico noted above. *Thomas Shelmerdine*, Corporation Surveyor, was architect. The councillors' benches, arranged in a curve, face the Lord Mayor's seat. Mahogany-panelled walls, with each round-arched window framed by unfluted columns and a serpentine entablature. Elaborate light fittings, vaguely Art Nouveau, by *Singer* of Frome. Charles Reilly in 1927 described the overall effect as 'in the best saloon-bar style'. Tucked between the Council Chamber and the main stairs is the **Hall of Remembrance**, where the names of Liverpool's First World War dead are inscribed. The **murals** by *Frank O. Salisbury*, with titles including Duty's Call, Sacrifice, Immortality and Triumph, were completed in 1923. From here stairs lead to the basement, with cloakrooms round a vaulted foyer, formed in 1913 by *Romaine-Walker & Jenkins*. (The kitchens have been in the basement since the 1820s; on the w side, off the sunken area, is a brick-vaulted ice house.)

Wyatt's **Staircase Hall** opens directly from the Vestibule and occupies the site of the central open court of Wood's Exchange. This is one of the great architectural spaces of Liverpool. The staircase rises in a single broad flight between two pairs of unfluted Corinthian columns (which support the upper landing) to a half-landing. From here two narrower flights, not attached to the walls, return towards the upper landing, which takes the form of a broad gallery running round three sides. The walls here have segmental heads with Diocletian windows. Pendentives carry the soaring drum with its large expanses of glazing, and high over all is the coffered interior of the dome. In 1913 *Romaine-Walker & Jenkins* laid a new marble floor and added extensions supported on Tuscan columns to both ends of the half-landing; the motto of the city round the base of the drum was redone in raised letters, and cherubs' heads and swags in relief added between the windows. The four impressive **paintings** in the pendentives by *Charles Wellington Furse*, planned as part of *F.M. Simpson*'s redecoration, were installed in 1902. The subjects – energetic scenes of dock labour – are striking in this ceremonial setting. The early C19 surfaces were much plainer: drum and walls were finished with rough stucco, and painted to imitate stone. In niches at the foot of the stairs are two extraordinary cast-iron **stoves** each in the form of a Greek Doric column surmounted by a trident head and standing on a plinth. These and other stoves were apparently supplied by *Moser & Co.*, and it has been suggested that all were designed by *J.M. Gandy*, who received payments for unspecified designs in connection with the Town Hall, 1811–13. On the half-landing a marble **statue** of George Canning, 1832, by *Francis Chantrey*.

The **first floor** [29] is entirely occupied by entertaining rooms, designed by *Wyatt* and executed under Foster's supervision (designs apparently approved 1805). They have interconnecting doors, so the visitor makes a complete circuit. The landing opens into the roughly square **Central Reception Room**, directly behind the s portico. It has a circular ceiling with fluted pendentives, and beautiful Neoclassical plasterwork by *Francesco Bernasconi*, who was responsible for most of the stucco throughout. Stoves stand in niches on either side of the central door, with cylindrical bases and elaborate superstructures incorporating winged female herms. Doors on the right lead into the **West Reception Room**, of similar shape but with a segmental vaulted ceiling. The white marble chimneypiece has rich fittings of brass and cast iron. The **Dining Room**, entered from here, occupies the w side [30]. The most sumptuous room in the building, with Corinthian pilasters of yellow Carniola marble (an artificial material), a coved ceiling divided into moulded compartments, and an elaborate plaster frieze with scrolls, urns and crouching dogs. Between the capitals of the pilasters are roundels painted with pairs of cupids, possibly by *Matthew Cotes Wyatt*, James Wyatt's son, who devised a much more ambitious scheme of allegorical decoration in 1811. Built into pairs of niches at either end are mahogany cabinets with brass fittings (intended for warming plates), supporting candelabra in the form of red scagliola vases, ordered from *Joseph Brown* in 1813. Between the windows is another pair of **stoves** of extraordinary Neoclassical design: the grate is contained in the square base, with elaborate perforated doors and slender candelabra rising from each corner, on top of which stands a sturdy column with a swirling skirt of fleshy acanthus leaves. A door at the NE corner leads to a top-lit room, running w–e above the Hall of Remembrance, which was given its present form – and its elegant plaster decoration – in 1913 by *Romaine-Walker & Jenkins*. The central N door of the Dining Room leads to a landing at the top of the secondary stairs, also rebuilt in 1913.

30. Town Hall, the Dining Room, by James Wyatt (design approved 1805)

From here the **Large Ballroom** is entered, occupying the whole upper floor of Wyatt's N extension. The decoration, with giant Corinthian pilasters of yellow Carniola, was not completed until 1820. In the middle of the s side is a balconied niche with a coffered semi-dome, for the musicians, between white marble chimneypieces carved by *William Hetherington*. From the segmental-vaulted ceiling, with stucco work by *James Queen*, hang three spectacular chandeliers, supplied by *Thomas Hawkes & Co.* in 1820. The huge mirrors at either end seem to be later C19. Doors at the SE corner open into the **Small Ballroom**, which fills the E side. It has pilasters of red Carniola and a segmental vault with shallow end apses; in the N apse are two niches for musicians – the same arrangement as Wyatt's saloon at Heveningham Hall, Suffolk. It opens into the **East Reception Room**, which balances the West Reception Room and completes the circuit. Most of the **furniture** in these rooms was designed and made for the Town Hall *c.* 1817–*c.* 1820, and is of superb quality.

The combination of richly decorated apartments for entertaining and more functional spaces for civic administration, council meetings, etc., is found in other late C18 public buildings – the Newark Town Hall by Carr of York, for instance, and formerly in the Chelmsford Shire Hall – but not on the magnificent scale seen here. This is probably the grandest such suite of civic rooms in the country, an outstanding and complete example of late Georgian decoration and a powerful demonstration of the wealth of Liverpool at the opening of the C19.

St George's Hall and the Plateau

Lime Street

Early C19 Liverpool lacked a suitable venue for its triennial music festivals and other large assemblies. Following a public meeting in 1836, a company was formed to raise subscriptions for a hall, and early in 1839 a competition was announced for a building dedicated to meetings, festivals, dinners and concerts, to be called St George's Hall. The winner was a twenty-five-year-old London architect, *Harvey Lonsdale Elmes*. New assize courts became necessary at about the same time, Liverpool having become an assize town in 1835. A second competition was held, and this too was won by *Elmes*. The planning of Elmes's court building was heavily criticized in the press, and the Corporation Surveyor, *Joseph Franklin*, was asked to make new designs. Elmes protested, however, and, given the chance to revise his original proposals, he was ultimately awarded the commission.

The chosen **site** was extremely prominent, elevated above the town and adjoining the newly built Lime Street Station. The initial idea was to set the buildings at right angles, the courts on the w side of Lime Street (previously occupied by the Infirmary of 1759) and the hall just s of where the Wellington Column now stands. They would have enclosed

31. St George's Hall, by Harvey Lonsdale Elmes (1841–54), photographed *c.* 1855

two sides of a formal *place*, with the façade of the station (1835–6, by *John Foster Jun.*; demolished) making a third. In 1840, however, Elmes was asked to explore alternatives, and his suggestion to combine hall and courts in one exceptionally large building on the w side was adopted.

Size was important if St George's Hall was to express adequately the pride and confidence of the thriving town. Elmes made a drawing in which the cross-section was superimposed on other great buildings, drawn to scale: Westminster Hall, St Paul's Cathedral and most significantly the new Birmingham Town Hall (begun 1832) were all to be surpassed. The inscription over the s portico, *Artibus, Legibus, Consiliis* (To Arts, Laws and Counsels), proclaimed unequivocally that this huge edifice was a monument to civilized values, in a town where the previous largest buildings had been dedicated to commerce. Construction began in 1841 and the building opened in 1854 (the Small Concert Room in 1856). In 1847 Elmes died in Jamaica, where he had gone in hope of recovering his health. By this date the interior was not far advanced. Work continued under the supervision of *Robert Rawlinson* and the Corporation Surveyor, *John Weightman*. From 1849 *C.R. Cockerell* was invited to give advice, and in 1851 he was appointed architect. The decoration of the interiors is largely due to him. *W.H. Wordley*, who had been Elmes's assistant, continued under both Weightman and Cockerell. As many as 299 men laboured on the site at its busiest, and the cost was almost £290,000. This compares with over £700,000 for the Albert Dock and its warehouses, built at the same time.

Elmes's competition designs had been conventional Greek Revival, but the combined building designed in 1840–1 is altogether more inventive, drawing on Roman sources as well as Greek. Certain features of the competition designs are retained: the long lateral portico and pedimented s end from the first St George's Hall, and the long windowless attic of the Assize Courts. But the unifying feature – the giant Corinthian order – is not present in either design, and is thoroughly Roman in derivation. The s portico is pushed beyond the original edge of the site where the ground falls away. Towering above St John's Lane, it recalls visionary C19 reconstructions of the temples in the Roman Forum. That Elmes relished such magnificent effects is clear from his perspective drawings.

To explain the novelty of Elmes's classicism the influence of the great Prussian architect K.F. Schinkel has sometimes been cited. Elmes did not visit Germany until 1842, after the external design was largely finalized, but he may have known Schinkel's work through illustrations. Square pillars of the sort used by Elmes are found in Schinkel, but also in William Wilkins's The Grange, Hampshire (begun 1809), which Elmes probably knew. Whatever influences he was exposed to, however, Elmes's design seems to have grown out of the unusual requirements of the brief, coupled with deep archaeological knowledge and an experimental attitude to Antiquity. Such is clear from Elmes's

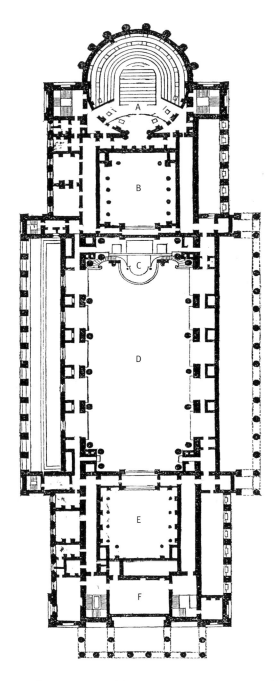

32. St George's Hall, plan from *The Builder*, 1855: A, Small Concert Room; B, Civil Court; C, Organ; D, Concert Hall; E, Crown Court; F, Grand Jury Room

letter to his collaborator Rawlinson: 'How frequently I observe the great & true end & aim of Art entirely lost sight of in the discussion of some insignificant detail or quaint Antiquarianism. Bold and original conceptions never can find favour while so much stress is laid upon precedent'. Elmes's inventiveness is clear if one compares St George's Hall with earlier, more literal interpretations of temple architecture, such as the British Museum, or, closer to home, St Bride (*see* Walk 6, p. 240).

St George's Hall Relief Sculptures

33. Joy follows the growth of Justice, led by Conscience, directed by Wisdom, relief by Thomas Stirling Lee (installed by 1885)

Elmes's design provided for extensive exterior sculpture, but apart from the s pediment none was installed until the 1880s. In 1882 the City Council held a competition for reliefs at the s end of the E façade, won by *Thomas Stirling Lee*. Young and unknown, Lee had trained mostly in France and was an adherent of the New Sculpture movement (*see* Introduction, p. 29). He proposed six reliefs illustrating the Progress of Justice, portrayed as a female figure growing to maturity. In the first panel [33] she takes the form of a nude girl, in the second an equally nude young woman. When these were unveiled the unidealized figures aroused great controversy – it was alleged they would encourage the sale of pornography – and Lee's contract was terminated. In the end, he was allowed to complete the series, the remaining panels being paid for by Philip Henry Rathbone, Chairman of the Walker Art Gallery's committee. They feature draped figures, and lack the narrative drive of the first two. The six panels at the N end of the E façade illustrate National Prosperity, and were designed and carved 1895–1901: *C.J. Allen, Conrad Dressler* and *Lee* were each responsible for two, with *Lee* having a supervisory role.

34. St George's Hall, E front

Exterior

The Concert Hall is placed lengthways in the centre (indicated by the great windowless attic), with the Crown Court to the s and the Civil Court to the N. At the N end is an apsidal entrance hall with the elliptical Small Concert Room above. All four **elevations** are different, and expressive of the various spaces within, but tied together by the unbroken horizontal of the entablature. The **s front** [31] has an eight-columned portico, two columns deep, raised on steps above a rusticated podium. Sculpture for the pediment, designed by *Cockerell* and executed by *W.G. Nicholl*, became unsafe and was taken down in 1950. The substructure of the portico is not as *Elmes* intended. The steps surrounding it are due to *Cockerell* and date from after 1849. Cockerell also introduced paired flights of steps in front of the podium, replaced in the late 1850s by the rusticated wall facing St John's Lane. The main **entrance front** [34] is on the E, facing the station. It has a portico of sixteen columns, corresponding to the Concert Hall inside. On either side, correspon- ding with the courts, the order continues in square, unfluted pillars. Their lower parts are embedded and read as pilasters, but their upper parts are free-standing. Between the pilasters are **reliefs**, added 1882–1901 (*see* topic box, facing). The outer bays are blank and solid. The w side now overlooks St John's Gardens but until 1899 faced the church of the same name (*see* Major Buildings, p. 65). Smaller rooms for court purposes occupy the ground and first floors here, lit by large windows. The projecting central part has the same square pillars as the ends of the E front, but here they support only a massive entablature and no roof, so admitting light to the Concert Hall behind. The entablature viewed from below, outlined against the sky, is an extraordinary sight. The N **front** has a semicircular apse with three-quarter columns, and three doorways. These are flanked by **statues** of nereids and tritons bearing lamps, by *Nicholl,* matching statues under the S and E porticoes.

Interiors

The main entrance, central behind the E portico, is the least satisfactory part of Elmes's plan. Instead of a spacious and dignified vestibule, it leads into a **corridor** running N–S to the courts at each end. A matching corridor runs along the W side. Crossing the corridor and entering the **Concert Hall** [35] brings further disappointment, because the entrance is on the short rather than the long axis. The space is so magnificent, however, that disappointment is quickly forgotten. This is one of the greatest Victorian interiors, and perhaps more expressive of C19 civic pride and aspiration than any other. It is roofed with a mighty tunnel vault, planned by Elmes before his death but constructed under *Rawlinson*'s supervision. To lessen the weight Rawlinson used hollow bricks throughout; when the centring was struck in 1849 the vault settled by just three-eighths of an inch (1 cm.) at its crown. Elmes's inspiration for this vaulted space seems to have been Blouet's reconstruction of the frigidarium of the Baths of Caracalla in Rome, published in 1828. The vault is carried on columns of polished red granite, placed in front of massive piers, and there are arches between the piers – five on each side – with transverse tunnel vaults running to the outer walls. Within these arches are balconies, positioned above the outer corridors. On the W side the arches also contain windows. The projecting balcony fronts with balustrades of coloured marbles, and the three-dimensional, polychrome treatment of the lower walls with niches for sculpture, are due to *Cockerell.* So is the richly panelled plasterwork of the vault, with its allegorical spandrel figures of Virtues, Science and Arts (Elmes's intentions were more restrained). Also by *Cockerell* is the *Minton* tile **floor**, with its pattern of interlocking circles against a diapered background, in shades of buff, brown and blue. *Ludwig Grüner* (Prince Albert's mentor in art) is said to have advised on its design, and *Alfred Stevens* has been credited with the figure panels of tritons, sea nymphs and boys on dolphins. The sunken central area is usually hidden under a removable floor.

By *Cockerell,* too, are the fantastically rich bronze **doors**, and the **gasoliers**, converted to electricity in 1896. The doors have openwork panels of foliage, incorporating tridents and the letters SPQL (the Senate and the People of Liverpool), boastfully adapting the SPQR badge of ancient Rome. The gasoliers hang from brackets in the form of ships'

35. St George's Hall, the Concert Hall

prows. *Cockerell* placed the massive **organ** at the N end, on a circular platform carried by short columns. Heroically muscled atlantes, carved by *E.B. Stephens* to *Cockerell*'s design, support the pipes on either side. Installing the organ entailed removing two of Elmes's red granite columns, eventually reused in the entrance gates to Sefton Park (*see* Walk 10, p. 282). The organ blocks the axial view from Crown Court to Civil Court. It was a view to which Elmes attached great importance, echoing the vistas in Blouet's restoration of the Baths of Caracalla. The s end of the Concert Hall is as Elmes intended, with a great round arch enclosing a screen of two columns supporting an entablature. Gates between the columns open directly into the Crown Court.

The niches round the walls contain twelve **statues** of C19 worthies. They are, anticlockwise from the N end of the w side: William Roscoe by *Chantrey*, 1841 (transferred from the Liverpool Royal Institution, 1893); Sir William Brown by *Patrick MacDowell*, 1860; Peel by *Matthew Noble*, 1853; George Stephenson by *John Gibson*, 1851 (in classical dress: Gibson, the arch-Grecian, said his aim was to make the railway engineer look like Archimedes); Rev. Hugh McNeile by *George Gamon Adams*, 1870; E. Whitley by *A. Bruce Joy*, 1895; S.R. Graves by *G.G. Fontana*, 1875; Rev. Jonathan Brooks by *B.E. Spence*, 1858; Gladstone by *John Adams-Acton*, 1868; the 14th Earl of Derby by *William Theed the Younger*, 1869; the 16th Earl of Derby by *F.W. Pomeroy*, 1911; Joseph Mayer by *Fontana*, 1869.

Strongly coloured pictorial **stained glass** was added to the semi-circular windows at each end in 1883–4 by *Forrest & Son* of Liverpool. The s window represents St George and the Dragon, the N window above the organ has the Arms of Liverpool. Windows on the w side, originally with small polygonal panes, were fitted with plate glass in 1875. The present painted decoration on walls and vault, of 1974–5, is based on redecoration carried out in 1875.

The **Crown Court** and **Civil Court** differ in design. The Crown Court has a tunnel vault on red granite columns, the Civil Court a coved ceiling and a greater number of grey granite columns. Beyond the courts are two entrance halls. The **South Hall** is a disappointment, being relatively low and leading from the temple portico of the s front dead against a blank wall. It has Ionic columns in the corners. Above it is the **Grand Jury Room**, with a rich marble chimneypiece designed by *Wordley*. Only the **North Hall** makes an appropriately dignified impression. It has Greek Doric columns on the landing and a Greek Doric ambulatory in the semicircle of the apse. A copy of part of the Parthenon frieze runs round the walls, and there are splendid lamp standards by *Cockerell*. On the axis is a statue of Henry Booth, 1874, by *Theed the Younger*, placed here 1877. Booth was an engineer and the chief promoter of the Liverpool & Manchester Railway. His left hand rests on a screw coupling of his own invention, beneath which is a scroll with a drawing of Stephenson's locomotive *Rocket*, designed with Booth's assistance.

St George's Hall, the Small Concert Room

The most beautiful interior is the **Small Concert Room** [36], reached from the North Hall by stairs w and e. It is virtually circular in plan, half projecting to form the external apse, another echo of the Baths of Caracalla. Its shape is due to *Elmes*, but *Cockerell* was responsible for the lavish and sensuous decoration, completed in 1856. A balcony runs round, supported on **caryatids** which are more Baroque than Greek in their lively naturalism. They are cast in an artificial material, and are said to have been modelled by *M. Joyon*. The balcony front of cast-iron latticework swells outwards between each support, creating an

St George's Hall: Heating and Ventilation

A hidden marvel of the Hall was the heating and ventilation system designed by *Dr Boswell Reid*. Fresh air was drawn into the basement from around the perimeter, principally through shafts at each end of the E portico. There were no inlets on the W side overlooking St John's burial ground, which was seen as a health hazard. According to the season, the air could either be heated by passing it over batteries of hot water pipes (in cold weather steam could be used) or cooled by cold water pipes. The air was propelled by four giant fans, 10 ft (3 metres) in diameter, driven by a steam engine under the Concert Hall. Insulated ducts conveyed it throughout the building, the flow being controlled by canvas flaps, operated by an army of staff. Inlets are discreetly positioned, for instance behind the statues in the Concert Hall and in the steps leading to the sunken part of the floor. The system was zoned, so parts could be heated separately. For economy, heated air could be recycled while the building was being warmed up; when occupied, the vitiated air rose through ceiling vents (the hollow bricks of the Concert Hall vault were ideal for this purpose) and was dispelled via shafts at the corners of the Concert Hall, concealed behind the parapet.

undulating effect. Behind the platform are attached columns, the lower third decorated with arabesques. They support a frieze with griffins, and the space between is filled with mirrors. The griffin frieze continues round the auditorium on pilasters, with wood panelling between, elaborately grained. The ceiling has a flat central area divided into radial panels, with grilles for ventilation.

Below, the cavernous **basement** is a Piranesian region of soaring brick piers and arches, as Roman in its way as the building above. Here was the steam engine that powered the Hall's elaborate heating and ventilation system (*see* topic box). Along the W side are cells for prisoners awaiting trial, served by a roadway with arched entrances in William Brown Street and St John's Lane.

With the opening of the Queen Elizabeth II Law Courts in 1984 (*see* Derby Square, p. 150), large parts of St George's Hall became redundant. A programme of repairs and alterations is currently under way (2004), with the aim of improving access and returning more of the building to use. The architects are *Purcell Miller Tritton*. The most significant external change will be a new pavement-level entrance from St John's Lane into a vaulted space under the S portico, originally intended by Elmes as an entrance hall, but subsequently abandoned as the design evolved. The brickwork never received its decoration, and the construction is here clearly exposed.

The Plateau

Even after it was decided to combine the Assize Courts with St George's Hall, the possibility of a formal *place* between the Hall and Lime Street was not abandoned. In 1840 Elmes was asked to design Daily Courts to stand on the site of Islington Market, enclosing the N end of this open space (*see* also Major Buildings, p. 60). He made drawings for a building with an enormous octagonal tower, linked with St George's Hall by tunnel, to act as a flue for Reid's ventilation system, but this extraordinary scheme was abandoned in 1843. The area E of the Hall was laid out by *Cockerell*, but after criticism it was altered within a few years, gates and other boundary features being removed. The gatepiers were originally crowned with the triton and nereid statues that now flank the doors of the Hall. Cockerell designed the four **lions**, carved by *Nicholl* and set up from 1856 (moved to their present positions by 1864), and the cast-iron **lamp standards** with dolphin bases.

The forum-like space of the Plateau became the location for important public **monuments**. An equestrian bronze of Prince Albert by *Thomas Thornycroft*, 1866, is balanced by one of Queen Victoria, 1869, also by *Thornycroft*. In 1883 Disraeli, by *C.B. Birch* (now on the Hall steps) joined them. All three are suitably dignified. In 1887 a far too animated Major-General William Earle, by *Birch* again, was installed at the s end of the Hall's E front. Between the two equestrian statues, where Disraeli once stood, is the **Cenotaph**, unveiled 1930. Architect *L.B. Budden*, sculptor *H. Tyson Smith*. A simple horizontal block suggesting an altar or a tomb, with a continuous bronze relief over 31 ft (9.4 metres) long on each side. The relief facing Lime Street shows mourners of all ages in everyday dress, against a military cemetery with gravestones receding to infinity. The other side has marching soldiers, barely individualized, moving collectively like automata [23]. It is one of the most remarkable war memorials in the country, unflinching in its depiction of the scale of loss and grief, and in its refusal of allegory or heroic idealization.

The William Brown Street Group and St John's Gardens

(For plan, see City Centre map, fig. 79)

Until the mid C19 William Brown Street was Shaw's Brow, a steep hill with a ragged collection of buildings on the N side, and the C18 Infirmary and St John's church on the s. In 1843, as St George's Hall began to rise on the Infirmary site, Samuel Holme hoped it would become the focus of a sort of forum, 'round which should be clustered our handsomest edifices, and within the area of which our public monuments ought to be placed.' This is exactly what came to pass over the next sixty years. However, instead of combining to enclose a formal space, the new public buildings were strung out in an irregular line along the slope [37]. Their effect is therefore not that of a forum so much as a splendid architectural backdrop to the Hall. Individually they are not in the same league as Elmes's masterpiece, but taken together as a piece of romantic classical urban scenery, they have no equal in England. In the late C20 the street was closed to through traffic and partly paved over.

37. William Brown Street, showing, left to right, the Museum Extension and Central Technical School, Museum and Library, Picton Reading Room, Walker Art Gallery and County Sessions House. In front, the Steble Fountain and Wellington Column

38. Museum and Library, by John Weightman (1857–60)

The first building, 1857–60, was the Library and Museum, in the middle, followed in 1861–3 by the Wellington Column to the N. The Walker Art Gallery and Picton Reading Room, both 1870s, lie E of the Library; the County Sessions House of the 1880s further E again. Last came the Museum Extension of 1896–1901 at the opposite, W, end.

We begin with the **Museum and Library** [38]. The Free Public Library, established in 1850, was temporarily housed from 1852 in the old Union News Room in Duke Street (*see* Walk 4, p. 206), along with important natural history collections bequeathed by the 13th Earl of Derby. The Shaw's Brow site was acquired, and in 1856 an architectural competition was held. The terms noted that it would 'form one side of an open space at right angles with St George's Hall', so it seems that a formal *place* was under consideration (and indeed the local architect *Henry Sumners* had already published designs for one). *Thomas Allom*'s winning scheme was too costly, so the Corporation Surveyor *John Weightman* produced a revised design, built 1857–60. The merchant and banker William Brown offered to meet the cost, and the street was renamed in his honour. Allom had proposed an Italianate façade, with much sculpture.* Weightman produced a broadly similar composition – a six-column Corinthian portico with attic, flanked by five-bay wings and projecting end bays – but in a severely Graeco-Roman style, in the mould of St George's Hall. The great flight of steps in front was not formed until *c.* 1902; originally there was a broad, elevated terrace here. Bombed in 1941, the Library was rebuilt 1957–60 and the Museum 1963–9 by *Ronald Bradbury*, behind Weightman's preserved façade. The C19 skyline was wrecked in the process by a rooftop addition. Rear extension to the Library 1978.

*Illustrated in the *Building News*, 2 January 1857.

Adjoining the Museum on the left is the former **Museum Extension and Central Technical School** [39], now given over entirely to museum use. It was won in competition by *E.W. Mountford*, 1896, and opened 1901. Baroque, with Mannerist touches: notice how the rustication wraps round the first-floor window jambs, leaving only the capitals and bases of the hypothetical columns exposed. The original main entrance is in the convex w façade to Byrom Street (a feature echoed in Mountford's Old Bailey, London, 1900–7) which has giant Ionic columns in pairs above. At each end of the William Brown Street elevation are advancing pedimented bays, with extravagantly blocked columns flanking big, deep niches lined with windows. Allegorical **sculpture** in pediments and above windows is by *F. W. Pomeroy*; also the beautiful bronze **lamp standards** by the Byrom Street entrance. The lower floors, entered from Byrom Street, were for the Technical School: a lofty entrance hall, followed by the long, low, marble-lined vestibule, leads to the former lecture room and examination hall. These spaces have plaster reliefs by *Pomeroy*, some coloured by *Robert Anning Bell*. The upper floors, entered from the neighbouring Museum, are U-shaped galleries. In 2000–1 *Law & Dunbar-Nasmith* transformed one of two central open courts into an atrium, bridged by high-level walkways. The space is impressive, though the curved glass roof unfortunately compounds the damage done to the skyline by Bradbury's earlier addition. At the same time a new entrance from William Brown Street was formed.

On the E side of the Museum is the **Picton Reading Room** [40], by *Cornelius Sherlock*, 1875–9. Circular plan, after the British Museum Reading Room (1854–7). The semicircular façade with Corinthian colonnade nicely accommodates the street's change of direction, and echoes the apsidal N end of St George's Hall opposite. The roof is a shallow dome covered with zinc on a framework of iron, with a glazed oculus. Behind the colonnade are niches with weathered plaster statues by *Benjamin Edward Spence*, presented by the sculptor's widow in

39. Museum Extension and Central Technical School, by E.W. Mountford (opened 1901)

1870: Jeanie Deans, The Lady of the Lake, Highland Mary. Inside, the 100 ft- (30 metre-) diameter reading room retains its bookcases and cast-iron gallery (a second, higher gallery was added later). It was lit with electricity from the start (gas was laid on as a back up) by three arc lamps in the glazed dish that still stands on an octagonal wooden structure in the centre. The basement was originally a lecture theatre, kept free of obtrusive columns by supporting the floor of the reading room on arched wrought-iron girders (engineer *James N. Shoolbred*), now boxed in. Attached to the rear is the **Hornby Library**, opened 1906, funded by Hugh Frederick Hornby to house his bequest of books and prints. By *Thomas Shelmerdine*. Impressive stone-faced Edwardian Baroque interior, a five-bay aisled hall under a plaster barrel vault. Halfway up the columns a balustraded gallery runs all round. Outside the door, an Art Nouveau copper **plaque** of 1907 by *C.E. Thompson* commemorates Hornby's gift.

Next the **Walker Art Gallery** by *Sherlock* and *H.H. Vale*, 1874–7, paid for by the Mayor, the brewer Andrew Barclay Walker. It served originally for exhibitions of contemporary art, but rapidly acquired a permanent collection. With the decision to site it where the street veers away from St George's Hall, any thought of creating a forum-like enclosure seems to have been abandoned. More decorative than the Museum and Library, it is still chastely Neoclassical for its date. Corinthian portico of six columns with pediment. Extensive sculpture by *John Warrington Wood*: on either side of the steps, weathered seated figures of Raphael and Michelangelo; above the portico, Liverpool (a copy, *c.* 1996). Over the windows, four long reliefs, left to right: The Laying of the Foundation Stone of the Walker Art Gallery by the Duke of Edinburgh, 1874; The Visit of Queen Victoria, 1851; King John Granting Liverpool's First Charter, 1207; The Embarkation of King William III at Hoylake, 1690. Extended at the back by Sherlock, 1882–4, doubling its size. In 1931–3 an even larger rear extension was added by *Arnold Thornely*. At the same time he remodelled the entrance, creating

40. Picton Reading Room, by Cornelius Sherlock (1875–9)

41. County Sessions House, by F. & G. Holme (1882–4), staircase hall

a spacious travertine-lined hall with flanking staircases, lit from above through a circular opening in the landing. It is a good example of the American-influenced classicism so ably handled by Liverpool architects between the wars. In 2001–2 the wedge-shaped gap between Thornely's extension and the C19 building was partly filled in by *Law & Dunbar-Nasmith*, creating a new first-floor foyer for the exhibition rooms at the rear. It is top-lit and paved in pale stone.

Detached on the E of the Walker Art Gallery stands the **County Sessions House**, 1882–4 by *F. & G. Holme.* Unlike its neighbour, it is exuberantly late Victorian, its style derived from Renaissance Venice rather than ancient Greece and Rome. Portico with coupled columns. The front is lavishly decorated but the sides and rear are bare brick (the NE side was originally hidden by buildings). Complex internal layout, largely preserved, with separate circulation for prisoners, public, solicitors

*Actually in Islington, but visually part of the William Brown Street group.

and witnesses, and barristers and magistrates. Staircase hall, rich with marble, mosaic and *sgraffito* decoration, under little saucer-domes [41]. Magistrates' room with panelling and C17-style plaster ceiling. Two court-rooms, the larger with dado of *Burmantofts*' tiles. Cells in basement.

In front of the Walker Art Gallery and Sessions House is a triangular space formerly occupied by the old Islington Market. On this commanding site the **Wellington Column** was erected in 1861–3: a very late example of a column-monument for Britain. The Duke died in 1852, but funds were slow to come in, and a design competition in 1856, won by *Andrew Lawson* of Edinburgh, was followed by further delays while a site was secured. It is a Roman Doric column supporting a bronze statue of the Duke (the subject of a second competition in 1861) by *George Anderson Lawson*, 132 ft (40 metres) high overall. Bronze plaques on the pedestal display the names of Wellington's victories, and on the s face is a relief of Waterloo by *G.A. Lawson*, installed 1865. The form was no doubt intended to echo Nelson's column in Trafalgar Square, but also complements its very Roman setting near St George's Hall. w of the Wellington Monument is the cast-iron **Steble Fountain**, unveiled 1879. Neptune, Amphitrite, Acis and Galatea are seated round the base. Designed by *Paul Liénard*; other versions in Boston, Geneva, Launceston (Tasmania) and elsewhere.

Views of the w side of St George's Hall were long obscured by the C18 Gothic Revival church of St John, 1775–84, possibly by *Timothy Lightoler*. It was demolished in 1899, and its extensive churchyard laid out by *Thomas Shelmerdine* as **St John's Gardens**. Opened in 1904, they at last provided the formal public space envisaged for half a century as an adjunct to St George's Hall. Shelmerdine's surrounding walls in debased classical style (now missing their railings) contrast unhappily with the Hall and the buildings in William Brown Street, but the late Victorian and Edwardian sculpture within is of exceptional interest. The gardens were conceived as a site for commemorative **statues** – 'Liverpool's al fresco Valhalla', as a local newspaper put it in 1899 – and leading sculptors were employed. At the NE corner is William Rathbone, by *George Frampton*, 1899–1900, with reliefs illustrating his philanthropic work. Frampton designed the plinth incorporating a bench. Continuing clockwise: Sir Arthur Bower Forwood, 1903, also *Frampton*; Monsignor James Nugent, 1905, by *Frederick William Pomeroy*; Canon T. Major Lester, 1907, *Frampton* again; and Alexander Balfour, by *Albert Bruce Joy*, 1889 (erected in St John's churchyard before the gardens were formed). The grey granite plinth is by *Alfred Waterhouse*. In the middle are the **Gladstone Memorial**, by *Thomas Brock*, unveiled 1904, and the lively **King's Liverpool Regiment Memorial**, by *William Goscombe John*, 1905: Britannia presides, with soldiers in C17 and early C20 dress below, and a vigorous figure of an C18 drummer boy.

Pier Head

(For plan, see City Centre map, fig. 79)

The buildings at the Pier Head (more properly George's Pier Head) occupy the site of George's Dock, opened in 1771 and obsolete by the end of the C19. In 1899 the Corporation drained it, and extended Water Street and Brunswick Street across it in the form of viaducts, creating three superb sites for new buildings fronting the river. Because the dock was not quite a rectangle and the streets were not parallel, the sites varied in shape, and this militated against a unified, symmetrical development. More importantly, no restrictions were imposed to ensure that the buildings harmonized or formed a coherent group, and the result is an amazingly disparate trio [42]. They are, from N to S, the Royal Liver Building, 1908–11, the Cunard Building, 1914–16, and the former Mersey Docks and Harbour Board headquarters, 1903–7. The Pier Head in the early C20 was a bustling interchange for trains, trams, ferries and ocean liners, and the buildings were conceived as landmarks, commanding attention and giving international travellers their first or last impression of the city. Seen from the water they form an unforgettable group, a symbol of maritime Liverpool at the height of its prosperity and self-confidence. As Pevsner wrote in 1969, 'They represent the great Edwardian Imperial optimism and might indeed stand at Durban or Hongkong just as naturally as at Liverpool'. (For proposals to add to the group, see topic box, p. 70.)

First to be erected, 1903–7, were the offices of the **Mersey Docks and Harbour Board** (MDHB, now the Port of Liverpool Building) at the S end [46]. They were the subject of a local competition, won in 1900 by *Briggs & Wolstenholme*, with *Hobbs & Thornely*. The winning design had its main entrance at the SW corner, but boundary changes led to a radical reworking, resulting in the symmetrical riverside façade. The structure is of steel encased in concrete, with a facing of Portland stone. It is a very large rectangular block, proudly Baroque, with polygonal corner turrets crowned by stone cupolas. These originally had lanterns on top. In the centre is a much bigger, copper-covered dome, on a high drum with coupled columns and pedimented aedicules. It was added

42. The Pier Head group: left to right, the Royal Liver Building, Cunard Building, and former Mersey Docks and Harbour Board headquarters

43. Royal Liver Building under construction: granite cladding being attached to the frame

The frame of the Royal Liver Building was designed by the engineers *L.G. Mouchel & Partners* using the system of ferro-concrete construction (concrete reinforced with steel) devised by the French builder *François Hennebique*. It was one of the most ambitious examples to date of this relatively new technology. It is a monolithic structure of columns, beams and arches, cast *in situ*, supporting the weight of the towers, floors and external granite walls. The building site was organized on industrial lines. Sand, cement and aggregate were delivered into the basement; the concrete was mixed here, then raised by electric hoists to the level needed; and narrow-gauge railway tracks were laid on each floor as completed, so materials could be moved more efficiently. Construction proceeded with remarkable speed, and the skeleton of the ten main storeys was built at an average of one floor every nineteen working days. The exterior granite is simply a cladding, no more than 14 in. (35 cm.) thick.

at the last minute to make the design more imposing, and gives the building a strong family resemblance to Brumwell Thomas's Belfast City Hall, won in competition in 1896. The riverside front has a rounded pediment at each end and a triangular one over the entrance. The top floor above the cornice, a later alteration, injures the proportions. Above and around the entrance are **sculptures** by *C.J. Allen*, including weathered statues of Commerce and Industry. Corridors from this entrance and from the NE and SE corners form a Y-plan, dividing the hollow centre into three light-wells. The corridors meet in a lofty octagonal hall, overlooked by galleries on each floor. This is directly under the great central dome, which however is hidden by a lower domed ceiling. In what is effectively a secular cathedral of commerce, this hall takes the place of the crossing, and the quasi-ecclesiastical impression

44. Royal Liver Building, by Walter Aubrey Thomas (1908–11), clock tower

is reinforced by the words of Psalm 107, They that go down to the Sea
in Ships . . ., inscribed within the lowest tier of arches. Off the E side is
a semicircular staircase, open to the hall. **Stained glass** on the stairs
and landings, by *G. Wragge & Co.* of Salford, displays the arms of
British colonies and dominions. The same firm supplied the decorative
metalwork inside and out.

In 1906 the site N of Water Street was acquired by the Royal Liver Friendly Society for its new headquarters. The **Royal Liver Building** of 1908–11, designed by *Walter Aubrey Thomas*, is perhaps the most extraordinary office block of its date in the country. It is almost certainly also the tallest, and was referred to as a skyscraper in the contemporary press. It displeased the MDHB, which had hoped for a building that would balance its own, not an attention-grabbing monster like this. Far bigger than was necessary for the Society's accommodation, it provided abundant lettable space, as well as being an advertisement to a worldwide public. It consists of an oblong block orientated w–E, eight storeys high to the main cornice. Piled on top are two further storeys with corner domes, and two extravagant clock towers w and E that reach 295 ft (90 metres) above the pavement [44]. The structure is of reinforced concrete faced with granite (*see* topic box, p. 68). The style is impossible to label. The round-arched windows and the short columns below the main cornice recall Louis Sullivan's Auditorium Building of 1886–9 in Chicago. Pevsner detected faintly Byzantine motifs in the towers, which also seem to have echoes of Hawksmoor's London churches. The semicircular porch facing the river

Pier Head Expansion

Even before the Pier Head buildings were complete, visionary proposals were put forward for enlarging the group. *Stanley Adshead* in 1910 and *Harold Chalton Bradshaw* in 1913 both suggested a succession of grand, blocks extending N along the waterfront, but nothing was built. Plans for a very prominent new building immediately s of the MDHB offices, to a competition-winning design by *Will Alsop*, were abandoned in 2004. However, Liverpool's greatest public open space is now threatened by a proposed canal linking Prince's Dock and Canning Dock, intended to slice through the Pier Head between fussily landscaped banks.

Former
Mersey Docks
and Harbour
Board head-
quarters,
Briggs &
Wolstenholme
with Hobbs &
Thornely
(1903–7)

is more straightforwardly Baroque. A N–S corridor divides the building,
with light-wells on each side. Originally lined with white glazed brick,
these were refaced with curtain glazing during refurbishment in
1977–82 by *Arup Associates*. The two giant Liver birds, symbols of the
Friendly Society which add a surreal flourish to the clock towers, are of
sheet copper (originally gilded) on steel armatures. They were made by
the *Bromsgrove Guild*.

The remaining site, between Water Street and Brunswick Street, was
acquired in 1914 by the Cunard Steamship Company for its head office.
The resulting **Cunard Building** [45], completed 1916, has generally
been described as the work of the local firm *Willink & Thicknesse*, with
Arthur J. Davis of *Mewès & Davis* as consultant. However, recently
discovered drawings, apparently by Davis, show that the design had
been brought close to its final form well before the contract with
Willink & Thicknesse was signed. The broadly Italian Renaissance style
and the emphatically horizontal palazzo shape with mighty crowning
cornice were chosen to contrast with the discordant buildings on either
side, rather than attempt to reconcile them. The style also invites
comparison with the work of Americans such as McKim, Mead &
White. The structure is again of reinforced concrete, clad in Portland
stone. The stonework, particularly the rustication of the battered
ground floor and the angles, was designed to be enhanced by the
inevitable accumulation of soot. Subsequent cleaning has evened out
the intended contrast of light and dark. The frieze is carved with the
shields of countries allied in the First World War, by *Edward O. Griffith*,
models for the eagles at the corners being supplied by *C.J. Allen*. Those
parts occupied by Cunard served both as headquarters and as a
passenger terminal. The w entrance led to the toplit public office, with
first-class passengers' lounge adjoining. Other classes were accommodated in the basement along with baggage handling and storage. A
stately marble-lined corridor with Doric columns links the N and S
entrances, giving access to lifts and stairs.

Just E of the former MDHB offices is the **George's Dock Ventilation and Control Station** [21], the most ambitious of the buildings for the first Mersey road tunnel by *Herbert J. Rowse* (*see* Old Haymarket, pp. 161–2). The design, approved in 1932, shares the streamlined, Art Deco character of the other tunnel structures. Reconstructed in 1951–2 by *Rowse* after war damage, it contains offices, and huge fans that extract foul air and force clean air in. It is Portland stone-faced, and has notable **sculptures** by *Edmund C. Thompson*, assisted by *George T. Capstick*. On the W front, a figure with helmet and goggles represents Speed, and black basalt statues of Night and Day in niches allude to the ever-open tunnel; on the N and S fronts, four panels illustrate Civil Engineering, Construction, Architecture and Decoration.

The Pier Head became a favoured location for **public monuments** in succession to St John's Gardens (*see* Major Buildings, p. 65). At the N end in St Nicholas Place is the **Memorial to the Heroes of the Marine Engine Room**, by *William Goscombe John*, unveiled 1916. Conceived as a monument to the engineers of the *Titanic*, and paid for by international subscription, it is a granite obelisk topped by a gilded flame. At the corners, nude figures symbolizing Earth, Air, Fire and Water emerge from a background of stylized waves. By contrast, on the W and E sides, two pairs of engineers are portrayed with striking naturalism, their dress and attributes carefully studied from life [1]. In British public sculpture this is an exceptionally early monument to the heroic working man.

The very different equestrian bronze **statue of Edward VII** in the middle of the Pier Head is also by *John*. Intended to stand on the podium at the S end of St George's Hall, it was placed here instead in 1921. Behind, directly in front of the Cunard Building, is the **Cunard War Memorial**, a rostral column by *Arthur J. Davis* with a nude Victory in bronze by *Henry Pegram*, unveiled 1921. W of the Mersey Docks and Harbour Board building is the bronze **Alfred Jones Memorial** by *George Frampton*, unveiled 1913. Jones was a shipowner and founder of the Liverpool School of Tropical Medicine. His likeness is confined to a medallion on the plinth, while flanking statues of Research and the Fruits of Industry represent his achievements allegorically. On top, a female figure in medieval dress carrying a ship symbolizes Liverpool. SW is the **Merchant Navy War Memorial**, unveiled 1952, a column like a lighthouse, in a semicircular enclosure. Designed by *Stanley H. Smith* and *Charles F. Blythin*, with sculpture by *H. Tyson Smith*.

The present landscaping of the open space between the Pier Head buildings and the river dates from 1995 and is by *Allies & Morrison*. The shabby restaurant overlooking the Mersey belongs to an earlier remodelling of the area carried out from 1963 by the City Architect, *Ronald Bradbury*. For the Mersey Ferry Terminal *see* Walk 2, p. 121.

Anglican Cathedral

Upper Duke Street

Liverpool Cathedral, the life's work of *Sir Giles Gilbert Scott*, represents the final flowering of the Gothic Revival as a vital, creative movement, and is one of the great buildings of the C20 [47]. Construction began in 1904 at the height of the city's prosperity, and finished in 1978 as her long economic decline reached its lowest point. Funded to a large extent by the city's merchant class, it marks the climax of the private patronage of public architecture that flourished in C19 Liverpool.

The diocese was established in 1880. At first the church of St Peter (*see* topic box, p. 179) served as pro-cathedral, then in 1884–6 a competition

47. Anglican Cathedral, by Sir Giles Gilbert Scott (1904–78)

was held for a new building on the site of St John, next to St George's Hall. It was won by *William Emerson* with a domed Gothic design, but the project lapsed in 1888. In 1901 the present magnificent site was selected, a rocky ridge elevated above the city, ensuring that the cathedral dominates the skyline seen from the river. The ridge determines the building's N–S orientation, compass N being ritual w (in the following description N means ritual N, etc.). On the landward side the former quarry of St James's Cemetery (see Walk 6, pp. 242–4) adds further drama. A two-stage competition was held, in which architects were asked initially to submit portfolios, including cathedral designs if they wished. At first Gothic was stipulated, but this aroused objections and the condition was dropped. The assessors were G.F. Bodley and Norman Shaw, and out of the 103 entrants they shortlisted five: *Austin & Paley*, *C.A. Nicholson*, *Malcolm Stark*, *W.J. Tapper* and *Scott*, all of whom had submitted Gothic drawings. Among those rejected were *Beresford Pite* (Byzantine), *C.H. Reilly* (classical) and a team effort by *W.R. Lethaby* and others (a strange, organic design, apparently to be built in concrete). Scott – a Roman Catholic – was chosen as winner in 1903, but since he was only twenty-two, the aged *Bodley* was nominated joint architect. Not surprisingly it was an unhappy collaboration. When Bodley died in 1907, Scott became sole architect.

The winning design was for a cruciform cathedral with a six-bay nave and three-bay choir. Its most distinctive feature was a pair of towers over the transepts. There were also subsidiary transepts not projecting beyond the aisles, three to the nave and one to the choir. After the competition the plan was modified, and the Lady Chapel moved from behind the high altar to the SE corner. It was built first and opened in 1910. Amazingly, in 1909–10 Scott decided to redesign the cathedral completely. Work had begun on the choir, so he did not have an entirely free hand, but he made such sweeping changes that virtually nothing of the competition-winning design is recognisable. His governing aim was to replace the twin towers with a bigger, central tower. The crossing of the original transept was too narrow for this, so Scott positioned it further w, with a second transept matching the original one to frame it. This produced a very broad, uninterrupted central space, something which the terms of the competition had called for, and which Scott's winning design failed to provide. He placed the main porches N and s between the transepts. All this left the nave reduced to three bays, the same as the choir. The result is a plan symmetrical about both axes, shaped as much by aesthetics as by function. According to the new scheme construction progressed from E to w over seven decades, though Scott continued to revise and refine the design until his death in 1960: the choir and E transepts were consecrated in 1924; under-tower and w transepts were opened in 1941; the final pinnacle of the tower was set in place in 1942; and constructing the nave took from 1948 to 1978.

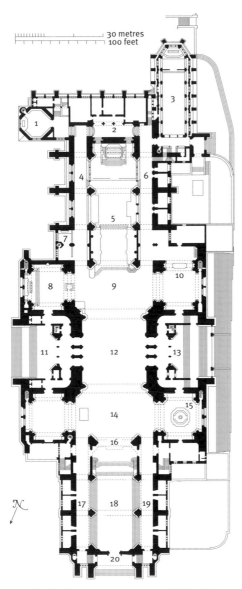

1	Chapter House	11	Welsford Porch
2	Ambulatory	12	Under Tower
3	Lady Chapel	13	Rankin Porch
4	North Choir Aisle	14	Western Transept
5	Choir	15	Baptistery
6	South Choir Aisle	16	Nave Bridge
7	Chapel of the Holy Spirit	17	North Nave Aisle
8	War Memorial Chapel	18	Nave
9	Eastern Transept	19	South Nave Aisle
10	Derby Memorial	20	West Porch

48. Anglican Cathedral plan

Exterior

The overall impression is of massive, brooding bulk, and a certain sombreness due to the colour of the stone (red sandstone, mostly quarried at Woolton SE of the city; brick and concrete are used where they cannot be seen). The total external length is 619ft (189 metres).We begin at the E end and work W, following the course of construction. The earliest part is the **Lady Chapel**, tall and narrow with a polygonal apse, in style akin to late Bodley. Closely spaced buttresses with numerous slight weatherings, pierced top and bottom by galleries with openwork balustrades. Dec tracery, varying from window to window. Porch with a lofty two-arched balcony above, with **sculptures** of children by *Lillie Reed* in C15 Italian Renaissance style. The **Chapter House** is connected with the choir by a passage which continues as an ambulatory behind the sanctuary. In Scott's 1904 scheme it was to have been rectangular, balancing the Lady Chapel, but instead an octagonal plan was adopted. This better exploits the picturesque possibilities of its location by the cemetery, from the edge of which, in distant views, it appears to grow like the tower of a fantasy medieval castle. It has a higher stair-turret on one side, and, like the Lady Chapel, an arcaded balcony near the top, linked to the choir by a bridge high up.

The E elevation of the **choir** is dominated by a very large Dec window, divided by a mullion with statues in niches. This is flanked by buttresses and corner turrets with short spires. By contrast the N and S elevations are in a more personal, 'modern' Gothic, adopted with the redesign of 1909–10. This style, used for the rest of the cathedral, is characterized by large, unbroken expanses of wall, with knots of intricate decoration concentrated towards the top. The choir side windows have quadrant jambs into which the arch mouldings die, a motif used throughout and derived from advanced late C19 Gothicists (among them Scott's father). They also have simpler tracery than the E window, a rather bald late C13 Geometrical consisting of two lights with a sexfoil above. Widely spaced buttresses separate them, and a gallery of small arches runs above. The carved ornament often seems influenced by Spanish late Gothic examples, and indeed Scott visited Spain soon after construction began.

The composition of the two **transepts** flanking the tower and the S porch – the **Rankin Porch** – is impressive in the extreme, and unlike anything in medieval church architecture. Although generally kept shut, this, and not the W end, is the main entrance front (the interior tells a different story, as will be seen). The transept ends are sheer cliffs of masonry, each with a long, narrow two-light window, between which the cavernous porch is recessed in deep shadow under a broad segmental arch. Scott's enthusiasm for Spanish detail is again evident from the grille that closes the arch, and from the three doorways within, their heads merging into the tracery of a single large window above. The flat roof is reinforced concrete. Low, arched entrances projecting left and right of the transepts lead to the undercroft. The whole composition,

The triple portals under the tower have figure sculpture designed in the 1930s by *Edward Carter Preston* (1885–1965), following a programme devised by Sir Frederick Radcliffe, chairman of the Cathedral Committee. On the ritual N side, the figures flanking the doors illustrate from left to right the Natural Virtues (and under each, the corresponding vice) – Humility, Bounty, Temperance, Justice, Prudence, Fortitude, Concord and Chastity – while the figures above the doors represent the Supernatural Virtues, Faith, Charity [49] and Hope. On the s side, the theme is the Liberal Arts and the Sciences. The upper figures here are left to right Philosophy, Theology and Natural Science; below are Architecture, Painting, Music, Poetry, Astronomy, Mathematics, History and Medicine. Outside, the Welsford Porch, on the ritual N overlooking St James's Cemetery, takes the Resurrection as its theme. Above the doors are the risen Christ and two angels; below, Old

49. Model for *Charity*, by Edward Carter Preston (1934–5)

Testament prophets of his coming – David, Isaiah, Jeremiah, Ezekiel and Daniel – and New Testament writers who bore witness to the Resurrection: John, Luke, Mark, Matthew and Paul. The Rankin Porch on the s illustrates the Active Life. Above the doors are a teaching figure of Christ and two angels. Below, flanking the doors, figures from Christ's parables: Housewife, Merchant, Builder, Labourer, Sower, Fisherman, Shepherd, Good Neighbour, Steward and Servant. In the side walls of the porch are two further doors, with figures of George V and Queen Mary, and George VI and Queen Elizabeth the Queen Mother (the latter pair added 1953). The style is strongly influenced by C13 French portal figures at (e.g.) Chartres, with little undercutting and much emphasis on linear drapery folds.

minus the undercroft entrances, is repeated for the sake of symmetry on the N side in the **Welsford Porch**. This has little functional justification since it opens straight into the abyss of the cemetery. Both porches have **sculpture** by *Edward Carter Preston* (*see* topic box, p. 77).

The **tower** (paid for by the Vestey family, Liverpool meat importers) is a magnificent landmark. Its design was repeatedly revised by Scott, resulting in greater height (331 ft; 101 metres) and a more subtly tapered outline. The lower part is square, with large windows N and S, of three lancets with a rose above. The eight-sided upper stage has tapering octagonal turrets at the angles, ending in delicate lanterns.

The **nave** follows the choir, but is more simply detailed: the buttresses have fewer weatherings and neither they nor the window mullions have figure sculpture. Scott redesigned the **w front** in 1942, with a projecting *porte-cochère*, but by the time building reached this point costs had risen so much that a simpler design by *F.G. Thomas* and *Roger Pinckney*, finalized in 1968, was adopted. It has a giant arched recess flanked by pairs of buttresses. The w window fills the recess and consists of three lancets under a decorative horizontal cresting (a composition adapted from the tower windows), above which the tympanum of the arch is fully glazed. Over the central door a bronze **statue** of Christ by *Elisabeth Frink*, installed 1993. This door is only used on ceremonial occasions. Those at each side, one of which serves as the main public entrance, lead by awkward right-angled turns into the aisles.

Interior

Internally, Scott's version of Gothic is characterized not by columns and arcades, but by solid walls and vaults. The nave and choir derive from medieval churches such as Albi in SW France: piers (short walls projecting from the outer walls) support the main rib vault and are pierced at the bottom to form aisle passages. Cross-vaults roof the spaces between these piers and support a triforium, but no clerestory. Looking from w to E, the side windows are mostly hidden from view, and masonry predominates [50]. The spatial effects are awe-inspiring, but on a practical level the plan is less convincing. The nave feels detached, and the huge transepts, out of sight of the sanctuary, seem redundant (the NW one has been adapted as a shop). The N and S porches, so dominant externally, seem poorly related to the interior, bringing one in at the mid-point of what is, internally, an emphatically longitudinal building. In the end, however, practical considerations seem less important than emotional responses. As Goodhart-Rendel wrote of the unfinished cathedral in 1953: '. . . it stands aloof from architectural reality, having neither the functional nor the constructional inevitability of the ancient buildings whence its forms are ultimately derived – it is either a great engine of emotion or nothing'.

Entered at the w end, the cathedral unfolds in reverse chronological order. The distance from w door to E window is 457 ft (139 metres). The

50. Anglican Cathedral, interior looking E from the nave

sunken floor of the **nave** – 4 ft (1.2 metres) lower than the aisles – was planned by Scott in 1942, with the probable intention of making a semi-independent space for less formal events. A highly theatrical round-arched **bridge** across the E end, supporting a balcony reached by long flights of stairs, sets it apart even more. Originally meant to carry an organ, this serves also to frame the distant view of the altar and delay the moment at which the full height of the central space is revealed. The rib vault has two quadripartite bays for each of the three bays below. Sadly, to reduce costs, the two westernmost vault bays were constructed from moulded glass-fibre rather than stone.

The **transepts** and the immensely high **under-tower** are sublimely impressive, the octagonal rib vault of the latter rising to 175 ft (53.3 metres). Foundations for the choir and E transept had already been laid before Scott's redesign of 1909–10. This explains the massive NE and SE transept piers, originally planned to carry the twin towers, and the curious vaulting devised to overcome the difficulty of the central space being wider than the choir. For the sake of balance these were repeated westward, but with variations in detail. The doors of the Rankin Porch are generally closed, but the identically planned Welsford Porch, N, is accessible. Approached from outside, its three external doors open into a vaulted vestibule, now used as a café. A left or right turn leads by a curving passage to one or other of the transepts, while straight ahead are three inner doors opening into the under-tower. Seen from inside the

51. Anglican Cathedral, the Lady Chapel

cathedral, these have the same Spanish-influenced decoration as the outer ones, and similar sculpture by *Carter Preston* (*see* topic box, p. 77). They match the doors of the Rankin Porch opposite. The interior of the **choir**, like its exterior, has more decorative carving than the nave. Bishop's Throne in the middle bay on the s. The aisles are connected behind the altar by the vaulted **ambulatory**. Off the NE corner is the **Chapter House**, with a circular balcony just below its concrete domed ceiling.

The **Lady Chapel** [51] is reached from the s choir aisle. The first part of the cathedral to be completed, it is a good deal richer than what followed, possibly reflecting the early involvement of *Bodley*. The slope of the site means its floor lies below choir level, and it is reached by stairs at the w end. These pass behind an arcaded w gallery, with a striking view down into the chapel. Like the choir and nave it has wall-piers, but here they are not so deep and the windows are proportionally bigger, so the effect is brighter and less ponderous. The piers are pierced with narrow passage aisles, and linked by arches supporting a balcony. This is screened by arcading, with a floridly carved foliage cresting and an elaborate inscription below. The stone-carving here, as in the choir, seems to have been directed by *Joseph Phillips*. Its rough naturalism contrasts with the later, more precise work of Carter Preston. The elaborate vault has sinuously curving ribs of a kind which occur in Spain, but hardly in England. The floor is asymmetrically patterned in black and white marble. The door in the second N bay has a marvellous lock and wrought-iron hinges.

Furnishings and Monuments

Most were designed by Scott or executed under his close supervision, giving a remarkable stylistic unity. Like the architecture, they use traditional forms without directly imitating historical models. They are described here approximately from ritual E to W.

Choir. Main **reredos** of distinctly Spanish appearance, the composition apparently derived from the gateway of the College of St Gregory, Valladolid. Stone, partly gilt, with sculpture conceived by *Walter Gilbert*, modelled by *Louis Weingartner*, and carved by *Arthur Turner* and others at *H.H. Martyn*'s of Cheltenham. – **Communion rail**, with figures representing the Ten Commandments, by *Gilbert* and *Weingartner*. – Bronze **gates** from sanctuary to choir aisles by the *Bromsgrove Guild*. – **Stalls** by *Waring & Gillow*; in 1996 two **paintings** by *Christopher Le Brun* were incorporated, The Good Samaritan and The Prodigal Son. – **Organ case**, on both sides above the stalls, designed by *Scott*.

Lady Chapel. Monuments to Helen Swift Neilson, d. 1945, by *Carter Preston*, with a relief of musicians, and to First World War Nurses by *David Evans*, 1928, with an austere relief of a nurse bandaging a soldier's head. – **Organ case** by *Scott*. – Kneeling **statue** of the Virgin, glazed terracotta, late C15–early C16 Florentine, ascribed to *Giovanni della Robbia*. – **Altarpiece**, carved and painted wood with elaborately crested top, German- or Flemish-looking. Designed by *Bodley* and *Scott* and made by *Rattee & Kett*, the reliefs from models by *G.W. Wilson*. – Gilded wrought-iron **electroliers** by *W. Bainbridge Reynolds*.

S **choir aisle**. Forming the back of the Bishop's Throne, **monument** to Bishop Chavasse, d. 1928, carved by *P. Induni* and *J. Phillips* from a model by *Evans*, incorporating a representation of the E part of the cathedral. **Monuments** by *Carter Preston* to Sir Robert Jones, d. 1933; Bishop Ryle, d. 1900, an impressive recumbent effigy, carved 1930–1; and Dean Dwelly, d. 1957.

N **choir aisle**. **Monument**, E end, A.J.M. Melly, d. 1936, by *Carter Preston*. **Reredos**, Chapel of the Holy Spirit, with an alabaster relief of Christ praying, by *William Gough*.

E **transepts**. **Reredos**, War Memorial Chapel, NE transept, with sculpture by *Gilbert* and *Weingartner*. – **Monument** to the 16th Earl of Derby, d. 1908, SE transept. Unveiled 1929. Designed by *Scott*, the figure apparently modelled by *Thomas Tyrrell* and a Mr *Wilson*. Recumbent bronze effigy on a classical marble tomb-chest. At the head a model of the cathedral, its W end tantalizingly veiled. Above the arch on the transept's w side, **memorial** of the 55th (West Lancashire) Division, with sculpture designed by *Gilbert* and *Weingartner*. ᴇ of the Derby monument, **monument** to Sir Max Horton, by *Carter Preston*, 1957.

w **transepts**. **Font**, sw transept. Marble, with relief figures by *Carter Preston*. **Canopy**, designed by *Scott*, square with flamboyant top. – **Statue** of the Holy Family, near the ɴᴡ transept arch, by *Josefina de Vasconcellos*. A fibreglass moulding, installed by 1965.

Stained Glass

Much of the glass was made by *James Powell & Sons* (*Whitefriars*). Their earliest surviving is in the ᴇ and ɴ windows of the choir, designed by *John William Brown* and made 1911–21. Sombre in colouring, it is decidedly subordinate to the architecture. The ɴ window in the ɴᴇ transept, 1921–2, brighter and more translucent, is by *Brown* and *James H. Hogan*. *Hogan* developed this approach further in the huge under-tower windows, designed 1933, and particularly in his replacements for bomb-damaged windows on the choir s side, sᴇ transept, and Lady Chapel s side, begun 1941. The damaged windows of the Lady Chapel apse and ɴ side were replaced from *c.* 1948 to designs by *Carl Edwards*. The large windows in the ɴᴡ and sᴡ transepts with their chunky figure style are by *Herbert Hendrie*. The nave windows are much more brightly coloured towards the w, probably because they were made after Scott's death and without his controlling influence. The most easterly on the s side is by *William Wilson*; all the rest are by *Edwards*, culminating in the great w, or Benedicite window, installed for the dedication of the finished building in 1978. Its intense colour and fluid design, and the colossal scale of the Christ figure at the top, mark a radical departure from all previous glass in the cathedral.

Burlison & Grylls did the ambulatory windows and *C.E. Kempe & Co.* the window on the Chapter House stairs, all completed in 1916. *Morris & Co.* produced the Chapter House windows from 1915 onwards.

The Cathedral Precinct

The land sloping down to Great George Street was originally occupied by early ᴄ19 terraced houses. Scott prepared speculative designs for new housing here, but nothing resulted. In 1982 a redevelopment competition was won by *Brock Carmichael Associates* with the landscape architects *Derek Lovejoy & Partners*. The resulting three-storey brick housing is grouped into oval courts, enclosing car-parking and private gardens. The level open space in front of the cathedral, known as **Queen's Walk**, is part of the scheme. An intended grand processional route from the corner of Upper Duke Street and Great George Street to the Rankin Porch has not materialized.

Metropolitan Cathedral (R.C.)

Mount Pleasant

Liverpool's Metropolitan Cathedral, designed by *Frederick Gibberd* and built 1962–7, was the greatest Roman Catholic postwar architectural commission in Britain. It was also the first cathedral to break with longitudinal planning (a tradition upheld by Basil Spence in his design of 1951 for Coventry Cathedral) in favour of a centralized arrangement,

52. Metropolitan Cathedral, by Frederick Gibberd (1962–7); steps by Falconer Chester (2003)

as encouraged by the Liturgical Movement. Gibberd's revolutionary plan was realized with modern materials – the building belongs in the mainstream of 1960s monumental concrete design – and was complemented by mainly abstract furnishings. It stands on top of the beginnings of an earlier, profoundly different, and hugely ambitious cathedral, designed by *Edwin Lutyens*.

The size of Liverpool's Catholic population, even before the immigration that followed the Irish famine of the 1840s, is clear from such ambitious churches as St Peter (*see* Walk 4, p. 202), St Patrick (*see* Walk 9, p. 271) and St Anthony (*see* Walk 7, p. 254). In 1845 *A.W.N. Pugin* was reported to have made designs for a cathedral in Liverpool, and after the formation of the Catholic diocese of Liverpool (1850) a cathedral was actually begun to the designs of his son *E.W. Pugin* in 1856 in St Domingo Road, Everton. Building progressed no further than the eastern chapels, which served as part of the parish church of Our Lady Immaculate until demolition in the 1980s. The role of pro-cathedral was filled by the church of St Nicholas in Hawke Street, an early C19 Gothic Revival building, demolished in 1972.

The Lutyens Cathedral

In 1928 the dynamic Richard Downey was appointed archbishop and made it his aim to build 'a cathedral in our time'. The magnificent site at the top of Mount Pleasant and Brownlow Hill, formerly occupied by the workhouse, was bought in 1930. This ensured that the building would be seen in relation to the Anglican Cathedral, rising half a mile (800 metres) to the s, and that the two great churches would crown the skyline. The commission was given to *Edwin Lutyens* – no competition was held – and his design was exhibited at the Royal Academy in 1932.

Lutyens's vision of the cathedral is preserved in numerous working drawings, in watercolour perspectives by Cyril Farey, and above all in the gigantic wooden model [53] now in the care of the Walker Art Gallery. Though classical in detail, it was a design of remarkable inventiveness, described by John Summerson as 'perhaps . . . the latest and supreme attempt to embrace Rome, Byzantium, the Romanesque and the Renaissance in one triumphal and triumphant synthesis'. The building would have been colossal, 680 ft long by 400 ft wide (207 by 122 metres), with a dome 168 ft (51 metres) in diameter and rising to 510 ft (155 metres) externally, dwarfing the tower of the Anglican Cathedral and outstripping St Peter's in Rome. The plan was longitudinal but compact: a short nave with double aisles, transepts also with double aisles, the dome to the diameter of the nave and inner aisles, and a short chancel with apse and circular chapter house behind. Before the nave there was to be a great narthex, the transept ends were to have angle chapels, and the apse was to be flanked by large apsed chapels and sacristies. The materials were to be buff brick with grey granite dressings.

53. Model of Lutyens's design for the Metropolitan Cathedral, by J.B. Thorp (1933–4)

The design of interior and exterior, excluding the dome, was a development – on a stupendous scale – of the three-dimensional triumphal arch motif Lutyens used for the Memorial to the Missing of the Somme at Thiepval.

Work began in 1933, but only the **crypt** was completed. It stands partly above, partly below ground, at the N end, beneath where the choir and chapter house would have been. The grey granite exterior should be understood as no more than the plinth from which the cliff-like walls of the ritual E end would have soared (the cathedral was – and is – not orientated; ritual E equals compass N, ritual W equals S, etc.). The entrance is from a sunken court on the ritual S side. Pevsner was shocked by what he called the 'exasperating whimsy' of Lutyens's unconventional detailing here: the tapering pillars that flank the doors, partly free-standing and partly absorbed, and the transom of the great semicircular window, seemingly forced into a downward curve by the keystone above. But such details are surely personal and expressive distortions of the classical language, in the tradition of Michelangelo or Giulio Romano. The doors lead straight into the **Chapel of St Nicholas**, with nave and aisles terminating in three apses. The piers are so massive that the space seems hollowed out of the earth rather than built. Granite dressings are used, but walls and vaults are of brick (left bare, not plastered as Lutyens intended). An identical space (now the **Concert Room**) occupies the corresponding area on the ritual N side, and on the central axis, between the chapel apses, are two great circular chambers, directly below what would have been chapter house and choir. One was intended to contain the organ, the sound of which would have risen through a grille; the other was to be the electrical switch room. On each side of the chapels, two immense vaulted halls run the full width of the building. The one on the ritual E side, originally intended as the lower sacristy, is lit by five semicircular windows and has stairs at either end. These are cantilevered around a circular well, and each flight starts with convex and ends with concave steps. The hall on the opposite side has groups of columns at each end, creating shadowy three-naved fragments [22]. Opening off its ritual w side is the **Chapel of the Relics** – the burial place of the archbishops – directly under what would have been Lutyens's high altar. The remarkable **gate** is a circular slab of Travertine that rolls open and shut, fretted with carving in the form of a cross. Inside, the chapel is faced with marble and Travertine and has pairs of Doric columns in recesses. Deep semicircular arches above these columns enclose sculpted sarcophagi. It is a solemnly impressive interior.

The Gibberd Cathedral

Work on the crypt ceased during the Second World War; Lutyens died in 1944, Archbishop Downey in 1953. By now it was clear that Lutyens's scheme was impossibly large and costly. A scaled-down version by *Adrian Gilbert Scott*, published in 1955, was not pursued. Finally, in 1959 a competition was held for an entirely new design.

The terms reflected the liturgical trend of the late 1950s and beyond, which favoured the closer involvement of the faithful in the Mass. Architects were required to provide for a congregation of 3,000 (later reduced to 2,000), all within sight of the altar. In a letter sent to competitors, Archbishop Heenan impressed upon them that 'the high altar is not an ornament to embellish the cathedral building. The cathedral, on the contrary, is built to enshrine the altar of sacrifice. The attention of all who enter should be arrested and held by the altar.' The winner was *Frederick Gibberd*, whose circular plan with central altar met this requirement in the simplest and most obvious way. Another stipulation was that the Lutyens crypt be incorporated, and this Gibberd achieved with notable success. He transformed the crypt roof into an elevated piazza (already proposed by *Scott* in 1955), extending this level platform across the rest of the site to form a podium [54]. The cathedral stands at one end, raised high above the uneven contours of the site, and set apart in a way appropriate for a sacred building. At the other end, the crypt stairs are nicely finished off with a pair of stone-faced pyramids. An outdoor altar is set against the ritual E end of the new cathedral. Within the podium are a car park, sacristies, and other offices, linked internally with both crypt and cathedral.

The plan of Gibberd's building can be read from the outside. It is a circle 195 ft (59.4 metres) in diameter surrounded by thirteen chapels, the main entrance and two side porches. The structural elements are exposed. Sixteen boomerang-shaped concrete trusses rise vertically from the podium then slant inwards, supporting the conical roof of the central space. They are tied together by a ring beam at the height of the bend of the boomerangs and again at the top. The boomerangs are helped in their work by flying buttresses from the lower ring down to the ground, continuing unbroken the diagonal line of the roof, so that they resemble the poles of a tepee or the taut guy ropes of a tent. These buttresses – the most striking exterior feature – were not part of Gibberd's original conception, but were suggested by the engineer *James Lowe*. They give a superficial similarity to Oscar Niemeyer's Brasilia cathedral, 1958, but Niemeyer's graceful, organic curves are very different from Gibberd's jutting, angular shapes. From the upper ring the trusses extend upwards to form the glazed lantern tower, ending in a spiky crown of pinnacles (the cathedral is dedicated to Christ the King) with cobwebby stainless steel between. Gibberd's cylindrical tower with its pinnacles responds to the tower of the Anglican Cathedral, and in views both near and distant the two buildings appear linked. He intended that his cathedral should have a ceremonial approach from Hope Street, but a pre-existing building in Mount Pleasant prevented this. Eventually in 2003 a broad, axial flight of steps was provided by *Falconer Chester*, rising from a new square at pavement level. (The single-storey Visitor Centre flanking the square on the E forms part of the scheme, with a garden above incorporating ramped access, and a curved façade of coursed slate to Mount Pleasant).

Gibberd's chapels and entrance porches, positioned between the flying buttresses, are of varied shapes and have different arrangements of windows. However, their consistently tall, narrow proportions and Portland stone facing helps unify them. The main doors are at the base of the great wedge-shaped bell tower that closes the view N along Hope Street [52]. The bells hang in openings punched through the thin apex of the tower (recalling Marcel Breuer's St John, Collegeville, Minnesota, 1953–61) and the surface below is carved with an angular, geometric relief designed by *William Mitchell*, incorporating three crosses. The discipline of this contrasts with the huge sliding **doors** below, also by

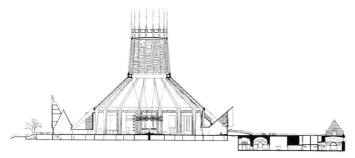

54. Section through the Gibberd cathedral and the Lutyens crypt

Mitchell. They feature the symbols of the Evangelists, treated in an expressionist style that made Pevsner think of 'the introduction to some cruel Mexican ritual'. They look like bronze, but are fibreglass.

The entrance leads through a low porch directly into nave and sanctuary [55]. The first uplifting impression is of vast height and space, and of intense colour from the stained glass, contrasting with the darkness of the roof. The disappointment is that almost everything can be taken in at once: the building does not reveal itself gradually or hold many surprises in store. The boomerang-shaped trusses (here of exposed concrete poured into smooth shuttering) appear in full clarity. That the chapels and porches are treated as independent buildings, unconnected with the main structural frame, is made wonderfully clear, because each is bordered left, right and top by strips of intense blue glass with flecks of red (by *John Piper* and *Patrick Reyntiens*). Some are open to the nave, others present a largely blank wall, others still are horizontally divided, with a low, enclosed space below a balcony. The focus of everything is the central **altar**, a single block of pure white marble, 10 ft (3 metres) long, quarried at Skopje in Macedonia. It is raised on a stepped platform.* The ethereal **crucifix** of pale gilt bronze – just a figure, without a cross – is by *Elisabeth Frink*. Her intention was 'to make a silhouette rather than a solid sculptural shape'. Suspended above is Gibberd's **baldacchino**, a crown-like canopy of aluminium rods incorporating lights and loudspeakers. The concentric curved **benches** (by *Frank Knight*) and the radial-patterned grey and white marble **floor** (by *David Atkins*) also lead the eye towards the altar. So, of course, does the luminous **tower** directly over it, a cylinder of abstract stained glass by *Piper* and *Reyntiens*, with three great bursts of colour (yellow, blue and red) symbolizing the Trinity. The design, which has echoes of the artists' earlier work in the baptistery at Coventry Cathedral, spreads right round, taking no account of the ribs, and changing continuously as one makes a circuit. The individual pieces of glass, 1 in. (2.5 cm.) thick, are bonded with epoxy resin (visible as a network of fine black lines) and set in concrete frames. The result is that glass predominates over concrete, which was not the case in Gibberd's original tower design. The same technique is used for the blue glass framing the chapels.

Gibberd's preference for abstract, allusive art was not always in step with the Cathedral Committee's taste, and the harmony he achieved between architecture, furnishings, sculpture and glass is therefore all the more remarkable. Since the building opened it has acquired a good deal of more conventional religious art – figurative, narrative or overtly symbolic – some of which sits uncomfortably in the context of Gibberd's Modernism. In the following description, furnishings are contemporary with Gibberd's building unless later dates are given.

*The circular plan brings with it functional difficulties – when the cathedral is full the priest has his back to a large part of the congregation – and there are acoustic problems too.

The expressionist **Stations of the Cross** in cast and welded metal, 1993–5, are by *Sean Rice*, who also designed the **lectern** near the high altar with two intertwining eagles. Walking clockwise round the nave from the main entrance, the vivid red stained glass in the **Chapel of St Paul of the Cross** (now Chapel of Reconciliation) is by *Margaret Traherne*. The **Chapel of St Joseph**, right of the ritual N porch, has wood panelling, and a funnel-like pyramid ceiling. In 1983 the panelling of the rear wall was carved and painted by *Stephen Foster* with scenes from the life of St Joseph in a folk-art style; the side walls were similarly carved in 1995. Next comes the **Lady Chapel**, with a terracotta **statue** of the Virgin and Child by *Robert Brumby*. The tall narrow windows have stained glass in subdued browns by *Margaret Traherne*. In the recess right of the Lady Chapel (not strictly speaking a chapel) is a **statue** of Abraham in various metals, cast and welded, by *Rice* again, 1990s. After this comes the **Blessed Sacrament Chapel**, directly opposite the main door. The entrance is low under the organ, beyond which the chapel widens and the roof slopes steeply upwards to the altar wall, faced with pitted stone. The abstract painted **reredos** and **stained glass** by *Ceri Richards* were conceived as a single composition – a triptych – 'suggesting a mysterious infinity of cool space' in Gibberd's words. *Richards* also designed the **tabernacle doors** with their more straightforward eucharistic imagery. Small statue of the Risen Christ by *Arthur Dooley*, presented 1986. Continuing round the nave, in the **Chapel of St Thomas Aquinas** (now

Speed and economy were important factors in construction – building took just five years, and the total cost was £1.9 million. Unfortunately, the use of new materials and techniques led before long to leaks and other chronic problems with the fabric. A campaign of repairs from the 1990s has changed the external appearance significantly. The frame was originally faced with off-white mosaic, large areas of which became detached. The mosaic proved impossible to repair, and the frame has now been clad in mottled grey glass-reinforced plastic. This makes the members slightly thicker, and the joints in the new material give a misleading impression of masonry construction rather than poured concrete. The conical roof, originally covered with aluminium, has been renewed in stainless steel, and the podium has been repaved with concrete flags, replacing the original random slate. The restoration of the Gibberd cathedral was conducted by *Vis Williams Prichard*, the repair of the Lutyens crypt and piazza by *O'Mahony Fozzard*.

Chapel of Unity) is a bronze holy-water **stoup** by *Virginio Ciminaghi*, and a **mosaic** of Pentecost by *George Mayer Marton*, 1957, brought in 1989 from the demolished church of the Holy Ghost, Netherton. The final chapel, next to the main entrance, is the cylindrical **baptistery**, with gates by *David Atkins*. Its skylight is hidden by a suspended cone which diffuses the light. In the crypt is a set of Stations of the Cross designed by *Howard Faulkner*, 1930s, and carved in oak by *Frederick G. Pugh* and *James Barnett*, in a style recalling Eric Gill's for Westminster Cathedral.

E of the cathedral, but linked, are **Cathedral House** and the (former) **Convent of Christ the King**, and just N of these, the **Catholic Chaplaincy** of the University of Liverpool. All were designed by *Gibberd*, and all are faced with Portland stone. Relatively small in scale, of two storeys: a good foil for the main building. Convent and Cathedral House have narrow vertical windows to the ground floor, and there is an enclosed garden between Cathedral House and the podium. The Chaplaincy has more blank walling, and arched windows facing the Lutyens crypt.

The Docks

RICHARD POLLARD

Introduction

Liverpool emerged from insignificance in the C17 to become the country's third port by 1700. A century later it was second only to London and was Europe's foremost transatlantic port. Its strategic advantages – proximity to Ireland, easy Atlantic access and excellent communications with a booming industrial hinterland – outweighed its substantial natural limitations. Overcoming these required the development of the largest single system of enclosed docks in the world, one of Britain's greatest engineering achievements. In the later C20 technological innovation and the collapse of traditional industries and trading patterns sent much of the port into dramatic decline. Today parts of the docks are thriving, others lie derelict and many acres are being redeveloped in one of the biggest such exercises in the country outside London's Docklands.

Until the second half of the C17 Chester was the leading port of NW England; Liverpool had a tiny fleet (only one ship, of 30 tons, was recorded in 1609), sheltered in the Pool [6]. By the end of the century Liverpool had leapt ahead, first on the strength of Cheshire salt exports and Irish trading, and then, from the 1670s, on the transatlantic plantation trades that would be the backbone of future growth (*see* pp. 5 and 10). Expansion continued rapidly through the C18 and C19, propelled by the industrialization of northern England, for which Liverpool was the principal entrepôt. This expansion both required the creation of the docks and financed their development. By 1700 the hostile river and small silting Pool were totally inadequate for the growing ocean-going merchant fleet; only expensive enclosed docks could provide the required deep, safe berths, but their huge cost necessitated corporate action. Thus, unlike London and its private wharfs, from the outset Liverpool's docks were a unified public enterprise, owned and managed until 1858 by the Dock Trustees (the Corporation by another name) and thereafter by the independent Mersey Docks and Harbour Board (MDHB). This enabled the town to expand the docks, the key to its economic growth, on a scale that only London would better, and with a technological and stylistic coherence none could match. From the outset works were financed by surplus local capital generated by the

56. Albert River Wall, recess for steps, by Jesse Hartley (*c.* 1843)

57. *East quay, Prince's Dock*. Watercolour by Samuel Austin (1833)

port's expansion, invested in bonds issued by the trustees and the MDHB. £31.5 million was raised in this fashion between 1858 and 1914 alone.

The port's zenith, encapsulated in the Edwardian pomp of the MDHB's offices on the Pier Head (*see* Major Buildings, p. 67), was the beginning of the C20, when Liverpool's tonnage surpassed those of the next six ports put together. Decline was presaged by the emergence of new rivals, especially Manchester, which built the Ship Canal (opened in 1894) specifically to bypass Liverpool, and Southampton, nearer to London, taking away the prestigious transatlantic liners from 1907. The Second World War, in which the port was the county's principal gateway for men and *matériel*, left widespread destruction. A surge of postwar prosperity ended abruptly in 1971 when the MDHB collapsed under spiralling debt and crippling labour disputes. Thirty years on, the successor Mersey Docks and Harbour Company has begun to post record cargo figures, though the port today handles a far smaller percentage of the country's maritime trade. The cost of recovery has been dockers' jobs – perhaps 95 per cent lost since 1948 – and hundreds of acres of obsolete facilities. In 1972 all docks s of the Pier Head were closed, joined in 1988 by the oldest to its N.

Engineering and Shipping

The development of the dock system was shaped by the interaction of surging demand with evolving ship design, and the severe environmental handicaps of the Mersey estuary. The estuary's strong currents, stiff westerlies, shifting sandbanks and 30 ft (9.1 metre) tidal range meant that expensive **enclosed docks** were the only means of providing safe berths. Moreover, high ground inland forced expansion into a ribbon of foreshore 7 m. (11.3 km.) long and seldom more than ½ m. (0.8 km.) wide, on ground reclaimed from within the tidal margins: a truly heroic undertaking. So dependent was Liverpool on its dock engineers to overcome these problems that *G.F. Lyster*, who was paid a staggering £4,500 in 1873, was easily the best remunerated salaried engineer of his time.

At the invitation of the Town Council, in 1708–9 *Henry Huss* and *George Sorocold* surveyed and designed schemes to improve the silting Pool, though in the end *Thomas Steers* was commissioned to build a 'wet' dock, that is one enclosed behind gates, within it. This, the 3.5 acre (1.4 hectare) **Old Dock** [58], was begun in 1710, opened in 1715 and completed the following year. Its layout set the pattern for the **sail era**: roughly rectangular, and approached through gates from a **tidal basin** (*see* topic box, p. 117). Earlier docks – London's Blackwall Dock, *c.* 1650, and Howland Great Wet Dock, 1697–1700, and others in the naval dockyards – were for laying up and repairing ships, so Steers's was the world's first commercial enclosed dock, designed for loading and unloading at any state of tide. A second, South (later Salthouse) Dock followed (1739–54). By the time the next three had been completed under Steers's successors *Henry Berry* (1750–89) and *Thomas Morris* (1789–99), Liverpool's docks covered some 25.7 acres (10.4 hectares); no other port had more than one. *John Rennie* and *John Foster Sen.*'s Prince's Dock (*c.* 1810–21) [57], at 11.4 acres (4.6 hectares), introduced the first substantial increase in size. The first **half-tide dock** (*see* topic box, p. 117) was Union (*c.* 1823). Very little pre-1840 fabric has survived radical C19 and C20 reconstruction; the best remaining C18 **quay walls** line Duke's Dock (1773), the first and only survivor of a number of small **private docks** and basins.

The delays and allegations of corruption that dogged the construction of Prince's Dock brought about Foster's resignation in 1824 and the appointment of *Jesse Hartley* (1780–1860), a bridge builder from Pontefract, trained as a mason, but with no previous experience of dock

58. The Old Dock (1710–16) and the Dry Dock, a tidal basin, by Thomas Steers. Detail from J. Chadwick's map (1725)

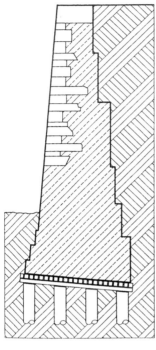

59. Albert Dock, west quay wall, by Jesse Hartley (*c.* 1843), section

Liverpool's prosperity was founded on the ability to construct dock and river walls capable of resisting the forces of water, tides and storms, superimposed loads (cargo, buildings, etc.) and the fill behind the wall, all at an affordable cost. The engineering issues were long recognized when *Thomas Steers* began the Old Dock in 1710. Nevertheless, its walls, the first and last to be built of brick (with rubble backing), collapsed frequently for want of proper drainage and foundations. Sandstone replaced brick from the 1730s, laid in dressed courses bound to rubble masonry behind.

c18 walls had a pronounced concave profile to brace against collapse, but by the 1840s *Jesse Hartley* was building straight faces with only a slight batter; these became essential with the advent of deep, square-hulled steamships. Cruciform-profiled buttresses called counterforts were set into the rear, and wooden or (from 1823) iron-sheet piling was used where necessary. Hartley, an outstanding mason, insisted on superlative construction standards; these enabled him to build comparatively thin walls that hardly ever failed. At Clarence Dock, completed in 1830, he introduced harder-wearing granite facing in place of sandstone (though shortages of granite ensured the use of both into the 1880s); he insisted on leasing a quarry in Kirkmabreck in sw Scotland to supply it. His distinctive cyclopean construction [64] consists of massive bonding headers (up to 6 ft – 1.8 metres – deep), knitted together precisely with small irregular pieces of rubble like a jigsaw puzzle, and set in the thinnest lime-mortar joints. It may look extravagant, but it cost no more than sandstone. 'Hartley' granite continued to be employed, e.g. for dock entrances, for a while even after concrete was adopted, beginning with the Harrington Dock river wall in 1876. Traditional continuous-face construction was retained until the Royal Seaforth Dock in 1967–71 introduced the 'diaphragm' wall: a row of huge, vertical, semi-cylindrical sections, with a fin extending from the rear of each.

building. Hartley nevertheless became the world's first full-time professional dock engineer. Within months he presented plans for expanding the docks into a fully integrated system. From 1846 he became increasingly reliant on his son and assistant *J.B. Hartley*, who succeeded him for a year after his death. By then he had built or rebuilt twenty-six docks, increasing their acreage from 46 to 212 (18.6 to 85.9 hectares).

Hartley's achievements in Liverpool mark him out as one of the greatest C19 engineers. His success was based on craft experience, insistence on quality, attention to detail, openness to new ideas, a fearsome capacity for work and sound management. His docks were superbly built, relatively cheap and of conventional layout, and only his last, Canada Dock (1859), was at 17.4 acres (7 hectares) substantially larger than Prince's. Nevertheless, there were innovations. From Waterloo (1834), docks were interconnected, without separate river entrances, reducing operating costs. He built **specialized docks**: Clarence (1830), exclusively for steamers, at a distance N for fear of fire; three, beginning at Brunswick (1832), for unloading timber through ships' bows onto sloping quays; three warehouse docks for bonded goods (*see* below), starting at Albert (1843–7); and Stanley (1844–8) as an interchange with rail – the first of its kind – and canal. He also developed an integrated depot, the Dock Yard, responsible for design, construction and maintenance.

Hartley also raised the standard of design on the Dock Estate to **architecture** of the highest calibre. His two styles share an overwhelming monumentality symbolic of confidence and prosperity. The earlier Greek Revival structures – e.g. the utterly massive 1830s gatepiers in the dock wall and the utilitarian classicism of the Albert warehouses [64] – were,

60. The entrance to Stanley Dock, and policemen's lodges. Lithograph from W. Herdman, *Views in Modern Liverpool*, 1864

Pevsner declared, endowed with 'a sense of the cyclopean, the primeval, which is unparalleled'. The Gothic castle idiom [60] that emerged in the 1840s was more overtly emblematic of security (e.g. the accumulator towers at Stanley and Wapping) and often arrestingly whimsical e.g. the Wapping Policeman's Lodge [68] (the most fantastical, the Canada Dock accumulator tower, is demolished). Hartley's architectural talent was not matched by his succesors.

The emergence in the mid C19 of **iron-hulled steamships** stimulated the first radical change in dock design. The new ships were of a previously unimaginable, and growing, size. They cost huge sums to build and operate and ran to regular timetables, making rapid turnarounds imperative. The solution to this, and to unrelenting demand for more berths, was three building programmes undertaken following Acts of 1873, 1891 and 1898 by *G.F. Lyster* and his more talented son *A.G. Lyster,* Dock Engineers 1861–97 and 1897–1913 respectively. These programmes were characterized by three developments: the **branch-dock** plan, with fingers off a vestibule; two-storey transit sheds for more rapid goods handling; and river **locks** to eliminate delays associated with half-tide docks (*see* topic box, p. 117). The principal **new docks**, of unprecedented size, were downstream where the channel was deeper and the foreshore wider, e.g. Alexandra (1874–82), 44 acres (17.8 hectares), and Gladstone (1910–27), the spectacular 49 acre (19.8 hectares) culmination of the steamship programme. Selected older docks were comprehensively rebuilt along similar lines e.g. King's, *c.* 1898–1906.

In the 1960s a revolution spread through shipping, replacing loose mixed cargoes with standardized, pre-packed **containers**. This made narrow finger quays crowded with transit sheds obsolete: the speed at which container ships load and unload requires large open quays for transfer and storage. The layout of the Royal Seaforth Dock was revised during design and it opened in 1971 with the key new characteristics: specialist (container and bulk) berths around a single 85 acre (34.4 hectare) polygonal dock with massive gantry cranes and vast areas of hardstanding for storage of containers and timber.

Storing and Moving Cargoes

Because Liverpool's docks were almost exclusively publicly owned, the private quayside warehouses common in older ports such as Hull were almost non-existent. Nearly all private warehouses in Liverpool (*see* topic box, p. 205) were built inland instead. The first **warehouse** on the Dock Estate was at King's Dock (1793, demolished), erected by the Corporation to store tobacco. The next to be built were required by the 1803 Warehousing Act, which extended the privilege to hold goods in bond – that is in a secure warehouse without paying duty – to a variety of commodities provided that the **closed-dock system** was adopted. This system consisted of an integrated walled complex of dock and warehouses, as pioneered in London at the West India Dock (1799–1809).

61. Albert Dock, by Jesse Hartley (1843–7)

Vested interests, e.g. carters, warehouse-owners and unscrupulous merchants, blocked full implementation in Liverpool until *Hartley*'s magnificent Albert Dock was erected in the 1840s (*see* topic box, p. 205, for interim arrangements). With the destruction of most of the equivalent London warehouses, Albert is now the best location to evoke the ambition and monumentality of the system [61]. Similar iron and brick warehouses followed at Wapping and Stanley Docks. Subsequent warehouses were for particular goods, e.g. the vast Waterloo **grain warehouses** by *G.F. Lyster*, 1866–8 [72]. *A.G. Lyster* built the even larger **Tobacco Warehouse** at Stanley Dock, *c*. 1897–1901, introducing steel and concrete [74]. Like many Lyster buildings, it was enlivened by free Renaissance detail in terracotta, probably by *John Arthur Berrington*, employed as an architectural draughtsman for forty-six years from 1872 [70]. The ultimate development was bulk storage, beginning in 1881 with **casemates** cut into the rock at Herculaneum Dock for petroleum and followed in the C20 by oil-tank farms, grain silos and Tate & Lyle's sublime parabolic **Sugar Silo** of 1955–7 [78] (just outside the Dock Estate).

Transit sheds, for the temporary shelter of goods on the quayside, were always more widespread, though rarely of any architectural pretension. The many built by *Hartley* had composite iron and wood structures. Only a rebuilt gable at Salthouse Dock (1855) survives of these. The *Lysters*' steamship docks had standard enclosed brick and iron or steel designs, of one or two storeys. The pioneers of the latter, built at Harrington and Toxteth docks in the 1880s, were the world's first to be designed to work on two levels simultaneously, by ships' tackle below and travelling hydraulic roof cranes above. They survive as business units. C20 developments – electric cranes, reinforced concrete and forklift operations – culminated at Huskisson Dock in the 1950s. Since containerization, transit sheds, mainly at Royal Seaforth Dock, have been generic single-storey, portal-frame structures of up to 100,000 sq. ft (9,290 sq. metres), designed around articulated lorries, containers, pallets and forklift trucks.

Most goods have always left the docks by road. For this, **bridges** were provided across passages. In the C18 they were wooden drawbridges; beginning with an order for Queen's Dock in 1809, a standard cast-iron swing bridge was introduced based on a *John Rennie* design. An 1840s

The Liverpool Overhead Railway

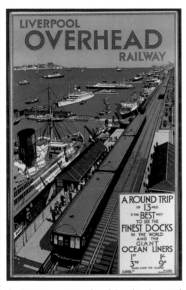

62. Interwar poster advertising the Liverpool Overhead Railway

An elevated railway was first proposed in 1853 above the dock railway to alleviate chronic congestion on the dock road. However, the Dock Board's interest remained half-hearted until it leased the rights to build and operate a passenger-only line to the Liverpool Overhead Railway Company in 1888. The company's decision to adopt electric traction to reduce weight and fire risks made it the world's first elevated electric railway. The line opened in 1893, and was subsequently extended until it ran for 9 m. (14.5 km.) from Dingle to Seaforth. *Sir Douglas Fox* and *J.H. Greathead* were the consultant engineers, and *Francis Fox* and *S.B. Cottrell* the resident engineers. Trains ran along an iron and steel viaduct spanning the dock railway on columns supporting transverse girders. The railway became a much-loved Liverpool institution, affectionately known as the Docker's Umbrella, and was promoted as a tourist attraction because of its unrivalled views of docks and shipping. It closed in 1956, requiring at least £2 million of repairs, and was demolished to a chorus of protest. Stanchions survive in the dock wall alongside Prince's Dock and Wapping Warehouse.

An excellent history is Adrian Jarvis, *Portrait of the Liverpool Overhead Railway*, 1996.

example survives at Albert Dock. Wider passages for steamships were spanned by hydraulically powered swing bridges, and on occasions in the C20 by lifting bridges, e.g. Stanley Dock [74]. The first link to the **canal** network was an indirect one, the Duke of Bridgewater's Duke's Dock of 1773. A direct connection opened in 1848 to the Leeds and Liverpool Canal at Stanley Dock. The world's first mainline **railway**, the Liverpool & Manchester, opened in 1830 with a goods station serving the docks (*see* topic box, p. 188) and by the end of the C19 an internal railway extended the length of the docks. For workers, the elevated **Liverpool Overhead Railway** operated along the docks from 1893 to 1956 (*see* topic box, facing).

Redevelopment since 1972

After closure the South Docks, upstream of the Pier Head, were colonized by small business, whilst their redevelopment was debated. In 1981 Michael Heseltine as Environment Minister created the **Merseyside Development Corporation**, one of the first Urban Development Corporations (UDCs), to take over ownership and lead **regeneration**. In 1988 its remit was extended to the obsolete docks N from the Pier Head to Stanley Dock. To attract investment the MDC set about environmental and infrastructure improvements, demolition and selective restoration. Central to its approach was the exploitation of water as an attractive backdrop for development, a lesson learnt from pioneering harbour regeneration schemes e.g. Baltimore Inner Harbor. Many docks were restored, requiring the removal of more than three million cubic metres of silt. Development of the South Docks was zoned – s of Queen's for business and industry, N for leisure and housing, though in execution the emphasis across the whole area switched to the latter (e.g. Brunswick Dock). An early priority was the restoration of Albert Dock as a flagship mixed-use development. The first phase was completed in 1984; by 1988 it had become the second most popular free attraction in the UK. The MDC was wound up in 1998 and its responsibilities split between the City Council, English Partnerships and the private sector. By 2004 most sites s of the Pier Head had been developed, the glaring exception being King's Dock. N of the Pier Head, progress to 2004 was limited to Prince's and Waterloo docks.

Regeneration has been economically successful, but the **architecture** is extremely disappointing. There has been a widespread failure to rise to the potential of the extraordinary location. The best by far is **conservation**: the magnificent repair and conversion of Albert Dock [64], but also the residential conversion of Wapping Warehouse by *Kingham Knight Associates*. The best **new building** is *David Marks Julia Barfield Architects*' Liverpool Watersport Centre, 1993–4, at Queen's Dock [69]. *Eduard Ross*'s bridge at Prince's Dock (2001) is noteworthy too. Otherwise the lack of commitment to good design is sorely evident in banal office and housing schemes and, unlike in London's Docklands, standards have yet to improve.

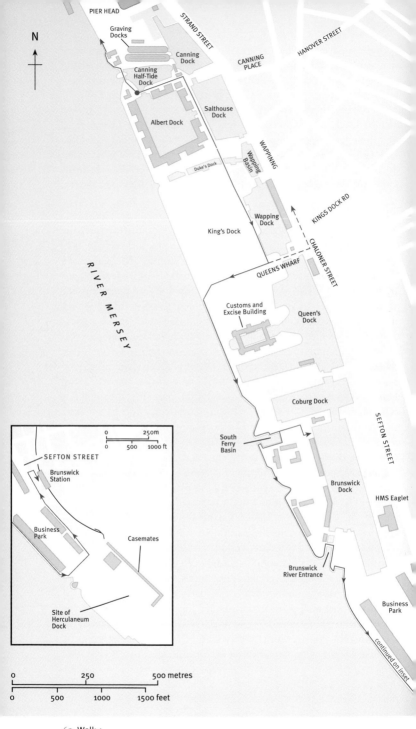

N

PIER HEAD

STRAND STREET

Graving
Docks

Canning
Dock

CANNING
PLACE

HANOVER STREET

Canning
Half-Tide
Dock

Salthouse
Dock

Albert Dock

WAPINNG

Wapping
Basin

Duke's Dock

KINGS DOCK RD

Wapping
Dock

King's Dock

CHALONER STREET

QUEENS WHARF

R I V E R   M E R S E Y

Customs and
Excise Building

Queen's
Dock

Coburg Dock

SEFTON STREET

South
Ferry
Basin

Brunswick
Dock

HMS Eaglet

0   250m
0   500   1000 ft

SEFTON STREET

Brunswick
Station

Business
Park

Casemates

Brunswick
River Entrance

Business
Park

Site of
Herculaneum
Dock

continued on inset

0   250   500 metres
0   500   1000   1500 feet

63. Walk 1

The South Docks: Albert Dock to Herculaneum Dock

This long walk explores the South Docks, from the Pier Head s along the reclaimed foreshore for 2.5 m. (4 km.) to Dingle, where rock out-cropping prevented further expansion up river. It begins at the peerless Albert Dock and follows the broadly chronological development upstream. By 1900 the South Docks were already struggling to cope with the growing size of steamships. Their slow decline ended abruptly in 1972 with complete closure, a stark emblem of the collapse of the port and with it Liverpool's economy. Of the efforts of the Merseyside Development Corporation to regenerate the semi-derelict estate from 1981 the most significant was the restoration of Albert Dock, a self-conscious symbol of rebirth and redirection. Today the South Docks contain homes, businesses, shops, restaurants and museums; economically, if not always architecturally, a success.

Albert Dock

Jesse Hartley's **Albert Dock** is one of the great monuments of C19 engineering; its sublime grandeur unquestionably the architectural climax of the Liverpool docks. In 1969 Pevsner wrote that 'For sheer punch there is little in the early commercial architecture of Europe to emulate it'. In its bare bones it is an integrated warehouse–dock complex, built in 1843–7 without any combustible material, for the secure storage of high-value bonded goods [61]. At the centre is a 7.75 acre (3.1 hectare) dock, with 40 ft (12.2 metre) walls constructed in Hartley's habitual cyclopean granite (*see* topic box, p. 96). Grouped around this – and standing on almost 5,300 beech piles – are five 60 ft-(18.3 metre-) high warehouse stacks, with vaults below, each constructed of a brick skin wrapped around a cast-iron frame. They contain over one million sq. ft (92,900 sq. metres) of floorspace. Ancillary buildings and a perimeter wall erected to prevent theft surround the warehouses.

But what solicits admiration now, apart of course from the scale, is the monumental solemnity of the warehouses, the manner in which they have been pared down to a synthesis of austere classicism and technological functionalism. This has not always been the case: J. A.

Picton, the c19 Liverpool architect and historian, described them as 'simply a hideous pile of naked brickwork'.

A good place from which to consider the whole ensemble is the **swing bridge** of 1843 across the Canning–Albert passage in the dock's NW corner. This is itself an interesting object: a cast-iron two-leaf structure supplied by the *Haigh Foundry*, Wigan, the last surviving example of a pattern, once common in the docks, which was derived via Hull from *John Rennie*'s pioneering design for the London Dock (1803–4). The N railings could be pivoted flat so as not to foul ships' ropes when swung open. Restored to working order 1984.

History. In 1841 local opposition to the creation of a 'closed-dock system' in Liverpool, in pursuance of the 1803 Warehousing Act (*see* pp. 98 and 205), was finally overcome. Parliamentary consent was obtained to construct a purpose-built dock, overturning earlier proposals to erect warehouses at Prince's Dock. The site chosen, mostly occupied by ship-builders, was constricted by docks to its N, S and E and by the Mersey to the W. Work began immediately when Canning and Salthouse docks were run dry. Excavation of the new dock began in 1843, the first warehouse stacks came into operation at the opening by Prince Albert in 1846, and the last were finished the following year. The complex cost in excess of £700,000.

The dock was initially a great success, specializing in the Far East trade, and extensions were added to the S stack in 1853–5, but within two decades its entrances were too small and awkward for the latest ocean-going steamships. The presence of the warehouses made rebuilding impractical (making Albert one of the very few Liverpool docks to remain in its original form) and by 1914 hardly any ships unloaded here. Nevertheless Hartley's warehouses continued to make a profit until the 1950s, storing bonded tobacco, wines and spirits. They finally closed in 1972. By this time they were far from pristine: the N stack was converted into a cold store as early as 1899 (evidence of the rail connection remains at its rear), the SE stack had not been repaired since a bomb in 1941 had blown a corner off, and parts were derelict.

Demolition was a threat from 1960 as a myriad of development proposals came and went (*see* topic box, p. 106) until, in 1983, the newly created Merseyside Development Corporation (MDC), in partnership with the Arrowcroft Group, embarked on an ambitious programme to convert the complex, a task that to 1997 had cost £177 million. The first phase opened in 1984, but in 2004 a few sections still remained undeveloped. It is arguably the largest single conservation project ever undertaken in the UK and essentially extremely successful. New uses include hotels and bars, shops, offices and apartments, many by the *Franklin Stafford Partnership*, the Merseyside Maritime Museum by *Brock Carmichael*

64. Albert Dock, the west warehouse, by Jesse Hartley (1843–7)

Associates and *James Stirling*'s Tate Liverpool art gallery. The dock has become Merseyside's premier tourist attraction, but an isolated one: the windswept dock road remains a hostile barrier to the hoped-for extension of the city centre into the dock and on to the riverfront.

The **Warehouses**. Hartley's design marries two engineering traditions, those of warehouse planning and fireproof textile-mill construction, and was arrived at by a process of investigation, consultation and experimentation. The closed-dock systems of London had been described in a report to the Dock Committee in 1839 and a deputation was sent to study the most recent, the St Katharine Docks, where *Philip Hardwick* had designed warehouses in 1826–7. These formed the basis of Hartley's design. As Hartley had no previous experience in the field, Hardwick himself was consulted, along with his successor at St Katharine, George Aitchison Sen., and others.

Hartley laid out five separate **warehouse stacks**, each five storeys high on basement vaults. No two stacks are identical because of the irregular plan of the basin and interruptions for the passages [61]. Each has large yards for carts cut out of the rear, an idea taken from the St Katharine Docks. The massive load-bearing brick walls are over 3 ft (0.9

Redeveloping Albert, Canning and Salthouse Docks, 1960–80

Obsolete and semi-derelict by 1960, Albert, Canning and Salthouse docks became the focus of a succession of failed, and often improbable, redevelopment proposals. The site was enticing: large, on the riverfront and adjacent to the city centre. In 1966 *Harry Hyams* unveiled *Richard Seifert*'s designs for River City, an ambitious slice of Manhattan housing 50,000 workers in a dozen towers (one of forty-four storeys) to be built in the place of Hartley's warehouses, and trumpeted as the largest office centre outside London. The absurdly unrealistic plan, scaled down as Aquarius City, died in 1970. Two years later the Heron Corporation proposed a tower for civil servants on Canning Dock. Much more serious – and sympathetic – was Liverpool Polytechnic's decade-long ambition to convert the Albert stacks as the centrepiece of a new campus, killed by political vacillation in 1976. Then came three rival proposals: to turn the warehouses into an exhibition hall and offices around a piazza created by infilling the basin; to restore it as a marina and apartments; and for a 1,831 ft (558 metre) tower, by *Seifert* again, publicized as the world's tallest building. But the scale of the restoration challenge and of the economic collapse on Merseyside defeated any development until the massive injection of public funding through the MDC made private investment viable.

metres) wide at ground level, diminishing to 1 ft 7 in. (0.48 metres). On the quayside is a **colonnade** [64] of hollow cast-iron columns 15 ft (4.6 metres) high, filled with masonry.* These are unfluted Greek Doric of the most Primitivist kind, with powerfully squat proportions. The colonnade was the key concept borrowed from Hardwick's warehouses, though the idea had been first suggested by Ralph Dodd for London's Legal Quays in 1799. For both Hardwick and Hartley its principal advantage was that on a constricted site warehouse accommodation could be maximized whilst still providing quayside space for unloading, inspecting, weighing and sorting cargo. The colonnade functioned like a transit shed, from which goods, once landed, could be transferred by means of internal hoists and external cranes for storage above or in the vaults below, or onto carts for onward distribution. The broad elliptical **arches** that break the colonnade and bite into the floor above were Hartley's innovation, allowing cranes and ships' tackle to swing goods over the quay.

Above the colonnades the massive **façades** are stripped bare, relying solely on function for proportion and articulation. The crane arches create the principal stresses, the slightly recessed hoist doors the secondary. The one, slightly incongruous, concession was the cupola'd clock tower, designed by *Hardwick*, above the NE stack (removed *c.* 1960). Note everywhere Hartley's fastidious attention to detail: granite replaces brick or sandstone where quoins or other elements were susceptible to damage by carts, and the corners of the E stacks flanking the Salthouse passage are rounded so as not to foul ships' rigging. Where windows weren't required initially he provided blanks, not bonded-in.

So to the **interiors**. The basic plan followed St Katharine, with five storeys plus vaults and a **mezzanine floor** behind the colonnade [65]. Hartley developed the mezzanine concept further by merely providing footings (in the form of flared capitals) halfway up the internal columns, leaving future users to determine if and when to insert a floor. However, for the structure Hartley looked elsewhere, to contemporary textile-mill construction. The St Katharine stacks had wooden floors and roofs, but a series of serious warehouse fires made expensive **fireproof construction** of the Albert stacks imperative (a decision reinforced in 1842 by the Great Fire of Hamburg and a devastating blaze in Liverpool). Therefore, between 1841 and 1843, Hartley drew up six alternative designs to consider different degrees and types of fireproofing. Full-scale mock-ups of two of these were then tested to destruction before a system of cast-iron columns and beams supporting brick- ('jack'-) arch floors was chosen. This was already established as best practice in textile-mill design. The *Haigh Foundry* and the *Gospel Oak Iron Works*, Staffordshire, supplied the structural ironwork.

---

*In the infill of 1855 in the sw corner the ground-floor columns, inside as well as along the quayside, are granite, from which spring brick groin vaults.

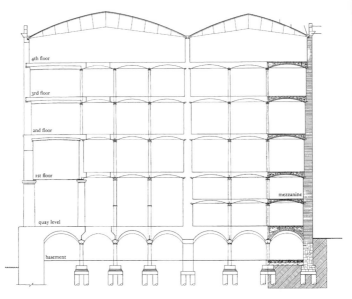

65. Albert Dock warehouses, by Jesse Hartley (1843–7), transverse section

This frame was built up above magnificent sandstone and brick **vaults**, which spring from elegant, cambered cast-iron beams spanning cast-iron columns. Arching in two directions, they swell rhythmically like the barrels they once stored. Above, the **cast-iron frame** rises on a module of 18 ft by 12 ft (5.5 by 3.7 metres), the columns supporting beams of inverted Y- and V- profile. From these spring the shallow jack arches, covered with ash and aggregate and laid with tiles. Hartley arranged the arches in the outer bays at right angles to the walls and provided plenty of iron tie-rods across all arches to restrain the lateral thrusts that had caused notorious mill collapses, but what makes his frame stand apart from mill structures is the outstanding aesthetic quality of the ironwork: muscular and elegant, fluid and sculptural, beautifully detailed. And to cap it, he invented a wholly new and remarkable stressed-skin **roof**, made of wrought-iron plates riveted together and tied across the eaves by slender wrought-iron rods suspended on hangers from ribs attached to the underside. Unlike conventional roofs that derive their strength from trusses, in Hartley's the strength lies within the curvature of the riveted iron skin itself. Though of an undeniable delicate beauty, it suffered problems with thermal expansion and, after the Stanley Dock warehouses (1852–4), the concept was abandoned until revived by C20 engineers. Cast-iron window frames, stone parapets and staircases, lateral and spine brick firebreak walls and wrought-iron firedoors completed the fireproof construction. The best place to examine the internal structure is the Merseyside Maritime Museum in the N stack.

Lifts and hoists were initially manually powered, but in 1848–9 the warehouses became the world's first to be fitted with **hydraulic cranes** and hoists, ordered from *William Armstrong* in Newcastle. The hydraulic jiggers of *c.* 1878 (*see* topic box, p. 115) in the colonnade were part of a later expansion of the system.

Now the **conversions**, beginning, clockwise, with the N stack and the **Merseyside Maritime Museum**, chiefly 1984–6, by *Brock Carmichael Associates.* A museum had been considered as early as 1884, and a site N of Albert was acquired for the purpose in the 1960s. Albert's N stack emerged as the preferred home in 1978 in a study commissioned from *Building Design Partnership*. Brock Carmichael's scheme is generally a success. The fully glazed wall behind the colonnade is sympathetic and confident and removing the mezzanine creates a lofty foyer [66]. Throughout, columns, beams, arches and walls (and Hartley's iron roof) are exposed. So too, unashamedly, are the services. Some bulky exhibition designs have masked the structure, cluttering the interiors and diluting the original approach. However, the staircase is a triumph. It slices through the structure in flights staggered sideways by one bay per storey, opening up views right through the building. It has an appropriately nautical flavour, like companionways ascending from deep inside a ship's hull, and by making Hartley's structure instantly

Albert Dock: Repair and Reuse

This mammoth undertaking was a two-stage process. In stage one, the MDC restored docks, locks and bridges, installed services, landscaped the site (in a not quite overwhelmingly 'heritage' style) and undertook restoration and repair of the warehouses, the two museums were created, and Arrowcroft converted ground and mezzanine floors for shop and office use. In stage two, the remaining floorspace was converted by Arrowcroft and various leaseholders. Stage one began in 1983 and was completed in 1988; stage two is still under way.

To ensure continuity the MDC retained *Holford Associates* and *W.G. Curtin & Partners* throughout as consultant architects and engineers respectively. The fabric was seamlessly repaired and bomb damage made good. Holfords and Curtins did the N stack (Merseyside Maritime Museum) 1983–4 and the N end of the W stack (the Tate) 1985–6. The rest was undertaken by the *Franklin Stafford Partnership* with *Ward, Ashcroft & Parkman* as engineers, 1983–7. Around the basin all window frames were replaced in aluminium to the original pattern. Franklin Stafford fitted new glazing of contemporary design to the rear elevations of the E, S and W stacks and recessed angled glazing to the loading doors, creating welcome shadow and depth. All blank windows were opened up.

66. Albert Dock N Warehouse (Jesse Hartley, 1843–7), entrance foyer of the Merseyside Maritime Museum (conversion by Brock Carmichael Associates, 1984–6)

comprehensible, it also succeeds in turning the building itself into a major exhibit.

Next, the NE, SE and S stacks, and S end of the W stack. *Franklin Stafford* have done most, beginning with **shops** and **offices** on the ground floor and mezzanine, in phases, clockwise, 1983–8. Some of this has been lost to later bar, restaurant and shop fit-outs with generally frameless glazed façades, but where it survives it is undoubtedly the least successful element. Intrusive, clumsy concrete mezzanines. Wooden-framed glazed partitions, desperately crude alongside Hartley. In the upper floors the practice created offices in the SE stack, 1992–3, and the NE stack, 2001, and **apartments** in the S end of the W stack, 1987–96. In the W end of the S stack is a hotel, by the American *Hausman Group*, 1998.

Lastly, **Tate Liverpool**, in the N end of the W stack. 1984–8 by *James Stirling of Stirling, Wilford & Associates*. The gallery selected the dock for its first regional outpost in 1981. Stirling, who was working on the development of the gallery's London home, was asked in 1984 to convert Albert and produced an admirably simple and clear plan. Running along the back of the spine wall is a core one structural bay wide, containing a staircase and other services. Flanking this are the galleries and secondary spaces stacked straightforwardly within Hartley's structural system. The spaces are clean, calm and elegant. As at the Maritime Museum the structure is celebrated, though the screens for picture hanging and controlling natural light (which also hide servicing) necessarily interfere, forming a new inner wall. Services and lighting are gathered in hefty, angular ducts slung beneath the jack arches. The museum's façade was a panelled blue and orange screen (much of it replaced by glazing in 1997–8) with portholes and bold and elegant signage, self-effacingly set back behind the colonnade [64]. Behind this is the foyer, originally spanned by a mezzanine café in the form of a swelling blue balcony (nicknamed the 'blue bum' by Stirling), and lofty ground-floor galleries created by removing the mezzanine. As part of the controversial **phase-two** works, 1997–8, *Michael Wilford & Partners** relocated the balconies to create a more spacious foyer. The ground-floor galleries to the left became a bookshop and a new, larger café, into which the balcony was re-inserted, folded back on itself above an island bar. The vacant top floor was fitted out as galleries for temporary exhibitions, retaining Hartley's stressed-skin roof E of the spine and creating a new north-light roof w of it.

This was an intensely personal commission for Stirling, a Liverpudlian who had played around the dock as a child, and trained in the city. It was his only project in his home town, and throughout his response is notable for its restraint. Both Hartley and Stirling had famously powerful personalities, but at Liverpool Stirling put aside his usual exuberance in deference to Hartley's masterpiece.

Related structures. Security against theft was a fundamental purpose of the dock and so the warehouses were enclosed by a 12 ft (3.7 metre) **perimeter wall**, erected across the cart bays on the N, E and S sides, but free-standing along the riverfront (intended as a public promenade; magnificent views of the w stack from here). It was pierced by gates, whose massive **gatepiers**, with wild rustication and characteristic slots for sliding gates, can be seen w of the swing bridge and in the SE and SW corners. **Police lodges** are built alongside the gates against the inside of the wall.

Other ancillary buildings included a simple, two-storey **cooperage** (1846) inside the wall in the NW corner and, beyond on the pierhead, residences for key employees. Only one remains (the last of over forty on the Dock Estate), the three-storey **Piermaster's House** of 1852–3 with dog-tooth eaves corbelling; to the left is the Piermaster's Office. Restored from dereliction by *Brock Carmichael Associates* to their appearance *c.* 1910, for the Merseyside Maritime Museum, 1983–4. An imposing foil to the warehouses in the NE corner is the **Dock Traffic Office** [17], completed in 1848 to a slightly hunched design of two storeys over a basement by *Philip Hardwick*. He was preferred by the Dock Committee over Hartley here (and for the clock tower) possibly because for Architecture it wanted an Architect. The pedimented Tuscan portico is a *tour de force* in cast iron; each column is made of two sections over 17 ft (5.2 metres) high and the architrave is a single casting. A year later *Hartley* introduced some hauteur by adding a second storey containing a flat for the principal clerk. With that came the splendid

*Stirling died in 1992.

tapering chimneystacks and probably the first-floor cornice, which is far bolder than that proposed by Hardwick. The core is a large galleried hall, a double cube with coved ceiling. The derelict building was converted by the *Building Design Partnership* as Granada Television news studios in 1984–5.

Beyond Albert Dock

So to the docks around Albert. First, N, **Canning Half-Tide Dock** (*see* topic box, p. 117), the entrance to the Albert system, created in 1842–4 by *Jesse Hartley* out of the Gut, the narrow entrance to the Dry Dock (*see* below). The **lamp standards** are replicas of *Hartley*'s elegant tapering design. On the pierhead s is *Tony Cragg*'s **sculpture** Raleigh, 1986, evoking the working docks in reclaimed granite and recast cast iron. The **river entrance** is a typical Hartley design of two 45 ft (13.7 metre) passages divided by a masonry island. N passage sealed; gate and stayed swing bridge of 1983–4 across the s passage. Note the quality of Hartley's granite **masonry** (*see* topic box, p. 96) and the attention to detail, e.g. the upward sweep of the island coping, making a warning of the edge and a foothold when handling heavy hawsers in wet weather. The octagonal **gatemen's shelters** flanking the entrance and the **light-house** on the island are excellent examples of *Hartley*'s architectural style. Superb stonework, with highly original detailing: e.g. the roofs of massive overlapping granite slabs, the finials, and the tapering sides and oriental eaves brackets of the lighthouse. In appearance and function they echo entrance lodges to a country estate.

N of Canning Half-Tide Dock are **Canning Nos. 1 & 2 Graving Docks** [67], built 1765–9, subsequently lengthened, and finally deepened by *Hartley* in the 1840s*. Between them and the river is the three-storey **Pilotage Building** of 1883, with projecting pedimented, cupola'd centre and Renaissance detail, probably by *John Arthur Berrington*. Converted in 1980 by the *Building Design Partnership*, along with sheds to the N, for museum use (currently the **Museum of Liverpool Life**). On the river wall outside stands a memorial to Irish emigration by *Mark de Graffenried*, 2001. Bronze. A heroic young family. The car park, N, is the site of the small **Manchester Dock**, built before 1785 for barges and flats and filled with spoil from the Mersey Tunnel excavations in 1928–36. On its SE side, mid-C19 railway offices attached to a **Great Western Railway warehouse** of *c.* 1891, restored as offices a century later. Brick. In the GWR's house style. Inland from the car park is **Mann Island**, once surrounded by docks. The tall brick building is *Grayson & Ould's* **pump house** for the Mersey Railway, *c.* 1885 (*see* City Centre, p. 152). To the N is the Pier Head (*see* Major Buildings, p. 67).

---

*Graving (or dry) docks are required for the inspection and repair of the parts of ships' hulls normally under water. They are pumped dry when in use, and have sides descending in steps, know as altars.

67. Canning No. 1 Graving Dock, as deepened by Jesse Hartley, 1840s

Retracing our steps to the Albert Dock Traffic Office to begin walking s, on the quayside opposite is the former **Albert Hydraulic Power Centre**, by *G.F. Lyster*, 1878. Tall chimney. Tacky restoration as the Pumphouse Inn in 1986. Spanning the Canning passage alongside is a delightful iron rodstay **footbridge**, a two-leaf swing bridge of *c.* 1845, probably by *Hartley*. E of the passage is **Canning Dock**, created in 1829 by locking the Dry Dock, the tidal entrance basin to the Old Dock of 1710–16 [58]. This lay inland across what is now Strand Street on the site of Canning Place until *c.* 1826 (*see* p. 136). The largest blocks of the NW quay wall are thought to be of *c.* 1737, making them the oldest surviving stonework in the docks.

s from Canning is **Salthouse Dock** (the passage between filled in 1984). Begun as the South Dock by *Thomas Steers* in 1739 and finished by *Henry Berry* in 1754, in part to serve a salt works. Remodelled and enlarged by *Hartley* 1841–2 as Albert's export dock. This was part of a one-way system: ships entered at Canning Half-Tide, discharged in Albert, proceeded through its E passage to take on cargo in Salthouse before leaving via Canning and Canning Half-Tide. All that remains of the encompassing transit sheds is the gable dated 1855 in Hartley granite in the SE corner, reconstructed in 1980. The removal of sheds has opened up views of the Albert warehouses unknown before closure. SE across the dock road is the mid-C19 **Baltic Fleet** pub, a survivor of the dozens that served the famously thirsty dockers.

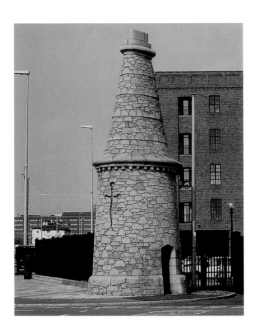

Duke's Dock runs behind Albert's s stack through car parks. Best
seen from the steel footbridge. Named after Francis Egerton, 3rd Duke
of Bridgewater, who completed a private transhipment dock in 1773 for
goods carried by barge to Manchester via his Bridgewater Canal. This
forms the central section today. Its narrow dimensions are unlike any
other surviving dock; in conception it is much more a canal basin.*
Although much patched, the best remaining example of c18 dock-wall
construction. The E section is a 1790s extension, the w is *Hartley's* half-
tide dock of 1843–5. None of the 166 buildings noted in 1899 survives.

Walking s from the footbridge, on the l. is **Royal Quay**, seven- and
eight-storey apartment blocks by *Patrick Davies Architecture,* 2000–2.
White and tritely Deco nautical. s of these is **Wapping Dock**, built by
Hartley together with **Wapping basin** to its N in 1851–5 to link the docks
N and s of Duke's Dock. On the E quay is **Wapping Warehouse**,
completed in 1856 by *Hartley.* Like its siblings at Stanley Dock (*see*
p. 124), a simplified, more utilitarian version of Albert: unbroken rear
elevation to incorporate railway sidings, no mezzanine, simpler vaults,
a conventional roof and quayside columns of concave, not convex,
section (a more satisfactory structural form for hollow cast-iron
shafts). Sensitively converted into apartments by *Kingham Knight
Associates,* 1986–9, when the bomb-damaged s end was demolished
(the quayside columns are preserved) and a new well-matched s wall
built.

*Ritchie-Noakes gives *John Gilbert*, the Duke's resident engineer, as the probable designer.

The vast temporary car park on the w side of Wapping Dock is **King's Dock**. From 1906 these two docks were remodelled as one body of water when King's was rebuilt with two branches. It was originally constructed in 1785–8. The MDC filled the branches in 1986, but a series of ambitious proposals for retail and leisure development, most recently for a conference centre and indoor arena, have as yet come to nothing.

At **Queens Wharf** a diversion inland. First, on the left, two of *Hartley's* architectural flights of fancy. The **Wapping Hydraulic Power Centre**, 1855–6, provided power for Wapping Warehouse. The embattled octagonal brick folly is the accumulator tower, the turret on top the boiler chimney. Boiler and engine house in granite with Tudor arches. Restored 1988. Next, the extraordinary **Policeman's Lodge** [68], the central pier of a demolished double gate in the dock wall. Oval, with a blank, snaking arrow-slit motif and a bizarre conical roof of overlapping masonry bands terminating in a flattened finial-cum-chimney. Again, the granite masonry is itself a thing of great beauty. Now on to the **dock road**, here actually Wapping. Alongside Wapping Warehouse (note the fantastically shaped quoins of its cart arches) are fragments of *Hartley's* granite **dock wall**, now lowered. Kings Dock Street opposite is

Hydraulic Power

Hydraulic power was fundamental to efficient steamship docks. In the age of sail, cranes, gates, bridges and capstans were hand operated, but the larger iron steamships required greater power to manoeuvre them around the docks (via capstans) and to operate the massive new dock gates and bridges, as well as for speedier goods handling. Hydraulics arrived in Liverpool after *Jesse Hartley* inspected *William Armstrong's* pioneering crane at Newcastle upon Tyne in 1847. Impressed, he ordered two lifts and two cranes for the Albert Dock, the first hydraulic warehouse equipment in the world. They were operated by 'jiggers', rams to which a chain was attached by pulleys (examples of c. 1878 in the Albert Dock colonnade). Water came from the town supply, but this was weak and unreliable; it required Armstrong's 1850 invention, the accumulator which delivered a constant high-pressure supply by using steam engines to pump water into a weight-loaded tank – to make widespread application practical. The first accumulator appeared in Liverpool at Queen's Dock in 1852, others soon followed, and by 1906 they were connected by a hydraulic main. Most importantly, from 1859 these powered the hydraulic capstans and the massive bridges and gates of the steamship era. Quayside hydraulic cranes, however, were adopted more slowly: dockers were cheap and ships' steam winches efficient. In the c20 electric power gradually replaced hydraulic equipment, except for lock gates and some bridges.

69. Queen's Dock. Liverpool Watersport Centre, left, by David Marks Julia Barfield Architects (1993–4) and, right, the Customs and Excise Building by PSA Projects, Birmingham (1991–3)

the site of Wapping Goods Station, opened in 1830 as part of the Liverpool & Manchester Railway (*see* topic box, p. 188), now an industrial estate. In the retaining wall at the E end is the blocked entrance to the 1828 **Wapping Tunnel**, up which wagons were rope-hauled to Edge Hill.

Returning up Queens Wharf, to the s is **Queen's Dock**, completed 1795–6 by *Thomas Morris* under the same programme as King's. Doubled in size 1810–16; rebuilt for steamships 1898–1906, with two branches and a graving dock. Redevelopment has been aesthetically the least successful here. A few truly feeble buildings occupy the E side including a casino (2003), with a glass façade leaning out over the dock, dwarfed by water and quay. The N branch has been partially infilled as a car park, an appropriately dreary setting for the **Customs and Excise Building**, 1991–3 by *PSA Projects*, *Birmingham*. This has the scale but none of the quality that a major public commission on such a prominent site demands. A five-storey quadrangle, the E and w wings bridging the flooded graving dock in exposed steel frames, the mean N and s wings in buff concrete blocks. Beige, faceless, remote, it is a sadly apposite home for the taxman. Outside the w façade, **sculpture**: Time and Tide, 1993 by *Philip Bews*. Two bronze figures raised on columns and a frieze (made by *Diane Gorvin*). These face the **Riverside Walk**, the promenade created by the MDC in the 1980s between the Pier Head and Dingle, opening up over three miles of riverfront to the public.

In the dock's SE corner is the **Liverpool Watersport Centre** of 1993–4, the best new building completed under the MDC. An early work by *David Marks Julia Barfield Architects*, designers of the London

Eye. A pavilion visually 'floating' in the dock (though actually built on piles), so emphasizing its purpose. Exposed steel frame cleanly articulated. Clear vertical separation between 'wet' and 'dry' areas, the latter a deck above, supported on steel trees.

Continuing s along the Riverside Walk, the next dock is **Coburg Dock**. A complex history, beginning with construction *c.* 1817–23 as Union Half-Tide Dock and Brunswick Basin, is reflected in the materials of the **quay walls**: sandstone, limestone, granite and concrete. Connected to the s to **Brunswick Dock**, first suggested in 1809 and built by *Hartley* 1827–32 for timber imports. Present form: 1905 rebuild and s extension in concrete, with river lock, by *A.G. Lyster.*

Today these two docks succeed as a place because quayside housing creates a sense of enclosure, and because the expanses of water are alive with boats in the **Liverpool Marina**. This is despite the weakness of the architecture. The illiterate 1980s Marina and Harbourside Club stands between the two docks, in a key location requiring something far more accomplished. In Brunswick's SE corner can be seen **HMS Eaglet**, the

Getting from River to Dock: an Engineering Challenge

With the Mersey's swift currents, great tidal range and exposed position, getting ships in and out of the docks has always presented significant technical challenges. Three successive engineering solutions have been adopted. The **tidal basin** [58] had a wide entrance to enable ships to manoeuvre in under sail. Once moored inside they could be hauled through gates into the dock itself. However, as *William Jessop* told the Dock Trustees in 1800, they were very prone to silting. He therefore recommended **half-tide docks**. These function something like locks: ships enter through river gates opened only on the top half of the tide, these are then closed and further gates to the inner docks opened to allow the vessels to proceed to their berths. The first, Union Half-Tide Dock, opened in 1823. Canning Half-Tide Dock (1842–4) is the sole operational survivor. Their operation had to be synchronized with the tides, imposing operational delays that were critical to the owners of expensive steamships running to regular timetables. The solution was the angled river **lock**, like a vast canal lock. It was made practical by powerful steam tugs and the manoeuvrability of steamships, and enabled ships to enter the system at most states of the tide. The first, at Canada Dock, opened in 1859 but was prone to silting and awkward to use. These shortcomings were substantially overcome by *G.F. Lyster* at the Langton River Entrance, opened in 1879, by angling the lock upstream. Further locks followed, notably the massive Gladstone River Entrance, completed in 1927. At 1,070 ft (326 metres) long it remains large enough to be used by the biggest vessels visiting the docks today.

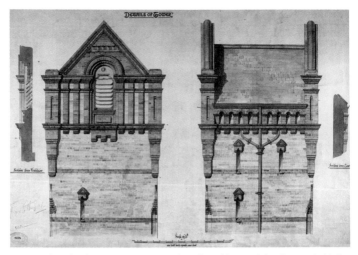

70. Toxteth Hydraulic Power Centre, Toxteth Dock. Architectural drawings probably by John Arthur Berrington (1889)

Royal Naval Headquarters, Merseyside, by *Bannister Storr Associates*, 1996–8, more heavy-footed public architecture. Clustered roofs, banded walls. Much of the **housing** is feeble, e.g. Brunswick E quay: too suburban, lost above the massive quay walls. Brunswick W quay is at least of an appropriate scale and density. Bolder too is **Mariner's Wharf**, Coburg N quay, 1989–97 by *David Backhouse*, the first housing in the South Docks. A terrace treated as pavilions dominated by gabled projections over fat columns, intended to evoke warehouses, in the vein of Troughton McAslan and Jeremy Dixon in London's Docklands.

    South Ferry Island is between Brunswick and the river. At the N end on the river wall is the unaltered **South Ferry Basin**, constructed *c.* 1817–23 for ferries and fishermen. Then more bad apartment blocks. They are built on the site of the Dock Yard (*see* Docks, Introduction, p. 97), itself built around *Hartley*'s now infilled Brunswick Half-Tide Dock of *c.* 1832. Two of his characteristic **gatemen's shelters** survive on the river wall, flanking the old entrance. N of these are his magnificent sweeping **river steps**, each step a massive block laid at a dramatically acute angle, like uprooted bedrock.

    At the S tip of the island is *Lyster*'s **Brunswick River Entrance**, the principal entrance to the South Docks until closure. One lock reopened for small craft in 1987 by the MDC, with a *Brock Carmichael Associates* control room meant to evoke the form of a ship. Cross the bridge to the preserved top rail of a lock gate. Superlative joinery. Beyond is the **Brunswick Business Park**, created 1981–96. A fenced development with limited access, so we follow the Riverside Walk, from which there are views in. The first phase, completed 1982, was the appropriately robust, industrial conversion (see N elevation) of the Brunswick **SW6 Transit**

Shed of *c.* 1908, E of the River Entrance, into a business centre. The rest was established on *G.F. Lyster's* **Toxteth** and **Harrington docks**, constructed 1882–8 and 1875–83 respectively, obliterating four small C19 predecessors. The MDC infilled the docks and in 1986–94 converted *Lyster's* four brick and iron **transit sheds** into offices and industrial units. On the landward quays are two import sheds, 1883–9, the first two-storey transit sheds in Liverpool (*see* pp. 99–100). Best preserved is the N one, **East Toxteth Shed** (now Century Building), with a clock tower pleasantly enriched in *John Arthur Berrington* fashion. Single-storey **export sheds**, typical of many built by the MDHB, were erected on the W quays. **West Harrington Shed**, *c.* 1884–8 (now Glacier Building), has had the most architectural makeover, by the *Owen Ellis Partnership*, 1993–4. Porthole windows, and cable-stay masts supporting a canopy. Also, in the NW corner, the lively **Toxteth Hydraulic Power Centre** [70], 1889, extended 1911, and alongside it the **Customs Depot** of 1890. Crisp *Berrington* Renaissance detailing.

And so onwards S to the site of **Herculaneum Dock**, the most southerly in the system. Built by the MDHB following a failed private scheme; named after the pottery that had occupied the site. Graving docks and a coaling dock, opened 1866 and expanded in stages until 1902, cut deep into outcropping rock. *G.F. Lyster's* first major work, though the river entrance (NW corner, filled, but quays still visible) was pure Hartley in plan and construction. Infilled by the MDC for access to the 1984 International Garden Festival (*see* Walk 10, p. 294) and redeveloped with insipid offices and housing. On the old entrance island is the **Chung Ku Restaurant**, 2000 by *DTR Sheard Walshaw*. A two-storey drum, with fully-glazed riverside dining rooms. Rear service wedge, finishing in a sharp prow sheltering the entrance. E of Sefton Road, **Greens Health and Fitness Centre**, *Carden Croft*, 2000. Around the S and E perimeter, sixty-one curious **casemates** cut into the rock, faced in concrete with pilasters between. By *G.F. Lyster*, 1881–2, for the storage of petroleum. Above, the noble entrance to the **Dingle Tunnel** of the Liverpool Overhead Railway, 1896 (*see* topic box, p. 100), and above that the Edwardian bylaw terraces of Dingle rising up.

To return to central Liverpool head N up **Sefton Street** past Harrington and Toxteth transit sheds. On the E side, an **incline** to Horsfall Street, erected 1866. Channelled ashlar and rustication, with urinals and a horse trough. Then, **Brunswick Station**, from which Central Station is a short journey. A new station for the redeveloped docks, by *Brock Carmichael Architects,* built 1997–8. Despite a tight budget, robust but elegant, thoughtful and well detailed.

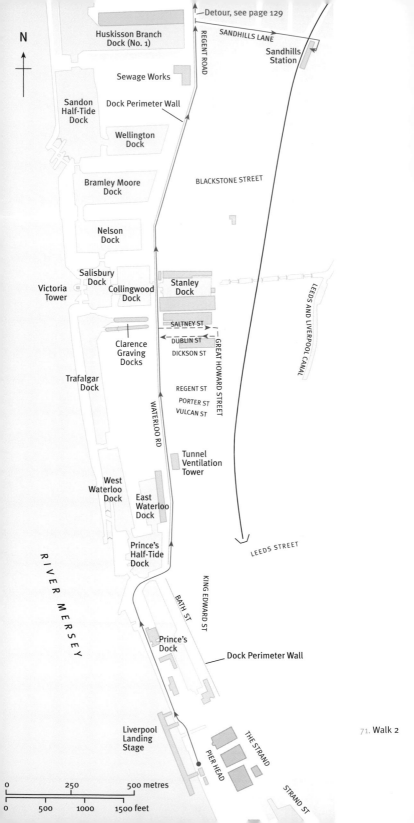

N

Huskisson Branch
Dock (No. 1)

Sewage Works

Sandon
Half-Tide
Dock

Dock Perimeter Wall

Wellington
Dock

Bramley Moore
Dock

Nelson
Dock

Salisbury
Dock

Victoria
Tower

Collingwood
Dock

Clarence
Graving
Docks

Trafalgar
Dock

West
Waterloo
Dock

East
Waterloo
Dock

Prince's
Half-Tide
Dock

R I V E R

M E R S E Y

Liverpool
Landing
Stage

REGENT ROAD

Detour, see page 129

SANDHILLS LANE

Sandhills
Station

BLACKSTONE STREET

LEEDS AND LIVERPOOL CANAL

Stanley
Dock

SALTNEY ST

DUBLIN ST

DICKSON ST

GREAT HOWARD STREET

REGENT ST

PORTER ST

VULCAN ST

WATERLOO RD

Tunnel
Ventilation
Tower

LEEDS STREET

KING EDWARD ST

BATH ST

Prince's
Dock

Dock Perimeter Wall

PIER HEAD

THE STRAND

STRAND ST

71. Walk 2

0   250   500 metres

0   500   1000   1500 feet

Walk 2.

The North Docks and the Dock Road

This long walk begins at the Pier Head. Most of it is along the dock road and the reader may prefer to follow it by car. Parking is possible almost anywhere along the route. For those on foot, the return trip is by train.

In 1796 this journey was described as a pleasant ride along beaches lined with bathing machines, but over the next two hundred years these gave way to the ever deeper and bigger docks stretching eventually to the mouth of the river. Today operations are consolidated in the largest, most northerly docks, and the oldest, nearest the centre, are being redeveloped. A number though, particularly Stanley, remain evocatively semi-derelict. Beyond, the dusty dock road retains its bustling industrial character.

The three iconic buildings of the **Pier Head** (*see* Major Buildings, p. 67) were built on the site of George's Dock, constructed in 1762–71 and infilled 1900 (parts of its walls are preserved in the lower basement of the Cunard Building). Ferries have crossed to the Wirral from this point since at least the C13, at their peak carrying over sixteen million people a year, but by the 1980s rail and road tunnels had reduced the famous service to the verge of bankruptcy. It was relaunched as a tourist attraction, for which the **Mersey Ferry Terminal** on the river wall was refurbished in 1991. The building, and adjoining restaurant, are by *Ronald Bradbury*, mid-1960s. *Brock Carmichael Architects* did the make-over, with tented roof. The motif is continued for the shelter on the **Liverpool Landing Stage** itself, today used by river and Isle of Man ferries, but once the berth of transatlantic liners and the point of departure for millions of C19 emigrants and of arrival for millions of troops in two world wars. The current 1975 concrete pontoon, to be extended for cruise liners, replaced an iron structure first floated in 1847 and eventually lengthened to over 2,500 ft (762 metres). Defining the N boundary of the Pier Head is a narrow masonry well built by *G.F. Lyster* in *Jesse Hartley's* distinctive granite (*see* topic box, p. 96) in 1873–6 to house a **floating roadway** down to it. Inland are the drum piers that flanked the approach, and one of a chain of 1990s Neo-Hartley sewer-interceptor stations.

N of the **Memorial to the Heroes of the Marine Engine Room** [1] (*see* p. 72) along the river wall is **Princes Parade**, landscaped 2000, and inland from this **Prince's Dock**, the first C19 dock. Both *William Jessop* and *John Rennie* were consulted over plans for a new dock here before construction to Rennie's outline designs began under *John Foster Sen.*, c. 1810. Delayed partly by the Napoleonic Wars, work was still not finished when it opened in 1821. The North Atlantic trade for which Prince's Dock was built migrated to newer, larger docks as ships grew, and by the c20 the dock was home to coastal and Irish traffic, for which quays were modernized early in the century. Nothing more than single-storey transit sheds and the very utilitarian Riverside Station (1895–1972) was ever built around it. The last regular user, the Belfast ferry, left in 1981.

In 1988 the dock passed to the Merseyside Development Corporation, since when the buildings have been cleared, the E quay widened and commercial redevelopment begun to a masterplan by *Taylor Young*. The results so far, though, are inadequate. The architecture is both bland and overly fussy, and the lifeless monoculture could be a business park anywhere. Adjoining the Pier Head, architectural standards should be far higher. So far three offices: in the sw corner, No. 8 by *Kingham Knight Associates*, 1996–7, next to it No. 10 by *Austin-Smith:Lord*, 1999–2000, and then No. 12 by *Atherden Fuller Leng*, 2002–3. All instantly forgettable corporate architecture. Across the dock, the **Crowne Plaza Liverpool Hotel**, 1997–8, by *Kingham Knight* also. Messy entrance court to The Strand. In 2004 the first tower was going up: twenty storeys of apartments by *Atherden Fuller Leng*. Most interesting is the **footbridge**, 2001, designed by *Eduard Ross* whilst still a student. *Ian Wroot*, his senior lecturer at Liverpool John Moores University, was project architect. A white steel carcass linking jutting quays to divide the dock, visually, in two. Of the dock's archaeology, note at the s end the blocked passage to George's Basin (subsequently a graving, then a branch dock) and the original coursed Runcorn stone quay wall.

Along the riverside walk where derelict river steps survive it is possible to glimpse *Rennie* and *Foster*'s red sandstone **river wall**. At the N end are the remains of **Prince's Pier**, marking the end of the Liverpool Landing Stage until 1975. The wharf, of 1899–1900, was the first reinforced concrete structure in the docks, and is one of the earliest surviving British examples of the *Hennebique* system. Designed by the French company's agent *Louis Gustave Mouchel*, with *A.G. Lyster*. Its success led Lyster to adopt concrete swiftly and extensively, which may have encouraged its early use elsewhere in the city (*see* topic box, p. 68). As Princes Parade curves around the head of Prince's Dock there are excellent views of the docks to the N. The nearest is the derelict **Prince's Half-Tide Dock** (*see* topic box, p. 117), built as a tidal basin and rebuilt in 1868 by *G.F. Lyster*, in Hartley fashion: e.g. a triple entrance based on Salisbury Dock (*see* below) and granite walls. Entrance sealed 1949. Beyond is **Waterloo Dock**, dominated by the mighty **Waterloo Grain Warehouse** of 1866–8 [72]. The dock, by *Hartley*, opened to general traffic in 1834 orientated E–W, but was rebuilt as a specialist grain dock with two branches aligned N–s by *G.F. Lyster* in 1863–8. With the repeal of the Corn Laws, the MDHB shrewdly foresaw North America as the principal source of

72. Waterloo Grain Warehouse, Waterloo East Dock, by G.F. Lyster (1866–8)

imported grain, and reconstructed Waterloo as the world's first bulk-grain dock to handle it. The surviving warehouse, also by *Lyster*, was the E of three: the N stack was demolished after war damage, the W stack in 1969. In their place now stand hipped-roofed apartment blocks completed in 2001. These cannot match the warehouse's massiveness or quality of detailing, but, being built right up to the quayside, they are substantial and regular enough to maintain a sense of ordered enclosure. The warehouse was converted into apartments by *Kingham Knight Associates*, 1989–98. With five storeys of brick above a mightily rock-faced granite ground-floor arcade, it has as much floorspace as all the Albert stacks combined. The arcade, originally open, functioned like a transit shed. Above rise windows gathered regularly in round-arched pairs, and pilaster strips flanking the five hoist bays, two of which climb high above the bold parapet to house machinery. The structure is fire-proof: cast-iron columns and beams, brick arches and cement floors. The chief novelty was an innovative system of hydraulic elevators and conveyor belts, developed and supplied by *Sir W.G. Armstrong & Co.* to move grain in, out and around. It never worked properly, however, and the dock was rapidly made obsolete by its inadequate depth and by newer facilities elsewhere.

Leaving Prince's Dock by the gates of 2001, to the right is the **dock perimeter wall** by *John Foster Sen.*, begun 1816. Brick, stone coping. Stone **gatepiers** halfway along with curious rustication. This was the first perimeter wall erected around a Liverpool dock, a measure required by the 1803 Warehousing Act (*see* p. 98). It was extended N and s by *Hartley* and the *Lysters* until it stretched the length of the docks, a physical and psychological barrier *c.* 18 ft (5.5 metres) high, behind which the docks were a mysterious world to most Liverpudlians. The novelist Nathaniel Hawthorne, American consul in Liverpool in the 1850s, likened it to the Great Wall of China. Chased into the dockside face are the remains of the stanchions that supported the Liverpool Overhead Railway (*see* topic box, p. 100). We follow it N from here along the **dock road** (actually Waterloo Road and Regent Road). This longest remaining section, by *Hartley*, is a remarkable sight, extending almost two miles and punctuated by further, colossal, **gatepiers**. The first are a mixture of Hartley's earlier Greek Revival style, *c.* 1834, and his later fat granite idiom, of 1841–8, all with slots for sliding gates. Beyond the wall, the tremendous scale of the Waterloo warehouse is apparent. The 1990s railings and gates are feeble. Opposite is the imposingly sculptural **ventilation tower** [73] of the Kingsway Tunnel, 1971, by *Bradshaw, Rowse & Harker*. Like a rocket on its launch pad. The next gatepiers bear the names of **Victoria Dock** and **Trafalgar Dock**, opened in 1836 as part of the same programme as Waterloo, to a similar design by *Hartley*. Little has survived modernization.

Opposite Trafalgar Dock a fragment of the C19 dock road flanks the bottom of **Vulcan Street**, including a handsome mid-century pedimented fireproof warehouse (iron frame and lintels, brick floors) and in **Porter Street** – a gulley of cut-down warehouses – a non-fireproof warehouse (iron columns but wooden floors) dated 1884 on the lively gable.

Next was **Clarence Dock**, Liverpool's first steamship dock, proposed 1821 and completed by *Hartley* in 1830. Closed in 1928 when a power station (demolished 1994) was erected on the site. In the dock wall a small, scalloped cast-iron drinking fountain, one of thirty-three sanctioned in 1859 by the MDHB in a vain effort to keep dockers out of the pubs. Immediately to the N, **Clarence Graving Docks**, *c.* 1830 by *Hartley*, with magnificent masonry. Subsequently lengthened. Here we encounter the southern edge of the operational docks. The perimeter wall changes to granite rubble and the **gatepiers** [60] become peculiarly castle-like – massively round turrets with vestigial castellation. Slit windows and door in the central pier, which doubles as a policeman's hut.

The next eight docks were built by *Hartley* between 1844 and 1858. His tenure reached its zenith on 4 August 1848 when the first five opened simultaneously. All were built in granite with 33 ft (10 metre) quay walls behind a 37 ft (11.3 metre) river wall. The best place to view the first three is from the 1930s rolling bascule **lifting bridge** [74]. Easily the most impressive, and the most evocatively derelict dock in Liverpool in 2004, is **Stanley Dock**, inland from the bridge. The **perimeter wall** is intact, with the same castle-like **gatepiers**. Conceived as an integrated interchange with rail and the Leeds and Liverpool Canal (*see* pp. 251–2). A flight of four **locks** [151] by *J.B. Hartley* rising E of Great Howard Street connects the latter, but subsidiary railway and barge docks were never built (the blocked passages remain in the N and E quays respectively). Instead, two **warehouses** were erected in 1852–4 (E end of N

73. Kingsway Tunnel ventilation tower, by Bradshaw, Rowse & Harker (1971)

stack demolished following war damage). Like the near-identical Wapping Warehouse these are a simplified version of Albert (*see* pp. 103–12). They were also the first dock warehouses designed for rail and hydraulic power, the latter provided by the picturesque **Stanley Hydraulic Power Centre**, 1854, N of the bridge. Embattled accumulator tower with turret chimney (cf. Wapping Dock, p. 114). Extended in brick with another chimney, 1913. A twin, s, was demolished for the gargantuan **Tobacco Warehouse** [74], built on land reclaimed from the dock in front of Hartley's s stack, *c.* 1897–1901 by *A.G. Lyster*. Free Renaissance detailing, probably *John Arthur Berrington*, is concentrated in a heavy cornice – what Osbert Lancaster once called 'above the snow

74. Tobacco Warehouse, Stanley Dock, by A.J. Lyster (c. 1897–1901). View from the Regent Road lifting bridge

line'. Rising 125 ft (38 metres) through thirteen storeys over a basement, with a floor area of 36 acres (14.6 hectares) and constructed of 27 million bricks, it was claimed to be the largest single brick building in the world. Fireproof construction: steel and concrete floors; cast-iron columns. Since closure in 1980 its size and deep plan have not been the only barriers to reuse: the floors are only 7 ft 2 in. (2.2 metres) high because the 77,000 casks were stored in single tiers to avoid breakage.

A short detour E up Saltney Road, s of Stanley, is rewarded by the sight of the warehouses from Great Howard Street, and the locks to the canal. In the dock's SE corner is the **King's Pipe**, the chimney of the *c.* 1900 furnace in which tobacco scraps were destroyed. One block s are the enormous **Clarence Warehouses**, easily the largest group of private warehouses left in the city, and when designed and built *c.* 1844 by S. & J. Holme for P.W. Brancker, the largest to date. Eleven separate stacks of six storeys within one shell relieved by only the most meagre embellishment. They were among the first fireproof (*see* topic box, p. 167) warehouses in the town and were probably intended for multiple letting. Together with the Stanley stacks they make up the last large-scale remnant of a distinctive Liverpool townscape, once characteristic of the streets inland from the docks.

Returning to the lifting bridge, there are two docks on the riverside, **Collingwood Dock,** and **Salisbury Dock** beyond. Collingwood has derelict gates and barge locks at either end. Salisbury was the entrance

Dock Construction and Safety

75. Canada Half-Tide Dock (now demolished) under construction in 1875–6

Construction of a dock in the c18–c20 was a massive, complex and dangerous operation, though the essence remained simple: erect a coffer dam, dig a hole and line it with walls, back fill and finish. The scale could be heroic: in three years from 1844 three million cubic yards of soil were excavated for the five docks of the Stanley–Salisbury complex. Steam power was first adopted by *John Foster Sen.* at Prince's Dock in 1811 to lift spoil, and later used for pumping and excavating, but the operation remained labour-intensive well into the c20, partly because labour remained cheap. It was also very dangerous, involving blasting, excavating and manoeuvring massive stone blocks, and often subject to flooding. Evidence given to the Select Committee on Railway Labourers in 1846 sheds light on c19 working practices, from which *Jesse Hartley* and the Dock Trustees emerge as progressive and generous employers. In 1844–6 4,600 men worked on the construction of the Stanley–Salisbury docks. As was normal, the 2,800 navvies employed by contractors excavated, and the rest – working for Hartley and the Trustees – constructed. In that time twenty-nine contractors' men were killed and a hundred seriously injured, compared respectively to two and none of Hartley's. The navvies were paid by the cubic yard; output was everything and safety ignored. By contrast, the men under Hartley's rigorous management were well supervised, better paid, and contributed to a sickness and injury fund from which they could not benefit if dismissed for misconduct.

dock. On the island between the river gates stands *Hartley*'s **Victoria Tower** [76], an idiosyncratic Gothic clock tower in his usual granite. Built 1847–8; based on a *Philip Hardwick* drawing dated 1846. Round below, hexagonal above. Clock faces on all sides and an elongated belfry stage. Projecting castellated parapet. As Pevsner concluded, 'It is all ham, but it tells of the commercial pride of the decades'. On the

76. Victoria Tower, Salisbury Dock river entrance, by Philip Hardwick and Jesse Hartley (1846–8)

river wall s is *Hartley*'s **Dock Master's Office**, 1848. Rectangular and embattled medievalism.

Now to resume the walk N, following the granite perimeter wall, broken by gatepiers of the type already seen. Names and dates of the docks are marked by stone plaques. First comes **Nelson Dock**, then the last of the 1848 group, **Bramley-Moore Dock**, with C20 transit sheds. From 1856 it had a high-level railway link for the export of coal. A derelict *Lyster* **accumulator tower** survives. Then comes **Wellington Dock**, 1850, on the corner **Sandon Dock**, 1851, and behind them **Sandon Half-Tide Dock**, 1901–2 (replacing a basin). Sandon was infilled in 1989 for a sewage-treatment works, with Postmodern trim, by *Athanassios Migos* for *Kingham Knight Associates*. Sandon was built with six graving docks, but *c.* 1900–2 **Huskisson Dock** was extended s with branches at their expense by *A.G. Lyster*. Huskisson had opened in 1852 for the timber trade. In 1941 a munitions ship exploded destroying the central branch, which was filled in and replaced by two **transit sheds**. Designed 1953–4, presumably by the Dock Engineer *Adrian J. Porter*, and completed 1957 and *c.* 1960. Built with generous dimensions for forklift operation. Two storeys, entirely reinforced concrete, including the vaulting roofs.

To return to the city centre from here turn E up **Sandhills Lane** to Sandhills Station. By car, drive s down Derby Road/Great Howard Street.

Detour

Continue N up the dock road to the unmissable form of the redundant **Tate & Lyle Sugar Silo** [78], a titanic structure designed to house 100,000 tons of raw sugar. 1955–7 by the *Tate & Lyle Engineering Dept*. A reinforced concrete parabolic tunnel, 528 ft long by 87 ft high inside (161 by 26.5 metres), believed to be the largest such structure in Europe. The pre-stressed concrete floor acts as the tie of the arch. Richly sculptural surface of deep, closely spaced ribs. Sugar was delivered to the crown on conveyor belts from ships in Huskisson Dock; the clear span simplified removal by bulldozer.

Now comes **Canada Dock**, *Hartley*'s last, opened 1859 and built for the North American timber trade. A reminder, a statue of a moustachioed lumberjack leaning on his axe, crowns the gable of the former Canada Dock Hotel, *c.* 1860, on the corner of Bankfield Street opposite. Rebuilt

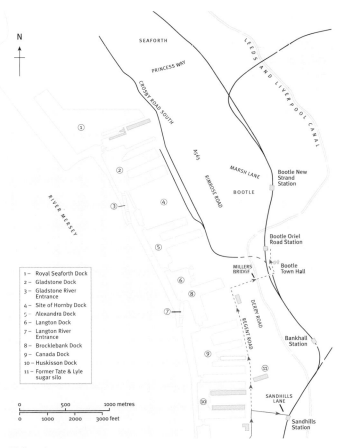

1 – Royal Seaforth Dock
2 – Gladstone Dock
3 – Gladstone River Entrance
4 – Site of Hornby Dock
5 – Alexandra Dock
6 – Langton Dock
7 – Langton River Entrance
8 – Brocklebank Dock
9 – Canada Dock
10 – Huskisson Dock
11 – Former Tate & Lyle sugar silo

77. Walk 2, detour

78. Tate & Lyle sugar silo, Regent Road, by Tate & Lyle Engineering Dept (1955–7)

with branches and a **graving dock** around the turn of the C20. Next is **Brocklebank Dock**, opened for timber in 1862, rebuilt 1904–8, and again with the construction of the second **Langton River Entrance** in 1949–62. Today partly filled with industrial plant. Finally, *G.F. Lyster's* **Langton Dock**, opened 1879. The battered industrial remnants on the E side of the dock road include, N of Raleigh Street, the offices of the otherwise demolished **Harland & Wolff Shipbuilding and Engineering Works**, opened in 1913.

At this point progress up the dock road is barred. The final 1.5 m. (2.4 km.) were absorbed into the Liverpool Freeport in 1998. Along it are the largest and most modern docks, the heart of the present port: first **Alexandra Dock**, 1874–82, then the site of **Hornby Dock**, 1880–3, and then the huge **Gladstone Dock** system, begun 1910, completed 1927. Lastly, the larger still **Royal Seaforth Dock**, opened 1971 (*see* p. 98).

To return to the city centre by train, head up **Millers Bridge**, crossing the **Leeds & Liverpool Canal**. Turn left on to **Oriel Road** to Bootle Oriel Road Station, passing the cluster of Bootle's C19 civic buildings (*see* the forthcoming *Buildings of England: Lancashire: Liverpool and the South West*).

City Centre

(Area bounded by Leeds Street (N); Byrom Street, Old
Haymarket, Whitechapel and Paradise Street (E and SE);
Canning Place (S); and Strand Street, The Strand, George's
Dock Gates, New Quay and King Edward Street (W))

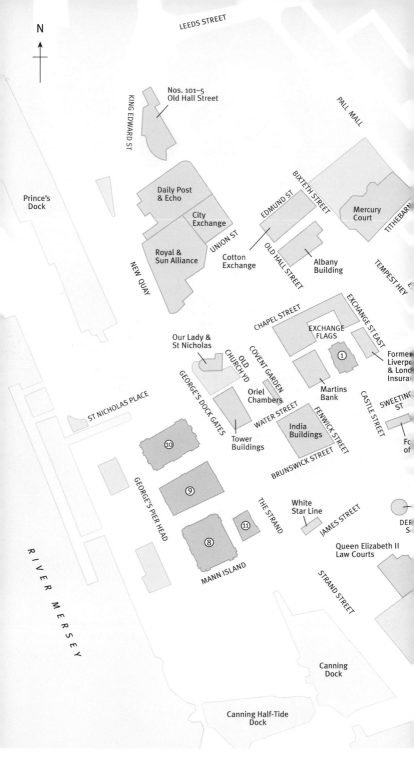

N

LEEDS STREET

KING EDWARD ST

Nos. 101–5
Old Hall Street

PALL MALL

Prince's
Dock

Daily Post
& Echo

City
Exchange

Royal &
Sun Alliance

BIXTETH STREET

EDMUND ST

Mercury
Court

TITHEBARN

UNION ST

Cotton
Exchange

OLD HALL STREET

Albany
Building

TEMPEST HEY

NEW QUAY

CHAPEL STREET

EXCHANGE ST EAST

Our Lady &
St Nicholas

OLD
CHURCHYD

COVENT GARDEN

EXCHANGE
FLAGS

①

Former
Liverpool
& London
Insurance

GEORGE'S DOCK GATES

Oriel
Chambers

Martins
Bank

CASTLE STREET

SWEETING
ST

ST NICHOLAS PLACE

Tower
Buildings

WATER STREET

India
Buildings

FENWICK STREET

For
of

⑩

BRUNSWICK STREET

GEORGE'S PIER HEAD

⑨

THE STRAND

White
Star Line

JAMES STREET

DER
S

⑪

⑧

Queen Elizabeth II
Law Courts

MANN ISLAND

STRAND STREET

R I V E R   M E R S E Y

Canning
Dock

Canning Half-Tide
Dock

79. City Centre

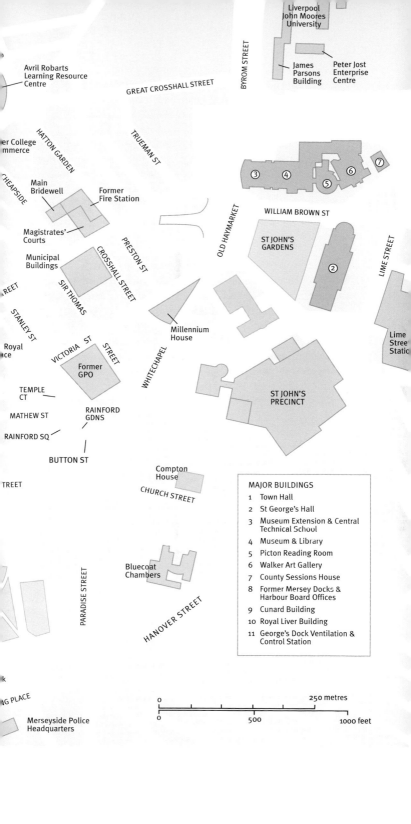

Liverpool John Moores University

BYROM STREET

James Parsons Building

Peter Jost Enterprise Centre

Avril Robarts Learning Resource Centre

GREAT CROSSHALL STREET

HATTON GARDEN

TRUEMAN ST

er College mmerce

CHEAPSIDE

Main Bridewell

Former Fire Station

Magistrates' Courts

Municipal Buildings

CROSSHALL STREET

PRESTON ST

SIR THOMAS

REET

STANLEY ST

Royal ce

VICTORIA ST

STREET

Former GPO

TEMPLE CT

MATHEW ST

RAINFORD GDNS

RAINFORD SQ

BUTTON ST

WHITECHAPEL

Millennium House

OLD HAYMARKET

WILLIAM BROWN ST

③ ④ ⑤ ⑥ ⑦

ST JOHN'S GARDENS

②

LIME STREET

Lime Stree Statio

ST JOHN'S PRECINCT

TREET

Compton House

CHURCH STREET

MAJOR BUILDINGS

1 Town Hall
2 St George's Hall
3 Museum Extension & Central Technical School
4 Museum & Library
5 Picton Reading Room
6 Walker Art Gallery
7 County Sessions House
8 Former Mersey Docks & Harbour Board Offices
9 Cunard Building
10 Royal Liver Building
11 George's Dock Ventilation & Control Station

PARADISE STREET

Bluecoat Chambers

HANOVER STREET

k

G PLACE

Merseyside Police Headquarters

0   250 metres
0   500   1000 feet

City Centre

The business core occupies the area of the pre-c18 town, a triangular tongue of land between the river and the former tidal inlet known as the Pool [6]. Today it is bounded on the w by King Edward Street and the dock road, called at different points New Quay, George's Dock Gates, The Strand and Strand Street. The E and SE boundary is formed by Byrom Street, Old Haymarket, Whitechapel (described in Walk 3) and Paradise Street, following the course of the Pool. Canning Place, the site of the Old Dock within the Pool mouth, marks the s point of the triangle, and for the purposes of this guide the N side is formed by Leeds Street. Within these boundaries the pattern of Liverpool's seven ancient streets (*see* topic box, p. 6) is discernable, and the oldest building, the Town Hall (*see* Major Buildings, p. 42), stands at the junction of four of them.

At the E end of Dale Street are the Municipal Buildings and a cluster of public offices, but otherwise the area is largely commercial, a character it assumed from the early c19. Palatial banks, exchanges, speculative offices and the premises of shipping and insurance companies, mostly Victorian and early c20, are concentrated in and around Castle Street, Water Street, Dale Street, Old Hall Street and Victoria Street; utilitarian warehouses survive off Dale Street and Victoria Street. Bombing, demolition and rebuilding have erased everything pre-war from below the line of James Street, Derby Square and Lord Street, including the original street pattern, and much of this s part awaits redevelopment. To the N, most of Liverpool's high postwar office blocks are concentrated round Old Hall Street. In recent years a number of older commercial buildings have been converted to residential and leisure uses, and new residential buildings are under construction or planned.

The streets are described here in alphabetical order.

Bixteth Street

Berey's Buildings (entrance in George Street) is a big, muscular office block of 1864. *W. Culshaw* signed the drawings, but the design is likely to be by his future partner *Henry Sumners*. Ten bays by six, of red brick with sandstone bands above a grey stone basement. Square-headed windows under segmental arches; other details, such as the pointed arches to the end bays, are Gothic. Recently converted into flats, with a floor set back above the cornice. Next door, **Lombard Chambers**, Venetian Gothic in polychrome brick, presumably 1860s.

For the Cotton Exchange *see* Old Hall Street, p. 159; for Orleans House, *see* Edmund Street, p. 150.

Brunswick Street

Created in the 1780s, at the same time that Castle Street was widened. The E view is impressively closed by Cockerell's Bank of England (*see* Castle Street, p. 137).

On the s side, between Fenwick Street and Lower Castle Street, the former private **bank** of Arthur Heywood, Sons & Co. [80], simple and dignified ashlar of 1798–1800, possibly to a design of 1789 by *John Foster Sen*. Five bays, three storeys, the ground floor with channelled rustication and round-arched windows. Doorcase with pilasters, clearly later. Attached, on Fenwick Street, a matching house of three narrow bays, stuccoed, the stone ground floor presumably once with a doorway. This is an exceptionally early purpose-built bank, and though it combines office and living accommodation in the traditional way, the house is an appendage to the business part, rather than the other way around.

On the N side, directly opposite, the former **Union Bank** head office, *c.* 1870, probably by *John Cunningham* (replacing premises by *Cunningham & Holme*, 1840). A well-detailed five-bay palazzo with rounded, inset corners, surprisingly correct and restrained for its date. Doric pilasters to ground floor, Corinthian aedicules framing first-floor windows. At the back, along Fenwick Street, an extension by *G.E. Grayson*. He probably also added the carved panel on the corner displaying the bank's name, and altered the adjacent ground-floor windows. Inside, noble banking hall with polished red granite columns, glazed dome, and rich plasterwork.

For the Corn Exchange *see* Fenwick Street, p. 151; for India Buildings *see* Water Street, p. 170; for the former Adelphi Bank and former Leyland & Bullin's Bank, *see* Castle Street, pp. 138–9.

Button Street

The block bounded by Button Street, Rainford Square and Rainford Gardens has polychrome brick warehouses built for Edward Graham, beginning with a group dated 1863 in Rainford Square and ending in Rainford Gardens in 1880.

Byrom Street

E side mostly occupied by the Liverpool John Moores University. The **James Parsons Building** (originally College of Technology) by *Ronald Bradbury*, was put up in phases: brick-faced s part 1956–9, curtain-walled N section opened 1965, followed by further additions. The result is large and dull. Not so the **Peter Jost Enterprise Centre** just behind, 1994–5 by *Austin-Smith:Lord*. Three floors reducing to two across the sloping site. Lower floors and projecting rounded stairtowers sleekly clad in silver-coloured aluminium panels. The top floor is completely glazed, with a curved monopitch roof. This has a lattice of tubular beams on its underside, and continues beyond the glass walls to be supported externally on angled struts, leaving the interior column-free. At the N end of the site **Security Control Centre**, by *Cass Associates*, completed 1997. Triangular, with a boldly oversailing roof.

Byrom Street is crossed at its s end by two **flyovers** with pedestrian walkways, 1967–71, designed by the City Engineer *N.H. Stockley* in conjunction with *Shankland Cox & Associates*, with *W.S. Atkins & Partners* as Consulting Engineers. The aim was to separate city-centre traffic from traffic using the first Mersey Tunnel. On the w side between the two flyovers (actually in Fontenoy Street) a **sculpture**, Palanzana, by *Stephen Cox*. Made for the Liverpool International Garden Festival, 1984, relocated 1998. A tree-like form wrapped around a large sphere, carved from volcanic stone quarried at Palanzana, near Viterbo in Italy.

Canning Place

The site of the Old Dock, the first commercial wet dock in the world (*see* Docks Introduction, p. 95), infilled in the 1820s to create a spacious *place* where *John Foster Jun.* built his vast Greek Revival Custom House, 1828–39 (demolished following Second World War damage). A huge late 1960s office scheme has in turn been demolished. Now little more than a wasteland, currently (2005) the subject of ambitious proposals for redevelopment. On the s is the **Merseyside Police Headquarters**, 1980s, by the *City Architect*. High and impressively forbidding, and brick-clad in deference to nearby Albert Dock.

Castle Street

One of the seven ancient streets (*see* topic box, p. 6), named from the castle on the site of Derby Square (*see* topic box, p. 4). Very narrow until 1786, when the w side was rebuilt on its present line, opening up the view N to the Town Hall. *Samuel Hope* of Manchester was paid 20 guineas by Liverpool Corporation for designs for the new elevations, though whether these were followed is not clear, since *John Foster Sen.*

was also asked to make designs. The buildings were brick with stone dressings, subsequently stuccoed. From the 1840s Castle Street became the chief financial street, and was almost entirely rebuilt by banks and insurance companies who vied with each other in the splendour of their offices. In recent years many have been adapted to new uses.

E **side.** At the corner of Dale Street, the former premises of the art dealers **Agnew's** (now part of the HSBC building in Dale Street), 1877, by *Salomons, Wornum & Ely*. Very similar to their contemporary building for Agnew's in Bond Street, London: Queen Anne style, red brick, carved decoration rather than moulded terracotta. After this, the former **British & Foreign Marine Insurance Co.,** 1888–90, by *Grayson & Ould*. Red brick with red sandstone and terracotta. Mosaic frieze above the first floor with shipping scenes, designed by *Frank Murray* and made by *Salviati*. Next door, the same architects' **Queen Insurance Building** and **Arcade**, 1887–8, with lively terracotta decoration. Shops on the ground floor, and an archway leading through to Queen Avenue, with attractive offices in cream glazed brick and red sandstone (for the remainder of Queen Avenue, *see* Dale Street, p. 145). Back in Castle Street, the former **Scottish Equitable Chambers**, *c.* 1878, classical with bands of polished granite, and the former **Scottish Provident Building**, 1874, both by *G.E. Grayson* before his partnership with Ould. After these, at No. 27, a three-bay building of 1846 with Corinthian columns and pediment.The order is that of the Choragic Monument of Lysicrates. Built by the lawyer and developer Ambrose Lace for his own offices, originally entered from Union Court, with ground-floor shops facing Castle Street. Convincingly ascribed to *Arthur H. Holme*.

Between Union Court and Cook Street is the former Liverpool branch of the **Bank of England** by *C.R. Cockerell*, built 1846–8 [81]. One of the masterpieces of Victorian commercial architecture, and among Cockerell's greatest works, combining Greek, Roman and Renaissance in a remarkably vigorous and inventive way. Only three bays wide, but overwhelmingly massive and powerful. Ground and first floors are tied together by attached Roman Doric columns, framed by rusticated angle pilasters. Second floor recessed, with a central Ionic aedicule window set in a round arch that pushes up into the open pediment. This impressive composition is developed from Cockerell's Manchester branch of the Bank and his earlier Westminster Insurance office. Seven bays to Cook Street, with three great tripartite windows under rusticated arches (the middle one originally lit the tunnel-vaulted banking hall). The huge crowning cornice on pairs of curved brackets is more prominent here. The front contained the residence of the Bank's Liverpool agent, entered from Union Court, with the sub-agent's house at the opposite end, entered from Cook Street. The first-floor windows to these residential parts have curved balconies with graceful ironwork.

On the other corner of Cook Street, No. 43, **Castle Chambers**, 1955–9 by *Felix Holt*. A very large Portland stone block, its upper floors set back

in the middle of the long Cook Street elevation. Next door, on the corner of Harrington Street, the former **Equity & Law Building**, 1970, by *Quiggin & Gee*. The projecting windows echo Peter Ellis's Oriel Chambers of 1864 (*see* Water Street, p. 171), by this date regarded as admirably proto-modern. For Pearl Assurance House, *see* Derby Square, p. 149.

w **side.** On the corner of Derby Square, and making the most of its prominent site, No. 62, the exuberant **Trials Hotel**, built as the Alliance Bank by *Lucy & Littler*, 1868. 'Italian, of the Venetian type' according to *The Builder*, with high chimneys, balconies, and much carving. Domed banking hall with paired Corinthian columns. The two bays on the right are a matching addition by *G.E. Grayson*. At Nos. 48–50, a tall, narrow building four bays wide, 1864, by *J.A. Picton*, originally the Mercantile and Exchange Bank. Polished red granite columns frame the ground-floor windows, and the first-floor lunettes have carved heads in roundels. T. Mellard Reade wrote in 1866 that it had 'the not uncommon defect of appearing as though made in lengths and sawn off to suit consumers'. Was it conceived as part of a larger block to be erected in stages? It is sandwiched between altered fragments of the 1786 rebuilding, with ends of a pediment visible on either side. No. 44 has a late c19 faience façade with foliage in the gable. At No. 42, the former **Victoria Chambers**, dated 1893, by *Grayson & Ould* again. Renaissance style, large and straggling, with three gables incorporating sculptures of mermen. Ground floor altered.

Next door, at the corner of Brunswick Street, the former **Adelphi Bank** by *W.D. Caröe*, *c.* 1891–2, colourful and exotic [82]. Northern Renaissance with much decorative carving, including figures in niches by *Charles E.*

81. Former Bank of
England, Castle Street, by
C.R. Cockerell (1846–8)

82. Former Adelphi Bank,
Castle Street, by W.D.
Caröe (c. 1891–2)

Whiffen to Caröe's designs. Alternate bands of red and white stone, with green copper for the onion domes and finials that add a touch of fantasy to the roofline. The corner entrance has exceptionally beautiful bronze **doors** of 1892 by *Thomas Stirling Lee*, with scenes of brotherly love (Adelphi means 'brothers' in Greek) in sensuous low relief. On the other corner of Brunswick Street, the former **Leyland & Bullin's Bank** (now Bank of Scotland), dated 1895, with an extension dated 1900 in Brunswick Street. *Grayson & Ould* in Renaissance mode again. The gable to Brunswick Street is framed by domed angle turrets, echoing Shaw's contemporary White Star Line building (*see* James Street, p. 153). Next door building of similar date, but more disciplined, with round-arched windows. *Shaw* himself, in association with *Willink & Thicknesse*, was responsible for the neighbouring **NatWest Bank** (originally Parr's), 1898–1901 [18]. Classical, of five bays. Basement of smooth grey granite with round-arched entrance, richly rusticated. Above, bands of grey-green and cream marble, the window surrounds and cornice red terra-cotta. Circular, domed banking hall, with offices stacked above, ingeniously supported by steel trusses [83]. The remainder of this side is all *Grayson*: No. 14 of c. 1885, classical; the former **Edinburgh Life Assurance**, dated 1897 (and therefore done in partnership with *Ould*?), coarser and rather flabby; and finally, on the corner of Water Street, an exquisite François I-style block erected in 1882 for the jewellers Robert Jones & Sons. Ground floor with very elegant projecting display windows. Office floors subtly polychromed, with bands of contrasting stone. Delicate carving around the windows, and good wrought-iron balconies.

Chapel Street

One of the seven ancient streets (*see* topic box, p. 6); now a mix of C19 and early C20 commercial, later C20 rebuilding, and cleared sites.

Starting near the E end, **Yorkshire House**, at the corner of Rumford Place, is by *T. Wainwright & Sons* (*J.B. Hutchins*), 1929. Classical, in Portland stone. Giant square piers extend from first to third floor, enclosing expanses of metal-framed glazing. The site immediately w of this is to be cleared, 2004, for a mixed-use development by *Allford Hall Monaghan Morris*: two towers, one residential, one offices. The fine five-bay **Hargreaves Buildings** opposite, dated 1859, is by *J.A. Picton* in Venetian palazzo style [84]. Carved heads of Cortez, Columbus, etc., in roundels between the ground-floor windows, commemorate exploration of the Americas. Back on the N side, at the bottom, the **Thistle Hotel**, 1970–3, by *Victor Basil* and *Keith McTavish* of *William Holford & Associates*. Eleven-storey tower – a convex-sided triangle in plan – on a two-storey podium. Concrete cladding, windows in bands. Constructed using the British Lift Slab method, each complete floor being jacked up and fixed around the core.

The church of **Our Lady and St Nicholas**, opposite, is the parish church of Liverpool and occupies a venerable site. It was originally built *c.* 1360 as a chapel of ease to Walton. Before that there was another chapel, called St Mary del Key (i.e. Quay), first mentioned 1257, which Chapel Street was named after. It stood at the bottom, overlooking the river. Nothing is left of it, nor is there anything left of the St Nicholas of the C14. The oldest part of the present church is the steeple [84], for which the Greek revivalist *Thomas Harrison* of Chester made a Gothic design in 1810, after the previous spire and tower collapsed. The foundation

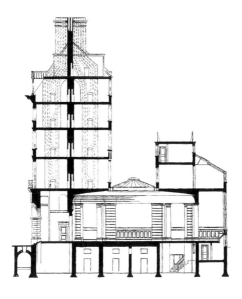

83. NatWest Bank (originally Parr's), Castle Street, by Norman Shaw with Willink & Thicknesse (1898–1901), section

stone was laid in 1811. It has panelled buttresses, which become octagonal higher up. In 1814 Harrison designed 'an elegant and appropriate Lantern' for the top. This delightful structure is a delicate cage of stone tracery, consisting of a spire on a recessed octagon. Flying buttresses connect to the corner pinnacles. The weathervane in the form of a ship is probably the original one made by *John Sutherland*. The rest, except for the vestries which flank the tower (presumably Harrison's), was bombed in 1940. A simple Gothic building by *Edward C. Butler*, completed 1952, replaced it. Flat elevations without buttresses, Perp windows. Narthex, three-bay nave with aisles, sanctuary with flanking chapels. Open timber roof with tie-beams. The orientation was reversed in the rebuilding, so the altar is against the tower wall.

Fittings: Screens with etched glass by *David Peace*, 1984. – **Stained glass**, window in s aisle, Our Lady and St Nicholas, 1951, by *Harcourt M. Doyle* of Liverpool. – **Statue**, in chapel right of the altar, Our Lady of the Key, by *Arthur Dooley*, 1993: a stark figure standing in the prow of a ship. – The only **monument** from the old church, in the vestry in the base of the tower, commemorates the Rev. R. Roughsedge, d. 1829, and is by *William Spence*. A bust against a tablet with Greek cresting, with a fine relief of Faith, Hope and Charity on the base.

The **churchyard** was laid out as a garden in 1891. On the w side, a **monument** to those who died in the Liverpool Blitz, bronze, by *Tom Murphy*, 2000: mother and children on a spiral stair. On the N side of the church, overlooking Chapel Street, a **statue**, Christ upon an Ass, early 1970s, by *Brian Burgess*. In the exterior of the churchyard wall, at the corner of Chapel Street and George's Dock Gates, the **William Simpson Memorial Fountain**, dated 1885, by *Thomas Cox*. Gothic, with

84. Chapel Street, with Hargreaves Buildings by J.A. Picton (1859), and tower of Our Lady and St Nicholas by Thomas Harrison (1811–15). Lithograph from W. Herdman, *Views in Modern Liverpool*, 1864

bronze portrait medallion by *Joseph Rogerson*. Gothic **archway** at the sw entrance, probably 1880s, but apparently a replica of an earlier one that stood at the corner of Chapel Street.

Cheapside

On the w side towards Tithebarn Street, **Cablehouse**, a 1960s electronics factory imaginatively converted into flats and live-work spaces by *Union North*, *c.* 2000. Much external cedar panelling, and a zinc-clad penthouse floor with pod-like projections containing windows. On the e side, the **Main Bridewell** [85], a grim and surprisingly large prison, part of a complex by *John Weightman*, begun 1857, including the Magistrates' Courts in Dale Street (q.v.). Red brick with stone dressings, set behind a high screen wall with rusticated piers. Front block with central pediment and small, barred window openings. By this date castellated Gothic was the usual prison style, but classicism still held sway in Liverpool. Opposite, a couple of robust polychrome brick warehouses, one dated 1884: industrial storage and incarceration rubbing shoulders, in sight of the palatial Municipal Buildings (Dale Street).

Cook Street

No. 16, on the s side near the e end, dates probably from 1864–6 and is by *Peter Ellis* [86]. Tall, narrow front divided into three great arches, rising through five storeys from pavement to gable. The middle arch is wider and higher, and pushes the cornice up to form a curving gable with a little obelisk crowning the keystone. The proportions are those of a warehouse (the central arch recalls a loading bay) but the building was designed as offices. As with Ellis's Oriel Chambers (*see* Water Street, p. 171), there is an amazing amount of plate glass to stonework, so that the façade resembles one huge mullioned window. The offices facing

85. Main Bridewell, Cheapside, by John Weightman (late 1850s)

86. No. 16 Cook Street, by Peter Ellis (probably 1864–6)

the rear courtyard have large areas of glazing too, and a remarkable spiral staircase, cantilevered and expressed externally, and now entirely glazed. Externally completely utilitarian, the ironwork inside is quite decorative, with a Gothic balustrade, and mullions in the form of slender spiral columns. No. 14, almost contemporary, could not be more different. It was built as the **National Bank**. The drawings, dated 1863, are signed by *William Culshaw*, but the designer was probably *Henry Sumners*. Five bays, Italianate. The Queen Anne windows between the ground-floor columns are later.

Crosshall Street

For the Conservation Centre *see* Walk 3, pp. 190–1; for Millennium House, *see* Victoria Street, p. 168.

On the E side, N of Victoria Street, is **Crosshall Buildings**, by *F. & G. Holme*, put up in two phases *c.* 1878–80. Offices combined with warehouses, the latter entered at the rear. Fireproof construction, façades of red brick and terracotta. Next door, the former **Victoria Chapel** of the Welsh Calvinists, 1878–80, by *W.H. Picton*. Surprisingly late for a new place of worship in the commercial centre. David Roberts (*see* below) helped secure the site. Early Gothic, with round-arched windows and stiff-leaf capitals. After this, and with a façade to Dale Street, **Westminster Buildings**, 1879–80, by *Richard Owens*. A well-detailed Gothic block with attractive carving by *Joseph Rogerson*. Built for David Roberts, Son & Co., surveyors, leading players in Liverpool's Welsh-dominated house-building industry. Originally there was a spire over the main entrance. A good example of a building combining shops and offices with warehousing at the rear, very characteristic of later C19 Liverpool.

Dale Street

One of the seven ancient streets (*see* topic box, p. 6). Lanes and narrow streets run off N and S, echoes of medieval burgage plots.

From W to E: No. 1, next to the Town Hall (q.v., Major Buildings), is *C.R. Cockerell*'s great office complex for the **Liverpool & London Insurance Co.**, 1856–8. He was assisted by his son *F.P. Cockerell* and by *Christopher F. Hayward* (resident architect *Joseph Boult*). Four linked buildings filling an entire block, the richest one (now Royal Bank of Scotland) facing Dale Street, the other three a little plainer and intended as lettable offices. The Dale Street building [87] is a Venetian-looking palazzo with attached columns between the second-floor windows, and a memorable central entrance: a Doric doorcase of polished red granite with open pediment, in a rusticated niche carved with heavy garlands. Originally there were similar garlands between the attic windows of the frieze (a strong echo of St Mark's Library) and over the side entrances facing the Town Hall. Carving mostly by *Edwin Stirling*, with some by Cockerell's favourite sculptor, *W.G. Nicholl*. The overall

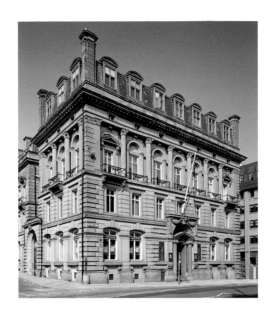

87. Former
Liverpool & London
Insurance Co, Dale
Street, by C.R.
Cockerell (1856–8)

proportions were marred by a mansard roof in the 1920s. Towards the
Town Hall the NW stairs are expressed externally, as at the Château
de Chambord, the balustrades and treads both visible, framed by
expanses of plate glass. The buildings originally enclosed a glass-roofed
court, faced with glazed white tiles and lined with access galleries. The
court became wider as the upper galleries stepped back, to maximize
daylight [13]. Interior of fireproof construction, some of the cast-iron
columns originally serving as flues.

On the opposite side of Dale Street, **HSBC**, *c.* 1971, by *Bradshaw,
Rowse & Harker*, a startlingly aggressive façade of twenty-eight identical, faceted windows of reflective glass, framed in stainless steel – a
Space Age descendant of Oriel Chambers (*see* Water Street, p. 171). Next
door a large, stone classical building with giant attached Corinthian
columns, much carved decoration (wreaths, fleshy acanthus scrolls)
and a big sculptured royal arms on the parapet. It is part of a group of
offices by *Samuel Rowland, c.* 1837–8, originally for the **Royal Bank**. On
the right an archway leads into Queen Avenue, with simpler offices on
each side and the former bank itself at the end, an exquisite Greek
Revival design [88]. Five bays, the centre breaking forward under a pediment, with Doric columns below Ionic. Superb masonry. The detail
here is much more refined and correct , and it is difficult to believe both
parts are by the same architect. Main hall with four Corinthian
columns near the corners and sumptuous plaster work, recently spoiled
when a mezzanine was introduced.

Returning to Dale Street, at No. 14 the former **State Insurance**,
1903–5, by *Walter Aubrey Thomas*. Wiry, sinuous Gothic. Originally

symmetrical, with a balancing gable left of the slim octagonal tower. Ground-floor restaurant (now a night club) at the back – part of the original scheme – with sumptuous multicoloured marble decoration, incorporating circular reliefs by *Alfred R. Martin*. This was top-lit, with offices above arranged round a glass-roofed court. Next door, at the corner of North John Street, **State House**. A seven-storey tower above a podium, by *Edmund Kirby & Sons, c.* 1962. Opposite, No. 11 at the corner of Hackins Hey, built for the Queen Insurance Co., 1859. Perhaps the best of *J.A. Picton*'s surviving office buildings: Italian Renaissance and Gothic details, with upper balconies and a bold machicolated parapet. Then, at Nos. 21–25, **Rigby's Buildings**, refronted in stucco 1865, with offices and a warehouse grouped round an inner courtyard. On the same side, No. 31, an impressive red brick palazzo of 1879, designed by *Edmund Kirby* as the **Reform Club**. Rather sombre, except for the continuous first-floor balcony with its delicate wrought-iron balustrade. The façade of the neighbouring **Guardian Assurance Buildings**, 1893, probably by *Grayson & Ould*, has pretty carved decoration. It was absorbed *c.* 1990 into a coarse Postmodern office block with a bulbous dome on the corner of Moorfields.

Returning to the s side, for the former Royal Insurance building *see* North John Street, p. 156. Next door, **The Temple**, by *J.A. Picton*, 1860s, with a central domed tower. One of several office buildings by Picton for the banker Sir William Brown. Refurbishment by *Falconer Chester*, completed 2001, including a rear extension, tall and thin and curved in plan, with aluminium cladding. Then the Gothic **Prudential Assurance**, by *Alfred Waterhouse*, dated 1886, in the same red brick and terracotta as the company's London headquarters. Extension, including tower, added by *Paul Waterhouse*, 1904–6, closing the view down Moorfields. Vaguely Art Nouveau details. On the N side, facing down Stanley Street, a stucco façade with two giant Corinthian columns, probably 1820s, incorporated into a dull red brick office block by *Bradshaw, Rowse & Harker*, completed 1985. (Behind is Moorfields underground station, part of the Merseyrail system opened in 1977. The station concourse at first-floor level was intended to be reached by elevated walkways in neighbouring buildings, but these were never constructed.) Opposite, on the corner of Stanley Street, the red sandstone **Musker's Buildings**, 1881–2 by *Thomas E. Murray*, in 'a coarse and florid sort of "Manchester Gothic"' (*The Builder*). Originally intended as shops and offices, it seems to have been adapted as the Junior Conservative Club during construction, then used as the Junior Reform Club. Next door, **Imperial Chambers**, *c*. 1870. Gothic details but mostly square-headed windows. Central entrance leading to a glass-roofed court surrounded by offices (now flats). After this, at the corner of Sir Thomas Street, the former **Conservative Club**, won in competition by *F. & G. Holme*, 1880, and opened 1883. Lavish French Renaissance, with a balcony, and cherubs in the first-floor spandrels in the manner of Sansovino. Impressive staircase inside. Stained glass.

Occupying the whole block between Sir Thomas Street and Crosshall Street, the **Municipal Buildings**, designed 1862 by the Corporation Surveyor *John Weightman*, modified by his successor *E.R. Robson*, and completed 1867–8 [89]. The aim was to unite the scattered offices of the expanding Corporation. Large rectangular block with giant attached columns and pilasters, corner pavilions, and a clock tower in the middle of the Dale Street front, with a curious pyramid spire strongly reminiscent of Charles Barry's slightly earlier Halifax Town Hall. Statues representing Industry, Commerce, Navigation, etc., decorate the attic. The style is hard to pin down – *The Builder* could do no better than 'Corinthianesque, treated very freely'. The columns do indeed have Corinthian capitals (carved by *Earp* of London), but with English ferns rather than acanthus, and each one different: a Gothic rather than a classical feature. At the same time there is a fashionably French character to the whole, especially the big, curved roofs of the corner pavilions. Inside, offices and committee rooms surround the central, top-lit Treasurer's Public Office. Stairs and corridors have unusual ceramic-tiled dados resembling parquetry, probably made by a technique of printing from the grain of natural wood, patented by *William Scarratt* and *William Dean* in 1865.

Opposite, between Hockenhall Alley and Cheapside, **Princes Buildings**, 1882, designed by *Henry Shelmerdine* as shops, offices and leather works. A rather ungainly red brick pile, with giant granite pilasters and sandstone and terracotta details. Large mullioned and transomed windows in the mansard, with pedimented gables. Absorbed

89. Municipal Buildings, Dale Street, by John Weightman and E.R. Robson (1862–8)

into the **Hockenhall Alley** elevation, left, is an extraordinary survival, a three-storey house of the meanest kind, just one bay wide, probably early C19. On the opposite corner of Cheapside, a short terrace with ground-floor shops, apparently part of a street-widening programme begun in 1818. After these, at the corner of Hatton Garden, the **Magistrates' Courts**. Simple but dignified ashlar façade, built as part of a group that included the Bridewell in Cheapside (q.v.), offices and quarters for the police, and a fire station (later replaced). All designed by *John Weightman* and supervised by his assistant, *G.H. Rollett*, 1857–9.

Back on the s side, for Westminster Buildings *see* Crosshall Street, p. 144. Then, on a triangular site, the **Travelodge**, a hotel by *Shed KM*, completed 2002. Two distinct blocks, raised above a set-back ground floor. That facing Dale Street is cubic, faced in blue render, and punched with square windows. The other, set at an angle, faces Manchester Street. It is mostly of glass, an all-over grid of squares, masking the division into bedrooms. At the back, stairs and lifts in a sleek aluminium-clad tower. Adjoining in **Preston Street** is **Preston Point**, two C19 warehouses converted into flats by *Shed KM*, with balconies concealed behind horizontally slatted timber screens.

At this point the s side comes to an end above the entrance to the Mersey Tunnel (*see* Old Haymarket, p. 161), and the carriageway is joined by a flyover (*see* Byrom Street, p. 136). On the N side, No. 127 at the corner of North Street is the offices of **National Museums Liverpool**, a seven-storey tower of 1964–5 by *Ormrod & Partners* (*D.H. Mills*). Polished granite facing. Nos. 135–139 are a terrace of three brick houses of *c.* 1788, including, at the corner of Trueman Street, the grandest surviving Georgian house in the business district [8], built for the distiller John Houghton, whose works adjoined. The houses were set back, allowing Dale Street to be widened. The Trueman Street elevation has a three-bay pediment and a Venetian window over the tripartite doorway. Finally, at the corner of Fontenoy Street, No. 151, built for the Blackburn Assurance Co. by *William P. Horsburgh*, *c.* 1932. Classical, with iron-framed glazing between giant pilasters. The corner entrance leads to a very impressive Travertine-lined spiral staircase, rising to a stained-glass dome.

Derby Square

A historic nodal point, site of the castle (*see* topic box, p. 4) and later of St George (*see* topic box, p. 179). From here, Castle Street leads N to the Town Hall, and from opposite, South Castle Street formerly led to the Custom House in Canning Place. The E side was rebuilt by *John Foster Jun.*, 1826, with two quadrants flanking Lord Street, forming St George's Crescent. In the Second World War the area was severely damaged [24], and in the rebuilding South Castle Street was obliterated and the Queen Elizabeth II Law Courts built in its place.

In the centre, the **Queen Victoria Monument**, 1902–6, by *F.M. Simpson*, with *Willink & Thicknesse* [90]. Bronze sculpture by *C.J. Allen*. Domed baldacchino on clusters of diagonally set columns, raised on a stepped podium enclosed by four concave walls with balustrades. Standing figure of the Queen under the dome, with Fame on the summit. The groups above the columns are Justice, Wisdom, Charity and Peace, and on the enclosing walls Agriculture, Industry, Education and Commerce. This was Allen's *magnum opus* and is one of the most ambitious British monuments to the Queen.

No. 2, **Pearl Assurance House**, *c.* 1954–5, by *Alfred Shennan & Partners*. A big Portland stone block, curved like the N half of Foster's crescent that it replaced. Pediments over the first-floor windows, and

other Neo-Georgian touches. **Castle Moat House**, 1838–40, by *Edward Corbett* of Manchester for the North and South Wales Bank, is a tall building on a narrow island site, with giant Corinthian pilasters on the Fenwick Street side and a pedimented front [16]. The front originally had a portico *in antis*, later infilled. The temple effect is undermined by three tiers of domestic-looking windows between the pilasters. The site lies partly over the castle moat, so the bank was given a deep, vaulted basement, used as bonded warehousing.

Filling the s side, the **Queen Elizabeth II Law Courts**, by *Farmer & Dark*. Design work began in 1973 but the courts did not open until 1984, by which date such assertive, concrete-clad buildings were less fashionable. Ten storeys, containing twenty-eight courtrooms in the core. Faced with vertically ribbed pre-cast panels of dark, pinkish concrete, with brown ceramic tiles used e.g. in strips between the stair windows, and lead-covered mansard roofs. On the N side the stair-towers of different heights dominate. On the s, some of the uprights stand clear, creating strong contrasts of light and shadow. Richly sculptural from most angles, though rather oppressive in bulk and colouring. Royal arms over the entrance by *Richard Kindersley*, cast in concrete.

Edmund Street

Orleans House, 1907, is a large E-plan office block with its long elevation facing Bixteth Street. By *Matear & Simon*, using the same cast-iron cladding panels as their Cotton Exchange opposite (*see* Old Hall

Street, p. 159). **Stanley Hall**, built as the headquarters of R. Silock & Sons, animal-feed producers, opened in 1938. By *Medcalf & Medcalf*. Frieze in the entrance with scenes of animal husbandry. Extended w in the 1950s by *Fraser, Son & Geary*. This part has an overdoor relief of a cow being fed; the style suggests *Herbert Tyson Smith*.

Exchange Flags

The present **Exchange Buildings**, enclosing three sides of the Flags, are by *Gunton & Gunton*. They occupy the site of two earlier Exchanges. The first – of 1803–8 by *John Foster Sen.*, possibly with *James Wyatt* – echoed the N portico of Wyatt's Town Hall extension, forming a noble Neoclassical quadrangle. It was replaced, 1864–7, with a florid French Renaissance building by *T.H. Wyatt*. The first phase of the present buildings opened in 1939 but construction was interrupted by war and not completed until 1955. Artificial stone on a steel frame, stripped classical, lumpish and ill-proportioned. The 1950s underground car park formed part of the pre-war plan, an early example. Reliefs by *Edmund C. Thompson* and *George T. Capstick* over entrances. In the centre of the N side, bronze **War Memorial**, 1924, by *Joseph Phillips*. Moved here from the old Exchange News Room in 1953, and placed between piers supporting stone sculptures by *Siegfried Charoux*.

In the middle stands the **Nelson Monument**, designed 1807–8 by *Matthew Cotes Wyatt*, executed in bronze by *Richard Westmacott*, and unveiled 1813. Cylindrical plinth with four battle reliefs, separated by life-size nude male captives in chains – memorable works of Romanticism. Above, the apotheosis of the hero of Trafalgar, with a skeletal figure of Death emerging from under a captured flag [10]. The contributions of Wyatt and Westmacott are difficult to disentangle. Wyatt claimed that his design was no 'embryo brought to maturity by another', but conceded that his ideas for the reliefs, at least, were very sketchy.

Exchange Street East

No. 26, former Royal Exchange Assurance, by *Willink & Dod*, 1927. Tall Portland stone façade, restrainedly classical. Converted into flats, with a penthouse added, 1990s. Next door, **Mason's Building**, offices, by *John Cunningham*, *c.* 1866. Renaissance style, with much carving. The *Building News* was not impressed: 'a great deal of showy but commonplace ornament . . . the whole having rather the effect of the regulation cement front of a gin-palace translated into stone.'

Fenwick Street

The **Corn Exchange**, 1953–9, by *H. Hinchliffe Davies*, succeeds earlier corn exchanges on the site by *John Foster Jun.* and *James A. Picton*. Probably the most imaginative of Liverpool's early postwar office buildings. A podium – three storeys in Drury Lane, reducing to two in Fenwick Street because of the sloping site – housed the news room and trading floor. Set back above is a seven-storey block, I-plan, with cylindrical tank rooms on the roof. It was intended to be higher. Ends subtly canted, with windows in a central, vertical panel. Stair windows correspond with the half landings, making a chequerboard pattern. Cladding of Portland stone, with grey-green faience panels between windows. Window frames recently replaced with uPVC.

Great Crosshall Street

Near the E end, N side, the former **St John's National School**, 1850, by *John Hay*. First floor with trefoil-headed arcade enclosing paired lancets. Ground floor originally arcaded, filled in by *William Culshaw*, 1854. Infants', boys' and girls' classrooms were on separate floors, reached by a spiral stair in a (demolished) rear turret.

Hatton Garden

Kingsway House, 1965–7, by *Derek Stephenson & Partners*, a large office block incorporating first-floor elevated walkways (*see* topic box, p. 160). The former **Fire Station**, 1895–8, officially by *Thomas Shelmerdine*, the Corporation Surveyor, but possibly designed in his office by *James Bain Hikins*. Red brick with generous stone dressings, long and low, in a free and imaginative Jacobean style. Watch tower with serpentine balconies. Opposite, No. 24, built 1905–7 as the City Tramway Offices. *Shelmerdine* again, this time classical and symmetrical. Imposing four-storey façade dominated by three projecting bays, those left and right having allegorical sculpture. Finally, the former **Parcel Sorting Office**, 1933–4, worked on by a succession of Office of Works architects, *C.P. Wilkinson*, *C.J. Mole* and finally *J. Bradley*. Large, handsome Neo-Georgian in red brick, with a screen of sturdy Greek Doric columns in grey granite. Recently converted into flats by *Falconer Chester*, who added the glazed penthouse.

James Street

The former **National Bank**, by *T. Arnold Ashworth & Sons*, *c.* 1920, closes the view w from Lord Street. Big, American-influenced classical, in Portland stone, coarser than the work of other Liverpool exponents of this style. Columned banking hall now a bar, upper floors now flats. **James Street Station**, further w, is the original Liverpool terminus of the Mersey Railway, the under-river line to Birkenhead, opened 1886. *James Brunlees* and *Charles Douglas Fox* were the engineers. The surface building, bombed in the Second World War, was replaced with a dull 1960s office block, **Moor House**, by *Gotch & Partners*. The tracks and platforms, excavated in the rock 92 ft (28 metres) below the pavement, survive more or less unaltered under a single, broad, brick-lined vault. Platform seating, etc., in the 1977 Merseyrail house style (*see* Walk 3, pp. 181–2); **mural sculpture**, Dream Passage, on platform 2 by *Tim Chalk* and *Paul Grime*, 1992.

No. 30, Albion House, was built as the **White Star Line**, 1895–8, by *Norman Shaw*, the local architect *James F. Doyle* superintending construction [91]. This mighty eight-storey block brought a new scale to Liverpool's commercial architecture. The *Architectural Review* thought it made 'everything round it look little and mean', and it still holds its own among its big neighbours. The composition with prominent domed angle turrets is a development of Shaw's New Scotland Yard, London (1888–90), but the Strand elevation also echoes the tall gabled warehouses then typical of this dockside street. Granite ashlar lower floors, rustication round the basement windows. The upper floors, as at New Scotland Yard, are banded with red brick and Portland stone. Colour aside, the absence of ornament is notable: apart from wrought-iron balconies to the second-floor and a continuous fifth-floor balcony, there are few projections from the cliff-like walls. The gable was crowned with a complicated aedicule, not rebuilt after war damage; a large clock projecting from the sw turret was removed at the same time. Entrance in James Street, with blocked surround and broken pediment. Inside, Shaw's ground-floor general office was severely functional: exposed cast-iron stanchions and girders, boldly riveted,

91. White Star Line offices, James Street, by Norman Shaw (1895–8)

92. Nos. 81–89 Lord Street, by Walter Aubrey Thomas (1901)

supported a fireproof ceiling of terracotta panels made by *J.C. Edwards* of Ruabon. This remarkable interior survives, obscured by partitions and suspended ceilings.

Lord Street

Laid out in 1668 by the 3rd Lord Molyneux. The s side, largely destroyed in the Second World War, was rebuilt in the 1950s with steel-framed, mostly Portland stone-faced blocks, none very exciting. **Merchants Court**, 1957–60, by *Quiggin & Gee*, has green marble columns on the ground floor and a wavy balcony to Derby Square. On the N side a few older survivors. At the corner of Dorans Lane, the former **Venice Chambers** with a Gothic parapet and yellow and white glazed brick-work in lozenge patterns à la Doge's Palace, 1882 by *Edmund Kirby*. The Dorans Lane elevation has projecting windows between glazed brick piers. At Nos. 81–89 a more ambitious Italian Gothic building of 1901 by *Walter Aubrey Thomas* [92]. Striped façade of red and white stone, composed of three giant round arches, with a band of small pointed windows above. It resembles three bays of the nave arcade and triforium of a church, with the middle bay slightly wider. Above, however, each bay has its own gable, like the w front of Peterborough Cathedral. The arches enclose full-width mullioned and transomed windows, recessed in the centre to form a giant niche. This originally led to a glass-roofed and galleried shopping arcade.

Mathew Street

This was a centre of the provision trade. Here, and in adjoining streets, is a cluster of warehouses from the first half of the C19.

Starting from Whitechapel, for Kansas Buildings *see* Stanley Street, p. 162. The curved block on the left at the corner of Rainford Gardens is a street improvement of *c.* 1830. Next is a red brick warehouse with blind Gothic tracery in the gable, and attached offices, late C19 by *Grayson & Ould*. No. 18, on the corner of Rainford Square, is a very large warehouse, apparently existing by 1836 and now used as a pub. Opposite is a smaller but more handsome warehouse, with a pediment to Mathew Street and a curved façade to Temple Court, with good ashlar doorcases and large office windows. It may date from *c.* 1840. Another similar warehouse at No. 23 (and two more in Temple Court, perhaps 1830s). For the rear of the Produce Exchange *see* Victoria Street, pp. 165–6.

At its w end the street is dominated by **Cavern Walks**, a shopping centre with offices above, designed by *David Backhouse* and built 1982–4. It is large, extending through to Harrington Street. The façades are broken up into tall, gabled elements, reminiscent of warehouses, and make use of Victorian-derived materials and motifs. Terracotta decoration round the entrances by *Cynthia Lennon*. Side elevations more original, with large areas of glazing sloping outwards towards the bottom. Inside, the core is an atrium, octagonal at ground level, narrowing and becoming square as it rises through seven floors [93]. It is an unusual and exciting space, let down by pseudo-Victorian ironwork and decorative touches. The present Cavern Club in the basement is a

93. Cavern Walks, Mathew Street, by David Backhouse (1982–4)

rebuilding of the demolished original, made famous in the early 1960s by The Beatles. The dreadful life-size bronze **sculpture** of them in the atrium, *c*. 1984, is by *John Doubleday*.

Mathew Street has more **sculptures** on the same theme: From Us to You, 1984, by *David Hughes*, above the doorway of No. 31; Carl Gustav Jung (whose 1927 description of Liverpool as 'the pool of life' has been taken as a prediction of the city's role in 1960s pop culture) by *Johnathon Drabkin*, set into the wall of No. 18; Four Lads Who Shook the World, 1974, by *Arthur Dooley* high up at the N end; and, close to the last named, John Lennon, *c*. 1996, by *David Webster*. These are striking as evidence of a cult. Between No. 18 and Cavern Walks is an **electricity sub-station**, refurbished 1998, its workings exposed like pieces of sculpture and enlivened at night by light projections.

North John Street

At the corner of Dale Street, the former **Royal Insurance** head office, 1896–1903, won in competition by *James F. Doyle* [94]. The assessor was *Norman Shaw* (for whom Doyle was working on the White Star Line offices, *see* James Street, p. 153); he was subsequently retained as 'advisory architect', though his contribution is unclear. Sumptuous Neo-Baroque on the grandest scale. Long façade to North John Street, with off-centre entrance under a gold-domed tower. High and narrow gabled façade with angle turrets to Dale Street – a composition derived from Shaw's White Star Line building and New Scotland Yard. Second-floor frieze by *C.J. Allen*, illustrating the theme of insurance. Despite appearances, the massive Portland stone walls (above an impressive basement of rugged grey granite) are not load-bearing: floors and chimneys are carried by a virtually self-supporting steel frame, possibly the first designed in Britain. This allows the former General Office, which fills most of the ground floor, to be completely free of columns. This, and the tunnel-vaulted Board Room (on the first floor, overlooking Dale Street) have neo–late C17 stucco decoration.

No. 17, **North House**, red brick Deco of *c*. 1932 by *Alfred Shennan*. Nos. 19–21, **Melbourne Buildings**, stuccoed, with (later) inscription giving the date 1854. Dramatic rooftop extension, highly sculptural and faced with slate-like tiles, added 1975 by *K.E. Martin & Associates*. Opposite, the windowless cliff of a **ventilating station** for the Mersey tunnel [95], 1931–4, by *Herbert J. Rowse* (*see* Old Haymarket, pp. 161–2). Next to this, **Union Chambers**, *c*. 1878, by *David Walker*, with oriels.

Back on the E side, Nos. 37–45, **Central Buildings**, a huge office block of 1884, by *Thomas C. Clarke*. The lower part of the twenty-bay front has no solid walls, only a giant Doric colonnade of polished granite. Ground floor and basement, recessed behind, are completely glazed. The architect's drawings show corner towers and a roof incorporating further floors, but it is not clear if these were built. Without them, the façade ends abruptly at the main cornice.

94. Former Royal Insurance, North John Street, by James F. Doyle (1896–1903)

The opposite side, between Cook Street and Lord Street, is representative of the commercial street architecture of 1820s–40s Liverpool. More such blocks – four storeys, usually stuccoed, with rounded corners – survived in the central area until the Second World War. The one at the corner of Cook Street has a rainwater head dated 1828; Nos. 24–26, **Harrington Chambers**, complete this block, with giant pilasters and shopfronts below. Nos. 28–40 form a single, almost symmetrical composition, elaborately stuccoed. Central attached Corinthian portico, with pilasters in the middle of each wing. An inscription inside the right part, **Marldon Chambers**, says this was built in 1841 – a likely date for the entire façade – and remodelled in 1884. The attractive doorway with Renaissance carving must belong to the remodelling.

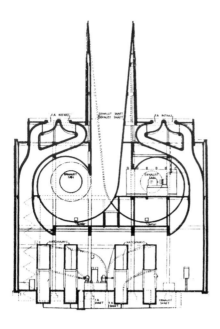

95. Mersey Tunnel
ventilating station,
by Herbert J. Rowse
(1931–4), section

96. Albany Building,
Old Hall Street, by
J.K. Colling (1856–8),
R.C. Naylor's mono-
gram

Old Church Yard

Mersey Chambers, *c.* 1878 by *G.E. Grayson*, was built as offices for the shipping firm of Thomas and James Harrison. Italianate with round-arched windows and a higher central feature. The utilitarian rear elevation to Covent Garden is more individual, with projecting windows partly of cast iron, set between yellow glazed-brick piers. Inside, glass-roofed court and fine cast-iron staircase. Board Room of *c.* 1920, classical in the Liverpool manner of this period: apsidal ends, coved ceiling, oak panelling incorporating First World War memorial.

Old Hall Street

One of Liverpool's seven ancient streets (*see* topic box, p. 6).

We begin near the s end. On the E side, the **Albany Building**, an exceptionally large speculative office block by *J.K. Colling*, 1856–8, for the banker R.C. Naylor [14]. His monogram appears left of the central entrance [96]. Imposing palazzo of red brick, dressed with sandstone and polished granite, and with much stylized foliage carving, a speciality of the architect. *The Builder* summed up: 'a very free treatment of the Renaissance, with Arabesque variations'. Side elevations plainer, with cast-iron hoists serving basement storage areas. Splendid gates on Old Hall Street, designed to look like wrought iron, but cast locally by *Rankin's Union Foundry*. They lead via a tunnel-vaulted passage with granite columns and elaborate plasterwork to a central courtyard. Within the long side blocks the offices are ranged on either side of broad spine corridors, pierced at intervals by light-wells.

Next, between Ormond Street and Edmund Street and extending back to Bixteth Street, the former **Cotton Exchange** by *Matear & Simon*, 1905–6. The front was demolished in 1967, an unforgivable act of vandalism. It was a magnificent classical design with Baroque angle towers, the architectural embodiment of the cotton trade, central to Liverpool's prosperity. Its replacement is a thoroughly unremarkable block of 1967–9 by *Newton-Dawson, Forbes & Tate*. The sides and rear of Matear & Simon's building, largely offices let to cotton traders, survive more or less unaltered. The six-storey façade to Edmund Street is notable, composed of classically detailed cast-iron panels decorated with wreaths, made by *Macfarlane's* of Glasgow [20]. They incorporate very large windows designed to admit the maximum of N light, necessary for examining cotton samples. Bixteth Street elevation of Portland stone, and more conventional; that to Ormond Street of brick. Immediately behind the front was the main exchange hall. This too was demolished in 1967, creating an open courtyard, but much of the colonnade that originally surrounded the trading floor survives behind the new elevations. The columns are superb monoliths of beautiful grey granite, quarried in Norway and polished in Aberdeen before being shipped to Liverpool. On the pavement at the corner of Old Hall Street and Edmund Street is a colossal **statue** representing the Mersey, by *William Birnie Rhind*, from the top of one of Matear & Simon's towers. In the courtyard, statues of Navigation and Commerce by *Rhind*, also from the façade, and the Liverpool Cotton Association **war memorial**, an advancing infantryman in bronze by *Derwent Wood*, 1921, originally on a tall pedestal in front of the building.

At the corner of Fazackerley Street, Nos. 21–23, **City Buildings**, remodelled by *Frederick G. Fraser*, c. 1908. He inserted large iron-framed windows to suit cotton traders attracted by the new Exchange. Nos. 25–31, between Fazackerley Street and Union Street, a former Midland Bank, by *Woolfall & Eccles*, 1925. Portland stone, classical, with round inset corners. In **Union Street** itself, No. 7, a two-bay brick house of c. 1760, a survivor from before mid-C19 commercial redevelopment.

Near the w end of Union Street, a **ventilating station** for the New Quay spur of the Mersey tunnel, by *Herbert J. Rowse*, 1931–4 (*see* Old Haymarket, pp. 161–2). Two square towers. Alone of the tunnel structures on the Liverpool side it is of brick, with geometrical ornament.

On the opposite corner of Union Street, **City Exchange**, by *KKA*, completed 2001. A large glass-walled concourse with a space-frame roof and split-level interior, giving access to two earlier buildings, the Royal Insurance headquarters, now **Royal & Sun Alliance**, by *Tripe & Wakeham*, 1972–6, and the **Liverpool Daily Post and Echo**, by *Farmer & Dark*, 1970–4. The former is a massive irregular stepped pyramid, thirteen storeys with three car-parking levels below, faced with ribbed panels of yellow-brown concrete [97]. Narrow slit windows give it a fortress air. At pavement level its blank walls give little pleasure, but from a distance – and especially from the river – its rugged bulk and distinctive silhouette contribute greatly to the skyline. As the monumentally self-important head office of a local insurance company, it follows worthily in the tradition of the Royal Liver Building. Inside, open-plan offices surround a central lift core. Impressive spaces for staff dining, recreation, etc., including a double-height sports hall entirely lined with wych-elm. Panelling in various woods designed by *Lyle Ellard*, some removed during refurbishment. The Post and Echo is more conventional, a speculative office tower on a podium containing newspaper accommodation. The tower has triangular fins faced with brown tiles, containing air-conditioning ducts. Both buildings were designed with elevated walkways, in accordance with the 1965 City Centre Plan (*see* topic box).

No. 100 is the Sir John Moores Building for Littlewoods, designed by *Littlewoods Department of Architecture & Planning* (*W.L. Stevenson*) and put up in two phases from 1962. Then Liverpool's highest multi-storey office block, it set the scale for much of the surrounding rebuilding. In

Elevated Walkways

In 1963 the Buchanan Report *Traffic in Towns* was published. Commissioned by the Minister of Transport, it analysed the problem of congestion in cities, and proposed 'traffic architecture' as a solution: cars and pedestrians would be separated, new buildings would incorporate elevated walkways giving access to shops and offices, while roads at ground level would be reserved for vehicles. The Liverpool City Centre Plan of 1965 enthusiastically adopted the idea, and in the 1970s new buildings were still being designed with sections of walkway at first-floor level, intended to form part of a comprehensive system that never materialized. Surviving examples include the entrance to the underground railway station in Moorfields (*see* Dale Street, p. 147) and Kingsway House (*see* Hatton Garden, p. 152).

97. Royal & Sun Alliance, Old Hall Street, by Tripe & Wakeham (1972–6)

front, a large aluminium sculpture by *Patrick Glyn Heesom*, the 1965 winner of a competition held by Littlewood's. Opposite, No. 105, completed 2004, a twenty-eight storey apartment tower, plus hotel and health club, designed by *Abbey Holford Rowe*; No. 101, by the same, is to be offices. Part of the site was occupied from *c.* 1790 by a basin of the Leeds and Liverpool Canal, and a brick canal building of *c.* 1800 remains (reconstructed) in front of the new hotel. It was originally one of a pair, flanking the entrance to Mr Clark's wharfside coalyard. On the E side, **Lancaster House**, 1936, built as a telephone exchange with training facilities for telephone engineers. Seven storeys, brick, with rounded corners, subdivided by bold fins from first to fourth floor.

Old Haymarket

Facing St John's Gardens and the w front of St George's Hall is the main entrance to the first **Mersey road tunnel** (Queensway) linking Liverpool with Birkenhead on the Cheshire bank. The tunnel was constructed 1925–34 by the engineers *Basil Mott* and *J.A. Brodie*, with *Bertram Hewett* as engineer-in-charge. It was one of the great engineering feats of its day, being at 2.1 m. (3.4 km.) – or 2.9 m. (4.6 km.) including its branches – the longest underwater road tunnel in the world. The entrance is by *Herbert J. Rowse*, appointed architect to the tunnel in 1931. Curved retaining walls of Portland stone – sleek and sheer, suggesting speed and efficiency – flank the semicircular arched entrance, with a relief of two winged bulls above, 'symbolic of swift and heavy traffic'. Art Deco carved decoration by *Edmund C. Thompson* and *George T. Capstick*. The walls end in sturdy arched lodges with fluted column-like buttresses. Overlooking the traffic from either side, bronze **statues** of George V and Queen Mary by *William Goscombe John*, 1939, originally behind the tunnel entrance, facing w. The layout in front has also changed, the most significant loss being the great lighting column faced with black granite opposite the entrance.

Rowse also designed a second entrance near the docks in New Quay with associated ventilating station (*see* Old Hall Street, p. 160), ventilating stations in North John Street (*see* p. 156) and at the Pier Head (*see* Major Buildings, p. 72), plus corresponding structures on the Birkenhead (Cheshire) side. All are characterized by cubic shapes and square towers. Rowse was also responsible for the tunnel interior, now altered, which had a black glass dado framed in stainless steel.

Rainford Square and Rainford Gardens
See Button Street and Mathew Street.

Sir Thomas Street
No. 14, the former City Education Offices, 1897–8, by *Charles E. Deacon*. High, narrow façade in a French late Gothic-early Renaissance style, with much carving. Impressive central staircase enclosing a lift – the original arrangement. Board Room with elaborate Renaissance plasterwork, and a beautiful chimneypiece, delicately carved. No. 20, **Minerva Chambers**, *c.* 1885. A striking design: a sort of palazzo, but with a very irregular window rhythm. Thin columns rise one above the other from basement to first floor, their proportions more like cast iron than stone. Transoms cut across where the first- and second-floor window arches spring. Parapet panels carved with ferns.

Stanley Street
Nos. 6–20, **Granite Buildings**, *c.* 1882, by *G.E. Grayson*. Built as offices and warehousing for the fruit and provision trade. The façade originally had three gables, the middle one now lacking. It is entirely of granite, polished, rough, or fitted together in an irregular jigsaw, reminiscent of Jesse Hartley's dock buildings. Tripartite windows divided by cylindrical columns. The style is a sort of simplified classicism, perhaps determined by the intractability of the granite. The rear is a complete contrast: the n end has office-type windows but the rest comprises a row of gabled warehouses. Utilitarian white glazed-brick facing. **Kansas Buildings**, at the corner of Mathew Street, is a good office-warehouse block in crisp red brick and terracotta, probably 1890s. Halfway along the side elevation of the former General Post Office (*see* Victoria Street, p. 167) a **sculpture**, Eleanor Rigby, a poignant seated female figure in bronze, by *Tommy Steele*, 1982.

The Strand

As the name indicates, here was the shoreline of the Mersey before land was reclaimed for dock construction. The traffic island in the middle marks the site of the Goree Warehouses, a mighty early C19 arcaded range, demolished following Second World War bomb damage

For West Africa House *see* Water Street, p. 172; for the White Star Line offices *see* James Street, p. 153. No. 7, **Wellington Buildings**, a twelve-storey classical block of *c.* 1923 by *Colin S. Brothers*. **Beetham Plaza**, built as offices in 1965–7 by *Gotch & Partners*, was converted into apartments by *Brock Carmichael Associates*, completed 2000. Facing the courtyard opening to Drury Lane, ground-floor restaurant with wavy glass wall. Also an ingenious **fountain** by *Richard Huws*, completed 1966. Pivoted cups of various sizes, mounted on posts, fill with water until they overbalance, producing random cascades.

Sweeting Street

Barned's Buildings, *c.* 1840, an early purpose-built office block. Three storeys, with a pedimented centre and classical details. It looks like a terrace of houses, except for the cast-iron hoists indicating the basement was used for warehousing. Recently converted into flats.

Tempest Hey

Mostly demolished. One unusual survivor, a block of four storeys plus basement, with narrow round-arched windows to the stone-fronted ground floor. Designed in 1849 by *William Culshaw* for Messrs Rowlinson, brokers. Their offices were on the ground floor, with a sales room above, the remaining floors being for storage and warehousing.

Facing the s end of Tempest Hey is the five-bay, palazzo-style N elevation of **Percy Buildings**, probably mid-C19. The long return elevation to **Eberle Street** has brick piers, separating huge windows with central cast-iron mullions. Here are the premises of the Liverpool Artists' Club, containing a bronze war memorial of 1919 by *C. J. Allen*.

Temple Court

See Mathew Street and Victoria Street.

Tithebarn Street

One of Liverpool's seven ancient streets (*see* topic box, p. 6).

Nos. 7–17, **Silkhouse Court**, by *Quiggin & Gee*; designed by 1964, built 1967–70. Fifteen-storey tower with three-storey corner blocks. Glazing and concrete cladding in alternate bands, the panels faced with chippings of granite. Next door, **Mercury Court**: façadism on a monumental scale. This was originally a hotel and offices above ground-floor shops fronting Exchange Station, the terminus of the Lancashire & Yorkshire Railway (closed 1977). The first station opened in 1850. To avoid interfering with neighbouring streets and the Leeds and Liverpool Canal, tracks and station were elevated high above Tithebarn Street. In 1882 it was decided to rebuild on a larger scale, level with the street, and *Henry Shelmerdine* was appointed architect. The two phases were completed in 1886 and 1888. Shelmerdine's façade is stone, classical, eighteen bays long, with a higher central section marking the twin-arched main entrance. Office complex behind *c.* 1985, by *Kingham Knight Associates*. Opposite, at the corner of Moorfields, two good Victorian pubs: **The Railway**, with stained glass illustrating the 1886 Exchange Station and its forerunner, and **The Lion**, mid-C19 with a rich and well-preserved interior of *c.* 1900.

On the N side, at the corner of Pall Mall, the former **Bradford Hotel**. Begun 1880s and extended. Italianate, with a little domed corner turret. (On the E side of Pall Mall, near the junction with Leeds Street, a very large apartment block by *Falconer Chester*, 2003; for the rest of Pall Mall *see* Walk 7, pp. 251–3.) Nos. 59–61, dated 1871, were built as a printing and bookbinding factory with integrated warehousing. Yellow brick; large windows with cast-iron mullions.

Further E at the corner of Smithfield Street, a fine, crisply detailed classical building, originally the **College of Commerce**, 1928–31 by the City Surveyor, *Albert D. Jenkins*. Brick and Portland stone. Corner crowned with a sculpture of Neptune in a ship's prow. Both elevations have applied porticoes, the one towards Tithebarn Street with reliefs of shipping by *Hooper & Webb*. Extension along Tithebarn Street by *Ronald Bradbury* completed in 1953, another at the back begun 1965. Attached, and united internally, is the **Avril Roberts Learning Resource Centre** of Liverpool John Moores University, by *Austin-Smith:Lord*, opened 1998. Curved plan, following the street line. Façade of brick at each end, glazed in the centre, with a clerestory right across. The brick parts have asymmetrical windows. Behind the glazed part is the impressive full-height entrance space, with an elegant but vertiginous steel staircase, lit by deep, circular skylights. The top-floor reading room has more of these skylights. It is a mezzanine or deep gallery, overlooking the floor below under the sweep of the monopitch roof. Concave rear elevation of brick, with glazed ground floor and windows of various shapes and sizes above, overlooking a garden.

Victoria Street

Victoria Street was cut through an area of narrow, congested streets to improve the flow of E–W traffic. Opened in 1868, it was mooted at least as early as the 1840s. The w part became the centre of the fruit and provision trade, lined with offices, warehouses and dealing rooms. Despite losses it remains one of the best-preserved Victorian streets in the city, especially rich in commercial buildings of the 1880s. The view E is closed by the Picton Reading Room dome (*see* Major Buildings, p. 62).

98. Fowler's Buildings, Victoria Street, by J.A. Picton (1865–9)

North John Street to Stanley Street. No. 1, N side, built as offices above a restaurant, 1881, by *Cornelius Sherlock* for the brewer Andrew Barclay Walker. Italianate, with splendid chimneystacks. Next door, **Fowler's Buildings**, the earliest building of any pretension in the new street [98]. A nine-bay stone palazzo with extensive polychrome brick warehousing behind, designed by *J.A. Picton* and built in two phases, 1865–9. Granite columns to the principal floor and curvy, almost Baroque window surrounds on the floor above. An odd segmental pediment supporting an urn sits on top of the cornice. After this, Nos. 11–13, built 1926–8 as Lloyds Bank by *Grayson & Barnish*. Handsome five-bay palazzo in grey brick with Portland stone dressings. The banking hall has giant Ionic columns. Next, **Victoria Buildings**, a quiet palazzo with the centre curiously recessed, then No. 21, **Union House**, dated 1882. Its conventional classical façade with a ground-floor colonnade of red granite conceals a more functional building: the side elevation to Progress Place (through archway, left) has large areas of glazing and exposed cast iron. Entrance vestibule, with good wrought-iron gates and a plaster frieze illustrating tea shipping, etc., leads to an impressive cast-iron staircase. No. 25, next door, is by *W.H. Picton*, 1881. Office block with rusticated granite ground floor, upper floors of brick with stone dressings. Simpler rear part containing offices and warehousing.

The s side starts at the corner of North John Street with **Century Buildings**, 1901 by *Henry Hartley*. Rather Glaswegian-looking on account of its red sandstone, with a polygonal turret and Renaissance details. Then No. 8, **Produce Exchange Building**, 1902, by *Henry Shelmerdine*. Big, loosely Baroque, with a little turret in the form of a tempietto. The ground floor of grey granite was a Lancashire &

99. Commercial Saleroom Buildings, Victoria Street, by James F. Doyle (opened 1879)

Yorkshire Railway goods depot, and a goods entrance survives at the back in Mathew Street. In the foyer a First World War memorial by *Edward Carter Preston*, a bronze plaque with classical figures. Next door, the former **Fruit Exchange**, *c.* 1888, also built as a goods depot, this time for the London & North Western Railway. Converted into an exchange by *J.B. Hutchins*, 1923. Thirteen-bay façade in Flemish Renaissance style with an oriel at each end. After this, a domestic-scaled building with rainwater head dated 1831, a survivor from before the creation of Victoria Street, rounds the corner into Temple Court. Between Temple Court and Stanley Street, **Commercial Saleroom Buildings**, by *James F. Doyle*, opened 1879 [99]. It cost £15,000. Queen Anne style, red brick with stone dressings above granite. Three principal storeys, crowned by a frieze carved with swags and a pretty balustraded parapet, and decked out with attractive wrought-iron gates and balconies. The ground floor contained a saleroom for fruit, connected by lifts with basement storerooms.

Stanley Street to Crosshall Street. The N side starts with **Lisbon Buildings**, 1882, and **Ashcroft Buildings**, 1883, the latter by *Hoult & Wise*, two exuberant red brick piles with plenty of carved stone decoration. Ashcroft Buildings was put up by James Ashcroft, cabinetmaker and manufacturer of billiard tables, for his showrooms and workshops. The flat roof was used for seasoning timber. Next, between

Cumberland Street and Sir Thomas Street, the comparatively sedate former **Bank of Liverpool**, 1881–2, by *George Enoch Grayson*. Classical, stone, with a central pediment and attached columns of polished grey granite. The car park between Sir Thomas Street and Crosshall Street is the site of Government Buildings, a very large classical block demolished in the 1940s, exposing the plain brick rear of the Municipal Buildings (*see* Dale Street, p. 147). On the s side, occupying the block between Stanley Street and Sir Thomas Street, are the remains of the former **General Post Office**, 1894–9 by *Henry Tanner*, with sculpture by *Edward O. Griffith*. The original design – livelier than Tanner's slightly earlier London GPO in St Martin's le Grand – resembled a Loire château with an eventful skyline of shaped gables, chimneys and pavilion roofs, but the top two floors were removed following war damage. The remaining two floors are to be converted into a shopping centre (*see* Walk 3, p. 191). At the corner of Peter Street, No. 40, Venetian Gothic in polychrome brick dated 1869, then the Conservation Centre (*see* Walk 3, p. 190).

Fireproofing

Warehouse fires were a scourge of C19 Liverpool, and with warehouses scattered throughout the town the threat was general. In the great Formby Street fire of 1842 goods and buildings to the value of almost half a million pounds were destroyed. A number of local Building Acts (1825, 1835, 1842 and 1843) aimed to control warehouse design and construction, to reduce the threat of fire and restrict its spread. Completely fireproof construction was not insisted upon, presumably because of the building costs involved. Instead, simple and practical regulations were introduced: for instance, height restrictions in relation to street width; walls of a minimum thickness, carried up above the eaves; and external features traditionally made of combustible timber (loading doors, window frames) made of iron instead. From 1843 warehouses were registered and graded according to their conformity with the Building Acts, those that were safer enjoying lower insurance premiums. The use of timber for the internal structure remained standard for most of the C19 (e.g. Edward Graham's range in Button Street, etc.); fireproof construction, with arched brick floors on cast-iron columns [65], was less common (e.g. P.W. Brancker's Clarence Warehouses, Great Howard Street. *See* Walk 2, p. 126).

Fireproof construction was also used for office buildings, for instance C.R. Cockerell's Liverpool & London Insurance Co. *The Builder* in 1865 noted that 'Fire-proof flooring is much in esteem in Liverpool. It comes, perhaps, of a community of merchants that chances should be calculated to a nicety, and that all risk should be reduced to the minimum as far as expenditure can insure that desirability'.

Crosshall Street to Manchester Street and Whitechapel. The N side begins with the former printing works of Tinling & Co., 1961–3 by *Morter & Dobie*, with a jagged sawtooth arrangement of windows to Crosshall Street. Then **Crown Buildings**, 1886, Gothic, with a corner turret, followed by the more characterful **Jerome Buildings**, 1883, and **Carlisle Buildings**, 1885, both by *John Clarke* for H. Rankin, whose Union Foundry close by supplied structural ironwork. Identical above the ground floor, they form a single composition. Red Ruabon brick, with red Runcorn stone dressings and red roof tiles. The most prominent feature is the row of six dormer windows, each with a pyramid-shaped roof. Next, Nos. 75–77, **Abbey Buildings**, 1885, Tudor Gothic, with three gables and an oriel over the entrance. All these have warehouse-type rear elevations with loading bays. This side ends with a restrained classical block by *F. & G. Holme*, turning the corner into Manchester Street. With Abbey Buildings it was elegantly converted into apartments by *Urban Splash Projects*, 1990s. They substituted a minimalist top floor for the original decorative chimneys and dormers.

On the S side, the triangular block bounded by Victoria Street, Crosshall Street and Whitechapel was transformed into City Council offices by *Falconer Chester*, 1990s, and named **Millennium House**. Some older buildings were replaced, the façades of others retained. The new parts are rather plain and mostly faced with green and buff brick, with a sweeping metal roof at the Crosshall Street end. The C19 frontages are a brick palazzo by *John Clarke*, 1878–9, with matching elevation in Whitechapel, and the classical **Imperial Buildings**, 1879 by *E. & H. Shelmerdine*, impressively sited at the sharp corner of Victoria Street and Whitechapel. It is faced with cream terracotta, by *Gibbs & Canning* who supplied the material for Waterhouse's Natural History Museum in South Kensington. Female figures representing Commerce and Industry stand sentinel below the corner dome.

Water Street

One of the seven ancient streets (*see* topic box, p. 6), sloping dramatically down to the Pier Head with tall buildings framing the river view.

Starting next to the Town Hall (*see* Major Buildings, p. 42), the former headquarters of **Martins Bank** (now Barclays), 1927–32, is the masterpiece of *Herbert J. Rowse*, and among the very best interwar classical buildings in the country. Won in a competition judged by Charles Reilly, the design perfectly expresses the American classicism promoted through Reilly's Liverpool School of Architecture, where Rowse studied before travelling in Canada and the United States. Portland stone on a steel frame, ten storeys, the upper ones set back. Ornament is judiciously concentrated at top and bottom, more emphasis being placed on beauty of proportion than on surface decoration. Interior more

100. Former Martins Bank, Water Street, by Herbert J. Rowse (1927–32)

opulent. The central entrance leads to a majestic top-lit banking hall, with island counter and vaulted arcades on four sides [100]. Travertine walls, floor and columns (the latter hollow, threaded on to the frame), relieved with gilding, bronze and coloured marbles. Every detail, down to the stationery holders, was overseen by Rowse. Circular corner lobbies, those at the sw and NE giving access to lettable offices on the upper floors. These cantilever out over the banking hall, up to the skylight edges. The eighth-floor board room is like the hall of a Renaissance palace, with large chimneypiece and painted, beamed ceiling. On the roof are penthouses for lift machinery and a flat for the manager, linked by colonnades enclosing a roof garden. Interior and exterior **sculpture**, illustrating themes of money and the sea, is by *Herbert Tyson Smith*, assisted by *Edmund Thomson* and *George Capstick*. The flat, linear style is influenced by the Paris Exhibition of 1925. The main bronze doors are specially notable.

No. 3, at the corner of Lower Castle Street, follows the old line of the s side, before 1920s street widening. It is a sober mid-C19 palazzo, with an elaborate E doorway added for the Manchester and Liverpool District Bank, 1883. No. 7, all in grey granite, is of two phases. The Fenwick Street elevation, *c*. 1896 by *Grayson & Ould*, originally for the Bank of Liverpool, has Celtic interlace ornament in the lunettes. The front block to Water Street was demolished and rebuilt further back *c*. 1933–4 by *Palmer & Holden*, for the National and Provincial Bank (the Bank of Liverpool, united with Martins in 1918, having moved across the road). It seems to be modelled on Sanmicheli's Palazzo Pompei, Verona. Of the same date the splendid bronze doors with ferocious lions' heads, and the barrel-vaulted banking hall with Art Deco reliefs.

Palmer & Holden's façade follows the building line established by its giant neighbour, **India Buildings** [101]. *Arnold Thornely* and *Herbert J. Rowse* won the competition for this in 1923 (assessor Giles Gilbert Scott). Completed 1930; extensively damaged by bombing in 1941, and reconstructed under Rowse's supervision. Built for the shipping firm Alfred Holt & Co., it is nine storeys and occupies an entire block, containing offices, shops, a bank (formerly), a post office, and access to the James Street underground station (*see* p. 152). In scale, combination of functions, and architectural treatment it emulates the most ambitious early C20 American commercial buildings. Steel-framed, cliff-like Portland stone walls, Italian Renaissance detail. Arched entrances in Brunswick Street and Water Street (bronze lamps by the *Bromsgrove Guild*, modelled on those of the Palazzo Strozzi, Florence) open into spacious elevator halls, vaulted and lined with Travertine, linked by a noble tunnel-vaulted arcade of shops through the centre (not part of the competition-winning design). Corner entrances, NE and SE, lead to polygonal lobbies. On the ground floor between them the former bank (now offices), with an impressive coffered ceiling. Office floors above,

101. Left, No. 7 Water Street, by Palmer & Holden (1933–4); right, India Buildings, by Arnold Thornely and Herbert J. Rowse (completed 1930)

round two light-wells. Sculpture of Neptune above the Water Street entrance by *Edmund C. Thompson*. Opposite, at Nos. 8–12, **Norwich House**, by *Edmund Kirby & Sons*, *c.* 1973. Pre-cast concrete cladding, with projecting lips framing the windows.

No. 14, at the corner of Covent Garden, is **Oriel Chambers**, 1864 by *Peter Ellis*. Liverpool's most celebrated Victorian office block, reviled in its day, but elevated to the status of a Modernist icon after bomb damage in 1941 exposed its cast-iron frame and attracted the attention of historians. In 1969 Pevsner described it as 'one of the most remarkable buildings of its date in Europe'. Its façades (basement and three and a half storeys) are mostly of glass. The tall oriel windows with their extremely slender cast-iron frames are individually boxed out ('suggesting the idea that they are trying to escape from the building', according to the *Building News*, 1868) and separated by narrow stone piers with nailhead decoration [15]. The piers end in ungainly pinnacles, and the parapet has battlements and an elaborate central gable, but otherwise few details are based on historical precedent. The dominant motif is the relentlessly repeated oriel, expressing the modular cast-iron frame and leading Charles Reilly to call the building 'a cellular habitation for the human insect'. Desks positioned in these projecting windows received light from top and sides as well as in front. The elevation to Covent Garden was originally almost twice as long: the bomb-damaged N part was replaced in 1959–61 with a sensitive addition by *James & Bywaters*. The C19 offices are arranged on each side of a corridor, aligned with the off-centre entrance on Water Street. The exposed

102. Tower Buildings, Water Street, by Walter Aubrey Thomas (designed 1906, completed by 1910)

utilitarian H-section stanchions of the frame support fireproof floors of shallow brick vaulting. On the w the offices overlook a courtyard, reached via a passage on the left of the Water Street façade. The elevations here are even more startling: the glazing is cantilevered out in front of the stanchions in horizontal bands – a pioneering instance of curtain walling.

Next door, **New Zealand House**, *c.* 1893 by *Walter Aubrey Thomas*, and surprisingly restrained for him. Then **Reliance House**, 1954–6 by *Morter & Dobie*, tasteful Neo-Georgian. H-plan, Portland stone in front, mostly brick behind. Flanking the side entrance in Tower Gardens are two mosaic panels depicting shipping, salvaged from the Edwardian Baroque predecessor, bombed 1941. Finally on this side, No. 22, **Tower Buildings**, by *Thomas* again, designed 1906, completed by 1910 [102]. Steel-framed, clad in white glazed terracotta by *Doultons* above grey granite, with a bizarre mix of Baroque and medieval motifs. The Water Street entrance has two generous round arches. Main elevation facing George's Dock Gates symmetrical, with three short towers having square, crenellated angle turrets. The medieval tower of the Stanley family, fortified 1406 and demolished 1819, was here. Opposite, **West Africa House**, by *Briggs, Wolstenholme & Thornely*, complete by 1920. Another good, American-influenced Portland stone block, this time with Greek rather than Italian Renaissance details.

Inner Districts

Walk 3.

Between Church Street and Lime Street

This walk covers the area E of Whitechapel and Paradise Street, roughly bounded by Hanover Street, Ranelagh Street, Lime Street and St John's Lane. Whitechapel and Paradise Street follow the course of a stream, covered over by 1725, which widened out into the tidal inlet known as the Pool on the site of Canning Place, before entering the Mersey. This stream effectively formed the E boundary of the town until the end of the C17. The land to the E came under Corporation control in 1672. It began to be laid out with streets from that date, and was built up during the course of the C18. During the C19 shops came to predominate, and Church Street became the city's main shopping street. Large-scale redevelopment, beginning in the 1960s, has erased the historic street pattern in the N and E of the area.

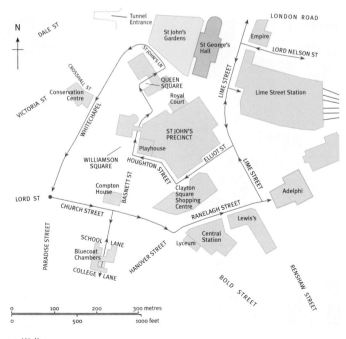

103. Walk 3

We begin at the w end of **Church Street**, where it joins Lord Street (*see* p. 154). Excavations here in 1851 uncovered the stone bridge built in 1672 by the 3rd Lord Molyneux, to carry Lord Street over the stream. It was a single sandstone arch, 12 ft (3.7 metres) wide. Church Street takes its name from the demolished St Peter (*see* topic box, p. 179). No. 2 on the corner of Paradise Street is the former **Seel's Building**, completed by 1872. A rare essay in commercial architecture by *Edward Welby Pugin*, best known for his R.C. churches. Gothic, rock-faced with ashlar dressings, with second-floor balconies and an angled corner entrance. The piers separating the two-light windows break forward to support the balconies, then recede, only to be corbelled out again on the third floor, creating an oddly undulating façade. The initial letter S of the Seel family is worked into the balcony tracery. Ground floor altered. Next door, the former **Cooper's** store (now W.H. Smith), *c.* 1920 by *Gerald de Courcy Fraser*. The principal, E elevation overlooking St Peter's churchyard was obliterated by an extension to the neighbouring store. The elevation to Church Street has a square tower and Mannerist details. Between here and Church Alley, occupying the site of St Peter and its churchyard, is the sprawling bulk of the former **Woolworth's**, 1923, by the firm's house architect *William Priddle* (now HMV, Top Shop, etc.). Coarse classical, with a large glazed area in the middle. Portland stone, rather than Woolworth's usual white faience. (It is an indication of Liverpool's prosperity at this date that Harrod's considered a branch on this site, and commissioned a design from *Willink & Thicknesse*.)

On the opposite side, at the corner of Williamson Street, a former branch of Lloyds Bank in red brick with a green copper roof strikes a colourful note. By *Herbert James Rowse*, 1930–1. Carved decoration in Portland stone, now unfortunately painted, by *Herbert Tyson Smith* and *Edmund C. Thompson*. The round-arched windows and parapet are Neo-Romanesque, but much of the ornament is Art Deco. After this, the Italianate shop now occupied by **Clarks** was designed by *Lewis Hornblower*, *c.* 1858, for the art metalworkers and electroplaters Elkington's. *The Builder* disliked the thin columns to the upper floors, 'which suggest rain-water pipes without being so'.

Filling the block between Tarleton Street and Basnett Street is the majestic **Compton House** (now Marks & Spencer) [104]. Built for the retailer J.R. Jeffery, whose premises on the same site burnt down in December 1865. The replacement was designed within two weeks by *Thomas Haigh & Co.*, builders, and opened just eighteen months later. It is of international significance as an exceptionally early purpose-built department store, finished five years before the Bon Marché in Paris. J.A. Kilpin, President of the Liverpool Architectural Society, described it in 1867 as a building 'which neither London, nor Paris, nor Genoa, nor Venice, nor Rotterdam, nor any other city . . . can excel in richness of architectural decoration, I mean as built for business purposes by a

104. Compton House, Church Street, by Thomas Haigh & Co. (opened 1867), C19 print

single firm'. The show front is a very elaborate affair in stone, eleven bays and four storeys with a big square tower at each end. These originally had high pavilion roofs, giving a distinctly French Renaissance look. In fact the façade bears a close resemblance to Les Magasins Réunis, a Parisian shop complex by *Gabriel Davioud*, begun in 1865. Much carved decoration (by Messrs *Williams*), including a figure of Commerce over the entrance. The interior, now altered, was thoroughly fireproofed. On the upper floors were extensive workshops, as well as sleeping accommodation and recreational facilities for live-in staff. Side elevations largely of brick, reduced in length.

Turn down Church Alley, opposite Compton House. On the right at the corner of School Lane is the **Athenaeum**, a private club designed by *Harold Dod* in 1924. This institution, the only one of Liverpool's subscription libraries and news rooms to survive into the C21, dates back to 1797; it originally occupied a building in Church Street by the elder *John Foster*, demolished for street widening. Chaste American classicism, with a strong French accent. The club occupies three floors above ground-floor shops. The simple, segment-headed entrance, its keystone carved with the head of Athena, said to be by *H. Tyson Smith*, leads via a broad corridor to an elegant elliptical staircase. The best interior is the second-floor Library [105]. Shallow segmental vaulted ceiling with Greek Revival decoration, and three subsidiary bays, separated by paired columns. Three large paintings by *Edward Halliday*, part of the original decoration, show The Contest between Athena and Poseidon, The Story of Marsyas, and Athena and Arachne. Their restrained classicism, without strong shadows or violent action, is a good match for the architecture.

105. The Athenaeum, Church Alley, by Harold Dod (1924), library

Closing the view down Church Alley is **Bluecoat Chambers**, begun 1716, the oldest surviving building in central Liverpool and, at the time it was erected, by far the largest secular building in the town [106]. Now a centre for the arts, it was built by Bryan Blundell, a sea captain, as a residential charity school for poor children. The original purpose is recorded in Latin across the façade, with the date 1717. The school opened in 1718, though building continued for a few years. It had fifty children by 1719, with room for 100 more. Despite alterations, extensions and reconstructions, it retains its early c18 appearance to a considerable degree. It is of brick with painted stone dressings and encloses three sides of a quadrangle, separated from School Lane by a low wall with railings and gatepiers. Two-storey central block with round-arched windows, the middle three bays breaking forward slightly under a pediment crowned with a pretty timber cupola. Two wings, just one bay wide and not quite parallel, extend forward on each side. They have three storeys rather than two, creating a discordant effect at the inner corners where the different levels collide. The ground- and first-floor windows of the wings are square-headed, those on the top floor oval, while the end elevations have arched windows that match the central block. All the large windows have keystones carved with cherubs' heads, presumably alluding to the building's function. The arched windows have unusual double surrounds: a moulding round the opening, and a separate, outer frame with pilasters supporting an arch. The main door has Ionic columns and a broken segmental pediment, apparently copied from St Peter's church, which stood opposite (*see* topic box, facing). The wings have three square-headed doors each, charmingly approached by ziggurat-like flights of steps.

The interior has been much altered, but vaulted cellars survive under the E wing and the original ground-floor plan can be traced in the shops which occupy both wings. When William Enfield described the school in 1773, the upper floor of the main block contained 'a large room, employed as a chapel and for other purposes'. This may have been the original arrangement, and is the same as the early C18 Grey Coat Hospital school, Westminster. Access would have been by the open newel staircase in the SE corner, extensively repaired but apparently incorporating early C18 work.

Who was the architect of this ambitious building? *Thomas Ripley* has been suggested, largely on the grounds that he is known to have designed the stylistically similar Custom House (demolished) shortly afterwards. Another candidate is *Thomas Steers*, the dock engineer, whose name appears in Blundell's account book for the school. However, there is no conclusive evidence that either was involved.

106. Bluecoat Chambers, School Lane (begun 1716)

107. St Paul, by
Timothy Lightoler
(1763–9).
Engraving by
E. Rooker after
P.P. Burdett (1773)

As Liverpool expanded in the C18, several ambitious churches were built in the centre, all since destroyed. In 1699 the town was made a parish, and the parish church of St Peter was erected (completed 1704). It stood in Church Street, at the corner of Church Alley. Possibly designed by *John Moffat*, it served as pro-cathedral from 1880, and was demolished in 1922. Fine woodcarving by *Richard Prescot*, formerly in the chancel, was removed to St Cuthbert and St Stephen-in-the-Banks, both in North Meols (*see* the forthcoming *Buildings of England: Lancashire: Liverpool and the South West*). In 1726–34 St George was built on the site of the castle. It was the chief architectural work of the dock engineer *Thomas Steers*, and had a classical tower and spire. Subsidence led to its reconstruction by *John Foster Jun.*, 1819–25. It was demolished in 1897, and the Queen Victoria monument now stands in its place. St Thomas, on the E side of Park Lane near Cleveland Square, also classical with a tall spire, was built 1748–50 by *Henry Sephton*. St Paul, in the centre of St Paul's Square, was an impressive domed building of 1763–9 by *Timothy Lightoler*, demolished in 1932 [107]. The same architect was probably responsible for the Gothic St John, built 1775–83, demolished 1898; its churchyard became St John's Gardens. The only C18 church remaining in the centre is the dignified but unassuming St Peter (R.C.) in Seel Street, begun 1788.

Originally it appeared less severe: there were statues at the corners of the pediment, and the brick parapet was interspersed with lengths of balustrade and had urns at the corners – details removed during major early C19 repairs and enlargements with which *John Foster* (Sen. or Jun.?) and the builder *Bartin Haigh* were involved. The biggest change was at the back. In *c.* 1723 thirty-six almshouses for rent to the parish had been added here, in the form of wings enclosing a quadrangle, open towards College Lane. The rear of the central block originally resembled the front, but in 1821 it was rebuilt by Haigh in its present convex form. It is not clear when the almshouses were removed, but the utilitarian buildings now enclosing the rear courtyard look early C19.

The Blue Coat School moved to Wavertree in 1906, and the future Lord Leverhulme bought the building and saved it from demolition. After bombing in 1941, a sensitive restoration by *Shepheard & Bower* was completed in 1951. This is commemorated by a tablet in the NE corner of the front courtyard, flanked by reliefs of a Blue Coat girl and boy by *Herbert Tyson Smith*. The same sculptor replaced some cherub keystones, and the cartouche with a Liver bird over the main door is his. In the 1990s the central steps were replaced with a ramp. The craft shop at the back of the rear courtyard has metal and glass screens towards College Lane, by *Helen Brown* and *Gareth Roberts*, completed 1999.

The area s of Bluecoat Chambers, bounded by College Lane, Hanover Street and Paradise Street, is largely derelict in 2004, but there are plans to redevelop it as an extension of the shopping area. In College Lane are two four-storey brick **warehouses**, apparently in existence by 1803 and, if so, among the earliest surviving in the city. They have central loading bays, the doors more or less flush with the façade.

Return to Church Street via Church Alley. On the right looms the enormous **Spinney House**, built for Littlewoods Mail Order Stores and designed by *Alfred Shennan*, 1951–5. One of the city's earliest large-scale postwar efforts, it is hardly a forward-looking landmark: faced in Portland stone with Art Deco-classical details, it might have been designed twenty years earlier. Carved decoration by *Herbert Tyson Smith*. Church Street entrance remodelled in the form of a tunnel by *OMI Architects*, *c.* 2003. Outside, a bronze **statue** of Sir John Moores, founder of Littlewoods, and his brother Cecil. By *Tom Murphy*, unveiled 1996.

Opposite this on the corner of Basnett Street stands a more interesting department store, now part of John Lewis, but built as the **Bon Marché** in 1912–18. By *Gerald de Courcy Fraser* again, Portland stone on a steel frame, decorated with an odd mix of French Renaissance trophies (one on Basnett Street includes a First World War tank) and ancient Egyptian motifs. Upper floors added *c.* 1922–3. Next door, a simpler Portland stone block of 1928 by *Hillier, Parker, May & Rowden* sweeps round into Parker Street. On the opposite corner, an attractive stuccoed building, possibly 1880s, with charming grotesque decoration in low relief. Six doors along from this in Church Street is an unusual shop, a scaled-down version of a starkly simple design published by *T. Myddelton Shallcross* in 1905. It has canted bay windows, sandwiched between square piers that rise above the cornice to frame a balustrade

108. Premier Buildings, Church Street, by Gerald de Courcy Fraser (1912–14)

of little square pillars. Simple elongated brackets support the cornice. Opposite, a good former branch of the Bank of Liverpool (now Alliance & Leicester), 1913–15, Baroque, the ground floor mutilated for a large window. Finally, at the Hanover Street corner, the best of *Gerald de Courcy Fraser*'s big classical blocks, **Premier Buildings** (now Lloyds TSB), 1912–14 [108]. It is tall – eight storeys – and the proportions are narrow, emphasized by thin vertical corner strips against channelled rustication. First-floor windows round-arched; those on the two floors below the main cornice recessed between square piers with quirky Mannerist capitals.

Marking the end of Church Street is a bronze **sculpture**, The Great Escape, by *Edward Cronshaw*, the result of a competition in 1994: a man restraining a rearing horse made of unravelled rope. For the Lyceum, *see* Walk 4, pp. 192–4.

Turn left into **Ranelagh Street**. The right side as far as Fairclough Street is occupied by **Liverpool Central**, a complex of shops above an underground station of the Merseyrail network, arranged round an L-shaped arcade under a glazed roof running through to Bold Street. Designed by *Edmund Percey Scherrer & Hicks* and completed *c.* 1984, it was refaced in 2001 by the *Owen Ellis Partnership*, who also redesigned the glazed roof. Street elevations rendered and painted white, with large areas of glass framed by steelwork. The arcade leads to the top-lit concourse of the station, linked by escalators to the platforms, all designed by *British Rail London Midland Region* architects and opened 1977. The same surface finishes are used throughout the underground: white ceramic tiles for concourses, yellow melamine cladding for corridors and escalators, and on the platforms modular units of dark brown fibreglass incorporating signage, seating and litter bins. What is now the Northern Line platform was opened in 1892 as the terminus of an eastward extension of the Mersey Railway connecting Liverpool with Birkenhead (*see* James Street, p. 152). The engineers were *James Brunlees* and *Sir Douglas Fox*, with *C.A. Rowlandson* and *J. Fright*. Here, partly obscured by the 1977 redesign, the sheer walls cut into solid sandstone can still be seen, roofed over with brick jack arches. Behind the present concourse and reached via Fairclough Street is the site of the demolished Liverpool Central Station, built for the Cheshire Lines Committee and opened in 1874. Its massive stone walls now enclose a car park. Abutments of the vanished glass and iron roof can be seen on the w side.

The left side of Ranelagh Street as far as Cases Street has mostly C19 shops, including a very tall, narrow, polychrome Gothic one dated 1868. Next door, turning the corner, is the **Abbey National**, handsome classical stucco with giant pilasters, 1843 by *William Culshaw*. (Closing the end of Cases Street, an entrance to the Clayton Square Shopping Centre, *see* below, p. 187.) The **Midland Hotel** on the opposite corner also looks mid-C19, but has a rich pub front of *c.* 1900: Ionic pilasters of shiny grey granite with bow windows squeezed between, and Art Nouveau copper and wrought-iron work. Next door, the **Central Hotel** bears the date 1675, for which there seems no justification, though its origins go back further than 1887, the other date on the façade. Probably converted from pub to hotel in response to the opening of Central Station. Interior 1970s Neo-Victorian, incorporating genuine C19 woodwork and brilliant-cut mirrors.

At the top of Ranelagh Street, on the corner of **Renshaw Street**, is **Lewis's** enormous department store. The present building, designed in 1947 by *Gerald de Courcy Fraser* and carried out by *Fraser, Sons & Geary*, replaced Lewis's previous store, also by *Fraser* and put up in stages 1910–23, which was devastated in the Liverpool blitz of May 1941. Part of the earlier façade survives at the E end of the Renshaw Street elevation: Portland stone, eight storeys, with slim red granite columns dividing the windows. When this extended round the corner in an unbroken sweep, Lewis's must have been the most impressive of Fraser's Liverpool department stores. The postwar rebuilding is also Portland stone, and to the same height. The divisions echo those of the older building, but the style is a stripped-down classicism. The corner was to have been concave, but was made flat as a setting for the giant bronze **statue** by *Jacob Epstein* above the former main entrance [109]. A nude male figure, striding forward purposefully on the jutting prow of a ship, it dates from 1954–6 and symbolizes Liverpool's resurgence after the war years. Below, three lively relief panels in *ciment fondu*, also by Epstein and made in 1955, show scenes of childhood. They represent the new generation for whom the city was being rebuilt. Inside, the former cafeteria on the fifth

floor (no longer accessible) has a huge tile mural in Festival of Britain style by *Carter's* of Poole, showing food and crockery.

In **Ranelagh Place**, closing the view up Ranelagh Street, is the **Adelphi Hotel** (now the Britannia Adelphi). It is the successor to two earlier Adelphi hotels, of 1826 and 1876. The latter was bought in 1892 by the Midland Railway Co., who replaced it in 1911–14 with the present building by *Frank Atkinson*. Then regarded as the country's most luxurious hotel outside London, its French-influenced classicism invited comparison with the most sophisticated Continental establishments. Its size and splendour reflect Liverpool's key position in transatlantic travel in the early C20. The hotel was unfinished at the outbreak of the First World War and the original plan was never completed. The decorative carving by *H.H. Martyn & Co.* is very restrained, and the exterior is more notable for its smooth, cliff-like walls of Portland stone in which the large windows are set almost flush. This flatness hints at the hidden steel frame. Inside, the main spaces of Atkinson's broadly symmetrical

plan survive, but his refined decoration has been much altered. From
the low entrance hall steps rise to the large, top-lit Central Court, lined
with pink marble pilasters. Glazed screens with French doors fill the
arches between, and open into large restaurants on either side. Ahead
lies the Hypostyle Hall, a square space with impressive Empire-style
decoration and four massive Ionic columns supporting the ceiling;
beyond this originally lay the open-air Fountain Court, surrounded on
three sides by terraces under vaulted ceilings. The Fountain Court was
to have been enclosed on its fourth side by a ballroom block, but this
was never built.

The chaste classicism of the Adelphi contrasts with the **Vines**, next
door on the corner of **Lime Street** and Copperas Hill [110]. This very
large, riotously Baroque pub was built in 1907 to the designs of *Walter
W. Thomas* for the Liverpool brewer Robert Cain. The ground floor of
polished red granite has bow windows (the brilliant-cut panes mostly
replaced with etched copies) and monstrously elongated keystones
above the doors. The skyline is enlivened by three big Dutch-looking
gables and a high cylindrical corner tower, capped with a dome and a
squat little obelisk. Inside, the sumptuous fittings include plaster reliefs
by the *Bromsgrove Guild* and *Gustave Hiller*. A little further along Lime
Street, on the same side, is the former **Futurist Cinema**, now disused.
Built as the City Picture House, 1912, by *Chadwick & Watson* of Leeds.

The classical terracotta façade has been painted. Central part altered probably c. 1920, when the shallow bow window was added. Opposite is one of the more appealing postwar commercial buildings, designed as a dress shop with offices above by *William L. Lowe & Partners*, c. 1952. Lemon yellow, red and pale blue cladding – ceramic? – with a recessed balcony on the top floor. Next door, rounding the corner into **Elliot Street**, the disused former **Forum Cinema** by *William R. Glen*, opened 1931. Sleek Portland stone façade with almost no decoration, subtly modelled in advancing and receding planes. Auditorium subdivided, but retains some original decoration. Back on the other side of Lime Street, on the corner of **Skelhorne Street**, the **Crown Hotel**. Taken over by Peter Walker & Sons 1905, it must have received its façade not long afterwards: an extravagant stucco panel bearing the brewery's name is on Skelhorne Street, presumably to entice passengers from the nearby railway station. Interior with lush plaster ceiling and beaten-copper bar front. On the opposite corner of Skelhorne Street, **Concourse House**, a thirteen-storey tower of 1967–8 by *R. Seifert & Partners*. Supported on distinctive columns each made up of two attenuated, interpenetrating triangles, faced in white mosaic. Serving as a podium to the tower is a curved row of single-storey shops with a roof terrace.

After this comes the principal (but rather makeshift) pedestrian entrance to **Lime Street Station**. The monumental building in front is by *Alfred Waterhouse*, 1868–71 [112]. Originally the station hotel, it reopened in 1996 following conversion into a student hall of residence. Symmetrical, except for the differing oriels in the end pavilions. Five storeys plus dormers, with pavilion-roofed corner towers, and two further towers with short spires flanking the central entrance: the splendid skyline is visible from far away. Windows mostly round-arched or with straight tops on quadrant curves. Statues over the main entrance by *Farmer & Brindley*, perhaps representing Europe and America. Waterhouse's competition-winning design was for a brick building with stone dressings, but presumably because of its proximity to St George's Hall the façade was carried out entirely in stone. Inside, a staircase with open well and cast-iron handrail leads visibly right up to the top floor.

As for the **station** itself, it is the successor to two earlier ones, the first opened 1836, the second completed 1850 (*see* topic box, p. 188). The present iron and glass train shed behind the former hotel was begun in 1867 by *William Baker* and *F. Stevenson* and had then the largest span in the world, though it was almost at once outstripped by London's St Pancras. The span is 200 ft (61 metres), carried by sickle-shaped beams on massive Doric columns. The shed curves in plan. A second shed, parallel and virtually identical, was added ten years later. This time the supervising engineer was *E.W. Ives* and the roof was put up at a rate of three bays per month, 1878–9. Restoration and re-glazing of the entire roof, completed in 2001, has revealed it as a thing of spectacular beauty [111]. Incorporated into the cast-iron colonnade on platform 1 is

111. Lime Street Station roof

a group of four columns, more closely spaced than the rest. Designed by *Edward Woods*, they date from the 1846–50 rebuilding, and are all that remains of a bridge which carried Hotham Street over the tracks. Enclosing platforms 1–6, a two-storey L-shaped building of black glass, containing booking office, restaurants, etc. Designed by *British Rail London Midland Region* architects, completed by 1984. Of the same date, a long glass screen dividing platforms 7–9 from the concourse, with an etched mural by *Dianne Redford, Lindsey Ball, Andrew Cooper* and *Clifford Rainey*, now sadly neglected. The design alludes to the early history of the station and of the tunnel linking it with Edge Hill.

Cross **Lord Nelson Street** (which has an early C19 terrace, and at Nos. 17–19 the former **Socialist Hall of Science**, *c.* 1840, subsequently used as a concert hall) to the **Empire Theatre**, which in its present form is by *W. & T.R. Milburn, c.* 1925. Portland stone façade with paired giant Ionic columns. Auditorium with graceful classical plasterwork. On the N side, rounding the corner into London Road, a weak glazed extension, 2002.

Return to Concourse House and cross Lime Street to **Elliot Street**. On the right is one flank of the massive St John's Precinct, seen better by descending the steps at the bottom.

The irregular open space at this lower level is a faint echo of Clayton Square, one of the few attempts at formal Georgian planning in central Liverpool. It was built up slowly from 1751 on land leased by Sarah Clayton. In the 1920s the NW half was built over with a single block (now **Tesco Metro**, etc.), designed by *Walter Aubrey Thomas* and originally intended as a hotel. With the plans amended by *Stewart McLauchlan*, it opened in 1925 as a department store. Portland stone, with giant three-storey pilasters turning into piers at the top, as on Thomas's earlier Crane Building in Hanover Street (*see* Walk 4, p. 200). It had a central light-well with a glazed roof. More recently, the SE half of the square was completely rebuilt by the *Seymour Harris Partnership* as the **Clayton Square Shopping Centre**, opened 1988. The walls have round-arched windows and are faced with bands of blue and red brick and light-coloured artificial stone, in imitation of High Victorian polychromy. Shops on two levels, round a cruciform arcade under glazed barrel vaults, with a glazed dome over the crossing. The inspiration no doubt came from Victorian precedents such as Manchester's Barton Arcade, but the steelwork here is comparatively clumsy. Originally, the shorter arm of the arcade was open from pavement to roof, but the first-floor shops were later extended across, giving the ground floor a confined, oppressive feel. The short arm continues the line of Cases Street, knitting the building into the old street pattern.

Overlooking the square from the N is the **St John's Precinct**, designed by *James A. Roberts* of Birmingham, but much altered. Permission was given in 1962 and it opened in stages from 1970. It combines a covered market, shops on two levels, a hotel and a multi-storey car park, and covers *c.* 6.2 acres (2.5 hectares). The sloping site was previously occupied by small streets surrounding the old St John's Market, a very large and severely functional building by *John Foster Jun.*, opened in 1822. The precinct is a bleak and brutal affair, monolithic, inward looking, and awkwardly related to the different levels of adjoining streets. The side facing Lime Street and St George's Place is truly disastrous, failing to establish any coherent relationship with the s portico of St George's Hall, and presenting an off-putting barrier in the form of access ramps

112. Former Lime Street Station Hotel, by Alfred Waterhouse (1868–71)

The Liverpool & Manchester Railway

Transport by canal between the Mersey and Manchester was slow, costly and unreliable: sometimes cargo took longer to get from Liverpool to Manchester than to cross the Atlantic. To improve communications the idea of a railway was promoted, largely by Liverpool businessmen. *George Stephenson* was appointed engineer, Parliamentary approval was obtained in 1826, and the line opened on 15 September 1830. At 31 m. (50 km.) long, it was the world's first major public railway: it ran to a timetable, carried passengers as well as freight, and provided a commercial and social link between two great centres. It ushered in the worldwide transformation of land transport in the C19.

The line approached Liverpool from the E, and at Edge Hill entered a tunnel 2,240 yd. (2,048 metres) long, terminating close to the docks at Wapping. This tunnel is no longer used. Parallel with it, a shorter tunnel went from Edge Hill to the passenger terminus at Crown Street, from which travellers were taken by omnibus to the centre. In 1832–5 the railway was brought by tunnel from Edge Hill to a new station in Lime Street, opened the following year. For many years trains were hauled through these tunnels by stationary engines situated at Edge Hill.

The first Lime Street station had a train shed 55 ft (17 metres) wide. The timber roof, partly glazed and carried on cast-iron columns, was by *Cunningham & Holme*. In front was a Neoclassical screen by *John Foster Jun.*, the first example of a monumental station façade. In 1846–50 the station was rebuilt behind. Offices by *William Tite* were erected facing Lord Nelson Street, and an iron roof by *Richard Turner* of Dublin constructed over the tracks. This had a single span of more than 153 ft (47 metres), and was then the largest iron roof in existence anywhere.

and a sunken roadway. The dominant feature – also dominating much of the city centre – is the so-called Beacon, over 450 ft (137 metres) high, really a giant chimney for the boilers. It was apparently modelled on the Euromast at Rotterdam. The revolving restaurant near the top was converted into a radio station *c.* 1999, and the metal structure above, triangular in plan, added to carry advertising. Earlier 1990s alterations, by *Bradshaw, Rowse & Harker*, aimed to give a friendlier look: clumsy external staircases and a ballroom on top of the car park were demolished, and large parts of the remainder clad in decorative brick and reflective glass. The strong horizontals were broken up by little gables, and brightly coloured metal pediments introduced above the entrances. Whatever interest Roberts's design may have had as an example of heroically scaled Modernism was lost through this prettification.

Leave Clayton Square by **Houghton Street**. On the left is a disparate group of buildings occupied by the **John Lewis Partnership** department store, formerly George Henry Lee's. The block on the corner with **Basnett Street** is dated 1897. It was apparently not occupied by Lee's until 1908, when it was reconstructed to designs by *Henry Hartley* with marble pilasters framing the display windows. Attractive plasterwork survives inside. In 1910 the façade was doubled along Basnett Street as far as **Leigh Street**, and in 1928 a more ambitious addition by *Gunton & Gunton* of London was built on the corner of **Houghton Lane**. Of Portland stone with giant Ionic columns, it is an adaptation of the façade of Selfridge's in London, which took over Lee's in 1919. It looks like a fragment of something meant to be bigger, and it was indeed intended that more of the store would be rebuilt to this pattern. For the John Lewis Partnership's building on the corner of Basnett Street and Church Street, *see* p. 180.

Houghton Street opens into **Williamson Square**, built up on the w side by 1765. Traffic-free since the 1970s, the first stage in a pedestrianization scheme that now covers much of the shopping area. c18 houses survive on the w, considerably altered. On the e side is the **Playhouse**, built 1865. It was reconstructed in 1895, which may be the date of the unexciting stuccoed façade. In 1910 it was acquired by the Liverpool Repertory Theatre, and in 1911 the auditorium and basement foyer were redesigned in an impressive Neoclassical manner by *Stanley D. Adshead*, Professor of Civic Design at the Liverpool School of Architecture. In 1968 a startling **extension** [113] by *Hall, O'Donahue & Wilson* was completed, comparable with Patrick Gwynne's exactly contemporary addition to the York Theatre Royal. The rear part houses dressing rooms and a large workshop, the front, foyer spaces and bars.

113. Playhouse extension, Williamson Square, by Hall, O'Donahue & Wilson (completed 1968)

It is a spectacular composition based around three cylinders. The largest starts at the first floor and is two storeys high. It is fully glazed and cantilevers from a central column over the pavement. To the left, a smaller cylinder, also cantilevered from a central column but only partly glazed, interlocks with the first. The third element is inside: a hollow column, originally containing the box office, around which stairs climb to the floors above. The interior creates an atmosphere of excitement and anticipation, exactly right for a theatre foyer, and at night the exterior is equally thrilling.

Leave the square by **Brythen Street**, past an entrance to the St John's Precinct, and turn right into **Roe Street**. On the right is the red brick Art Deco **Royal Court Theatre**, by *James B. Hutchins* of *Wainwright & Sons*, 1938. Its shorter façade was designed to face Great Charlotte Street, now largely absorbed by the precinct. The longer side faced **Queen Square**. The original square no longer exists but its name survives, attached to the wide, busy road lined with bus shelters, and to the recent buildings on the far side. The **bus shelters** and the **Queen Square Centre** with conical roof and clock turret, lower down on the same side as the theatre, are by *Brock Carmichael Associates*, *c*. 1995. The buildings on the far side were put up from *c*. 1995 on a site cleared thirty years earlier. Most prominent is the **Marriott Hotel** by *Falconer Chester*: a round tower with three wings, two containing bedrooms, the lower one a health club. It is linked to a multi-storey car park by the same architects, faced with brown and blue brick like a Victorian warehouse. A far cry from the Brutalist expression of levels in 1960s car parks, it follows a recent fashion for cloaking such buildings in historical dress. Between is a paved square containing a **sculpture**, Unknown Landscape 3, by *Nicholas Pope*, made for the Liverpool International Garden Festival 1983–4 and re-erected here 1998. Other new buildings fringing the square are depressingly tawdry.

Behind in **St John's Lane** is a lone Victorian survivor, the former **Pearl Life Assurance**, 1896–8, by *Alfred Waterhouse*. Stone, with an octagonal corner tower and spire, adapted from the architect's National Liberal Club in London. Part of the ground-floor interior survives, with colourful *Burmantofts* faience. Continue down St John's Lane. At the bottom on the left is the **Observatory**, offices by *Falconer Chester* completed in 2000. Its fully glazed façade sweeps round into **Whitechapel**.

On the corner of **Whitechapel** and Crosshall Street is the former Midland Railway goods warehouse, 1872–4 by *Culshaw & Sumners*, with matching addition of 1878 facing Peter Street. It is now the **Conservation Centre**, converted for the conservation studios of National Museums Liverpool by *Ken Martin*, *c*. 1995, with minimal changes to the polychrome brick and stone exterior [114]. More decorative than the average warehouse, it nevertheless gives an impression of great strength and solidity. The main façade is concave, following Crosshall Street, and has windows in giant round arches. Immense doorways to Whitechapel,

114. Former Midland Railway goods warehouse, Whitechapel, by Culshaw & Sumners (1872–4), converted to Conservation Centre by Ken Martin (*c.* 1995)

Peter Street and Victoria Street are high enough to admit the largest loads. Inside the double-height entrance hall are two weathered sculptures from elsewhere in the city: Liverpool, by *John Warrington Wood*, originally on the roof of the Walker Art Gallery, and Eros, by *Alfred Gilbert*, part of a copy of the Piccadilly Circus Shaftesbury Memorial set up in Sefton Park in 1932 (*see* Walk 10, p. 291). Next to the Conservation Centre at the corner of Peter Street, a building with incised Greek ornament, probably 1870s. On the other corner, Tudor Gothic offices (now flats) in red brick with yellow sandstone, by *John Clarke* for William Bennett, 1881–2. Further along the same side of Whitechapel, between **Sir Thomas Street** and **Stanley Street**, is intended to be the **Met Quarter**, a shopping centre designed by *Austin Associates*, part of which will occupy the shell of the former General Post Office on Victoria Street (q.v., p. 167). Construction began in 2000. Opposite, on the corner of **Richmond Street**, a large Gothic block of *c.* 1875 by *H.H. Vale*, of stone-dressed white brick, originally with black pointing.

Continue along Whitechapel and turn left into Church Street. This leads to Bold Street, where Walk 4 begins.

Bold Street – Duke Street Area

Spreading E from Canning Place, the site of the first enclosed dock, this area was developed between the mid C18 and the early C19. Some of the grandest early houses were on the SE side of Hanover Street, with long fields running uphill behind, a pattern reflected in the straight streets running NW–SE that are characteristic of the area. Affluent housing existed alongside industries associated with the port (ropewalks, timber yards, cooperages, foundries) and early merchants' dwellings were often physically linked to their warehouses and counting houses. By the mid C19 the rich had moved further out, leaving the district to industry, warehousing and the poor. Bold Street escaped this fate, becoming the favoured location of high-class shops. Regeneration began in the 1990s with the conversion of a few older industrial buildings to residential and leisure use. New developments are now transforming this area of extraordinary architectural and historical richness.

We begin at the NW end of **Bold Street**, which occupies the site of Joseph and Jonathan Brooks's rope walk [118]. Charles Eyes's 1785 map shows the street laid out, and according to Picton it was mostly built up by 1796. It was originally residential (above ground-floor level many late Georgian house fronts of brick or stucco remain) but soon the houses gave way to shops. In 1826 the *Liverpool Repository of Literature, Philosophy and Commerce* described it as 'this imperial trading street, where every year the shops are ousting from it clusters of dwelling-houses – and such shops! Paramount, princely, nay imperial in their way. Here taste, elegance and display are in their element.' Bold Street remained a byword for exclusive shopping until the Second World War. Its fortunes have since declined steeply, but architectural evidence of its former character survives throughout. It has largely retained its domestic scale, giving a feeling of intimacy which is enhanced by the pedestrianization of its lower half.

At the foot is the former **Lyceum** of 1800–2, designed by *Thomas Harrison* and built by *William Slater* [116]. A chaste Greek Revival structure in ashlar, and one of the finest early buildings of Liverpool. The principal façade faces NW: four demi-columns with windows between, and a pedimented window on either side. Above the central windows are reliefs of Geography, Apollo and Commerce, by *F.A. Legé*. The Bold

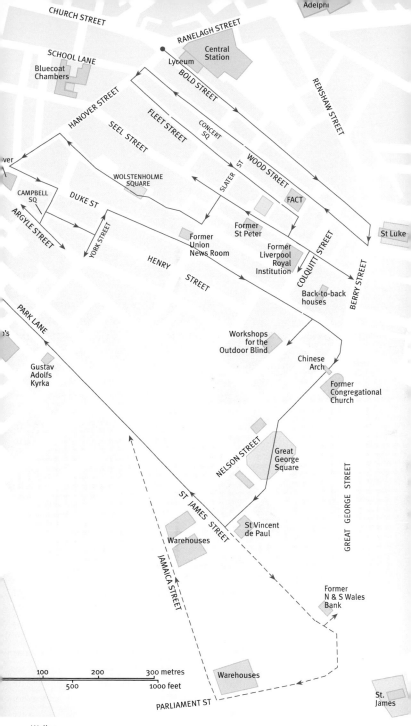

CHURCH STREET

RANELAGH STREET

Adelphi

SCHOOL LANE

Central Station

Bluecoat Chambers

Lyceum

BOLD STREET

HANOVER STREET

SEEL STREET

FLEET STREET

CONCERT SQ

WOOD STREET

RENSHAW STREET

WOLSTENHOLME SQUARE

ver

CAMPBELL SQ

DUKE ST

SLATER ST

FACT

St Luke

ARGYLE STREET

YORK STREET

HENRY

STREET

Former Union News Room

Former St Peter

Former Liverpool Royal Institution

COLQUITT STREET

BERRY STREET

Back-to-back houses

PARK LANE

o's

Gustav Adolfs Kyrka

Workshops for the Outdoor Blind

Chinese Arch

Former Congregational Church

NELSON STREET

Great George Square

GREAT GEORGE STREET

ST JAMES STREET

St Vincent de Paul

Warehouses

JAMAICA STREET

Former N & S Wales Bank

100   200   300 metres

500   1000 feet

Warehouses

St. James

PARLIAMENT ST

115. Walk 4

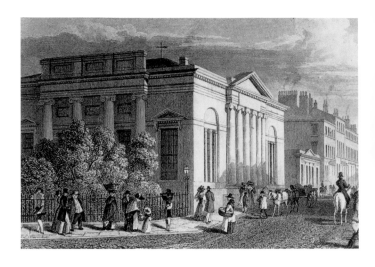

Street façade has a recessed Ionic portico of six columns, flanked by tripartite windows under segmental arches. Now converted to a variety of uses including a post office, it was designed to house two separate institutions, the Liverpool Library (a private subscription library founded in 1758, one of the oldest in the country) and a news room. The library occupied the galleried rotunda in the centre, lit by a glazed opening in the dome. The plaster and woodwork here are probably by *Slater* rather than Harrison. The former news room at the NW end, commanding the view down Church Street, has a segmental vaulted ceiling and a wide arched recess opposite the windows, with friezes painted rather naïvely in grisaille to imitate classical relief sculpture. They are mostly adapted from the Parthenon and the temple of Apollo Epicurius at Bassae. (The temple at Bassae was excavated in 1812 by the Liverpool architect John Foster Jun., in the company of C.R. Cockerell; casts of both the Parthenon and Bassae friezes were in the collection of the Liverpool Royal Institution by 1823.) The present ceiling is a restoration, part of a refurbishment by *Edmund Percey Scherrer Hicks*, completed 1990. The room had been subdivided horizontally in 1903, resulting in the loss of Harrison's original ceiling. The basement, entered from the NW end, has Edwardian-looking plasterwork and woodwork. Threatened with demolition for a shopping development in the 1970s, the Lyceum was only saved after a vigorous battle by conservationists.

The opposite side begins with a former branch of the North and South Wales Bank (now **HSBC**), 1903, by *James F. Doyle*. Edwardian Baroque in brick and stone, with attached columns above the corner entrance. Ground floor altered. Nos. 14–16 have an impressive shopfront with large areas of plate glass rising through two floors [117]. Built for John Cripps, Shawl Merchant and Manufacturer, who moved to these premises in 1848, the front was certainly in existence by 1861, and

116. The Lyceum, Bold Street, by Thomas Harrison (1800–2). Engraving by Henry Jorden, after G. & C. Pyne (1828)

117. Nos. 14–16 Bold Street

is therefore an exceptionally early survival of its type. The first-floor extension to the right is later, and the whole was carefully restored in 1981 by *Mansfield Design Partnership*. Such lavishly glazed fronts were made possible by new technology which facilitated the production of glass in larger sheets. Next door at Nos. 18–26 is the former **Radiant House**, by *Ernest Gee* of *Quiggin & Gee*, opened in 1938 as offices and showrooms for the Liverpool Gas Company. Faced in quartzite, with fluted columns of Swedish green marble to the ground floor, the sheer façade is broken only by a bronze balcony at first-floor level. Despite the setting back of the top two storeys it dwarfs its neighbours, bringing the scale of nearby c20 Church Street (Walk 3) into c18 Bold Street, but it is a stylish job. Higher up on the same side, at the corner of Concert Street, is the former **Music Hall**, 1852–3 by *Arthur Holme*, ornate Italianate in brick and stone, now painted. It replaced a Music Hall of 1785–6 by *Charles Eyes*, burned down in 1852. The auditorium of the present building was on the first floor, with shops below, but within a few years it was entirely given over to retail use. Entrance remodelled with paired columns, 1990s. At the back in Wood Street a colonnade, probably part of Eyes's building. *Pilkington's* supplied stained glass in 1853: could the large window above the colonnade be theirs? In Concert Street a cast-iron sculpture, Reconciliation, 1989, by *Stephen Broadbent*: two embracing figures.

Returning to Bold Street, No. 58 has an Arts and Crafts façade of *c.* 1900, attributable to *T. Myddelton Shallcross*. Leaded glazing across the first floor breaks forward into three shallow oriels; eaves cornice supported on deep brackets. The large Italianate block at Nos. 43–47, by *G.E. Grayson*, was completed in 1885 as a branch of the Union Bank of Liverpool. The ground floor had shops flanking a lofty central doorway leading to the banking hall. Now it is shops right across, though the segmental pediment of the doorway survives, with nice carving. Opposite, on the corner of Slater Street, a former branch of **Lloyds Bank**, designed in the late 1920s by *George Hastwell Grayson* (G.E. Grayson's son) in partnership with *Leonard Barnish*. Top two storeys set back above the cornice, which approximates to the height of Bold Street's Georgian buildings. Large flat expanses of Portland stone, subtly relieved with crisp carving (perhaps by *H. Tyson Smith*) and areas of horizontally channelled rustication. Higher up on the opposite side, Nos. 75–79 seem to be of 1833 and by *Joseph Franklin*. They are of stucco and form a Greek Revival composition of five bays, with a pediment supported by Ionic columns set in, and smaller pediments at each end supported by pairs of very thin pilasters.

No. 92 has an exceptional Graeco-Egyptian façade of *c.* 1879, strikingly similar to Alexander 'Greek' Thompson's work in Glasgow of twenty years earlier [119]. The glazing of the first floor runs unbroken

Rope Walks

118. Rope walks on the site of Bold Street, from George Perry's map (1769)

There were many roperies on the edges of the C18 and early C19 town, where rope for the rigging of sailing ships was manufactured. The work required a straight, narrow stretch of ground, somewhat longer than the rope to be made – the roperies that occupied the site of Bold Street were over 300 yd (274 metres) long. Plant fibres such as hemp were spun into yarn by the ropemaker walking backwards from a spinning wheel, paying out fibre from a bundle round his waist. Groups of yarns were then connected to a set of rotating hooks at one end of the ropery and a single swivelling hook at the other end and wound together, each group of yarns forming a strand. Finally, the strands were twisted tightly round each other to form a stable rope that would not unravel. This stage, known as 'laying' the rope, involved the ropemaker walking along the ropery, pushing a grooved tool called a 'top' between the wound-up strands. Because of the spinning and 'laying' stages of the process, roperies were known as rope walks.

119. No. 92 Bold Street, perhaps by W. & G. Audsley (*c.* 1879)

behind the masonry, and the top floor is an open loggia. Who designed this curiosity? The most likely candidates seem to be the brothers *W. & G. Audsley*. No. 96, dated 1866, has two red granite columns to the ground floor and sculpture with musical allusions above – it was the pianoforte warehouse of Messrs Dreaper. At No. 100, the Queen Anne style makes its only appearance in the street, in a façade of finely jointed small red bricks, dating from *c.* 1879. This is followed by an open space, Ropewalks Square, created in 2002 to provide a way through to FACT (*see* p. 199). Higher up on the opposite side, at the corner of Roscoe Place, is the former head office of the **Liverpool Savings Bank**, a six-bay palazzo by *William Culshaw*, 1861. The National Debt Commissioners, acting in the interests of depositors, at first stipulated that the building should be 'free from all useless ornament', but were persuaded to allow greater expenditure (the total was about £9,000) because the site had been acquired cheaply. A mixture of brick and stone was intended at first, but stone was used throughout. The unarchaeological capitals of the ground-floor windows seem to be adapted from Cockerell's recently completed Liverpool and London Insurance Co. (*see* Dale Street, p. 144). The sills on Bold Street have been lowered, making it look less like a bank and more like the shop it has become.

At the top, cross Berry Street to the church of **St Luke** [120], a proud building with a high, graceful tower, rising impressively from a steep flight of steps and dominating the view up Bold Street. Burned out in the Second World War and now a roofless shell. It was built by the Corporation, whose Surveyor, *John Foster Sen.*, made plans as early as 1802. The foundation stone was not laid until 1811, and work dragged on for a further twenty years, so it is unclear what, if anything, can be traced back to the 1802 design. In 1811 Rickman was shown what seem

120. St Luke, Berry Street (foundation stone laid 1811)

to have been new drawings, made by a 'young man' in Foster's office, to which he suggested amendments; Picton later wrote of St Luke that 'rumour ascribed the design to [Foster's] assistant, *Mr Edwards*'. For its date it is an unusually rich and ambitious Gothic Revival design in the Perpendicular style. Three-stage tower, the top richly panelled, with ogee hoodmoulds over the belfry windows. Octagonal clasping buttresses rise above the pierced and battlemented parapet to become tall turrets. Tucked into the angles between tower and aisles are single-storey porches. The aisles have very large windows, separated by buttresses carrying big pinnacles. In 1822 it was decided to add a chancel. One of the most striking features of the building, this is based (fairly loosely) on the c15 Beauchamp Chapel at Warwick. Such a large chancel, distinguished from the body of the church by its richer architectural treatment, is exceptional before the propaganda of the Ecclesiological Society. The elder Foster was succeeded as Corporation Surveyor by his son, *John Foster Jun.*, who completed the church, having in 1827 sought permission to make internal and external changes. The interior does not survive, but nave and aisles were of nearly identical height, with plaster vaults and a gallery at the w end only. A font (damaged), designed by *W. & G. Audsley* in the early 1870s and carved by *Norbury*, survived in 2001. The tower contains a cast-iron bell frame of 1828 by *George Gillebrand*. Around the site are Gothic cast-iron railings, by *Foster & Griffin*, and octagonal stone piers with lushly crocketed tops. This enclosure, never used for burials, was laid out as a garden in 1885. The ruins were earmarked for demolition in the 1950s and 1960s, but have come to be regarded as a war memorial. Early C19 houses overlook the church from **Bold Place**.

The E side of **Berry Street** was rebuilt to its present line *c*. 1900. On the opposite side, with a curved corner to Bold Street, is **Havelock Buildings**, *c*. 1858, four-storey stuccoed shops with showrooms and living accommodation above, by *Horace Field Sen.* of London. The original design had prominent chimneys and a pierced parapet. By 1861 it contained Stortz's Photographic Art Studio, with an exceptionally large glass house, 55 ft (16.8 metres) long, 'built on purpose for taking album portraits.' This room survives on the top floor, still partly glazed, and can be seen from the back. Between Wood Street and Seel Street are the premises of the mason and builder *John Walmsley*, designed and erected by himself *c*. 1798. They formed a U-shaped block, open to Berry Street, but the central yard was later filled in. The much-altered stucco façades of the wings, with pediments and pilasters, can still be traced.

Cross Berry Street and continue down **Wood Street**, which runs parallel to Bold Street. It is dominated at this end by the red brick mass of **Royal House**, a telephone exchange by *Building Design Partnership*, completed 1974. A large building on a confined site, its bulk broken down by the division of the two longer façades into projecting bays. Continue down Wood Street. On the left, just beyond Colquitt Street, is a well-proportioned brick warehouse with fireproof floors, all that remains of the **Apothecaries' Hall**, rebuilt following a fire in 1846. Extended and converted into flats 2004. The elaborate stone front to Colquitt Street, 1837 by *Cunningham & Holme*, was a war casualty.

Next is **FACT** (for Film, Art, Creative Technology), completed 2003, by *Austin-Smith:Lord*, containing cinemas and galleries for electronic media. The façade to Wood Street and Back Colquitt Street is a rather depressing grid of identical square zinc panels, sweeping unbroken round the corner above a blue brick plinth. Small windows take the place of a few panels, and there is a large, curved area of glazing over the corner entrance, but the overall impression is of a metallic screen, as regular as graph paper. By contrast the elevation to Fleet Street is mostly glass, and jutting through it at divergent angles above the ground floor are the blank end walls of two cinema auditoriums. Inside is a multi-level foyer, complex and exciting, defined by the curved undersides and walls of the auditoriums, which seem suspended overhead [26]. A curving staircase rises behind the big window on the corner of Wood Street.

Next door is the **Tea Factory**, a former warehouse, the earlier part (adjoining FACT) by *Gerald de Courcy Fraser*, *c*. 1930. Conversion into loft apartments and offices over ground-floor bars, by *Urban Splash Architects*, was completed in 2002. For most of its length, the opposite side has utilitarian workshops and warehouses of the second half of the C19 – the backs of Bold Street shops – but shortly above the junction with Slater Street are a couple of earlier, more domestic-looking façades. Were these offices, attached to merchants' houses in Bold Street? Crossing Slater Street, the **Liverpool Palace** shopping complex on the left occupies a four-storey, early C19 stuccoed block which housed the Liverpool Ophthalmic Infirmary from 1820 and the Institution for the Instruction of the Deaf and Dumb from 1825.

At the intersection with Concert Street, **Concert Square** opens on the left, a lively and informal space overlooked by refurbished industrial buildings. These include **Holme's Buildings**, polychrome brick warehouses dated 1867 and 1869, and on the opposite side a former chemical factory, now bars, restaurants and a gallery, with flats above. The earliest part of this, a boldly modelled four-storey red brick range with segmental arched windows facing Wood Street, dates from *c.* 1896. It is a fragment of a block designed by *Aston Webb*, grandson of the founder of the chemical firm Evans, Sons & Co. The conversion was completed in 1994 by the developers Urban Splash and designed by their in-house architects *Design Shed*, who also laid out the square. Apart from the docks, this was the first residential refurbishment of an industrial building in the city centre, and a catalyst for subsequent developments in the area. At one corner of the square is The Tango, a painted steel sculpture by *Allen Jones*, commissioned for the 1984 Liverpool International Garden Festival and relocated.

Continuing down Wood Street, on the left are the former premises of the *Liverpool Mercury*, dated 1879 on the chimney. The Italianate yellow brick front part, with round-arched cast-iron windows, contained the newspaper's offices; the factory-like block at the rear housed the presses. Closing the view down Wood Street is the former **Crane Building** (now Hanover House) in Hanover Street, 1913–15 by *Walter Aubrey Thomas*. Built as a store selling musical instruments, it is one of the most striking structures of its date in the city. Buff-coloured terracotta is used for the richly decorated lower floors, the capitals of the giant pilasters, and the massive cornice. These areas of decoration are separated by large expanses of plain wall, following American precedents for the treatment of tall buildings. On Hanover Street, the red brick pilasters emerge in their upper parts to become piers, a motif apparently derived from St George's Hall. Inside, a theatre with Neoclassical auditorium.

Turn left along **Hanover Street**, which in the C18 was lined with the substantial houses of merchants. The Hanover Hotel at the corner of Fleet Street is apparently a much-altered survival from this period. Opposite is **Abney Buildings**, 1883, almost certainly by *Henry Hartley*, a large red brick commercial block with minimal Queen Anne details in stone. Turn left into **Fleet Street**. On the right, opposite Roe Alley, an early C19 warehouse (now flats); further up on the same side, a warehouse conversion by *Shed KM*, 2003–4, with a glazed second-floor projection to the side elevation. Higher up on the left, after Concert Square, Vanilla

Factory: glass-fronted new-build offices by *Shed KM*, 2003–4. Next door, the **Baa Bar**, an industrial building of 1897, converted in 1991 by *Design Shed*. Steel supports of a type used in motorway construction hold up the façade at ground-floor level. This was probably the first 'designer' conversion of a Liverpool industrial building into an entertainment venue. Opposite is the side of the former **St Andrew's Schools**, a stuccoed classical block of 1818 paid for by the merchant John Gladstone. It provided places for 150 boys and 130 girls. The entrance is in Slater Street, next to the simple, pedimented **Charitable Institution**, funded by Gladstone and others, which provided free accommodation for Liverpool charities.

Cross Slater Street and continue up Fleet Street. First on the right is an early C19 warehouse, forming the return elevation of No. 13 Slater Street. Higher up on the same side, St Peter's Square is one of several landscaped spaces formed in 2002–3 to improve pedestrian movement through the area; another is under construction (2005) at the top, opposite the back of FACT. Turn right here along Back Colquitt Street and left into Seel Street. On the corner of Seel Street and **Colquitt Street**, part of a terrace of houses of *c.* 1800, described by Picton as 'commodious and respectable', now partly converted to commercial uses. Across Colquitt Street is the former Royal Telephone Exchange, 1939, by the *Office of Works*, of thin Roman bricks with recessed pointing, punctuated with tall, narrow windows: a well-mannered Modernist design which takes account of its Georgian neighbours. (For the adjoining new exchange, *see* above, p. 199). Continuing up Seel Street, this is followed by a terrace which seems to have formed the flank of Walmsley's yard (*see* above, p. 199). Near the junction with Berry Street, a good doorway with Composite columns and open pediment. The large pub of 1899 on the opposite side of Berry Street, vaguely Jacobean with a big curvy gable, closes the view along Seel Street.

Return down the other side of **Seel Street**, which begins with a 1790s terrace. On the corner of Colquitt Street stands the former **Liverpool Royal Institution**, built *c.* 1799 as the combined residence and business premises of Thomas Parr, and in Picton's words 'one of the best examples extant of the establishment of a first-class Liverpool merchant of the period' [121]. What was Parr's house faces Colquitt Street, with lower pavilion blocks on each side connected by single-storey screen walls with niches. That on the right was the carriage house, on the left the counting house. Behind the latter is Parr's five-storey warehouse, a dignified structure with pediments on three sides, unsympathetically converted into flats in the 1990s. The house occupies a surprisingly confined site, but when built it had a large garden on the opposite side of Colquitt Street. From 1815 the buildings were adapted as the Liverpool Royal Institution, dedicated to the promotion of literature, science and the arts. *Edmund Aikin* was architect for the remodelling, and the porch is his, an early and influential use of Greek Doric in Liverpool (*Thomas*

Rickman helped with the drawings); the ubiquitous *John Foster Jun.* was also involved from 1822. The most prominent addition is the large, windowless block behind, built to contain a lecture theatre with top-lit exhibition rooms above.

Further down Seel Street on the same side is the former **St Peter (R.C.)**, the oldest surviving church in the centre. As constructed in 1788 – three years before the Catholic Relief Act – it was a simple brick box with a pedimented gable, five bays long, with round-arched windows above and segmental ones below. It would have been virtually indistinguishable from a Methodist chapel. The exterior brickwork was later covered with render, scored to resemble masonry. In 1817 *John Slater* was paid £1,060 for extending the w end. He added an extra bay and transept-like projections, N and S, containing stairs up to the gallery. In the one facing the street is the main entrance, with fluted Doric columns and a frieze displaying the date of foundation (*Thomas Rickman* may have supplied the drawing for this). A large, square sanctuary, hidden behind the adjoining house on the E, was formed *c.* 1845 by 'Mr Picton' – presumably *J.A. Picton*. The interior has unfortunately been stripped of furnishings, but retains its three galleries on timber columns. The flat ceiling has been removed, revealing the kingpost roof. The sanctuary, with Corinthian pilasters and a pedimented aedicule that once framed an altarpiece, still has its segmental plaster ceiling. To the left of the church is the former school of 1831, distinguished by its pediment. The rest of Seel Street above Slater Street has houses of *c.* 1800, mostly derelict. On the corner of Slater Street, and also derelict, a building occupied by watchmakers in the second half of the C19, with generous windows to the former workshops. Beyond, on the same side, a terrace of five houses of the 1790s with pedimented doorcases in pairs.

Return to Slater Street and turn right, then right again at Parr Street and into **Wolstenholme Square**. Little remains to show that for a time

121. House and warehouse of Thomas Parr, Colquitt Street (*c.* 1799). Adapted as the Liverpool Royal Institution from 1815

122. No. 12 Hanover Street, by Edmund Kirby (1889–90)

in the C18 this was a select quarter. The s side was built up by 1765, and two altered houses survive at the SE corner. The square was the first in Liverpool with a central garden – trees were reinstated in 2001. Leave by Gradwell Street, continue to Hanover Street, and turn left. On the opposite side is Stanley Buildings, an office and warehouse block, presumably similar in date to Hanover Buildings of 1884, lower down.

The junction of **Hanover Street** and **Paradise Street**, previously narrow and congested, was re-planned in 1877–8. The N side of Hanover Street was set back to its present line and Paradise Street was extended southward across it to meet Park Lane. On the prominent corner sites two impressive brick and terracotta buildings were put up. **Church House**, with its main façade to Hanover Street and a shorter return to Paradise Street, is by *George Enoch Grayson*. Opened in 1885, the right half was an institute for the Mersey Mission to Seamen, containing a chapel and meeting rooms; the left half was a temperance pub. Blue, yellow and red brick under a red tiled roof, with round arched windows to the second floor and much moulded brick decoration. Opposite is No. 12 Hanover Street, on the corner of Duke Street, a splendid curved block by *Edmund Kirby* in hot red brick and terracotta from the *Ruabon Terracotta Works* [122]. Built 1889–90 for Eills & Co., shipowners and merchants, with ground-floor offices and warehousing above; an earlier warehouse of 1863 is incorporated round the corner in Argyle Street. Big round-arched windows to the ground floor with herringbone brickwork in the spandrels, three-light windows to the first and second floors, and four-light windows on top. The detail is somewhere between Gothic and Early Renaissance. A pretty wrought-iron balcony on brackets runs around the first floor. The piers between the windows extend above the openwork parapet as tall chimneys, creating a lively skyline. A sensitive refurbishment in the 1990s moved the entrance to the inner courtyard, reached via the former cartway in Duke Street.

123. Warehouse, Argyle Street (probably first half of c19). Right, the Bridewell (1861)

Duke Street in the c18 was affluent. A fashionable, tree-lined 'Ladies' Walk' extended for much of its length. In the c19 business activity shifted to the streets round the Exchange, and the rich moved up the hill to the spacious residential quarter building there (*see* Walks 5 and 6). The Duke Street area was increasingly taken over by warehousing and by the small industries which had always operated close to the docks, and the respectable houses began their decline.

Humyak House, a tall warehouse on the left dated 1864, is followed by five late c18 houses with columned and pedimented doorways. On the right, **Duke Street Lane** has a three-storey warehouse of 1863. This is attached to a large new red brick office building fronting Duke Street, ending with a short cylindrical tower at the corner of Campbell Street. It is part of a major regeneration project centred on Campbell, Henry, York, Argyle and Duke streets, combining new buildings with the refurbishment of old ones. Construction began in 2000, and the architects for the whole scheme are *Brock Carmichael Associates*. The area is especially rich in c19 warehouses, but many are very decayed, and it remains to be seen how much historic fabric will survive the rebuilding. Turn right into **Campbell Street**, which leads into the newly created **Campbell Square**. On the right, the former **Bridewell** of 1861, built as police cells and offices, now a restaurant. Viewed over the forbidding perimeter wall, which hid the ground-floor cells, it looks surprisingly picturesque: Italianate, asymmetrical, with two towers of different heights, the taller one for ventilation. On the left a new building with much grey metal cladding. In the middle of the square a sculpture, The Seed, 2002, by *Stephen Broadbent*: an egg-shaped pod, silvery outside, copper-coloured inside. Turn right into **Argyle Street**. Adjoining the Bridewell is a six-storey warehouse, probably from the first half of the c19, recently converted into flats [123]. A similar five-storey warehouse stands on the same side, just beyond Campbell Square.

Return to Campbell Square and turn right into **Henry Street**. Two houses on the right purport to be of *c.* 1766, but seem to have been entirely rebuilt recently. On the same side, and continuing round the corner into York Street, is a large block of late C19 four-storey warehouses. Polychrome brick, with buttresses between each bay and four big gables to Henry Street, altogether more decorative than the earlier warehouses nearby. Adjoining, and occupying the corner of York Street and Argyle Street, is a more austere block of particularly impressive warehouses of 1884, by *David Walker*. The strip of wall containing each vertical row of windows is recessed slightly, then corbelled out near the top to bring it flush with the parapet, giving an almost fortified look. **Lydia Anne Street**, to the SE, marks the boundary between this area of

Eighteenth- and Early Nineteenth-century Warehouses

Private warehouses, scattered throughout the centre, were one of the most characteristic building types of this period. In the C18 they were often attached to the owner's dwelling, the best of a very few surviving examples being Thomas Parr's, at the rear of his Colquitt Street house. The C18 warehouse form continued into the early C19, and can be seen in Henry Street, College Lane and Mathew Street. Typically such buildings occupied a deep, narrow plot, with a gabled street front. Storage space was maximized by building high: ten or more storeys are recorded, though among surviving early C19 examples five or six is usual. Loading doors for each floor were arranged in a vertical row under the gable (or sometimes two rows, left and right), with a pulley at the top by which goods could be hoisted and taken in at any level. In earlier buildings these doors were almost flush with the façade, and the pulley projected under a cover called a cathead; later, doors and pulley were recessed so that the hoisting process was less hazardous to passers by. A stair, often lit by small oval openings, gave access between floors. Windows were generally few and small, to prevent theft. Walls were of brick, roofs slated, floors of timber, supported by stout timber columns. The exterior was severely utilitarian, though the gable could be treated as a pediment for more dignified effect (e.g. Nos. 23 and 27 Mathew Street, q.v. Streets).

In 1805 the provisions of the 1803 Warehousing Act were extended to Liverpool, establishing bonded warehouses in which goods could remain under Crown locks until duty was paid on them. It seems that new warehouses were built to provide the increased security required for bonded storage (e.g. No. 46 Henry Street), while older ones were upgraded (e.g. No. 38 Henry Street, where large windows were replaced by smaller openings). For dock warehouses, *see* Docks Introduction, pp. 98–100.

high, densely packed warehouses on the one hand, and low, informally grouped housing of the late C20 on the other.

Return to **Duke Street** via York Street, which on both sides has C18 houses, some with warehousing. Thomas Leyland is said to have set up Leyland & Bullin's Bank in 1807 in the block on the NE, between Lydia Anne Street and Henry Street (being renovated, 2004). Turn right and continue up Duke Street. No. 64 on the right is an ornate five-bay palazzo by *John Elliott Reeve*, with carved decoration by *Norbury, Upton & Paterson*. Built in 1876 as offices and stores for the brewer Peter Walker, with an attached warehouse at the back in Henry Street. Higher up on the opposite side, at the corner of Slater Street, is the severe but well-proportioned ashlar **Union News Room** of 1800 by *John Foster Sen.* The main entrance was in the centre of the five-bay Duke Street façade, and had a large carving of the royal arms crowning the parapet above. The elevation to Slater Street breaks forward slightly under a central pediment and has a tripartite window on the first floor. In 1852 it was adapted as Liverpool's first public library, and the utilitarian brick extension at the rear was built to house the natural history collections of the 13th Earl of Derby presented to the town by his son. After library and museum moved to Shaw's Brow (*see* Major Buildings, p. 61) the Duke Street building was acquired for offices by Peter Walker in 1864. *R. T. Beckett* designed the three-bay Jacobean extension on the left, 1896, and further additions followed. The whole block was rebuilt behind the façades *c.* 1990, by *Kingham Knight Associates*.

Above Slater Street, Duke Street continues with more late Georgian houses, including some once-grand five-bay examples, now mostly very decayed. On the right, from Kent Street to Cornwallis Street, a very large development of flats around a central square, 2003. On the left, at the corner of Colquitt Street, a Neo-Georgian block by *Wilkinson Hindle Halsall Lloyd*, completed 2003. Virtually a replica of part of a longer mid-C18 terrace on this site, the derelict remains of which were demolished in the 1990s. The houses were notable for having individual gables facing the street, like warehouses. Behind and at right angles, and originally reached by a basement passage from Duke Street, a short terrace of smaller dwellings was built between 1836 and 1848. Remarkably this has survived (renovation completed 2003), and is the only example of back-to-back housing remaining in Liverpool. At a later date doors were punched through the spine wall, converting eighteen houses with one room to each floor into nine of twice the size with windows front and back. Now most of the surrounding buildings have been cleared, imagination is required to appreciate its original cramped setting. In Cornwallis Street are the yellow brick Gothic **Workshops for the Outdoor Blind** (i.e. blind people living in their own homes), 1870, by *George Tunstall Redmayne* of Manchester. They contained large rooms for making baskets, brushes and matting, and space for lectures and social gatherings. Upper part reconstructed after wartime bomb damage.

At the top of Duke Street, on the corner of Nelson Street, is a large and elaborately stuccoed classical building of *c.* 1858 by *Henry Sumners* (the date 1887 has recently been added on the Nelson Street side). It housed the furniture workshop and showrooms of Mr Abbott, and incorporated the proprietor's dwelling at the Duke Street end – a relatively late example of combined living and business accommodation. Next to it, spanning Nelson Street, is the very large **Chinese Arch**. Completed in 2000, it was designed and made in China by the *Shanghai Linyi Garden Building Co. Ltd* and erected here by Chinese craftspeople. It marks the long association of this area with Liverpool's Chinese community, who began to settle here at least a century ago.

Beside the arch, and impressively closing the view along Berry Street, is the former **Great George Street Congregational Church**, 1840–1, an outstandingly good building by *Joseph Franklin*, replacing a chapel of 1811–12 which burned down [124]. Oblong in plan, it turns the sharp corner of Nelson Street and Great George Street with a semicircular portico of fluted Corinthian columns enclosing a round inset tower – comparable to Nash's All Souls, Langham Place, in London, but more massive and imposing. The columns are monoliths, said to have come from a quarry in Park Road, Toxteth. The tower has a band of guilloche incorporating little wheel windows, and a shallow dome, now missing its finial. The sides have giant unfluted Corinthian pilasters and two tiers of windows, round-arched above, square-headed below. Minister's house attached at the back on the Great George Street side. Good classical cast-iron railings. In 1975 work began on conversion to an arts centre, resulting in horizontal subdivision of the galleried interior and the loss of all its fittings. The architects were *Kingham Knight Associates*. The ungainly new roof makes an unwelcome appearance

124. Former Great George Street Congregational Church, by Joseph Franklin (1840–1)

above the parapet. The only part of Franklin's interior that survives is the circular vestibule under the dome, with two stone staircases that gave access to the gallery.

Nelson Street has early C19 houses on the NW side, and leads into **Great George Square**, laid out by 1803 and built up by 1836. Once the grandest of Liverpool's residential squares, it was bombed in the Second World War and now only a handful of C19 houses survive. These originally formed unified terraces with central pediments: the elevations seem to have been approved by the Select Improvement Committee *c.* 1804. Cross the square diagonally, and turn down **Hardy Street**. At the junction with St James Street is the church of **St Vincent de Paul (R.C.)**, 1856–7, by *Edward Welby Pugin*. Gothic, with geometric tracery. The most striking feature outside is the high, delicate timber bellcote on the W gable. Inside, five-bay nave with octagonal piers, with deeply carved foliage capitals. An additional bay at the W end contains a choir loft with porch below. The sanctuary has a rich alabaster **reredos** with statues in niches, designed by *Pugin* in 1867, with carving by *Farmer*. Marble front of high altar added 1927. Above the reredos, a nine-light window with **glass** of 1925 completely fills the E wall. Chapels left and right, separated from the sanctuary by twin-arched openings, have statues in canopied niches, apparently 1890s. The **Lady Altar** of 1899, left, is particularly striking: standing Virgin under a lofty canopy, against a relief of the Annunciation in a circular field. The **presbytery**, also by *Pugin* and contemporary with the church, adjoins on the N. It is large, of red brick with stone dressings, and all the windows have trefoil heads.

At this point, those with the stamina for some contrasting buildings of the late C19 may be interested in the detour described below. For the main walk, from St Vincent de Paul turn N along **St James Street** and continue to **Park Lane**. On the left is the fancifully picturesque **Gustav Adolfs Kyrka**, the Swedish Seamen's Church, 1883–4, an early work by *W.D. Caröe* [125]. He obtained the commission through his father, then Danish Consul in Liverpool. Red brick, roughly square in plan, but rising to a higher octagonal centre under a pyramid roof. Scandinavian features include stepped gables and the concave-sided lead-covered timber spire over the entrance. Octagonal interior with pointed wooden vault, now horizontally divided at gallery level. The pastor's house, left, is integrated. Continue along Park Lane. On the left in Beckwith Street is **Heap's Rice Mill**, a big block of warehouse-like brick buildings put up in phases. The earlier parts look mid-C19. From Park Lane bear right into **Paradise Street**. On the right were much-altered mid-C18 houses (demolished 2004), the remains of **Cleveland Square**. On the left, **Chancery House**, 1899 by *James Strong* of Walker & Strong, built as the Gordon Smith Institute for Seamen, with library, reading room and assembly hall for sailors ashore. Red brick and terracotta, with red sandstone dressings. Two octagonal towers with pointed roofs frame the main façade, which has a generous round-arched entrance, blind

125. Gustav
Adolfs Kyrka,
Park Lane, by
W.D. Caröe
(1883–4)

Gothic tracery above the windows, and three big stepped gables. A simpler wing, originally lower, turns the corner into Hanover Street. Converted into offices by *Brock Carmichael Associates*, 1980–2.

From here, Hanover Street and Ranelagh Street lead to the Adelphi Hotel, where Walks 5 and 6 begin.

Detour

From St Vincent de Paul turn s along St James Street to **Great George Place**. Here in splendid isolation is a former branch of the **North and South Wales Bank**, a good Gothic building of *c.* 1878. Could it be by *J.P. Seddon*, who designed the bank's Birkenhead branch around the same time? Tall and narrow, it looks even more so now all its neighbours have been demolished. A mixture of square- and trefoil-headed windows, with a central gable. From here head s and turn right into **Parliament Street**. On the right is the most impressive surviving range of late C19 warehouses in the central area. They are huge and very plain, seven storeys high, of red brick, with blue brick around the small windows and the towering loading bays. Turn right into **Jamaica Street**. On the right in **Watkinson Street** and **Bridgewater Street** are further huge brick warehouses of the 1870s, etc. Jamaica Street leads to Park Lane, rejoining the main walk just above the end of the Wapping railway tunnel (*see* Walk 1, p. 116, and topic box, p. 188).

University of Liverpool via Mount Pleasant

This and the following walk take us through the outer fringes of C18 Liverpool. From the late C18, and especially after 1816, this ridge of high ground overlooking the crowded town was laid out with regular streets and developed as a favoured residential area. Alongside terraced housing it acquired churches (mostly demolished) and institutions, many associated with education and medicine. In the late C19 the new University College made its home here, and is now a dominant presence. Liverpool's two C20 cathedrals stand at the N and s ends of the ridge, visual anchors that give coherence to a large and architecturally diverse district.

We begin at the bottom (w) end of **Mount Pleasant**. On the right, rounding the corner of Renshaw Street, is the red brick and stone former **University Club**, 1903–5, by *Willink & Thicknesse* (perhaps with *F.M. Simpson*). Jacobean, with mullioned and transomed bow windows running through the upper floors. On the left, the tatty glazed triangular block at the corner of Brownlow Hill, containing cinemas and a night club, is by *Gillinson, Barnett & Partners* of Leeds, 1975. An elevated walkway on the N side (*see* topic box, p. 160) links it with a brutal multi-storey car park of 1972–4. Ascending Mount Pleasant, **Roscoe Gardens** on the right marks the site of the graveyard of the demolished Renshaw Street Unitarian Chapel, commemorated by a pretty octagonal domed monument with Tuscan columns, 1905 by *Ronald P. Jones*. Higher up on the same side, the block comprising Nos. 50–52 includes two altered five-bay houses, probably 1780s. No. 50 has a very unusual doorway, with an open pediment projecting on brackets turned outwards. Next on the right, the **YMCA**, 1874–7, by *H.H. Vale* (supervised by *W. & G. Audsley* after Vale's death in 1875). C13 Gothic, in brick with red sandstone dressings. Asymmetrically placed tower.

Opposite the YMCA, May Street leads to the disused **Pleasant Street Board School**, built as the Hibernian Schools in 1818 by the Liverpool Benevolent Society of Saint Patrick, to provide non-denominational education for children of Irish parents. Originally a simple, two-storey brick rectangle, with classrooms and master's house under the same roof. The domestic part, w, survives more or less unaltered, with a columned doorway to May Street. The teaching accommodation was extended and considerably altered from 1851.

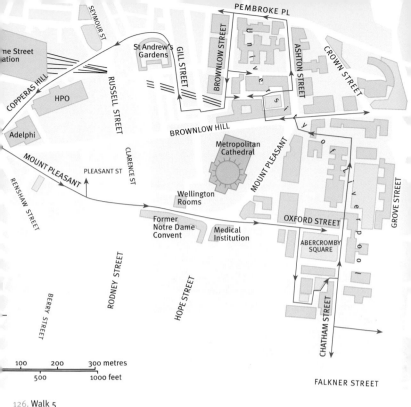

126. Walk 5

Returning to Mount Pleasant, the N side from May Street to Clarence Street has small terraced houses of *c.* 1800. Opposite, No. 62 was built 1767 for the merchant William Rice, making it the oldest in the street. Five bays and two storeys. A modest, rather rustic-looking building, made to appear more so by taller neighbours pressing forward on each side. No. 68, grander, was built *c.* 1788 for the merchant and future mayor, George Dunbar. Three storeys and five bays, the centre framed by a giant blind arch and breaking forward under a pediment. Charming doorway, carved with musical instruments and a frieze incorporating cherubs with globe and compasses. No. 70 was built as the Consumption Hospital, 1903–4, by *Grayson & Ould*. Harsh red brick and terracotta, with central pediment and advancing wings. The window in the centre of the first floor is said to have come from an early C19 house on the site.

Mount Pleasant here crosses Rodney Street (*see* Walk 6, p. 231) and its continuation, Clarence Street.* The S side of Mount Pleasant from Rodney Street to Hope Street is a confusing agglomeration of buildings, formerly the **Notre Dame Convent** and **Teacher Training College**, now

*On the E side of Clarence Street, three-bay terraced houses of *c.* 1800. On the W side, **Liverpool Community College**, by *Ellis Williams Architects*, completed 2000.

occupied by Liverpool John Moores University. The convent expanded from No. 96 Mount Pleasant, acquired in 1851. This five-bay late c18 house has a fine imperial staircase, possibly 1830s, with columns on the ground and first floors (those above have lotus capitals), Greek Revival doorcases, and a beautiful cast-iron balustrade of lushest acanthus. Four bays were added to the right, apparently in the early 1850s, for the convent school. To the left, a training college for female teachers was added by *J. & C. Hansom*, 1856–7. H-plan, with a stair-tower in the middle. Still essentially Georgian, but with Italianate touches such as a bracketed eaves cornice. A screen wall across the front gives a forbidding air. Right of the school is a block of 1865–7 by *M.E. Hadfield & Son* of Sheffield. Here, eventually, the nuns went Gothic. The street elevation is flat and unexciting, with timid polychrome brickwork, but the **chapel** wing at the rear, the slender flèche of which is visible, is more impressive. The chapel occupies only the upper floor. Round apse and buttresses with many set-offs. The red brick has bands of blue brick and yellow stone. In the centre of the apse wall a carving of Our Lady with two kneeling nuns, in severe medieval style by *Theodore Phyffers*. Interior with quadripartite vault of brick and stone (now unfortunately painted) carried by clustered shafts on corbels. Plate tracery in side windows; lancets in sanctuary, three with good early c20 stained glass said to be by *Early* of Dublin. The exceptionally rich furnishings have gone. (For the Aldham Robarts Learning Resource Centre s of the chapel *see* Walk 6, pp. 231–3). Subsequent additions to the convent are all more or less Gothic. Facing Mount Pleasant, right of the chapel block, two ranges by *Edmund Kirby*, 1870s–90s. Left of the training college, and turning the corner into Hope Street, further buildings by *James O'Byrne*, 1880s, and *Pugin & Pugin*, 1900s.

On the N side of Mount Pleasant, opposite the convent, the former **Wellington Rooms**, 1814–16, assembly rooms paid for by public subscription [127]. The subject of a competition won by *Edmund Aikin* of London, who then moved to Liverpool. Single-storey ashlar façade combining Roman and Greek elements. The ends break forward and have pairs of Corinthian pilasters, and the central door is in a semi-circular projection recalling the Monument of Lysicrates (originally an open colonnade, infilled in the 1820s because it gave insufficient shelter; porches on the w for sedan chairs and on the E for carriages have also been enclosed). Capitals after the Temple of Vesta at Tivoli, admired by Soane. In the blank walls to either side two fine panels of **sculpture**, sometimes ascribed to the young *John Gibson*. The pairs of winged female figures bearing garlands add a touch of gaiety to what is otherwise a rather solemn-looking place of entertainment. Inside, the plan largely survives. From the circular porch, doors right and left lead via cloakrooms to a central octagonal vestibule, which leads in turn to an ante-room. This is flanked on the right by the supper room (enlarged 1894 by *James F. Doyle*), and on the left by the card room. At

127. Wellington Rooms, Mount Pleasant, by Edmund Aikin (1814–16)

the back is the **ballroom** with plaster decoration of various dates. The frieze with dancing maidens may be Aikin's, but the garlands and wall panels look later.

After the Wellington Rooms comes the Metropolitan Cathedral (*see* Major Buildings, p. 83). Opposite, making excellent use of its position at the junction with Hope Street, is the **Medical Institution**, 1835–7, by *Clark Rampling*. Convex façade, with a central portico of six Ionic columns set in, and solid end blocks with pilasters. The plan is well-adapted to the wedge-shaped site: library and committee room flank the central hall and stairs, which lead to the double-height lecture theatre in the angle at the back. Council room remodelled by *Edmund Rathbone*, 1907, with panelling in the style of *c.* 1700 and an elaborate chimneypiece of beaten copper. In the entrance hall a memorial tablet (a sarcophagus with garlands) to the founder, Dr John Rutter, d. 1838, brought from St Peter (*see* topic box, p. 179). Turn E into **Oxford Street**, where a weak extension in artificial stone by *Robertson Young & Partners* was opened 1966. Opposite, No. 126 Mount Pleasant, built as the **School of Hygiene** and **City Laboratories**, is dated 1914. Begun under *Thomas Shelmerdine* and completed under *A.D. Jenkins*, successive Corporation Surveyors. Classical, in red brick with much stone. Big and lumpish and unworthy of its splendid site.

On entering Oxford Street we have reached the territory of the **University of Liverpool** (*see* plan, p. 214). It started as University College in 1881, became a member of the federal Victoria University (along with Owens College, Manchester) in 1884, and has been the University of Liverpool since 1903. Buildings erected between the 1880s and the Second World War are concentrated around Brownlow Hill, Ashton Street and Brownlow Street, and will be encountered later. Immediately after the war, *William Holford* was commissioned to plan the university's expansion. His report was published in 1949, and in 1950 the new Precinct was designated, stretching S and E of the earlier buildings; later enlarged, it now measures approximately 880 by 440 yds (800 by 400 metres). Holford offered a framework for growth rather

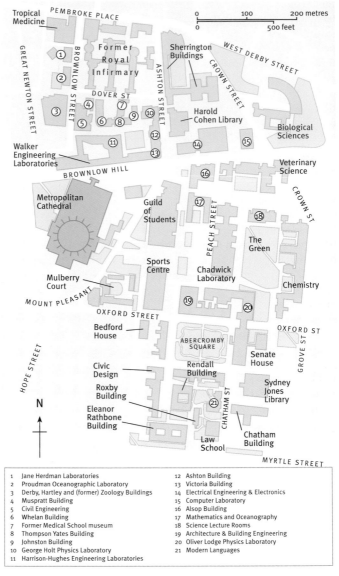

Tropical Medicine
PEMBROKE PLACE
Former Royal Infirmary
DOVER ST
GREAT NEWTON STREET
BROWNLOW STREET
ASHTON STREET
Sherrington Buildings
WEST DERBY STREET
CROWN STREET
Harold Cohen Library
Biological Sciences
Walker Engineering Laboratories
BROWNLOW HILL
Veterinary Science
CROWN ST
Metropolitan Cathedral
Guild of Students
PEACH STREET
The Green
Chemistry
Mulberry Court
Sports Centre
Chadwick Laboratory
MOUNT PLEASANT
OXFORD STREET
Bedford House
ABERCROMBY SQUARE
OXFORD ST
GROVE ST
HOPE STREET
Civic Design
Roxby Building
Eleanor Rathbone Building
Rendall Building
Senate House
Sydney Jones Library
CHATHAM ST
Chatham Building
Law School
MYRTLE STREET
N

0   100   200 metres
0   500 feet

1 Jane Herdman Laboratories	12 Ashton Building
2 Proudman Oceanographic Laboratory	13 Victoria Building
3 Derby, Hartley and (former) Zoology Buildings	14 Electrical Engineering & Electronics
4 Muspratt Building	15 Computer Laboratory
5 Civil Engineering	16 Alsop Building
6 Whelan Building	17 Mathematics and Oceanography
7 Former Medical School museum	18 Science Lecture Rooms
8 Thompson Yates Building	19 Architecture & Building Engineering
9 Johnston Building	20 Oliver Lodge Physics Laboratory
10 George Holt Physics Laboratory	21 Modern Languages
11 Harrison-Hughes Engineering Laboratories	

128. University of Liverpool

than rigid proposals, but a good deal of what we see today can be traced back to him. Most importantly, he did not envisage a formal layout, nor did he favour employing a single architect. The resulting visual diversity is partly due to this, partly to changes in funding, student numbers and land ownership. In 1969 Pevsner said of the Precinct: 'The whole is not a whole but a zoo, with species after species represented.' What makes the variety of the buildings more striking is that they occupy an area laid out in the early C19 with uniform terraces and a regular grid of streets (*see* Abercromby Square, below). Most of the Precinct is now pedestrianized and much planting has been carried out, obscuring the former thoroughfares. However, the university buildings are mostly aligned with these streets, and the late Georgian pattern provides a counterpoint to the clamouring individualism of their architecture. In the 1960s the University built its main halls of residence in the suburb of Mossley Hill (outside the area of this book) and very little student housing was provided in the Precinct. Recently, a good deal of accommodation has been built on the fringes, much by private developers, and of little architectural interest.

We begin in Oxford Street with Nos. 14–30, a terrace of *c.* 1820. Brick, two and a half storeys above a basement, with recessed doorways under arches, flanked by Doric columns. Typical of the housing that covered this area before the university. On the N side is **Mulberry Court**, student housing of two phases round a landscaped quadrangle. The block fronting the street is by *Manning Clamp & Partners*, 1978–81, with shops recessed behind a colonnade; a similar block at right angles behind. The other two sides are hostels of 1967–70 by *Gerald Beech*. Also by *Beech* is the glass-faced **Bedford House** on the s side of Oxford Street, 1965–6, originally a club for non-academic staff. Opposite stands the most startling and assertive of all the university's postwar buildings, the **Sports Centre** by *Denys Lasdun & Partners*, 1963–6 [129]. The plan is lucid and practical: sports hall and swimming pool balance each other on the N and s sides, with stairs, changing rooms, squash courts, etc., stacked between. As for the raw concrete and glass exterior with its dominant slanting lines, Pevsner considered it a calculated insult to the late Georgian rectangularity of nearby Abercromby Square. The pool and sports hall have tilted roofs that slope down towards the spine. N and s elevations lean inwards and are entirely glazed, the roofs carried by slender raking columns that pass just in front of the glass. The ground

129. Sports Centre, Oxford Street, by Denys Lasdun & Partners (1963–6)

floor is recessed behind this angled colonnade. w and e ends are almost windowless above the ground floor, with only a sliver of glazing just below the roof. Each is crowned by an overhanging water tank which seems to weigh down the two roofs at the point where they meet. Inside the sports hall is a splendid brick climbing wall devised by *Donald Mill*, with concrete projections, like a piece of abstract sculpture. A N extension by *Austin-Smith:Lord* was begun 2003, equal in size to Lasdun's building. It will have a catenary roof, suspended between A-frames.

So to **Abercromby Square**, now entirely occupied by the university. This is the most complete survival of the housing built all over the area in the early c19. Before 1800 this elevated tract was a heath known as Mosslake Fields. In that year the Select Improvement Committee recommended the adoption of plans made by the Corporation Surveyor, *John Foster Sen.*, for laying out the area between Crabtree Lane to the s (now Falkner Street) and Brownlow Hill to the N. Foster's plan was a straightforward grid running N–s and w–e, with a large and prestigious square, Abercromby Square, at its centre. Little progress was made until the lessees surrendered their interests in 1816. In 1819 *Foster* produced an elevation for a terrace on one side of the square. This was adopted for the w side with slight modifications, but those taking out leases were allowed more flexibility on the other sides. The centre of the e side was occupied by the Ionic portico of St Catherine's church, 1829–31, by *John Foster Jun.*, bombed in the Second World War and demolished for the Senate House (*see* below). Building on the three sides which survive was largely complete by 1830 [130]. The houses are brick, of three storeys plus basement, with a Greek Doric porch in the middle of each side, the other doorways having Doric pilasters. The stonework has been painted. In the middle of the communal garden is a pretty circular domed building, surrounded by a cast-iron trellis. Designed by the elder *Foster* in 1822, for storing garden tools.

130. Abercromby Square,
N side, mostly complete
by 1830

131. No. 19 Abercromby
Square, drawing by
William Culshaw (1862)

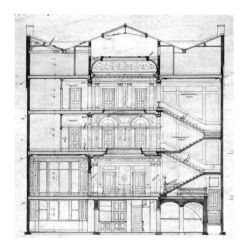

No. 19 on the N side, now the **Department of Education** and
Department of Corporate Communications, is seven bays wide and
higher than its neighbours. Designed in 1862–3 by *William Culshaw*
for C.K. Prioleau, a South Carolina-born businessman whose firm
encouraged support for the Confederate cause during the American
Civil War; early in the 1880s it was altered to become the Bishop's
Palace. It is perhaps the grandest surviving C19 house in the city centre,
with a fine top-lit hall with circular balustraded openings on the first
and second floors, and stairs off to the right [131]. Some ground-floor
rooms have painted ceilings (who was the artist?), the best being the
former dining room, with figures in classical dress seen through a
trompe l'œil oculus. The vestibule ceiling has a palmetto tree – as
featured on the flag adopted by South Carolina in 1861, when it seced-
ed from the Union. On the same side, No. 23 and adjoining houses were
given lavish late C17-style interiors for the School of Education *c.* 1921,
by *Ronald P. Jones*. No. 25 at the W end of the terrace is the **School
of Architecture and Building Engineering**, with a rear extension (the
Leverhulme Building) by *Reilly, Budden & Marshall*, opened in 1933. It
aims to harmonize with the square and yet be modern of a kind still
rare in England by this date. Note the horizontal window band. The
projecting glazed stair between new and old was added in the 1970s
by *Gerald Beech*. The 1930s extension was itself extended – inwards and
upwards – by *Dave King* and *Rod McAllister* (with the *Gerald Beech
Partnership*) in 1987–8. They added a three-storey open-plan studio
and gallery space, partly occupying the courtyard in the middle and
partly rising above the old roof level. It is a lightweight steel and glass
structure with exposed constructional details, services, etc., intended as
an object lesson for students.

The E side is filled by **Senate House**, by *Tom Mellor & Partners*,
1966–8. Proportions and materials respond sensitively to the terraced

Charles Reilly and the Liverpool School of Architecture

Charles Reilly (1874–1948) was from 1904 to 1933 the influential head of the Liverpool School of Architecture. Under his predecessor, F.M. Simpson, the School was aligned with the Arts and Crafts movement. Reilly, by contrast, rejected what he saw as the excessive individualism of much late C19 and early C20 architecture, favouring instead a purer classicism. Initially modern French architecture and the English Regency were his models, but on visiting the United States in 1909 he became a convert to the classicism of contemporary America. This he promoted through teaching and journalism as a truly modern, international style. He especially admired the large scale, lucid planning and scholarly refinement found in the work of American architects such as McKim, Mead & White. These were the qualities he encouraged his students to imitate, and in the 1920s he annually sent the best to gain experience in the offices of leading New York practices. He was a member of the Faculty of Architecture of the British School in Rome, which through its scholarships enabled Liverpool graduates to study ancient and Renaissance architecture at first hand.

Students of Reilly's who practised locally include *Harold Dod*, designer of the Athenaeum [105]; *H.H. Davies*, who specialized in pubs such as the Blackburne Arms; and above all *Herbert J. Rowse*, whose Martins Bank is probably the best example of C20 American-style classicism in the country [100]. The influence of America can also be seen in the work of *Willink & Thicknesse* and *Arnold Thornely*. At the end of his teaching career Reilly switched allegiance to the Modern Movement. This is reflected in the Leverhulme Building of the School of Architecture, opened 1933, which he designed in conjunction with *L.B. Budden* and *J.E. Marshall*, and in the work of graduates such as *William Crabtree*, responsible for the Peter Jones department store in London's Sloane Square, and *John Hughes*, who designed the St Andrew's Gardens housing scheme in Liverpool [135].

houses on the other sides, but the lack of a central entrance is keenly felt, especially since the portico of St Catherine was demolished to make way for it. Instead, there is an off-centre projecting platform, designed for a bronze **sculpture**, Squares with Two Circles, by *Barbara Hepworth*. The main entrance, perversely, is tucked away in the short return at the N end, facing Oxford Street. The **Senate Room**, a circular drum surrounded by a square colonnade, forms a pavilion at the back. An assembly hall was to have been built on the adjoining site, and together the buildings would have enclosed a square. This never happened, and the Senate Room now looks like a marginal appendage.

It is further compromised, like much of the Precinct, by a sea of parked cars.

Leaving the square at the sw corner, **Bedford Street South** begins with the **Department of Civic Design**, 1950–1, by *Gordon Stephenson*. Red brick, with a band of glazing to the first-floor library. The first new building in the Precinct to be completed after the war, it has the slightly undernourished look that marks that period of austerity. William Holford wrote in 1954 of the buildings of this time that they 'present elevations in the execution of which . . . a great deal of expense has been spared.' In the rear courtyard, a Portland stone **sculpture**, The Quickening, 1951, by *Mitzi Cunliffe*: a bird resting in the palm of a giant hand. *Cunliffe* also designed the handles of the main doors.

On the same side, a few early C19 stuccoed houses behind front gardens, now university departments. Across the end of the street, and defining the s edge of the Precinct, the **Eleanor Rathbone Building**, 1970–3, a lacklustre affair in blue-grey brick by *Yorke, Rosenberg & Mardall*, not a patch on their earlier work for the University (*see* below, pp. 222–3). Spreading E from Bedford Street South, a group of four blocks by *Bryan & Norman Westwood, Piet & Partners,* 1961–6. They constitute the most coherent and satisfying part of the Precinct, partly because their architecture is consistent and partly because the spaces between are planned with as much care as the buildings themselves. The **Rendall Building** (originally Arts Library and lecture rooms) is a hollow square. The outer walls are brick below and concrete above, much of the upper storey being faced with slabs which deviate slightly from the vertical, creating a kind of seasick feeling. Inside, large areas of glass overlook the quiet, cloister-like court. The upper floor, originally a spacious reading room, has been subdivided, and the abstract stained glass by *Gillian Rees-Thomas* can now be seen only with difficulty. On the E side the court is open at ground-floor level to a pleasant, irregular area of grass and trees, formed from the back gardens of houses in Abercromby Square, an idea proposed by *Holford* in 1949. It is enclosed by two taller slabs, the **Roxby Building** and **Modern Languages**. Just behind these is the last and most interesting of the group, the **Law School**. Square in plan and very restrained externally, with slender vertical fins of concrete to the upper floors. The roof hints at the intricate internal planning, with the library, lecture theatre, moot room and various circulation spaces interlocking like pieces of an ingenious puzzle.

On the opposite, E side of **Chatham Street** is the **Chatham Building**, 1860–1, originally a Welsh Presbyterian Chapel, by *Oliver & Lamb* of Newcastle. Brick and painted stone, coarse Italianate, with giant pilasters and a grotesque bellcote crowning the pediment. Large rear extension for the **Management School** by *McCormick Architecture*, completed 2002. L-shaped, with glazing between brick piers. Clerestory above a heavy projecting course of artificial stone.

From here two short detours can be made. First, Chatham Street continues s, and on the E side between Myrtle Street and Falkner Street has three-bay houses a few years earlier than Abercromby Square. Second, just behind the Management School is Grove Street, where No. 117 on the E side is **The Octagon**, an unusual house with Gothic details. Built in 1867 by a local GP, Dr. J.W. Hayward, to demonstrate his ideas on domestic heating and ventilation.* His system required a tall chimney, visible at the rear, in which were combined the smoke flue from the kitchen and a shaft for expelling foul air, extracted from all the rooms by a system of ducts. E of The Octagon is **Minster Court**, a complex of 1930s municipal flats, converted to private housing from 1982 by *Barratt*; *Kingham Knight Associates* were architectural consultants. The conversion involved transforming access decks into private balconies and adding glazed stair-towers.

Back on the main walk, immediately N of the Management School is the three-storey brick and concrete **Sydney Jones Library**, by *Basil Spence, Glover & Ferguson*, completed 1976. Set back from Chatham Street behind a sloping, brick-paved forecourt. A pair of stair-towers marks the central entrance. Down both sides projecting brick boxes contain individual work spaces – like the partly open drawers of a row of filing cabinets. On the forecourt a red-painted abstract **sculpture** in steel, Red Between, 1971–3, by *Phillip King*, installed 1977.

Chatham Street leads back to the E side of Abercromby Square, past a hexagonal **pillar box** of the type designed by *J.W. Penfold,* introduced in 1866. Passing Senate House and crossing Oxford Street we reach the **Oliver Lodge Physics Laboratory**, 1966–8, by *Tom Mellor & Partners* with the *United Kingdom Atomic Energy Authority* as executive architects. The same dark brick as Senate House (to which it is linked by a bridge over Oxford Street) with copper cladding above the windows.

A passage leads to **The Green**, an open space created in 1960 by clearing C19 housing. Along the W side is the **Chadwick Laboratory**, 1957–9, by *Basil Spence*. An eight-storey tower on stilts, from which a spine corridor runs N with single-storey laboratories branching off symmetrically. At the opposite end from the tower are lecture theatres, again symmetrical, with the raked auditoria cantilevered from the centre. Inside, the plan is admirably lucid, but from outside the building is mostly too low to have much impact, and the painted concrete and grey mosaic cladding to the tower have not aged well. Near the tower entrance, a cast aluminium **sculpture**, Three Uprights, by *Hubert Dalwood*, won in competition 1959. In the entrance hall leading to the lecture theatres, an impressive mosaic **mural** of the same date by *Geoffrey Clarke* (a cast-aluminium relief, also by *Clarke* and now in the

*With Dr Drysdale, Hayward published *Health and Comfort in House Building*, 1872.

entrance under the tower, was made originally for the Oliver Lodge Physics Laboratory, 1966–8). The E side of The Green is all **Chemistry**, by *Stephenson, Young & Partners*, in several phases. The red brick parts are 1951–4 and 1956–8, the curtain-walled **Robert Robinson Laboratories** at the S end 1960–2, and a small extension at the N end 1973–4. Closing the N side are the **Science Lecture Rooms**, 1965–7, by *Robert Gardner-Medwin* with *Saunders, Boston & Brock*. The N-facing entrance front is a strong, jaggedly Brutalist composition, mostly in raw concrete. It has a frieze of abstract sculpture by *David Le Marchant Brock* and *Frederick Bushe* on the ground floor, above which two of the auditoria jut out, one sideways, one head on. On the other three sides, panels of brick predominate. First-floor foyer with big windows overlooking The Green.

N of the Science Lecture Rooms a deep railway cutting originally ran E–W. It was covered over during the 1960s, resulting in a ragged space used mostly for car parking. N of this divide is **Veterinary Science**, 1958–60, by the Liverpool-trained *E. Maxwell Fry*. Fry was a pioneer of Modernism in Britain, but this is sadly unremarkable. The E and W ends of the rear elevation facing Brownlow Hill have reliefs of a horse and a bull carved into the brickwork by *Eric Peskett*. Attached to the main building on the E, the **Small Animal Hospital** of 1976–7 is by *Ormrod & Partners*. W of Veterinary Science is the **Alsop Building**, containing shops, a pub, a bank, etc., 1965–8, by *Tom Mellor & Partners*, and s of this are **Mathematics** and **Oceanography**, 1959–61, by *Bryan Westwood*. Two parallel blocks, six storeys and two storeys, linked by single-storey labs and a covered walkway, with a grassed courtyard in the middle. The cladding originally included large pyramidal panels on the ends of the higher block, intended to create chiaroscuro effects as they became stained with soot. They have been replaced with brick, but panels with smaller geometrical relief patterns survive on the long elevations. At the s end of the two-storey block is the university's original computer room, with copper-covered hyperbolic paraboloid roof. The penthouse on the higher block had a roof of similar form, for which a grossly inappropriate replacement has been substituted. The main entrance on the W has an iron **screen** by *John McCarthy* incorporating mathematical symbols, and the same artist made the five-panel **mural** in the entrance hall of the higher block, illustrating the growth of mathematical ideas.

This brings us to the **Guild of Students**. The earliest part (N end) dates from 1910–13. It is the major work of *Charles Reilly*, Roscoe Professor of Architecture, and illustrates his enthusiasm for a hybrid classicism combining Regency, Greek, and French Beaux-Arts elements. Markedly different W and E elevations are meant to reflect that the former was for women, the latter for men. This division is also evident in the plan. The women's side [132], facing Mount Pleasant, is composed like a Regency house and has squat Doric columns to the ground floor which continue round the bow window. The upper floor of the bow has

132. Guild of
Students,
Mount
Pleasant
front, by
Charles
Reilly
(1910–13)

slender baluster-like columns in pairs. The men's side, of six bays, has a massive Beaux-Arts balcony and bluntly pedimented windows to the first floor, and round windows over. The N elevation is a largely windowless brick wall (it originally overlooked the railway cutting) with two bowed staircase projections and a pedimented portion with brick columns high up in the middle. The best interior is the former **Gilmour Hall**, designed as a debating chamber, now unhappily converted into a bar with split-level floor. It has ponderous Doric columns in the corners and a richly compartmented ceiling. The original surface finish was Stuc – plaster with a stone-like finish, fashionable at the time. The two spiral staircases are also impressive, especially the men's, with its cast-iron latticework balustrade (perhaps inspired by the balcony fronts in the Small Concert Room of St George's Hall). Some rooms have classical reliefs by *Ethel Frimston*. The building was sensitively extended to the s by *Reilly, L.B. Budden* and *J.E. Marshall*, 1932–5. In 1962–5 a further large and elegant southward extension by *Bridgewater, Shepheard & Epstein* was added. Dark brick with bands of grey mosaic round the windows, and two opposing monopitch roofs. This was imaginatively adapted in the mid 1990s by *King McAllister*. They subdivided former restaurant spaces to provide accommodation for health, welfare and careers services, inserting free-standing mezzanines of meticulously detailed steelwork, and using translucent and reflective materials to distribute natural light. The courtyard was roofed with a huge wedge-shaped skylight, echoing the Metropolitan Cathedral's sloping roof and framing a view of its tower from within.

Returning to the paved area at the N end of the Guild of Students, we look across Brownlow Hill to **Electrical Engineering & Electronics**, 1962–5, by *Yorke, Rosenberg & Mardall*. Six-storey block with lower blocks grouped behind, all faced in the horizontal white-glazed tiles that were the practice's trademark at this time. The tiles are vertically aligned, not staggered like bricks, to emphasize their status as cladding; they also correspond to the module of the building, covering the surface entirely, without a single tile having to be cut. Windows mostly in bands, but the ground floor of the high block is fully glazed behind the uprights of the frame, to form a transparent foyer around the lecture theatres. The impression of purity and aloofness is underlined by the surrounding 'moat', across which the main entrance is reached by a footbridge. *Yorke, Rosenberg & Mardall* added the **Computer Laboratory** at the rear in 1967–9, and extended it 1973–4. This time the tiles have their long sides upright. Further E, across Crown Street is **Biological Sciences**. The original building, a higher block of 1965–9 by *R.R. Young*, was reduced in height 2003. A recent very large extension by *David Morley Architects* takes the form of a series of linked blocks in a curve.

It would be difficult to imagine a greater contrast than that between Yorke, Rosenberg & Mardall's clinical white boxes and the other ceramic-clad building which faces them across Ashton Street. This is the stridently red and assertively Gothic **Victoria Building**, 1889–92, by *Alfred Waterhouse*, the main teaching and administrative building of the fledgling University College [133]. It is faced with fiery Ruabon brick and terracotta, offset by common brick. Under this resilient skin the construction is fireproof, with iron frame and concrete floors; steel was apparently used in the Jubilee clock tower. This tower (terracotta modelling by *Farmer & Brindley*) with its lead-covered spire marks the main entrance. To the left, the former library with gabled dormers; to the right, the principal staircase and a semicircular lecture theatre, both expressed externally. Double-height apsidal **entrance hall** [19] faced in *Burmantofts* terracotta, glazed and unglazed, mostly browns with touches of pale blue. An arcaded first-floor landing runs round the s side and the apse. The stately staircase is also arcaded, allowing glimpses through to the hall. Corresponding with the apse is the stage of the **lecture theatre** above, an impressive space. The former library – now the **Tate Hall** – was stripped of fittings following the opening of the Harold Cohen Library in 1938 (*see* below), and the tie-beams removed from Waterhouse's open roof. The former librarian's room at the w end has C17 panelling installed in 1948, from the demolished Worden Hall at Leyland, Lancashire. – **Sculpture**: in the apse of the entrance hall (designed to receive it), life-size marble statue of Christopher Bushell, *c.* 1884, by *Albert Bruce-Joy*; opposite the main entrance, the University War Memorial, 1926–7, by *Gordon Hemm*, carving by *C.J. Allen*; on the stairs, plaques to Charles W. Jones, 1910, *Allen* again, and George Holt, 1897, a fine bronze relief portrait by *George Frampton*.

Adjoining the Victoria Building and facing Brownlow Hill are the **Walker Engineering Laboratories**, 1887–9. Also by *Waterhouse* and of brick and terracotta, but simpler. In the entrance hall a statue of

133. Victoria Building, Brownlow Hill, by Alfred Waterhouse (1889–92)

Leopold, Duke of Albany, by *Count Victor Gleichen*, 1886. In 1963–6 the laboratories were extended on the w by *Courtaulds Technical Services Ltd*, whose addition includes a seven-storey tower. A rib-vaulted passage between the Victoria Building and the laboratories leads to a quadrangle, enclosed on the s by the rear of the Victoria Building, and on the w and N by buildings more or less complementary in materials and styles, but comparatively dull. The **Harrison-Hughes Engineering Laboratories**, opened 1912, by *Briggs, Wolstenholme & Thornely*, are Gothic in brick and sandstone. The **Thompson Yates Building**, 1894–8, by *Alfred Waterhouse*, is brick and terracotta, with a terracotta **plaque** of 1896 by *C.J. Allen* (made by *J.C. Edwards* of Ruabon) showing female personifications of Physiology and Pathology. On the left is the **Whelan Building** (originally Anatomy), 1899–1904, by *Alfred & Paul Waterhouse*, with the former semicircular lecture theatres expressed externally, and on the right, the **Johnston Building** and the **George Holt Physics Laboratory**, completed 1904, by *Willink & Thicknesse* with *F.M. Simpson*.

The E side of the quadrangle is a complete contrast. The **Ashton Building**, erected for the Faculty of Arts 1912–14, is by *Briggs, Wolstenholme & Thornely* and *Frank W. Simon* (Simon was responsible for the exterior, according to Reilly). Here the University at last abandoned the Gothic agenda set by Waterhouse, turning instead to classicism of a type derived from Wren. Main block of four storeys and seven bays, with a bold cornice. Outer bays largely brick, the middle three of Portland stone with giant pilasters. Big pedimented window with Michelangelesque figure sculpture by *William Birnie Rhind*. A tunnel-vaulted passage on the left leads to Ashton Street where the façade is more conventional, with six giant pilasters supporting a pediment. On the parapet to either side, pairs of sphinxes by *Rhind*.

On the E side of Ashton Street, on the axis of the passage from the quadrangle, is the **Harold Cohen Library**, 1936–8, by *Harold Dod*. Symmetrical, Portland stone-faced, and vestigially classical. The wings, lower than the central block containing the reading room, were extended upwards and given curved roofs by the *Gilling Dod Partnership*, 1997. **Sculpture** over main entrance by *Eric Kennington*, a female figure superimposed on an open book, representing learning. The brick-faced book-stack block at the rear is entirely different: uncompromisingly functional, with windows in continuous bands. Inside on the stairs, memorial plaques to John Sampson, d. 1931, and William Garmon Jones, d. 1937, both by *H. Tyson Smith*. N of the library, the E side of Ashton Street is entirely occupied by the **Sherrington Buildings** of the Faculty of Medicine. Long, dull block fronting the street, 1951–7 by *Weightman & Bullen*. Inside on the first floor, excellent relocated memorial to Sir Rubert William Boyce, by *C.J. Allen*, 1913. A frieze of figures alludes to Boyce's work on tropical medicine, and mosquitoes decorate the border of his portrait. A rear wing, at right angles and raised on stilts, was added by *Weightman & Bullen* 1965–7. In 2001–2 the same architects rebuilt the N end of the front block.

Turning left into **Pembroke Place** brings us to the main entrance of the former **Royal Infirmary** [134] on the s side, the flank of which was visible in Ashton Street. It is by *Alfred Waterhouse* and dates from 1887–90. It was Liverpool's third purpose-built infirmary. The first opened in 1749 on the site now occupied by St George's Hall; the second, a Greek Revival building of 1824 by *John Foster Jun.*, stood on part of the

134. Former Royal Infirmary, Pembroke Place, by Alfred Waterhouse (1887–90)

present site. In 1978 Waterhouse's building was superseded by the new hospital in Prescot Street (*see* Walk 8, p. 260). After years of dereliction it was acquired in the 1990s by the University, whose Estates Department removed later accretions and admirably refurbished it for new uses. It now appears more or less as designed. Common brick with red terracotta dressings, very plain, with some Romanesque and Gothic touches, and round arches used extensively. Administration block with Gothic gables and *porte-cochère* facing Pembroke Place. Behind, six ward blocks branch N and S from a spine corridor running from W to E (the link between administration block and wards has been demolished). The S ward blocks end with external arcaded balconies flanked by towers. Typical pavilion plan, except that the NW and NE blocks are circular, the earliest use of this plan form for a large-scale new hospital in England. Circular wards had recently been used at the Antwerp Civil Hospital which Waterhouse had visited, but they did not win the approval of Florence Nightingale when he consulted her over his Liverpool designs. They were nevertheless adopted because pre-existing buildings constricted the site at these two corners. In Ashton Street, at the E end of the spine corridor, are the mortuary and boiler house, the latter with a Gothic chimney. Interiors throughout the building are faced with glazed brick. At the W end of the spine corridor, in the middle of the Brownlow Street front, is the former **chapel**. It has nave and aisles, and beautiful turquoise tile work by *Burmantofts*.

In the early C20 the corners of the site became available for expansion. At the corner of Pembroke Place and Brownlow Street, a new outpatients' department (now the **Foresight Centre**) was added by *James F. Doyle*, 1909–11. Waterhousian Gothic in red brick and terracotta, with octagonal angle turrets. Inside, it had a full-height central waiting room lined with cream and green tiles, only the ends of which survive. At the corner of Pembroke Place and Ashton Street a new nurses' home (now

Cedar House) by *Edmund Kirby & Sons* was begun in 1923. This alone among the Infirmary buildings is classical.

Further w along Pembroke Place, just beyond Brownlow Street, is the **School of Tropical Medicine**. The central, uninspired Baroque part by *Sidney W. Doyle* was built in phases, 1913–15 and 1939–40, and flanked by dull extensions in 1966 and 1978. Opposite, Nos. 35 and 37–39 **Pembroke Place** are of *c.* 1840. The narrow gap between led originally to court housing at the rear, part of the same development. An early C19 house just w of these has the later tiled shopfront of a Jewish butcher.

Return to Brownlow Street, where more university buildings face the w side of the Royal Infirmary. The elegant **Jane Herdman Laboratories** of 1927–9, by *Briggs & Thornely*, were built for Geology. Brick, with stone dressings, in a Neoclassical style reminiscent of American campus buildings. A rear extension by *Weightman & Bullen*, set diagonally and linked by a glazed stair, was completed 1985. Next door on the s, the **Proudman Oceanographic Laboratory** by *Architects Design Partnership*, 2003. It reuses the steel frame of a 1920s Neo-Georgian building by *Arnold Thornely*. In Dover Street, facing the back of the infirmary, is the rear of the former **Muspratt Building**, 1905–6, by *Willink & Thicknesse*, with corner domes. Beyond, the **museum** of the demolished Royal Infirmary Medical School, a small ashlar classical block of 1872–3, by *Thomas Cook*. Returning to Brownlow Street, the large and ungainly former **Zoology Building** (now School of Biological Sciences) on the w side is by *Willink & Thicknesse*, opened 1905. Off-centre entrance under a stubby square tower. The doors have metal roundels sculpted (by whom?) with delicate representations of animals. Adjoining on the s is the **Derby Building** (originally Electrotechnics), of the same date and by the same architects, but Georgian in style, and on the N the **Hartley Building** (originally for Botany), opened in 1901, by *F. W. Dixon*. Opposite this group is **Civil Engineering**, 1958–9, by *E. Maxwell Fry*. A T-plan tower, rising from a podium. The E face of the tower is windowless and slightly concave, and bears the names of great engineers in large raised concrete letters. In the entrance hall a **mural** by *Peter Lanyon*, The Conflict of Man with the Tides and the Sands, 1959–60. Enamel on ceramic tiles.

Brownlow Street at its s end turns right to meet Great Newton Street, which marks the w edge of the University Precinct. Cross Great Newton Street and continue w along Newton Way to Gill Street, then turn N to **St Andrew's Gardens** [135]. This and the former Myrtle Gardens (now Minster Court – *see* p. 220, above), are almost all that remains of several ambitious estates of walk-up flats built by the City between the wars under its Director of Housing, *Lancelot Keay*. St Andrew's Gardens was designed by Keay's assistant *John Hughes*, and completed in 1935. The buildings are faced with buff brick. The main element is a five-storey, D-shaped block (the model was Bruno Taut and Martin Wagner's Horseshoe Estate, Berlin, admired by Keay on a visit in 1931) with

135. St Andrew's Gardens, by John Hughes (completed 1935)

continuous balconies overlooking a central court. The court has arched
entrances, semicircular on N and S, parabolic on W and E. This block
was refurbished in the 1990s; the rectilinear blocks that made up the
rest of the estate were either reduced in height or demolished.

From the N side of St Andrew's Gardens follow Copperas Hill SW,
back to the city centre. **Seymour Street**, right, has a long terrace, begun
c. 1810, rebuilt behind preserved façades 1992. *John Foster Sen.* was one
of the developers, and probably the architect. On the grassy area in the
middle of the road a bronze **sculpture**, Sea Circle, 1984 by *Charlotte
Mayer*. Cross Russell Street and continue down Copperas Hill. On the
left is the **Postal Sorting Office**, 1973–7, by *IDC Ltd* from a design by
Twist & Whitley. A huge oblong block clad in concrete panels, with a
cluster of brown brick towers marking the N entrance, and further
service towers on the other sides. Approached from Skelhorne Street it
looks impressively fortress-like. Resited in the enclosure left of the
entrance is a rare early **pillar box** of 1863, one of the unusually large
'Liverpool Special' boxes, with rope mouldings and a crown on top. The
triangular site bounded by Copperas Hill, Skelhorne Street and Bolton
Street is all student housing, 2003, grossly over-scaled and crudely
detailed and with mean little prison-like windows.

Copperas Hill brings us back to the Adelphi Hotel, where Walk 6
begins.

Walk 6.

Georgian Residential Area

This walk is complementary to the previous, covering the area immediately s of it. Although institutional buildings are numerous here, late c18 and especially early–mid-c19 terraces survive in large numbers, and much of the area is still residential. The route crosses and re-crosses Hope Street – one of the main N–S streets – several times.

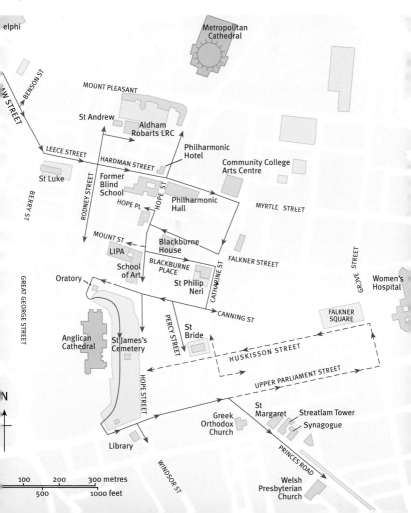

137. Former
Central Hall,
Renshaw
Street, by
Bradshaw &
Gass (opened
1905)

We begin at Ranelagh Place in front of the Adelphi Hotel (*see* Walk 3, p.
183), and head s along **Renshaw Street**. The tower of St Luke is visible
in the distance, and the Anglican Cathedral looms beyond. For Lewis's,
w side, *see* Walk 3, p. 182; for the former University Club, E, *see* Walk 5,
p. 210. On the s corner of Upper Newington is the former **Central Hall**
of the Liverpool Wesleyan Mission, by *Bradshaw & Gass* of Bolton,
opened 1905 [137]. Red brick and yellow terracotta, with a domed tower
over the corner entrance, a big dome over the main space, and further
subsidiary domes, some pointed. The style promiscuously mingles classical, Byzantine, Gothic and Jacobean, and much of the terracotta has a
swirly Art Nouveau character. It all looks thoroughly un-churchlike,
and might just as well have been a theatre or department store (the
large ground-floor windows were in fact designed for lettable shop
units). The Hall belongs to a national movement by the Methodists to
build such complexes around this time (Westminster is the most
famous example) which centralized their activities and created an iden-
tity distinct from the Church of England. As well as religious services,
concerts and other social activities provided a wholesome but attractive
alternative to pub and music-hall – hence, presumably, the secular
character of the architecture. Ironically, it is now a night club, with
ground-floor windows and decorative details playing up the Art
Nouveau aspects of the original design. The horseshoe-shaped main
auditorium seated 2,500.

Further along Renshaw Street, **Benson Street** turns off left. Nos. 8 and
10, *c.* 1842, were the offices (combined with a dwelling) of Samuel &

James Holme, leading mid-C19 building contractors. A handsome Greek Revival composition in ashlar, crowned by a pediment filled with acanthus scrolls, no doubt intended to advertise the firm's skills. *Arthur Hill Holme* (brother of Samuel and James) probably designed it, possibly with *John Cunningham*. Connected at the back is a big brick block with large arched openings, converted to residential use 2003. It probably formed part of Messrs Holme's extensive workshops, etc. Returning to Renshaw Street and continuing s, No. 75 is a narrow, gabled shop of 1904 by *Henry Hartley* for the ironmongers Quiggin Bros.

At the s end of Renshaw Street, turn left up the broad hill of **Leece Street**, with St Luke (*see* Walk 4, p. 197) on the right. This brings us to **Rodney Street**, which runs N–S. Laid out 1783–4 by William Roscoe and others, its length, width and straightness were unprecedented in Liverpool. It was developed piecemeal up to the 1820s with houses for the affluent, escaping the old town centre. A few have five bays with central doors, but most are three bays, erected in pairs or short runs and not always to a consistent building line. All are of brick. Many handsome doorcases, mostly recessed with columns, slender Ionic or slender Greek Doric, or Tuscan columns with pediments. In the longer s part, Nos. 51a–75 form a terrace with central pediment. No. 62, built for John Gladstone 1792–3, was probably designed by *John Whiteside Casson*. It was the birthplace of W.E. Gladstone. No. 31 has a porch with open pediment, probably 1914 by *Frank Rimmington*. No. 29, one of the five-bay houses, is said to have had a rainwater head dated 1811; the Greek Doric porch seems to be an addition, almost certainly that designed by *Edmund Aikin* and seen under construction by Thomas Rickman in 1817.

In the shorter, N part of Rodney Street stands the melancholy ruin of **St Andrew**, built for the Scottish Presbyterians, 1823–4, and burned out in 1983 [138]. The body, simple rendered brick with tiers of round-arched windows, was designed by the church's Committee of Management and their surveyor, *Daniel Stewart*. The once-imposing Greek Revival façade of blackened ashlar is by *John Foster Jun*. Picton considered it one of Foster's most successful efforts, and Schinkel sketched it during his 1826 visit to Liverpool. Recessed portico with Ionic columns, originally flanked by square towers with pedimented aedicules to each face, and small domes. N tower demolished. In the churchyard, single-storey **schools**, 1872, by *H.H. Vale*. Italianate with a Venetian window, and like the church ruinous. Also a notable **monument** to William Mackenzie, the railway contractor responsible for the Edge Hill-Lime Street tunnel (*see* topic box, p. 188), d. 1851. A large, plain granite pyramid, 1868.

Behind the church, approached from **Maryland Street**, is the most notable 1990s building in Liverpool, the white-rendered **Aldham Robarts Learning Resource Centre** of Liverpool John Moores University, 1992–3 by *Austin-Smith:Lord* [139]. It combines computer

138. St Andrew, Rodney Street, façade by John Foster Jun. (1823–4). Engraving by Henry Jorden after G. & C. Pyne (1828)

facilities with book stacks, and was intended to link physically with the restored church, forming a gateway to the university campus from Rodney Street. Square plan, divided into four subsidiary squares by internal 'streets' that cut across each floor N–S and W–E. Shallow curved

The Fosters

According to the C19 Liverpool architect and historian J.A. Picton, the Foster family 'for several generations managed the architectural and building affairs of the corporation'. Best known are *John Foster Sen.* (1758–1827), and his second son *John Foster Jun.* (*c.* 1787–1846). The former practised as builder and architect, apparently becoming Architect to the Corporation in 1789 and its Surveyor from 1801. He carried out alterations and additions to the Town Hall under James Wyatt, and built the Exchange (demolished) and the Union News Room in Duke Street. His son John studied under Jeffry Wyatt in London, and in 1809 went abroad and travelled in the eastern Mediterranean, spending time in Greece in the company of C.R. Cockerell and the German archaeologists Haller and Linckh. In 1810–11 he was involved with Cockerell in the excavation of the temples at Aegina and Bassae, with their exceptional sculptures. Returning in 1816, he joined the family building firm, succeeding his father as Corporation Surveyor in 1824 and holding the post until the Municipal Reform Act of 1835. Most of his numerous works were in an austere Greek Revival style, shaped by the travels of his youth. The majority have been demolished, including the second Royal Infirmary, Custom House, and the public baths at the Pier Head; among the few that survive are the derelict St Andrew in Rodney Street and the splendidly dramatic St James's Cemetery [146].

139. Aldham Robarts Learning Resource Centre, Maryland Street, by Austin-Smith:Lord (1992–3)

roofs identify these externally, and on N and S they end in glazed stair-towers. The main entrance is in the NE quarter, a three-storey atrium behind a wavy glass wall, set back under the oversailing space-frame roof. This links the building with its attractively landscaped grounds, and helps knit its uncompromisingly modern design into a largely C19 setting (for the university buildings to the N, *see* Walk 5, pp. 211–2).

Return along Rodney Street and turn left into **Hardman Street**. The fancy stuccoed block on the left at the W corner of Baltimore Street, dated 1866 on the gable end, was built as the Meyerbeer Hall. The name, and the decoration of the return elevation, indicate a musical use. On the E corner of Baltimore Street, a shopfront of 1888 in Queen Anne style, for the bakers Kirkland Bros. Immediately E of this stood St Philip, one of *John Cragg*'s cast-iron churches (*see* pp. 264 and 293), opened in 1816. Some ironwork fragments survive, inside the block built on the site of the churchyard after its closure in 1882.

Opposite, on the S side of Hardman Street, a stuccoed shop terrace with pediment, 1859 by *William Culshaw*. Next, the long Grecian frontage of the former **School for the Blind**, 1849–51 by *Arthur Hill Holme* (now the Merseyside Trade Union, Community and Unemployed Resource Centre), built when the school's original site in London Road was taken to extend Lime Street Station. The pedimented central section with rounded inset corners originally had single-storey three-bay wings, later extended by a further bay and raised to two storeys. Here was the committee room and a shop selling items made by pupils. Behind this show front of Bath stone the buildings are of brick, and more utilitarian. Four wings radiate from a domed rotunda, a plan reminiscent of mid-C19 workhouses. Those on the N, W and E contained dormitories, the S wing a concert room for perform-ances by pupils. A longer wing, at right angles to the S wing, was perhaps for rope-making. The entrance hall where the shop was located has pilasters and classical plasterwork, and the rotunda a cast-iron balcony with classical details. In 1986 the dome was painted in Socialist Realist style by *Mike Jones*, reflecting the present use: alongside marching Liverpool workers are the derelict Tate & Lyle sugar refinery (site of the Eldonian Village, *see* Walk 7, p. 256) and some mid-1980s City Council housing. On the Hope Street corner, left, an extension by the Liverpool-trained *Anthony Minoprio* and *Hugh Greville Spencely*, 1930–2: stripped classicism in Portland stone, the fluted pilasters echoing the vanished portico of *John Foster Jun.*'s Greek Doric chapel, 1818–19, moved here from the London Road site in 1850–1. Carvings by *John Skeaping* show activities at the school: brush-making, knitting, basket work, piano tuning and reading Braille. (Excellent bronze doors by *James Woodford* are now at the School's Wavertree premises; *see* the forthcoming *Buildings of England, Lancashire: Liverpool and the South West*.)

We have now reached **Hope Street**. It was straightened in the 1790s and houses began to appear *c*.1800 towards the N end. Facing the side of the Blind School extension is the **Philharmonic Hall**, 1936–9 by *Herbert J. Rowse* (its predecessor of 1846–9 by *John Cunningham* burned down in 1933). It owes something to Rowse's assistant *A.E. Rice*, who made a similar concert-hall design 1932–3, while at the Liverpool School of Architecture. Of brick, and starkly cubic except for two rounded stair-towers in front: the influence of the Dutch architect W.M. Dudok is clear. Rear extension by *Brock Carmichael Associates*, completed 1992. The main doors and first-floor windows of the Rowse building have **etched glass** by *Hector Whistler*. Just inside the entrance, a **memorial** to the musicians of the Titanic in repoussé copper, by *J.A. Hodel*. On the landings, gilded **reliefs** of Apollo by *Edmund C. Thompson* [140]. In contrast to the blocky exterior, the auditorium is sensuously curved. Walls and ceiling form a continuous shell, broken into gentle, over-lapping folds. Originally of fibrous plaster, this was entirely rebuilt in concrete by *Brock Carmichael*, working with acoustic consultants *Lawrence Kirkegaard Associates* (completed 1995). New recessed lights and other changes now sadly mar the smoothness of Rowse's design. Incised Art Deco female figures on the walls by *Thompson*, representing 'musical moods', were reinstated. These have been joined by a kinetic sculpture above the platform, Adagio, by *Marianne Forrest*, 1995. A cin-ema screen (part of the original equipment) can be raised from below.

On the NW corner of Hardman Street and Hope Street is the most richly decorated of Liverpool's Victorian pubs, the **Philharmonic Hotel**, *c*. 1898–1900 by *Walter W. Thomas*. It is of exceptional quality in national terms. Like the Vines in Lime Street (*see* walk 3, p. 184), built for the brewer Robert Cain, who aimed 'to so beautify the public houses under his control that they would be an ornament to the town of his birth'. Jauntily eclectic exterior with stepped gables, ogee domes, windows in many shapes and styles, and a serpentine balcony over the door. The

140. Philharmonic Hall, Hope
Street, by Herbert J. Rowse
(1936–9), panel by Edmund
C. Thompson

corner is excellent, with two canted bay windows almost touching
to form a sort of polygonal oriel. Superb Art Nouveau gates of wrought
iron and beaten copper (sometimes ascribed to *H. Bloomfield Bare*)
lead to the sumptuous interior, divided by mahogany and glass
partitions [141]. Music is a recurrent decorative theme, a reflection of
the name and of the nearby concert hall. The designers and craftsmen
were supervised by *G. Hall Neale* and *Arthur Stratton* (of the School of
Architecture and Applied Arts at University College). Repoussé copper
panels by *Bare* are set in panelling on either side of the fireplace. More
panels by *Bare* and *Thomas Huson* in the former billiard room; also
plasterwork by *C.J. Allen* – a frieze and two figure groups, The Murmur
of the Sea (over the fireplace) and attendants crowning a bust of Apollo
(over the door). The decorative richness even extends to the lavatories.

A short detour N along Hope Street (dramatically closed by the
Metropolitan Cathedral) takes us past early C19 houses to the **Masonic
Hall**, a four-bay palazzo of 1872 by Mr *Danson* of *Danson & Davies*
(entrance and interior altered by *Gilbert Fraser* and *W.P. Horsburgh*,
1927–31). Return and turn E into **Myrtle Street**, the continuation of
Hardman Street. First on the left is the former **Lying-in Hospital**, 1861
by *J.D. Jee*. Rock-faced with ashlar dressings, Tudor, with a little oriel
below the central gable. The Neo-Georgian rear addition (eight storeys,
but very narrow) is by *Rees & Holt*, 1931, the first stage of a planned
rebuilding for the Cancer Hospital. Next door, the former **Eye and Ear**

141. Philharmonic Hotel, Hope Street, by Walter W. Thomas (*c.* 1898–1900)

Infirmary, 1878–80 by *C.O. Ellison*. A lively design in Old English style à la Norman Shaw. Red brick with red sandstone and moulded terracotta, timber-framed gables, and splendid tall chimneys, corbelled out at the top. Converted to flats, 2003. After this, the Gothic **St Luke's Art Workshops**, 1880, by *Henry Sumners*. Built for *Norbury, Upton & Paterson*, architectural carvers, whose work adorns the façade. The front block, divided by an off-centre buttress with a statue in a niche, contained showrooms and offices. The ground floor, right, originally had a gateway to the masons' yard behind. On the opposite, s side, the former **Sheltering Home for Destitute Children**, 1888–9, *Ellison* again, this time on a tight budget: red and brown brick, rather grim. At the corner of Sugnall Street, facing the back of the Philharmonic Hall, it incorporates an 1840s house with nice ashlar details, including a segmental bow to the s. Further along on the N side of Myrtle Street, the **Arts Centre** of Liverpool Community College, 1999, by *Austin-Smith: Lord*. Red brick, with an oversailing aluminium roof supported by a slender column at the corner.

From Myrtle Street turn right into **Catharine Street**. On the E side is **Agnes Jones House**, formerly the Women's Hospital, 1932. Neo-Georgian by *Edmund Kirby & Sons*. Recently converted into student accommodation for the University of Liverpool by *Brock Carmichael*. Opposite, **Philharmonic Court**, early city-centre student housing for the University, begun 1973 by *Saunders & Boston*. C19 terraced houses here and in Falkner Street were converted into flats, with new three-storey blocks behind: a little like C19 court housing (*see* topic box, p. 8), though much more spacious, of course. The **Blackburne Arms**, on the s corner of Falkner Street, is an elegant Neo-Georgian pub by *Harold E. Davies & Son* (i.e. *Harold Hinchliffe Davies*), 1927.

Turn right into **Falkner Street**, where more C19 terraces lead back to Hope Street. Here, almost opposite, is the majestic former **Hahnemann Homeopathic Hospital**. Loire château style in red Ruabon brick and stone, by *F. & G. Holme*, dated 1887. Built at the expense of the sugar magnate Henry Tate. It was ventilated according to the system of Drs Drysdale and Hayward (*see* p. 220). The hospital stands on the s corner of Hope Place. On the N corner, a former carriage works of *c.* 1867, converted to a hotel 2003. Buff brick with round-arched first-floor windows – a sort of pared-down Venetian palazzo, surprisingly grand. **Hope Place** has terraced houses. On the right at the bottom is the **Joe H. Makin Drama Centre** of Liverpool John Moores University, formerly the Hebrew Schools by *Messes Hay*, begun 1852. Brick with stone dressings, Gothic, with Dec windows between buttresses and a central doorway under a gable. Next door, the **Unity Theatre** occupies a former synagogue of 1856–7 by *Thomas Wylie*. Yellow brick with stone dressings and touches of polychromy, in what *The Builder* called 'a modification of the Byzantine or Cinque-cento style'. The original vestry and Reader's house formed advancing wings, with an arcaded portico between. A high hemispherical dome with windows round the base, distinctly Byzantine, soon proved defective and was replaced with a shallower dome. Rebuilding *c.* 1997 by *Mills Beaumont Leavey Channon* of Manchester, in connection with the current use, did away with the dome and incorporated the portico into a projecting glazed foyer (painted top-floor window by *Terry Duffy*), with two performance spaces stacked behind. Joining of new and old is awkward.

Return to Hope Street. Opposite the end of Hope Place is **Federation House**, 1965–6, by *Gilling Dod & Partners* for the Building Trades Employers. Curtain walling; ground floor with an aggressive concrete relief by *William Mitchell*. Turn s along Hope Street. On the left, behind walled grounds, is **Blackburne House**. The s part, built as a private house *c.* 1800, has a portico of four columns facing s, and a central staircase hall under a domed skylight. In 1844 it became the girls' school of the Mechanics' Institution (*see* below), latterly the Liverpool Institute High School for Girls. In 1874–6 *W.I. Mason* added the central tower with French pavilion roof, and the N wing that balances the original house, which was partly re-faced to match. In 1994 *Pickles Martinez Architects* completed a sensitive adaptation as a women's training centre.

Where Hope Street widens at the top of Mount Street there is a curious **sculpture**, A Case History, by *John King*, completed 1998. Items of luggage, cast in fine-surfaced concrete, are piled on the pavement. Their labels refer to individuals and institutions linked with the area.

142. LIPA, Mount Street: former Mechanics' Institution by A.H. Holme (1835–7), converted by Brock Carmichael Associates (1992–6)

Turn right into **Mount Street**. Nos. 7–33 are small houses probably *c.* 1820, stepping downhill. On the s side is **LIPA**, the Liverpool Institute of Performing Arts, built 1835–7 as the Mechanics' Institution (the date 1825 on the façade refers to its inception) [142]. The competition was won by *Arthur Hill Holme*, then an apprentice in the Birmingham office of Thomas Rickman. *James Picton* was executant architect. Ashlar façade, restrained but imposing, with pairs of giant unfluted Ionic columns at the entrance, and no pediment. Intended to offer instruction to working men, the Institution developed into a notable day school, changing its name to the Liverpool Institute. Converted to its present use by *Brock Carmichael Associates* 1992–6. They rebuilt the rear parts (creating a new main entrance), added a ramped approach to Holme's entrance, and designed a new block to the right, with elevations to Mount Street and Pilgrim Street. This is mostly stone-faced, but the curved corner is glazed, enclosing a helical staircase. On the Pilgrim Street front, windows in vertical strips project at an angle. Between new and old, a glazed atrium. The c19 entrance hall has cast-iron gates between Ionic columns. Straight ahead is the U-shaped former lecture hall (now a theatre), with a gallery on slender iron columns, reached by two graceful open staircases outside the door.

Adjoining, e, is the earliest part of the **Liverpool Art School**, dated 1882, by *Thomas Cook*. Classical details, but no particular style. North-facing studio windows. The main entrance is now round the corner in Hope Street, in a wing by *Willink & Thicknesse* dated 1910. This is one of Liverpool's best buildings in the refined classical style promoted by

Charles Reilly (*see* topic box, p. 218). *Cook*'s return elevation is not parallel with Hope Street, and Willink & Thicknesse mirror this at the other end, so the Hope Street façade is gently concave. Square central porch, flanked by segmental bows with giant panelled pilasters. In 1961 a further extension along Hope Street was opened, designed by the City Architect's Department (*Ronald Bradbury*). Mostly curtain-walled, with brick at the s end. On the E side of Hope Street, facing the Art School, houses of the 1820s.

From Hope Street, turn E into Blackburne Place. On the left is Blackburne House (*see* above). Opposite, **Mildmay House**, 1880s, built to provide respectable lodgings for working women. Red brick with a corner turret. After this, set back behind a carriage drive, **Blackburne Terrace**: six houses, dated 1826. The middle four have paired Doric porches. Opposite, an impressive square **ventilation tower** to the 1826–9 railway tunnel from Edge Hill to the former goods station at Wapping. It presumably dates from the 1890s, when locomotives began working the tunnel in place of rope-hauled wagons.

At the s corner of Blackburne Place and Catharine Street is **St Philip Neri (R.C.)**. *Matthew Honan* exhibited drawings in 1912, simplified in execution by *M.J. Worthy* and *Alfred Rigby*, after Honan died in the First World War. The church opened in 1920. Neo-Byzantine, red brick with stone dressings, with a vault of reinforced concrete. Round-arched door flanked by baptistery and chapel, forming a single-storey projection across the front. The doorway carvings of Christ and the Virgin and Child, and a life-size Last Supper above, were completed by *Tom Murphy* after 1945. Broad nave of six bays with passage aisles (the left one added later) and arcades of square piers with chunky capitals, some carved. A segmental vault over the first three bays, a dome over the other three, and a semi-dome over the apsidal sanctuary. The nave vaults look like stone, but the surface is cork, applied to the concrete by *F.X. Velarde* to remedy damp. Above the arcades and in the apse, mosaics and coloured marbles create an atmosphere of Byzantine splendour. **Altar gates** said to have been designed by *Peter Kavanagh*. In the right aisle, attractive **murals** of biblical scenes (part of an uncompleted scheme), *c.* 1954 by *Robin McGhie*, who also designed the reliefs under the gallery.

Continue s along Catharine Street to **Canning Street**, one of the longest and best-preserved C19 residential streets in the area. The E continuation of Duke Street (*see* Walk 4, pp. 204–7), it was laid out in the late 1820s–early 1830s to link up with the town centre. Mostly lined with red brick three-bay terraces, of three storeys above a basement, with columned doorcases. Since the 1980s, through co-operation between owners, City Council and government agencies, much has been done here and in neighbouring streets to reverse years of decay. Turn left to glance at the E part, seemingly built up from the 1840s. The elevation of Nos. 18–50, on the s side up to Bedford Street, was approved

143. Nos. 3–17 Percy Street (probably early 1830s)

by the Corporation in 1845: two pediments, and cast-iron balconies of lush acanthus. The developer was the lawyer Ambrose Lace. Opposite is a stuccoed Italianate terrace, probably 1850s. In the earlier, w part of Canning Street, across Catharine Street, Nos. 4–16, unusually, are stone-faced. Nos. 1–43 opposite were mostly complete by 1836.

Turn s from the w part of Canning Street into **Percy Street**, the most distinguished in the area, with stone-faced houses, mostly in terraces of markedly original design. Nos. 2 and 4, Tudor Gothic, are dated 1835. The rest are Grecian, and seem to be mostly of *c.* 1830–6. Nos. 3–17, E side, form a tripartite composition, with a projecting pedimented centre and ends with giant pilasters [143]. Doric colonnades support balconies in front of the recessed parts. No. 6, w side, has four bays and first-floor pilasters. Nos. 8–18 have giant Corinthian pilasters and pediments framing the end houses. The porches have square columns. Nos. 20–32, simpler, have Soanian incised decoration round the doors. Who designed these houses, so unlike those in neighbouring streets? *John Foster Jun.* has been suggested, but his buildings show none of their inventiveness. Other possibilities are *Samuel Rowland*, architect of St Bride (*see* below), and *John Cunningham*, an Edinburgh-trained architect brought to Liverpool in the 1830s by the builder Samuel Holme, one of the Percy Street lessees.

On the E side is **St Bride**, 1829–30 by *Samuel Rowland* [144]. The best surviving Neoclassical church in the city. Set in a railed enclosure, with pedimented gatepiers of cast iron. A temple-like rectangular box, tower-less, with a monumental portico of six unfluted Ionic columns across

144. St Bride, Percy Street, by Samuel Rowland (1829–30)

the w end. Under the portico, two imposing doorways and a large central window, all with inward-sloping sides. The side elevations have six tall windows also with inward-sloping sides, with fine architraves on brackets. Bays one and six are flanked by giant pilasters, with bands of anthemion at the top. The slightly projecting chancel, E, has a large tripartite and pedimented window and is flanked by lower vestries. Inside, three galleries on slender cast-iron columns, connected by sweeping quadrant curves (the space underneath partitioned off in the 1980s). The chancel is framed by massive square piers with anthemion decoration, and the E window has unfluted Ionic columns. Carved and gilded **royal arms**, w end, dated 1817, from St John, Old Haymarket. – **Stained glass**: E window, *c.* 1905, Renaissance style. – **Monuments**: chancel, Rev. J.H. Stewart, d. 1854, by *Patteson* of Manchester, tablet with veiled urn. – Near the NE entrance, tablet by *William Spence* to W.M. Forster, his wife and servant, drowned in the wreck of the steamer Rothesay Castle, 1831.

Return N to Canning Street and turn w. The Anglican Cathedral (*see* Major Buildings, p. 73) now comes into view. Facing it across Hope Street and the wooded chasm of St James's Cemetery is **Gambier Terrace** [145]. Open views to the w made this a most desirable residential site, and in 1828 the developer Ambrose Lace obtained approval for a terrace here. Six houses were built in the early 1830s, four more in the late 1830s–early 1840s, but the terrace was not completed until the early 1870s, to a very different design. The architect of the original (N) part is unknown. It is of ashlar and stucco, and extremely grand. The first

145. Gambier Terrace (begun early 1830s)

seven bays have giant attached Ionic columns above, and a Greek Doric porch (also an enclosed Doric porch at the side, in Canning Street); then come twenty-one recessed bays with a Doric colonnade in front of the ground floor, supporting a continuous first-floor balcony (the same motif as Nos. 3–17 Percy Street); then six bays with giant Doric pilasters, suggesting the start of a centrepiece. No. 10, though it matches, in fact dates from the early 1870s. The rest of the 1870s section is of yellow brick, symmetrical in itself, with pavilion-roofed end blocks. Carriage drive with distinctive gateposts at the N end: fluted columns, with crown-like tops on inward-curving petals.

Continue w, downhill, from Canning Street into Upper Duke Street. **Mornington Terrace**, N, is a row of five brick houses, *c.* 1839–40, the middle one with a pediment. On the opposite side at the corner of Cathedral Gate is the **Dean Walters Building** of Liverpool John Moores University, *c.* 1990, by *Building Design Partnership*. Postmodern Neo-Georgian, out of respect for nearby Rodney Street. Two wings and a domed corner tower, in red brick with much white-painted concrete. A recent matching addition extends to Great George Street.

Opposite Mornington Terrace is the **Oratory**, the former chapel of **St James's Cemetery**, which it overlooks. The cemetery was laid out 1827–9, to the designs of *John Foster Jun.* Overcrowded burial-grounds attached to town churches were a major public health problem by the early C19, and St James's Cemetery is an exceptionally ambitious attempt at a sanitary alternative. For sheer drama its only rival is the Glasgow Necropolis, but whereas the Necropolis climbs a hill, the

Liverpool cemetery lies in the sombre depths of a rocky hollow – a former quarry, from which stone for the docks and other c18 buildings had been obtained. **The Oratory** (where services were held before interments took place) is *Foster*'s best surviving building, a perfect Greek Doric temple with a six-column portico at each end. The walls are windowless, the interior lit from above. Ionic columns support the coffered plaster ceiling. Rich collection of **monuments**, mostly Neoclassical reliefs, some brought in the 1980s from demolished buildings. They include: the Nicholson family, 1834 by *Francis Chantrey*, with mourners over an urn; William Earle d. 1839, by *John Gibson*, seated in profile, wrapped in a cloak and musing over a book; Dr William Stevenson d. 1853, by *J.A.P. Macbride*, a sickbed scene with the doctor in attendance (originally in St Mary, Birkenhead, where its Gothic frame would have seemed less alien); William Hammerton d. 1832, by *Gibson*, a fine relief of mother and children receiving charity, in classical dress; William Ewart d. 1823, by *Joseph Gott*, a vivid, informal statue sitting with legs crossed, amiably expounding something; Emily Robinson

Terraced Houses

Apart from isolated examples such as Clayton Square and the w side of Castle Street, terraced properties in c18 Liverpool were not generally built to a unified design. Even in prestigious Rodney Street most houses were erected singly or in small groups, and not always to the same building line. Most of Liverpool's late Georgian and early Victorian housing was developed speculatively, with large plots leased from the Corporation by financiers, who divided them into parcels for builders. This system did not favour consistency of architectural treatment, so for two prestigious early c19 developments, Great George Square and Abercromby Square, the Corporation required developers to conform with designs for symmetrical elevations, agreed in advance. The designs were quite simple, with just a pediment or porch marking the centre of each side. Terraces of the 1820s–40s around Canning Street are more or less uniform in height and building line, but rather than forming a grand composition, each generally consists of a standard house repeated as many times as necessary to complete the row. Such repetitiveness displeased the local architectural writer Samuel Huggins, who in 1849 criticized similar buildings in Shaw Street, Everton: 'With the exception of a couple of Ionic columns as a doorcase to each house, it is one dead merely perforated wall from end to end'. In Percy Street and Gambier Terrace in the 1830s a more sophisticated approach was adopted, comparable with early c19 Edinburgh, in which individual houses are subordinate to an overall palatial composition. In Falkner Square, built up in the 1840s, the earliest side has a flat, unified elevation, but bay windows disrupt the continuity of the other terraces and symmetry starts to break down.

146. St James's Cemetery, by John Foster Jun. (1827–9). Aquatint after T.T. Bury (before 1834)

d. 1829, by *Gibson*, seated in profile, modelled on a Greek stele; Agnes Jones d. 1868, by *Pietro Tenerani*, a free-standing Angel of the Resurrection with trumpet (originally in the chapel of the Brownlow Hill Workhouse). A red granite slab right of the entrance commemorates Foster, who 'on his return from long and arduous travels in the pursuit of his art . . . enriched his native town with the fruits of his genius, industry and integrity' (*see* topic box, p. 232).

On the s side of the Oratory we descend to the cemetery [146] by a path, lined with gravestones, which passes through a tunnel in the rock. From the bottom the Oratory appears perched on the edge of an Acropolis-like cliff, and the cathedral is seen in awesome perspective. The N, W and s faces are rough and wooded. The long E face, now heavily overgrown, was shaped by Foster into monumental terraces lined with catacombs and ramps. The catacombs have round-arched entrances with rusticated surrounds. The scale is colossal – was Foster influenced by ancient sites such as Palestrina? Regrettably, *c.* 1969–71 the cemetery floor was cleared of most of its gravestones for a public garden. In the middle stands the **Huskisson Mausoleum**, a circular domed temple of 1833–4 by *Foster*, based on the Choragic Monument of Lysicrates. It marks the grave of William Huskisson, the Liverpool MP fatally injured at the opening of the Liverpool & Manchester Railway. Originally it contained a marble statue by *Gibson*.

Leaving the cemetery at the sw corner through a splendid rusticated entrance **arch**, turn left past Foster's **lodge** to **Upper Parliament Street**, the extension of Parliament Street made in 1807. It marked the boundary between Liverpool and Toxteth Park until 1835. On the s side, at the corner of Windsor Street, is **Toxteth Library**, 1900–2, one of several branch libraries designed in the office of the Corporation Surveyor, *Thomas Shelmerdine*. Red brick and stone trim. Symmetrical to Windsor Street, with two big Venetian windows under gables with obelisks, the main entrance with a far-projecting hood. Small cupola above. Two more Venetian windows to Upper Parliament Street. The former reading room (N side) contains a mural by *W. Alison Martin* and *Clinton Balmer*, an allegory with Knowledge enthroned; also a copper plaque in Celtic Art Nouveau style by *C.E. Thompson*, commemorating the opening by Andrew Carnegie. (On the E side of Windsor Street, further S, interesting buildings for Toxteth TV by *Union North*, 2003. One block is polychrome brick, one timber-clad.)

Continue E along Upper Parliament Street, which has early C19 houses. At the W corner of Parliament Place is the **Third Church of Christ Scientist**, 1914, designed by *W.H. Ansell* as a Temple of Humanity for the Positivist church. A stark brick building, notable for having few historicist details. Windowless canted apse to Upper Parliament Street, Diocletian clerestory windows above the blank side aisles.

Turn right into **Princes Road**. On the E corner is the fine **Florence Nightingale Memorial**, 1913 by *Willink & Thicknesse*, with sculpture by *C.J. Allen*. Subtly detailed Ionic aedicule, framing a relief of her ministering to two men. It is built into the boundary wall of the former **Liverpool Queen Victoria District Nursing Association**, a nurses' home of 1900 by *James F. Doyle*, incorporating an earlier house on the left. The drive-in **NatWest Bank**, opposite, is of *c.* 1982 by *Gerald Beech*. Brick, with rounded corners clad in stainless steel, and a mansard roof. Next, with its entrance in **Berkley Street**, is the exotic **Greek Orthodox Church of St Nicholas** [147]. It is a close copy, considerably enlarged, of the former church of St Theodore in Constantinople, as illustrated in James Fergusson's *Handbook of Architecture* (1855). The idea of adopting this Byzantine model was due to *W. & J. Hay*, who won a competition in 1864, but building was carried out under *Henry Sumners*, and authorship was disputed when it opened in 1870. Red brick, with much stone. Three domes over the front, a fourth over the nave. They are raised on polygonal drums with round-arched windows on each face. *The Builder* described the stilted round-arched apse windows as 'an ugly and disproportioned feature to which no considerations of archaeology can reconcile us'. Interior spatially impressive, but without the richly coloured decoration that the exterior and the style lead one to expect. Under the W domes a narthex, with gallery overlooking the nave. The plan of nave and aisles is a cross within a rectangle. White marble columns with Byzantine capitals carry the central dome. The four arms have tunnel vaults. E end screened by the richly carved iconostasis.

Back on the opposite side of Princes Road is the attractive group of **St Margaret** with its **vicarage** connected and set at an angle, 1868–9 by *George Edmund Street*. Paid for by the stockbroker Robert Horsfall (*see* topic box, p. 247), this was the centre of Anglo-Catholicism in C19 Liverpool. *The Architect* wrote in 1869: 'Perhaps, indeed, Mr Street has seldom produced a more thoroughly natural and simple work . . .

147. Greek Orthodox Church of St Nicholas, Berkley Street, by Henry Sumners (opened 1870)

possessing architectural qualities which will hold their own when fast-Gothic and fast-Art of all kinds have given way to increasing knowledge'. Simple but dignified Dec. Gothic exterior of common brick with red stone dressings – the style more English-looking than French, unusually for Street. A timber bellcote marks the division between nave and chancel. In the centre of the w front a buttress with a statue of St Margaret in a niche, flanked by three-light windows and doors straight into each aisle. Interior much richer, though currently in sad decay (repairs carried out 2004). Five-bay nave without clerestory. Piers with clustered shafts of Irish marbles, laid in bands of alternating colours. Raised chancel, with sedilia and piscina, enclosed by a low marble wall. Divided from the E end of the s aisle by a two-bay arcade is a shallow, transept-like space (the corresponding N arches have been filled, and behind them the separate Jesus Chapel replaces the former 'transept'). Much C19 **painted decoration**: saints, biblical scenes, and Stations of the Cross, with stencilled borders. Particularly beautiful is the Marriage Feast at Cana, w wall. *Maddox & Pearce* appear to have been chiefly responsible, with some earlier work by *Clayton & Bell*; redecoration by *Campbell Smith*, 1967. – Wrought-iron sanctuary **gates** by *Skidmore* (also the **font cover**?). – **Pulpit** with busts of saints in gilded wood. – **High altar** with *opus sectile* reredos, postwar. – In the chancel floor, **brass** to Robert Horsfall, d. 1881, by *Barkentin & Krall*. Horsfall sits at the foot, holding a drawing of the church [148]. – Good **stained glass**, mostly *Clayton & Bell*. s aisle w window in German Renaissance style by *Percy Bacon Bros*. Two large E windows are postwar replacements, designed by *Gerald E.R. Smith* and *H.L. Pawle*, made by the *A.K.*

The Horsfalls: Liverpool Church Builders

The Horsfalls were exceptional patrons of church building in Liverpool over three generations. Charles H. Horsfall, a merchant living in Everton who became Mayor in 1832, was among the founders of St George, Heyworth Street, 1813–14 (*see* Walk 8, p. 264). In 1848 his sons, including Thomas Berry Horsfall (1805–78), Robert (1806/7–81) and George (1824–1900), built Christ Church, Great Homer Street, in memory of their father. This ambitious Gothic Revival building by *E.H. Shellard* of Manchester was bombed in 1941. Robert, a stock-

148. Robert Horsfall, d. 1881, from his memorial brass in St. Margaret, Princes Road

broker, later came under the influence of the Oxford Movement. He built the modest St James-the-Less on Stanley Road (demolished) and in 1868 employed *G.E. Street* to design St Margaret, Princes Road, as a focus for ritualism in Liverpool (*see* p. 245). George, by contrast, was an Evangelical. He paid for *Culshaw & Sumners*'s Christ Church, Linnet Lane (*see* Walk 10, p. 280).

Most munificent of all was Robert's son, H. Douglas Horsfall (1856–1936), who shared his father's Anglo-Catholicism. He and his mother built St Agnes, Ullet Road, designed by *J.L. Pearson*, with vicarage and church hall by *Norman Shaw* (*see* Walk 10, p. 284), and its daughter church of St Pancras, Lidderdale Road (demolished). He also employed Shaw to design his own house, Mere Bank (demolished), close to St Agnes. Later he paid for St Faith, Crosby, 1900, and St Paul, Stoneycroft, 1916 (both outside the scope of this guide), and beyond Merseyside he founded St Chad's theological college at Durham. He offered to pay for the reredos of Liverpool Cathedral, on condition it represented the Crucifixion, but this attempt to impose his Anglo-Catholic views was unsuccessful and his gift was declined. Robert and Douglas Horsfall are notable for employing leading national architects of their day, rather than only local designers.

Nicholson Studio. The **Jesus Chapel**, added on the N by *Hubert B. Adderley*, 1924–6, has C19 stained glass reset from the aisle, and an elaborate polychrome Gothic reredos.*

*Opposite St Margaret, the Kuumba Imani Millennium Centre, *Brock Carmichael*, under construction 2004.

Right of the church is **Streatlam Tower**, 1871, a large Gothic house of common brick and red sandstone, with a conical-roofed tower. Designed by *W. & G. Audsley* for the wool broker James L. Bowes and his collection of Japanese art. Incised disc patterns on the forward-projecting wing at the left may hint at Bowes's Japanese interests (this was possibly the entrance used by visitors to the collection).

Next door is the **synagogue**, the most memorable work of *W. & G. Audsley* surviving in Liverpool, and one of the finest examples of Orientalism in British synagogue architecture. It replaced one of 1807 in Seel Street, by *John Harrison*. The Audsleys won the competition in 1871, and the building opened in 1874. Common brick, with red brick, red sandstone and polished red granite, combining Gothic and Moorish elements. Façade with high, gabled centre and lower wings, reflecting the division into nave and aisles. Centre framed by octagonal turrets. These, and the outer square turrets, had arcaded and domed finials like minarets (removed in 1961, a sad loss). The w door and rose window above are Gothic, but incorporate Moorish lobed arches. Interior dazzlingly rich with polychrome stencilled decoration, restored, but said to follow the original [149]. Pointed horseshoe arcades spring from tapering octagonal columns of cast iron. Plaster tunnel vault over the nave, with transverse vaults. Seats in the aisles and galleries face inwards. The e end is divided off by a giant lobed horseshoe arch, framing the e rose window. Below this is the gleaming focus, the **Ark**, of multi-coloured marbles with five richly painted domes, like something out of the Arabian Nights. Carved by *Alfred Norbury*. In front, the equally rich **pulpit** and, further w in the central space, the sumptuous **Bimah**, or reading platform (presented in 1875 by David Lewis, founder of Lewis's department store), both also carved by *Norbury*. Stained glass with abstract and floral patterns, by *R.B. Edmundson & Son* to the Audsleys' designs.

Just s is the former **Adult Deaf and Dumb Institute**, 1886–7 by *E.H. Banner*. Gothic, red brick and terracotta. Basically octagonal, with four short two-storey wings, and single-storey projections between – the form recalls Caröe's Swedish Seamen's Church in Park Lane (*see* Walk 4, p. 208). The ground floor originally contained rooms for recreation, education, etc. The chapel above had tiered seating so the congregation could see the minister's sign language. On the opposite side of Princes Road at the corner of Upper Hill Street, the derelict former **Welsh Presbyterian Church**, opened 1868, by the *Audsleys* again. A proud and ambitious design, reflecting the success of Liverpool's C19 Welsh community. Early French Gothic in rock-faced stone. Nave and transepts form a T-plan, with an impressive nw steeple, the spire surrounded by pinnacles. Mostly plate tracery. w gable and crossing roof recently taken down. Brick lecture rooms and vestries behind.

149. Synagogue, Princes Road, by W. & G. Audsley (1871–4)

From here the journey back to the centre can be made by bus or on foot. Those with sufficient stamina who want to see more 1830s–40s housing can take the following **detour**:

Return to Upper Parliament Street and turn right. Nos. 96–98, s side, have at their core an ambitious five-bay house of *c.* 1840. Porch with paired Ionic columns, decorative window surrounds in ashlar, elaborate cast-iron balconies. Further E on the opposite side is **Falkner Terrace** (Nos. 155–177), stuccoed, with first-floor pilasters. Mostly in existence by 1831, it stood isolated for years before the surrounding streets were built up. Restoration by *TACP* completed 1986.

Turn N into Grove Street. On the right, the **Liverpool Women's Hospital**, 1992–5, by the *Percy Thomas Partnership* from a conceptual design by *HLM*: red brick and white cladding with light blue metal roofs (sculpture outside main E entrance, Mother and Child, 1999 by *Terry McDonald*). Grove Street leads to **Falkner Square**. The central garden is shown planted on a map of 1831, but the stuccoed houses did not begin to appear until the mid 1840s. The E side is a unified composition with a central pediment. The rest are looser, and several houses have canted bay windows, and balustraded balconies and parapets. Elevations for the s side were approved in 1845, and N and s sides were both under construction in 1845–6. Drawings for No. 29 are signed by *William Culshaw*, 1845. Was he responsible for the whole s elevation and therefore probably those on the N and w too, or did his drawings conform to an overall elevation by another?

Leave the square at the sw corner and follow **Huskisson Street** westward, with mid-C19 terraces on both sides. No. 3, N side, at the corner of Catharine Street, was built in 1839 for the Rev. John Jones, and altered in the 1850s–60s by *Culshaw & Sumners* for the hide broker Isaac Hadwen Jun. Turn s along Catharine Street and E into **Egerton Street**, which has modest two-storey houses of *c.* 1844 tucked behind the larger terraces of the main streets. No. 2 is an interesting pub, **Peter Kavanagh's**, with an early C20 tiled façade and murals of *c.* 1929 by *Eric Robertson* inside, with subjects from Dickens and Hogarth.

Back in Catharine Street, Nos. 44–50, just N of St Bride, are stuccoed with columned porches, *c.* 1840. Huskisson Street w of Catharine Street has a symmetrical terrace of *c.* 1832 at Nos. 30–42, facing the side of St Bride. Continue w along Huskisson Street to Hope Street. On the s corner is an early 1830s stuccoed terrace with continuous first-floor balcony; ahead, a fine view of the Anglican Cathedral across the cemetery.

Walk 7.

North of the Centre
Between the Docks and Scotland Road

Development of this area began with the construction of the Leeds and Liverpool Canal at the end of the C18. During the C19 the town advanced northward, shadowing the inexorable progress of the docks. The growth of industry around the canal, and the arrival of the railways with their goods yards from the 1840s, were accompanied by a tide of slum housing. Construction of the approach roads to the second Mersey Tunnel, Kingsway (first stage opened 1971; completed 1974) entailed much demolition, and economic decline in the late C20 erased more of the historic fabric. When Pevsner wrote in the 1960s, streets close to the river were still dominated by multi-storey brick warehouses. Today these have largely given way to low-rise sheds. In housing the changes have been even more marked. Early C20 and postwar council flats have been replaced by informally grouped co-operative housing, and private developers have built in the same style. Elsewhere, large tracts of cleared land await reuse. Against this transformed background a handful of C19 churches stand as reminders of the past.

The buildings of interest are widely scattered and can be found with the help of the map on p. 252.

The Leeds and Liverpool Canal

The **Leeds and Liverpool Canal** runs N–S through the area. Begun in 1770, the section from Liverpool to Wigan opened in 1774 and immediately became the principal route for coal into Liverpool. The full length opened in 1816, linking the growing port with the manufacturing towns of E Lancashire and Yorkshire. The terminus was in Old Hall Street (q.v., p. 161), and there were branches E of what is now Pall Mall. Manufacturing, including gas and chemical works, was drawn to the canal by the transport opportunities it offered, and by the ready availability of coal. These industries have all but disappeared, and the whole canal s of Burlington Street is now filled in, but evidence of its route can still be seen. On the E side of **Pall Mall**, N of Leeds Street, is a long range of mostly single-storey **warehouses** with cast-iron arched entrances. Some are late C19, others perhaps early C20. They were built on the w bank, with direct access to the wharf. Just N of these, in **Chisenhale Street**, is a former canal **bridge**, with pedimented abutments and Gothic cast-iron railings. Further N, where the waterway survives with

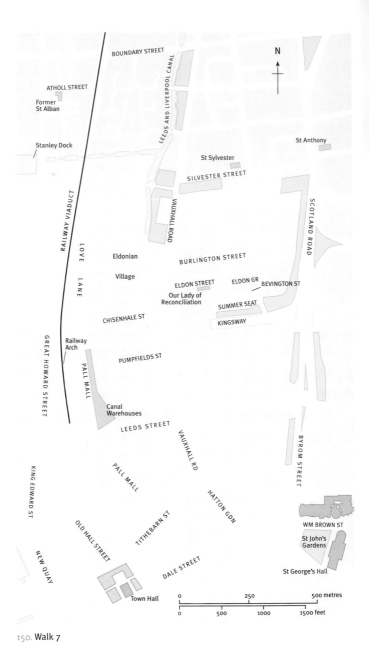

150. Walk 7

newly landscaped banks, are **Leigh Bridge** (1861) and **Boundary Bridge** (1836, widened 1861). In 1848 the canal was connected to the dock system and the Mersey by a sequence of four locks [151] designed by *J. B. Hartley*, linked with Stanley Dock (*see* Walk 2, p. 124).

Leeds and Liverpool Canal link to Stanley Dock, crossed by railway viaduct

Railway Viaduct

w of the canal and parallel with the river is a second transport artery, the **railway viaduct** of 1846–8 [151], built by *William McCormick* and *S. & J. Holme*; the chief engineer was *James Thomson*. Red brick with stone dressings, originally over a mile long, with 117 arches. It was built for the Liverpool & Bury Railway, but during construction this company was absorbed by the Manchester & Leeds, which in 1847 became the Lancashire & Yorkshire Railway. It is now linked to the Merseyrail underground system. At first the terminus was in Great Howard Street, just s of Chadwick Street, but the line was immediately continued s to a new station in Tithebarn Street (*see* pp. 163–4), and the Great Howard Street terminus was enlarged to become the L&YR's goods station. At this time the London & North Western Railway was constructing a goods line from Edge Hill to Waterloo Dock, which emerged from its tunnel just E of the Great Howard Street terminus. To carry the L&YR over the LNWR's line, a tremendous **arch** was built with a span of *c.* 100 ft (30 metres), containing, it was said, some five and a half million bricks. It is as impressive in its way as the exactly contemporary vault of St George's Hall (*see* Major Buildings, p. 54). The arch can be entered from the car park on the w side of Pall Mall, between Chadwick Street and Leeds Street. An oval plaque on each face, dated 1849, bears a Liver bird and the names of the engineer *John Hawkshaw* and the contractors *McCormick* and *Holmes* (sic). In the 1970s the line was cut back to this point, where the tracks now plunge below ground. In the 1880s an additional stretch of viaduct was built in connection with the enlargement of

Exchange Station. Some of its blue brick arches survive along the w side of Love Lane, N of Chadwick Street and E of the original viaduct.

Immediately s of the arch in Great Howard Street is an *ex situ* granite **drinking fountain** dated 1856. Such fountains were funded by the philanthropist Charles Melly from 1854, to promote temperance.

Churches

St Anthony (R.C.), Scotland Road, 1832–3, is by *John Broadbent*, a pupil of Rickman. When built it lay right at the N end of the town, corresponding to St Patrick at the s end (*see* Walk 9, p. 271). Gothic, with lancet windows throughout. w front of ashlar, with gabled and pinnacled centre breaking forward. Stuccoed, battlemented side elevations with pairs of lancets between buttresses. The interior is exceptionally impressive: a broad, lofty space under a flat, panelled ceiling, uninterrupted by columns or side galleries [152]. The E end is filled with three giant arched niches of equal height, the wider central one containing the high altar, with subsidiary altars left and right; statues in canopied niches flank the big arches. The altars have high and elaborate **reredoses** by *Broadbent*, the central one, perhaps designed in 1837, with three steep gables separated by pinnacled buttresses, like a cathedral façade in miniature. They are of carved stone, painted. On the rear wall of the w gallery, two **carved panels** of the Nativity and Epiphany, believed to be C17 Spanish or Portuguese. **Stained glass** of 1933 in the window over the high altar. Under the church, a brick vaulted **crypt** with over six hundred burial spaces.

(Just N of St Anthony, a former branch of the **Liverpool Savings Bank**, 1882, by *G.E. Grayson*. Stone, with a round corner tower.)

152. St Anthony,
Scotland Road,
by John
Broadbent
(1832–3)

153. Our Lady of
Reconciliation,
Eldon Street, by
E.W. Pugin
(1859–60)

St Alban (formerly R.C.) in Athol Street, NE of Stanley Dock, 1849 by *Weightman & Hadfield*. Gothic, in the irregular, squared masonry that A.W.N. Pugin approved of. Impressively sturdy looking, especially the side away from the river, which has big buttresses linked by a continuous plinth. Square, battlemented tower. Interior converted into a rock-climbing centre and largely obscured. High pointed arches on round columns. Very tall, narrow nave with open timber roof.

Our Lady of Reconciliation (R.C.), Eldon Street, 1859–60, by *E.W. Pugin* [153]. The church lies along the street. Clerestoried nave and aisles in rock-faced stone, with w rose window and a little bell-turret on the steep w gable. The clerestory windows are sexfoils. The impressive round E apse hints at the more interesting interior. Apse and nave form a single lofty space under one continuous roof. The relatively narrow aisles have arcades with widely spaced round columns, giving good sight-lines for a congregation of 1,800. This practical but dignified arrangement was Pugin's response to the need for large but economical urban churches. It is a very early example of the type (just predating J.L. Pearson's more famous St Peter, Vauxhall, in London) and was described by the Catholic journal *The Tablet* as representing 'a complete revolution in church-building'. Interior reordered.

St Sylvester (R.C.), Silvester Street, by *Pugin & Pugin*, opened 1889. Quite a large church (and yet close to St Anthony) in red Ruabon brick with red sandstone. Main entrance through the prominent pyramid-roofed tower that stands close to the street, connected to the church by a passage. Elaborate high altar and reredos, 1906.

154. Terraced housing, Summer Seat (1911)

Housing

The streets around Our Lady of Reconciliation had some of Liverpool's earliest municipal housing, but little remains. In **Eldon Grove** are three blocks of three-storey flats, currently derelict, built in 1910–12 as part of a slum-clearance scheme. They have access balconies across the front, reached by open stairs, and are surprisingly decorative with bay windows and half-timbered gables. Projecting towers at the rear, triangular in plan and originally open-sided, provided each flat with an outdoor yard, WC and access to a refuse chute. The blocks face s on to an open space, originally with separate playgrounds for boys and girls, with a bandstand in the middle. In **Bevington Street** and **Summer Seat**, s, are two-storey terraced houses forming part of the same scheme, dated 1911 [154]. They are cottagey-looking in brick and render, some with gables, set back slightly to break up the line of the terrace. They look like an economical attempt to imitate the style of Port Sunlight (*see* Excursions, p. 299) in an urban setting.

Between Vauxhall Road and Love Lane is the **Eldonian Village**, occupying the site of the Tate & Lyle sugar refinery closed in 1981 [155]. The first phase, s of Burlington Street, was built 1987–90; phase two, N, was finished in 1995. It was one of the biggest community-architecture schemes of the 1980s (*see* topic box, p. 272). Housing and layout were designed with the participation of future residents, who formed a co-operative for the purpose. Living in run-down municipal flats around Eldon Street, they were determined to be re-housed in their own area. Their architects were *Wilkinson Hindle Halsall Lloyd*. The Village has a mix of bungalows and houses, in pairs and short terraces. All have gardens, and are arranged round culs-de-sac called courts, branching off a winding spine road. To avoid the uniformity seen as typical of municipal housing, the planning is informal and the materials – mostly brick and stained wood – differ in colour from court to court. Internal layouts are varied to suit tenants' individual requirements. The architecture may not be aesthetically adventurous, but in its complete

155. Aerial view of Eldonian Village (1987–95)

transformation of an industrial wasteland and its preservation of an established community the Village is a remarkable achievement. A village hall and other community buildings, also by *Wilkinson Hindle Halsall Lloyd*, are on Vauxhall Road.

At the junction of Vauxhall Road and Pumpfields Road is a new building for **Liverpool Community College** by *Ellis Williams Architects*, completed 2002. Red brick, with much silvery cladding.

Via London Road to Everton

This walk takes us E from St George's Hall, along London Road and its continuation Prescot Street. This was the main route into town from the S and E, and London Road was also an important shopping street. After years of decline there has been much new building and refurbishment, following the setting up of the London Road Development Agency in 1992. Everton lies N of here, covering the highest part of the ridge of hills that surround the city centre. John Housman wrote in 1800: 'Everton is a remarkably pleasant village, finely situated on an agreeable eminence . . . and commands many fine prospects: it has of late years become a favourite residence for gentlemen of independent fortune.' From the mid C19 this semi-rural suburb was overtaken by the expanding town and covered with closely packed terraced streets. In the 1960s these were largely replaced with tower blocks, and since the 1980s most of the towers have been replaced with low-rise, low-density housing. Much of the hill's W slope is again open land, with spectacular views across the city to the river and beyond. Of the nineteen Everton churches described by Pevsner in 1969, only six remain.

We begin at the W end of London Road where it joins Lime Street. For the Empire Theatre, S, *see* Walk 3, p. 186. **Commutation Plaza**, N, combining offices and apartments, is by *Geoffrey Reid Associates*, completed 2002. Artificial stone, symmetrical, with round corner pavilions and a portico of copper-clad columns. It looks insubstantial by comparison with its grand C19 neighbours to the W in William Brown Street. Heading E along **London Road**, on the N side, flanking Norton Street, are two large residential blocks with commercial uses on the lower floors. Recent, by *Falconer Chester*. One, W, has a blue rendered finish and recessed balconies, the other, E, is faced with red brick and has a curved and glazed corner. On the S, at the corner of Seymour Street, a former branch of the **Union Bank**, dated 1890. Loire château style in stone, with a round corner tower. Possibly by *G.E. Grayson*, who did the bank's Bold Street branch a few years earlier. (For the adjoining terrace in Seymour Street, *see* Walk 5, p. 228.) On the same side, the **NatWest Bank** at the corner of Hart Street occupies a building of 1899 by *W. Hesketh & Co.*, for the Liverpool Furnishing Co. Fancy Northern

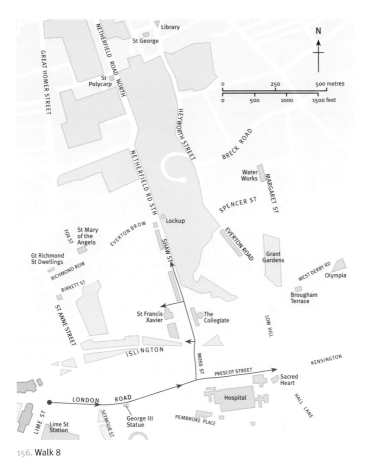

Walk 8

Renaissance with octagonal domed clock turret and elaborate gables, in fiery red terracotta supplied by *Jabez Thompson* of Northwich.

E of here the two sides of London Road diverge, the resulting triangular open space presided over by an impressive equestrian **monument** to George III. Fine bronze statue of the king by *Richard Westmacott*, commissioned 1818 and finished 1822, closely modelled on that of Marcus Aurelius in Rome. On the N side, filling the block between Stafford and Audley streets, is **Audley House**, a shop built in phases for the retailer Owen Owen and completed *c.* 1910; taken over by the present occupants T.J. Hughes in 1927. The architect seems to have been *Walter W. Thomas*, who designed the Philharmonic Hotel. Yellow brick, with much stone. Pedimented windows, octagonal corner turrets with pointed roofs, and a tower in Stafford Street, w. On the same side of London Road, No. 129 looks late C19 and has exuberant Renaissance decoration all over. After this, at the corner of Gildart Street, a former department store opened in 1937, an enterprisingly modern design by

Robert Threadgold who worked in the office of *A.E. Shennan*. A big rectangular block faced in smooth buff terracotta, with windows in horizontal strips. The corner has a glazed stair-tower. Converted to student accommodation in the 1990s.

Continue E along London Road. On the right, at the corner of Daulby Street, is the **Roy Castle International Centre for Lung Cancer Research**, completed 1997, by the *Franklin Stafford Partnership*. The peculiar tower, a pointed oval in plan, swoops up at the corner like the prow of a boat. Walls of rock-faced cast stone, glass above. The adjacent corner of London Road and Moss Street has a Gothic former pub with curved front. Opposite, at the corner of Moss Street and Prescot Street, an excellent former branch of the **Bank of Liverpool**, begun 1904, by *James F. Doyle*. Edwardian Baroque in Portland stone and grey granite, with an imaginatively detailed octagonal tower over the corner entrance. Convex balustraded balconies project between its columns, while each face of the entablature above is concave.

Continuing up **Prescot Street**, the whole s side is occupied by the enormous **Royal Liverpool University Hospital**, probably the biggest single 1960s public project in the city. The architects were *Holford Associates*. Planned 1963–5, opened 1978. A general teaching hospital with over 800 beds, it replaced the Royal Infirmary (*see* Walk 5, pp. 225–6) and three other C19 hospitals in the city. It followed the model of contemporary American hospitals in having a high (twelve-storey) ward block raised above a podium containing outpatient services, etc. Two wings containing teaching accommodation project forward, and a lower block in front houses the University of Liverpool's clinical departments. Entrance front remodelled 2003. Seen from the back (s) the ward block is undeniably impressive, if intimidating. Horizontal and vertical concrete members divide it into a grid of windows. The verticals are detached, and die into an outward-leaning parapet. The block is framed by two great ventilation ducts serving the podium, and in the space between these and the ends of the wards are external emergency stairs. Inside, wards are of the deep-plan 'racetrack' type adopted from America, with bed spaces round the edges and services in a central core. In front of the main hospital building is the bizarre **chapel**, a big windowless brick cube on a raked brick plinth. w towards Daulby Street is the grim **Duncan Building**, housing clinical sciences, with a sheer, windowless tower at the NW corner. At the sw corner of the site in Pembroke Place is the **Dental Hospital**, 1965–9, by the *Anthony Clark Partnership* but forming part of the Holford Associates complex. Ceramic **mural** by *Rhys Powell* in the entrance hall. To the E of the site, attached to the main building, a smaller block with similar leaning parapet runs N–S. Originally a training college, it was extended and converted to become the **Linda McCartney Centre** in 2001. s of this is a residential tower block. The powerful, rugged **boiler house** overlooks the site from the NE corner. The high chimney

157. Former Collegiate Institution, Shaw Street, by Harvey Lonsdale Elmes and Edward Argent (opened 1843); converted by Shed KM (1990s)

has water tanks cantilevered from its base, and looks like a giant upended hammer.

E of the boiler house is the **Sacred Heart Church (R.C.)**, 1885–6, by *Goldie, Child & Goldie.* Dec Gothic, the polychromy of yellow and red stone obscured by dirt. w end approached by steps, with porch, and corner spirelet. Polygonal apse. Nave with octagonal piers of polished red granite. The **high altar** with its spectacular Benediction throne and the gorgeous alabaster **reredos** were added in 1891 by *Pugin & Pugin*; carving by *Norbury, Paterson & Co.*, statues by *Boulton* of Cheltenham. – White marble **Lady Altar** with *opus sectile* panels of the Annunciation, *c.* 1908 by *Edmund Kirby & Sons.* – Outside the E end, First World War **memorial**: a Calvary. Small **Post Office** on the opposite corner of Hall Lane, 1883, by *Henry Tanner.* Brick and stone, Renaissance.

Return down Prescot Street and turn right along Moss Street. Cross Islington to **Islington Square** – now merely a widening on the N side of the dual carriageway. Here are two attractive buildings, apparently early 1830s. The left one is stuccoed, with slightly projecting end bays and a central porch. It was a music academy, and the first-floor cast-iron balconies incorporate lyres in their design. The other is a fine brick house, with a pediment across five of its six bays, and a handsome Greek Doric porch. Turn N into **Shaw Street**. On the right at the corner of College Street, a former **Baptist chapel** opened in 1847, converted into flats 2005. Red brick and red sandstone, with a pediment and two Ionic columns *in antis.*

Next to this, the former **Collegiate Institution**, an educational foundation comprising three distinct schools. A competition in 1840 was won by *Harvey Lonsdale Elmes*, fresh from his success in the St George's Hall and Assize Courts contests (*see* Major Buildings, p. 49). The building opened in 1843. Elmes only supervised construction of the façade, the rest being in the hands of the surveyor *Edward Argent*. Tudor Gothic in red sandstone, as stipulated in the terms of the competition. No doubt Gothic was chosen to signal its Anglican affiliation: a response to the secular (and Greek Revival) Mechanics' Institution (*see* Walk 6, p. 238). Thirteen-bay battlemented façade, with oriels at each end and a gatehouse-like feature – a tall, gabled arch flanked by octagonal buttresses – in the middle. Windows run through first and second floors, separated by buttresses that originally had high finials above the parapet. At the back is the octagonal lecture hall. Students in the three schools came from different social classes, and the building was subdivided to ensure segregation. Gutted by fire in 1994, the shell was imaginatively converted into flats in the late 1990s by the developers Urban Splash and their architects *Shed KM*. At the front, new windows are tactfully recessed behind Elmes's tracery, but the rear is uncompromisingly of today [157]. The roofless lecture theatre is now a walled garden. Inside, the original main staircase survives opposite the entrance, with a carved overmantel from the headmaster's room relocated to the landing.

Facing the Collegiate across Josephine Butler Square is the Jesuit church of **St Francis Xavier (R.C.)** and its former College and Schools. This was C19 Liverpool's most extensive group of religious buildings, set in the heart of a then populous area. The foundation stone of the **church** was laid in 1842. *J.J. Scoles* was appointed architect, his drawings are dated 1845, and the building opened in 1848. Rock-faced stone, with geometrical tracery. Nave and aisles under separate gabled roofs, with low confessionals down the ritual N side forming a sort of subsidiary aisle. The tower ('below criticism' according to *The Ecclesiologist*, 1853) stands outside the opposite aisle. Recessed spire planned from the outset but not added until 1883. For the Sodality Chapel on this side, *see* below. Inside [158], eight-bay nave of very slender columns, with huge bases and foliage capitals. The thinness of the columns suggests cast iron, but they are Drogheda limestone (now unfortunately painted, like much of the interior stonework). They minimize the division between aisles and nave, allowing a clear view of sanctuary and pulpit. Polygonal apse with high altar, flanked by Sacred Heart Chapel, left, and Rosary Chapel, right. The three very elaborate altars with reredoses are early 1850s. The drawings for the Sacred Heart altar, dated 1852–3, are by Scoles's pupil *S.J. Nicholl*. Next to it, and of the same date, a life-size relief of Christ with the Afflicted, after a painting by *Ary Scheffer*. – Above the sanctuary, carved and painted **rood** by *Early* of Dublin, installed 1866. – **Stained glass** above organ gallery, Christ the King,

158. St Francis Xavier, by J.J. Scoles (opened 1848)

1930, by *Hardman & Powell*; window left of this, unveiled 1999, by *Linda Walton*. – An arch right of the Rosary Chapel, now glazed, opens into the **Sodality Chapel**, 1885–7, a showpiece by *Edmund Kirby*. Virtually an independent building. The exterior shows it to have a polygonal centre with lower, asymmetrical ends. The two-light windows are gabled, with pinnacles between. Inside, the style is E.E., with soaring Purbeck marble shafts. The elongated octagonal centre has a high plaster rib vault, and a two-bay apsidal chancel with clerestory. Behind this is an ambulatory, and at the opposite end another, lower apse. The chapel houses the highly decorated altars of a number of sodalities (pious lay associations) and is richly evocative of the spiritual life of late C19 Liverpool Catholics. The chancel contains the **Altar of the Annunciation**, with marble reliefs carved by Messrs *Boulton* of Cheltenham, and a tabernacle door by *Conrad Dressler*; wrought-iron screens left and right incorporate electrotype **reliefs** of the Holy Family and The Presentation of the Virgin by *Dressler*, with *cloisonné* on the reverse. Opposite is the **Bona Mors Altar**, with a marble triptych, **stained glass** above designed by *Kirby*, made by *Burlison & Grylls*. – The **Chapel of St Joseph**, richly panelled in wood, opens off the ambulatory.

Behind the church is the former **College**, 1876–7, converted from 1999 into the Cornerstone building of Liverpool Hope University College. It was designed by *Henry Clutton*, to a plan by *Fr Richard Vaughan SJ*; architects for the conversion were *Downs Variava*. Red brick and terracotta. A strongly modelled classroom range faces Salisbury Street, with windows in threes between deep buttresses, and gabled dormers above a pierced parapet. (Simpler N addition, 1908, by

Matthew Honan.) Behind, and parallel, is a huge assembly and examination hall under a pointed timber roof with dormers. The long sides have internal buttresses in the manner of Albi, linked by lateral arches creating an arcade. The buttresses are pierced to form aisles and again for a first-floor gallery, but later infilling has obscured this. The N end survives to full height, the rest now has a mezzanine; large windows between allow the space to be read as a whole. Abutting the E side of the College in Haigh Street are altered remnants of the former **Schools**. Rock-faced red sandstone, simple trefoil-headed windows. These appear to be the school buildings begun in 1853 to designs by *Joseph Spencer*, and extended by him in 1857.

Return to **Shaw Street**. From 1826 the w side was built up with high-class three-storey brick terraces. After years of dereliction a few survivors have recently been restored; others have been reconstructed behind preserved façades or rebuilt entirely using salvaged materials. **Gardens** were laid out on the E side in the 1840s. Here stands a **memorial** to members of the Eighth (King's) Regiment killed in the Indian Mutiny, a Celtic cross in white marble by *H.S. Leifchild*, with weathered reliefs. First erected at Portsmouth in 1863, removed to Chelsea 1877, and finally to Liverpool 1911. Further N on the same side is the **lockup** of 1787, a round stone building with a conical roof, a relic of Everton's village centre. The line of Shaw Street is continued N by Netherfield Road. The E side for the next half mile (0.8 km.) is largely open land, cleared of housing and laid out as a public park from the mid 1980s. The idea is admirable, though the design with terraces, pergolas and grand flights of steps, is over-elaborate for such a rugged, windswept site.

The remaining buildings of interest in Everton are fairly widely scattered. They can be found with the help of the map on p. 259.

In Heyworth Street, near the highest point of the hill, is **St George**, 1813–14. This was the first of three churches erected by *John Cragg*, employing cast-iron parts manufactured at his Mersey Iron Foundry (the others were St Philip, p. 233, and St Michael-in-the-Hamlet, p. 293). Cragg had been planning a church for Toxteth Park. *J.M. Gandy* produced designs in 1809, and in 1812 Cragg met *Thomas Rickman* and had him make new drawings. Then the opportunity to build in Everton arose, and the church went ahead on the present site. It is impossible to disentangle Cragg, Gandy and Rickman's contributions. Some cast-iron elements shown in Gandy's drawings are very close to the executed building, but these could have been designed by Cragg before Gandy's involvement. Certainly Cragg had already cast some components before Rickman appeared on the scene.

The exterior is largely of stone, the style Perp. High w tower with pierced battlements (original?). Large Perp three-light windows along the sides, with cast-iron tracery. The buttresses between had cast-iron pinnacles, now removed. Six-light E window in short embattled chancel.

159. St George, Heyworth Street, built by John Cragg (1813–14)

The galleried interior is a delightful surprise, extraordinarily light and delicate due to the use of cast iron throughout [159]. Slender clustered columns divide nave from aisles. Traceried arches span between the columns to support the nave ceiling, and between the columns and the outer wall to carry the flat ceilings over the aisles (the tie-rods are a C20 insertion). Further traceried arches support the galleries, which cut across the windows. The ceilings are of slate slabs slotted between the cast-iron rafters, with cast-iron tracery on the underside. Thicker slabs of slate attached to the upper edge of the rafters form the roof – a system patented by Cragg in 1809. **Monuments.** Under the tower, John Rackham, d. 1815, a tablet with an ambitious Dec Gothic surround, designed by *Rickman* and carved by *S. & J. Franceys*. – In the s gallery, Thomas W. Wainwright (a surgeon), d. 1841, with a relief of the Good Samaritan by *W. Spence*. – In the N gallery, Walter Fergus MacGregor, d. 1863, an elaborate Gothic tabernacle incorporating a portrait roundel, by *E.E. Geflowski*. –

Water Supply

160. Water tower, Margaret Street, by Thomas Duncan (1857)

Until the end of the C18 water for domestic use was obtained from wells and sold from carts; in the first half of the C19 piped well water was supplied by two competing companies. By the 1840s supply could not keep pace with the growth of the town or satisfy the need for sanitary reform. To provide water for public purposes such as fire-fighting and street cleaning, the Highway Commissioners sank a well at Green Lane, West Derby, and built a reservoir at Kensington. Eventually, in 1847, the Corporation assumed responsibility: it bought the two companies, took over the Green Lane works, and obtained Parliamentary approval to construct reservoirs at Rivington, 25 m. (40 km.) to the NE. Work on the Rivington scheme began in 1852, and water was being delivered to Liverpool by 1857. *Thomas Duncan*, water engineer to the Corporation, designed architecturally imposing reservoirs in the highest parts of the town to receive and store water from local wells and from Rivington. Demand continued to grow, and in 1881 the damming of the River Vyrnwy was begun, creating a large reservoir in mid Wales. The first water from this source reached the city in 1891.

Stained glass mostly destroyed in the war. The third window on the N is the only complete survivor, 1863, by *A. Gibbs*. E window 1952, by *Shrigley & Hunt*.

Opposite the E end of St George is the disused **Everton Library**, opened 1896, perhaps the best of several by *Thomas Shelmerdine* [161]. Red brick and stone, with mullioned and transomed windows and other Jacobean touches. Three identical gables reflect the original plan (reading rooms flanking central lending departments) but the arrangement of windows below each is different. Octagonal corner tower, with stubby Tuscan columns making a porch, and a short lead-covered spire. Just s is the lively **Mere Bank** pub, dated 1881, with moulded terracotta panels, half-timbering and pargeting.

w of St George, along Netherfield Road North, are some of the few remaining public-housing tower blocks of the 1960s. The twenty-two-storey **Corinth Tower** uses the *Camus* system of prefabrication. At the s corner of Conway Street is the former church of **St Polycarp**, 1886 by *George Bradbury*, now in secular use. Common brick and red brick, Gothic, with geometrical tracery in the five-light window to the main street. Odd s aisle incorporating a gabled door. Interior said to be faced with white glazed bricks. Immediately w in Conway Street, two sixteen-storey tower blocks, converted to private housing 2003.

SE of the library, in Margaret Street, are the **Everton Water Works**, by *Thomas Duncan*, water engineer to the Corporation. A covered reservoir was built first, 1854, but only the **retaining walls** remain. It was followed in 1857 by the round **water tower**, 85 ft (26 metres) high to the tank, and one of the most impressive monuments of C19 Liverpool [160]. Mighty

161. Everton Library, by Thomas Shelmerdine (opened 1896)

rusticated arches support an upper tier of taller arches. Concentric with these are further piers linked by radial brick arches, the whole colossal structure recalling the prints of Piranesi. s are two **pump houses**. The first, attached, has a square Italianate tower, now missing its top part. The second was added in the 1860s.

sw of the Water Works in **Everton Road**, between Plumpton Street and Lytton Street, are some houses of the 1830s, survivors from Everton's period as a select middle-class suburb. No. 71 has a Doric porch; Nos. 47–65 form a terrace. s of these at the junction with West Derby Road, **Grant Gardens** occupies the site of the Necropolis, an early non-denominational cemetery opened in 1825. Nos. 8–10 **Brougham Terrace**, on the s side of West Derby Road, are the remains of a row of houses of c. 1830 by *J.A. Picton*. No. 8 served from 1889 as the Muslim Institute, and the lecture hall at the rear was used as a mosque. Internal alterations in 'Saracenic' style, made by *J.H. McGovern* in 1895, do not appear to survive. A little further E on West Derby Road, the **Olympia** is a theatre of 1905 by *Frank Matcham* with a good interior.

NW of St Francis Xavier, in **Fox Street**, is the redundant **St Mary of the Angels** (**R.C.**), 1910, by *Pugin & Pugin*. Brick and red sandstone, basilican plan, with round-arched arcades. The foundress was Amy Elizabeth Imrie, a Liverpool heiress and convert to Catholicism, who aimed to bring the religious art and architecture of Italy to this poor district. The church was apparently based on that of the Aracoeli in Rome, and Miss Imrie furnished it with altars and other artefacts acquired in Bologna, Rome and elsewhere. The **high altar** is said to have come from one of the chapels of Bologna cathedral. **Statue** above the Lady Altar by *Zaccagnini*. Good **stained glass** in w rose window by *Early & Co.* of Dublin, 1929. w of St Mary, on the E side of **St Anne Street** at the corner of Great Richmond Street, are the former **Great Richmond Street Dwellings**, 1930. Built as municipal housing, they are Neo-Georgian in contrast to the Modernist St Andrew's Gardens (*see* Walk 5, p. 227) of a few years later. Further s on the same side of St Anne Street, at the s corner of Birkett Street, is the former funeral carriage and coaching establishment of Messrs Busby, dated 1876. Gothic, red brick and red sandstone, with inscribed slate panels listing the services available. The square corner clock turret contained a chiming machine that played fourteen tunes, 'Irish, Scotch and English for weekdays, and the 104th psalm on Sundays'.

Walk 9.

South of the Centre, along Park Road

This area comprises a large part of Toxteth Park, a former royal hunting ground acquired by Sir Richard Molyneux in 1605. It remained undeveloped until 1771, when the land w of Mill Street, between Parliament Street and Northumberland Street, was laid out in a regular grid of broad streets. The intention was to form a new town, to be called Harrington, promoted by the builder *Cuthbert Bisbrown*. Apart from St James's church (*see* below) little was achieved. When these streets were eventually built up during the early C19, the large blocks were subdivided

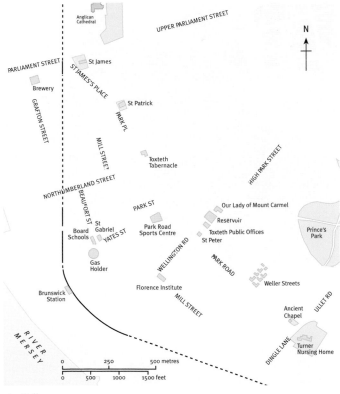

162. Walk 9

163. Brewery,
Stanhope
Street: detail of
façade (1902)

and filled with insanitary housing. During the second half of the C19, as the docks expanded and Liverpool pushed further S, the whole area W and E of Park Road was densely covered with terraced housing, and dotted with churches and institutions serving a predominantly poor population. Here and there this pattern survives, interspersed with cleared sites and the less formal housing layouts of the late C20.

Most buildings of interest lie on the busy main road made up of St James's Place, Park Place and Park Road, described here from N to S. A few short detours take in outlying buildings or clusters (*see* map, p. 269).

On the E of St James's Place is the redundant **St James**, 1774–5, built and perhaps designed by *Bisbrown*. Red brick with stone dressings. Battlemented W tower with pairs of round-arched belfry openings – was it intended to look Norman? Round-arched side windows in two tiers. Chancel 1899–1900 by *H. Havelock Sutton*. Conventionally Georgian interior, with galleries N, S and W on slender cast-iron columns, an early structural use. The columns are Gothic, quatrefoil in section (octagonal below, where originally hidden by pews), and perhaps derived from the published designs of Batty Langley. Open timber roof with Norman arches, introduced by *William Culshaw*, 1846. **Stained glass**: E window by *Henry Holiday*, 1881, presumably reset when the chancel was built. **Monuments**: George Pemberton d. 1795, with kneeling figure by an urn; Moses Benson d. 1806, with mourning figure by a sarcophagus; and J.E. Irving d. 1817(?), with seated figure.

At the corner of Stanhope Street and Grafton Street (reached via Parliament Street) is the **brewery** of Robert Cain, as ambitious as his famous pubs, the Philharmonic and the Vines (*see* Walk 3, p. 184 and Walk 6, p. 234). *James Redford* designed the rear part, completed 1887; the architect of the splendid five-storey red brick façade dated 1902, with elaborate Renaissance decoration in terracotta [163], is unknown. The height drops at the corner for **The Grapes**, the brewery tap. Taken over in the 1920s by Higson's, who inserted their name into the decoration, but Cain's monogram and gazelle symbol are everywhere.

On the E side of Park Place is the large church of **St Patrick (R.C.)**, 1821–7, by *John Slater* [164]. Brick, with stone dressings, and an unusual cruciform plan. The body resembles a Nonconformist chapel, with two tiers of windows and a pedimented gable. The original entrances (disused) are in the w sides of a pair of short, two-storey transepts. These contain stairs up to the galleries, an arrangement used by Slater in his 1817 additions to St Peter (*see* Walk 4, p. 202). Four Greek Doric columns form a porch in front of each entrance. Prominent on the w front is a **statue** of St Patrick, from the St Patrick Insurance Co. building, Dublin, presented in 1827 by the sugar-refiner James Brancker. Inside are w, N and s galleries on cast-iron columns (the space under the w one partitioned

164. St Patrick, Park Place, by John Slater (1821–7)

off) and a segmental plaster ceiling. At the E end, framed by giant Corinthian columns, a huge **altar painting** of the Crucifixion by *Nicaise de Keyser* of Antwerp, *c.* 1834. Said to have been commissioned for a church in Manchester and moved here after a fire; previously wider. In niches, high up to left and right, Neoclassical **statues** of St Matthew and St Mark. Sanctuary reordered: the present **altar** may incorporate parts of the 1867 high altar by *J.F. Bentley*. To the left, an arched marble **relief** of the Holy Family, probably from the 1891 altar of St Joseph by Messrs *Boulton* of Cheltenham. Opposite the church on the w side of Park Place, the **Memorial School** and **Hall**, 1927, by *Foden, Hemm & Williams*, vaguely Neo-Georgian, and the **presbytery**, a simple early C19 house.

Between Dombey and Dorrit streets is the **Toxteth Tabernacle**, 1870–1, a large Baptist chapel by *W.I. Mason*. A bizarre patchwork of styles in polychrome brick and stone. The front has a pediment, above pointed arches springing from pilasters with approximately Corinthian capitals. Between these are three round-arched doorways with foliage capitals. Next, at the corner of Northumberland Street, the four-storey brick warehouse of **Coleman's Fireproof Depository**, a landmark on

Housing Co-operatives and Community Architecture

Housing co-operatives played a significant role in Liverpool from the late 1970s to the mid 1980s, attracting national attention. They originated *c.* 1970 in Granby, Toxteth, where tenants living in dilapidated C19 terraces came together to bring about publicly funded improvements. The catalyst was the Shelter Neighbourhood Action Project (SNAP), a pioneering Granby-based venture by the national housing charity Shelter. After the wholesale clearances of the 1960s, the City Council adopted a policy of upgrading substandard older private housing, and loans from the Housing Corporation made it possible for co-ops to acquire properties and manage their refurbishment. In 1977 the Weller Streets Co-operative became the first to undertake a new-build scheme, an example followed by others, most famously the Eldonian Housing Co-operative (*see* Walk 7, p. 256). These co-operative new-build projects departed radically from the architecture of traditional local authority housing: it was the future residents – not housing professionals – who took charge of the design process, selecting their architects and working closely with them to develop plans that suited individual tastes and needs. And whereas Council re-housing schemes had resulted in long-established communities being split up, with residents uprooted and resettled in different parts of the city, the co-ops built on sites close to their existing homes, encouraging social cohesion and continuity.

account of the red and white ceramic lettering emblazoned across it. The topmost inscription says it was rebuilt in 1900. s of Upper Park Street, the former **Liverpool Savings Bank**, South Branch, *c.* 1882 by *G.E. Grayson*. Stone, Renaissance, with mullioned and transomed windows.

Opposite the bank, in Steble Street, is the **Park Road Sports Centre**. The older part opened in 1874 as public baths and washhouse. White brick with red sandstone dressings, stepped gables, minimally Gothic. Further sw in Beaufort Street is the brick and terracotta **St Gabriel**, 1883–4, by *H. & A.P. Fry*, and the burned-out Gothic **Beaufort Street Board Schools**, 1874, by *Aldridge & Deacon*. The church is on the corner of **Yates Street**. Here and in parallel **Corn Street** C19 terraces were upgraded *c.* 1976–7 by *Neighbourhood Housing Services Ltd* for the Corn & Yates Streets Housing Co-operative. Next to the school, a huge mid-1880s **gas holder** with two tiers of cast-iron Tuscan columns. SE, at the corner of Mill Street and Wellington Road, is the burned-out **Florence Institute for Boys**, 1889, probably by *H.W. Keef*. A really good building in bright red brick with delicate terracotta ornament, with three shaped gables, canted bay windows, and a polygonal turret. Founded by the former mayor Bernard Hall for the recreation and education of poor working boys. Wellington Road leads NE back to Park Road, past the **Wellington Road Church** (Methodist) by *W.I. Mason*, begun 1870, also ruinous. Red and white brick, Italianate.

At the highest point of Park Road, High Park Street turns off NE. **St Peter's Methodist Church**, on the NW side, 1877–8, is a quirky 'rogue' Gothic design in polychrome brick by *C.O. Ellison*. Over the door, a big window with plate tracery. A peculiar octagonal turret to its left grows out of a buttress dividing nave and aisle, supported on the left by a short flying buttress. At the corner of Letitia Street are the former **Toxteth Public Offices**, 1865–6, by *Thomas Layland*. Red sandstone, heavily Italianate, with channelled rustication. Single-storey wings; higher, pedimented centre with round-arched windows. Central room with C17-style garlands in plaster. On the other corner is the disused **Park Hill Reservoir**, 1853, by *Thomas Duncan*, built in readiness for the new water supply from Rivington (*see* topic box, p. 266). A steeply battered stone retaining wall encloses the cistern, which has a brick-vaulted roof on a forest of cast-iron columns. Corner tower, originally with conical roof. After this, **Our Lady of Mount Carmel (R.C.)**, 1876–8 by *James O'Byrne*. Plain exterior of red brick and red sandstone. Nave with clerestory and aisles, and a narthex across the (ritual) w end. Geometric tracery. Pevsner noted the doorways' 'quadrant jambs and arches dying into them, a motif typical of the most progressive work during the last quarter of the C19'. Inside, arcades with cylindrical polished granite columns, and foliage capitals carved by Mr *Hanley* of Chester. Virtually no division between nave and sanctuary. Elaborate altars, reredoses and altar rails of alabaster, added later. **Stained glass** in the six-light E

165. Ancient Chapel of Toxteth, Park Road (early c17, altered 1774)

window, apparently 1880s. **Stations of the Cross**, oil paintings by *May Greville Cooksey*, 1928, etc. **Presbytery**, left, added by *O'Byrne*, 1880–1.

Near the SE end of Park Road, bounded by Byles Street and Miles Street, is the earliest of Liverpool's new-build co-operative housing schemes, **Weller Streets**, opened 1982. The leading role of tenants in designing their new houses was pioneered here (*see* topic box, p. 272); the architect was *Bill Halsall* of *Wilkinson, Hindle & Partners*. The simple red brick houses are grouped into L-shaped blocks enclosing land-scaped courts, branching off a cul-de-sac.

At the foot of Park Road, on the corner of Ullet Road, is the **Ancient Chapel of Toxteth** (so called since the 1830s), the oldest ecclesiastical building in the area covered by this guide. Associated with Nonconformity from its earliest years, it was licensed as a Presbyterian meeting-house in 1672, and is now Unitarian. Built some time between 1604 and 1618 to serve what was then an isolated rural area, it was altered and largely rebuilt in 1774, when the walls were heightened. Some c17 masonry may have been reused. Externally, it is a simple box of coursed stone with superimposed pairs of round-arched windows in the sw and NE walls. A little louvred bell-turret on the SE gable; doorway below, enclosed by a porch dated 1906. The present entrance is at the opposite end, through a porch with organ loft above, added in 1841 on the site of a schoolhouse formerly attached to the chapel. Inside, a large arch opens into the chapel. The **pulpit** – the focus – is placed centrally against the sw wall, framed by the windows [165]. The other walls have **galleries** on wooden columns: those on the SE and NW seem to predate the 1774 rebuilding (the latter has a pew door dated 1700); the cross gallery only became practicable after the roof was raised. – **Box pews** throughout; one left of the pulpit has a door with the date 1650. – **Brass** to Edward Aspinwall, d. 1656, originally set in the floor, now on the SW wall. Just an inscription. – **Monuments**: several late C18 and early C19 tablets, including Alice Kennion, d. 1813, signed by *B. Baker*. Early C20 meeting room, etc., NW of the chapel. – Attractive graveyard, with a mid-C19 classical arcade on the NE side, paid for by Richard Vaughan Yates of Prince's Park fame (*see* Walk 10, p. 276), who is buried here. Nearer Park Road is the grave of the cartographer Richard Horwood, with an inscription referring to his exceptionally detailed 1803 map of Liverpool.

Opposite the end of Park Road in its own grounds is the **Turner Nursing Home** (formerly Turner Memorial Home), 1882–5 by *Alfred Waterhouse*. Erected by Mrs Charles Turner in memory of her husband, MP and chairman of the Dock Board, and their son. Picturesquely asymmetrical Gothic in red ashlar. Projecting timber porch, with an elaborate clock and the Perp E window of the chapel to the right, a conical-roofed turret to the left. In the entrance hall, marble **statue** of the Turners, father and son, 1885 by *Hamo Thornycroft*. They are seated, studying what are presumably plans of the Home (though it was designed after their deaths). The **chapel** is dignified inside, all ashlar, with a N aisle behind an arcade of octagonal columns, and clerestory above. Open timber roof. w gallery with organ. – Alabaster **reredos** with reliefs of Christ healing the sick. – **Stained glass** in E window, Life of Christ with Ascension, by *Heaton, Butler & Bayne*. Boards with the Ten Commandments, Creed and Lord's Prayer on either side – a traditional arrangement, old-fashioned by this date. – SE of the Waterhouse building a 1990s extension in brick. Attractive **lodge** on Dingle Lane, dated 1884.

From here, buses return along Park Road to the city centre. Alternatively, Ullet Road leads NE in the direction of Prince's Park, where Walk 10 begins.

Prince's Park and Sefton Park

This walk covers a large district s of the centre, part of Liverpool's semi-rural hinterland until the 1840s. Here Prince's Park was laid out from 1842, and the much larger Sefton Park from 1867. Fringed with affluent housing and impressive churches, they became the focus of a solidly middle-class residential area, spacious and leafy, and comfortably distant from the insalubrious city centre.

Prince's Park is reached from the centre by the twin thoroughfares of **Princes Road**, 'in the course of formation' in 1843, and **Princes Avenue**, which runs parallel and dates from the 1870s. They are separated by grass and trees, forming a wide, straight boulevard – a unique example of formal planning on a large scale in C19 Liverpool. For the group of important churches, etc., at the N end of Princes Road, *see* Walk 6, pp. 245–9. From here, the journey to the park can be made on foot or by bus. The boulevard is lined with three-storey terraced houses of the 1870s–80s, with some late C20 infill on a sadly reduced scale. Earlier houses are mostly of yellow brick and minimally Gothic; later ones, closer to the park, of red brick with columned porches and classical details in moulded terracotta. Behind, there is a sudden change of scale to the simplest of two-storey houses, in streets mostly laid out and built up during the 1860s–70s. Halfway down on the left is Princes Avenue Methodist Church, *c.* 1965, with a metal **sculpture** of Christ by *Arthur Dooley* attached. The pose suggests both Crucifixion and Resurrection.

At the s end of the boulevard is the main entrance to **Prince's Park**, the first public, or at least semi-public, park to be provided for the citizens of Liverpool [167]. It was the creation of Richard Vaughan Yates (1785–1856), iron merchant and philanthropic Dissenter, who lived nearby in Aigburth Road. He bought the site for £50,000 from the Earl of Sefton and in 1842 employed *Joseph Paxton* and *James Pennethorne* to lay it out, Paxton being the key figure. The name commemorates the birth of Edward, Prince of Wales, the previous year. This was Paxton's first park design and a precursor to his much larger and more influential Birkenhead Park across the Mersey. It follows the model of Nash's Regent's Park in London, with sites for housing around the edges. The sale of building plots was intended to offset the cost of laying out the park, with a proportion of rental income paying for its upkeep.

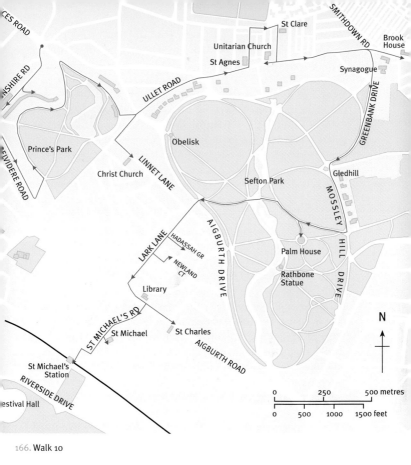

166. Walk 10

However, the take up was slow, and in 1843 it was decided to establish a company to carry forward the work. The degree of public access at this stage is not clear, but in the words of the *Liverpool Mercury*, 1844, it was 'delightful to see the labouring man, his wife and children in the evenings enjoying themselves in the pleasure grounds'.

The **plan** has a curving drive round the edge, and the houses are mostly outside this, facing the surrounding roads. Many have bow windows and verandas at the rear, to take advantage of the view. They do not follow Paxton's original layout, which envisaged more terraces and fewer detached and semi-detached villas. In 1843 a national competition was held for the design of the houses, won by *Wyatt Papworth* and *Henry Currey*, but except for one block by Papworth their proposals were not carried out. Progress was slow: some sites were not developed until the 1860s, and others were never built on.

The square **gatepiers** with curved flanking walls may be by *Pennethorne*; the handsome **gates** of a radial pattern are replicas of *c.* 1960. Rather than enter the park here, turn right into **Prince's Gate West** and continue into **Devonshire Road**. On the left is a brick and stone Gothic house of 1862–4 with later additions, by *Alfred Waterhouse* for the dock engineer George Fosbery Lyster. A little further along on the opposite side is a long, low, windowless brick range with classical stucco ornaments and a central entrance, all very derelict. These were livery stables, probably 1850s. Further along on the opposite side, at the corner of Sunnyside, is **Cavendish Gardens**, of before 1848. One of the earliest and best groups in the park, treated as a single, palatial composition. Stuccoed, of nine bays and three storeys, with giant Corinthian pilasters to the end elevations and a pediment with giant Corinthian columns on the park side. Following the serpentine curve of **Sunnyside** is a row of attractive, stuccoed, semi-detached houses with Italianate details, probably 1850s. The rest of Devonshire Road has large detached houses backing on to the park, none earlier than the late 1850s. One has an odd little Gothic gateway. On the opposite side, at the end, is an eighteen-bay terrace with projecting ends and centre, and cast-iron balconies in the recessed parts. It belongs to the earliest phase of development, and was complete by 1848. Facing the end of Devonshire Road on a prominent corner site is **Belvidere Road Independent Baptist Church**, built as St John's Wesleyan Methodist Chapel, 1861–3, by *Hayley & Son* of Manchester. Decorated Gothic, rock-faced. The octagonal towers framing the w end originally had tall spires. Attached at the back is a school. The whole strong and rugged group looks as if it had strayed from a Pennine mill town. Round the corner of Devonshire Road in **South Street**, immediately behind the grand houses, are 1870s terraces of the simplest two-storey workers' houses.

Return to the corner of Devonshire Road and **Belvidere Road**. Its houses are mostly of the 1860s, i.e. later than on the other sides of the park, and less distinguished. Halfway down on the sw side is a former **Presbyterian Church** by Messrs *Hay*, begun 1856: small, Gothic, rock-faced, with a rose window in the gable and a truncated square spire in

167. Prince's
Park, from the
Ordnance Survey
of 1846–8

168. Windermere Terrace, overlooking Prince's Park (1840s)

the angle of the porch.* On the same side, towards the junction with Ullet Road, is **Wellesley Terrace**, probably early 1850s: red brick with stucco dressings, symmetrical and quite impressive.

Entering the park opposite Wellesley Terrace and following the perimeter drive clockwise gives views of the backs of the houses in Belvidere Road, Devonshire Road and Sunnyside, the latter with elegant bow windows and verandas. After Sunnyside, and aligned with the main entrance gates, is a red granite **obelisk**, 1858, to the memory of Richard Vaughan Yates. Turn right here and continue along the perimeter drive. On the right is the **lake**, created by Paxton to be the main landscape feature. It has an island, and at the s end a **boathouse** in the style of a Swiss chalet, possibly by *John Robertson*, now ruinous. The banks were laid out with gardens and winding paths. On choice sites overlooking the lake are some of the earliest houses. **Princes Park Mansions**, a stuccoed terrace of eight houses by *Wyatt Papworth*, is the only result of the 1843 competition. Converted into flats from 1912. Immediately after this is a row of 1840s houses on the right of the drive, within the park itself: **Windermere Terrace** [168], with two bows facing the park, then **Windermere House**, a handsome three-bay house with

*Lower down on the opposite side, within the park itself, stood the principal church of the new suburb, St Paul. A large Gothic building of 1846–8 by *A.H. Holme*, with a dominating spire, it was demolished in 1974.

a porch of four Ionic columns, aligned with the E entrance to the park. Turn left here and leave the park. On the left, at the corner of Sefton Park Road, is **Park Lodge**. Unremarkable externally, it is supposed to incorporate masonry from one of the lodges of the former royal hunting ground of Toxteth Park.

Turn right along **Ullet Road**, and left into **Linnet Lane**. On the right is **Christ Church**, 1867–71 by *Culshaw & Sumners*. It was paid for by George Horsfall (*see* topic box, p. 247). A lively Dec Gothic design in stone, with quirky and original touches. The E elevation facing Linnet Lane [169] has an apse flanked on the s by vestries and on the N by an open porch, and a tower with tall broach spire, the broaches convex in outline. The w end, facing **East Albert Road**, has diagonally set corner porches. The aisles are cross-vaulted, each window having its own gable, and the clerestory windows are merely arched heads filled with tracery. Inside, the six-bay nave has a hammerbeam roof and slender

169. Christ Church, Linnet Lane, by Culshaw & Sumners (1867–71)

quatrefoil piers with foliage capitals. Sanctuary **floor** and **reredos** by
Bernard Miller, 1930. The apse **stained glass** seems contemporary with
the building and may be by *Hardman*. Two early C20 windows, s aisle,
by *Gustave Hiller* of Liverpool, one including a representation of the
recently completed E end of the Anglican Cathedral. *Shrigley & Hunt*
also supplied two windows. Return to Ullet Road, and turn right to the
main entrance of Sefton Park.

Sefton Park, occupying 269 acres (109 hectares) bought mostly from
the Earl of Sefton, was by far the biggest public park laid out anywhere
in the country since Regents Park in London at the beginning of the
C19. As with Prince's Park, the cost was to be recouped from the sale of
building plots around the edges. In 1867 a design competition was won
by *Lewis Hornblower* and *Edouard André*. It is not clear how the two
came to work together. Hornblower, a Liverpool architect, had taken
part in the 1843 competition for housing in connection with Prince's
Park and had designed the main entrance lodge of Paxton's Birkenhead
Park. André, aged just 26, was chief gardener to the city of Paris, where
he had been involved in the creation of such public parks as the Bois de
Boulogne and the Parc des Buttes-Chaumont.

 Spiralling costs meant that the winning design was not carried out in
full, and it was far from complete when the park opened in 1872. An
extensive botanical garden, lodges, and recreational buildings designed
by *Hornblower* in a range of picturesque styles, remained unbuilt.
Despite this, Sefton Park is a magnificent achievement of mid-Victorian
suburban planning and municipal enterprise. It should be remembered
that the landscape was created from a windswept tract of featureless
agricultural land: there were no groups of trees, and no lake. Now, in its
maturity, the park largely fulfils André's promise that its forest trees
would in time appear 'as if planted by nature'. The layout embodies the
principles of landscape design practised by André in Paris. The
Gardener's Chronicle huffily summed it up as a 'Gallicised version of the
Jardin Anglais, which, as in architecture and costume, we are bound to
accept with reverence, and to pronounce the fashion, however much the
stomach of a genuine John Bull may revolt against it'. The informality
is indeed derived from the English parks of Paxton and Loudon, but
instead of Paxton's serpentine paths André favoured long sweeping
curves which meet tangentially rather than intersecting, inducing the
visitor to follow a roundabout route and so making the park seem even
larger. The convergence of the paths was made less obvious by masking
them with embankments and by planting trees in clumps at these
points. Decorative planting of evergreens and shrubs was confined to
areas such as the banks of the lake and its feeder pools, created from two
streams that crossed the site.

 The main entrance from Ullet Road, 1875 [170], has Gothic **gate piers**
with a short central **tower**, its E.E. details debased with relish. The

170. Sefton Park gates and lodge, Ullet Road, by Thomas Shelmerdine (1875)

chunkily buttressed base supports two short, fat red granite columns with a thin sandstone one squeezed in between, all three holding up a steep little roof. (The granite columns are sections from much larger ones, removed from the interior of St George's Hall in the 1850s – *see* Major Buildings, p. 56.) To the right is a pretty **lodge** of 1874 – one of three at the entrances – in *cottage orné* style, of red brick and sandstone with half-timbering. Gates and lodges are by *Thomas Shelmerdine*, Corporation Surveyor. Just inside, aligned with the gates, is a red granite **obelisk** of 1909 to Samuel Smith MP, Liverpool cotton broker and philanthropist, by *Willink & Thicknesse*. The plinth had bronze relief sculptures by *C.J. Allen*. The straight path leading from the obelisk was not part of André and Hornblower's plan.

The fringes of the park, divided into villa plots, were sold off from 1872. J.A. Kilpin, President of the Liverpool Architectural Society, hoped they would be

> 'Soon adorned with villas, in infinite variety,
> And all designed by members of the Architectural Society.'

Among local architects known to have worked here are *Banner & Co.*, *James N. Crofts*, *F. & G. Holme*, *James Rhind*, *George Rushforth*, *Henry Sumners*, *Walter W. Thomas* and *H.H. Vale*, though unfortunately few designers of specific houses are recorded. On the whole the houses are more remarkable for size than for architectural quality. Most have been converted into flats or adapted for institutional use. Some of the earliest and most interesting lie immediately NE of the entrance gates on **Ullet Road**. Right beside the gates is **Ullet Grange**, 1876, for the cotton broker Edward Ellis Edwards. Red brick with bands of red

171. The Towers, Ullet Road, by G.A. Audsley (1874)

sandstone, elaborate timber gables, and high, dramatic chimneys. Next, three rather old-fashioned stuccoed Italianate houses of 1872. They were built for Greek merchants, which probably explains why two have Greek-looking busts in roundels above their entrances. After these is Rankin Hall, originally **The Towers**, 1874, a gigantic Gothic pile by *G.A. Audsley*, first occupied by the cotton broker Michael Belcher [171]. Red brick with red sandstone dressings. Arched entrance at the base of a high, square tower with a higher turret at one corner. Typical Audsley stained glass and stencilled decoration inside. Further along, at the corner of Ullet Road and **Croxteth Gate**, is **Sefton Court**, another stuccoed Italianate house, extended in 1889 for the shipping magnate Dashper Edward Glynn. Part of the interior was refurbished *c.* 1901 by the Liverpool Arts and Crafts architect *Edmund Rathbone*, with woodwork, metalwork and painting by the *Bromsgrove Guild*.

In 1958 the City Architect and Director of Housing, *Ronald Bradbury*, and the City Engineer and Surveyor, *Henry T. Hough*, proposed replacing all the park-side villas with much denser housing, mostly in the form of slab and tower blocks. This plan was partly carried out, and Ullet Road E of Croxteth Gate shows the results: a Corbusian vision of high residential towers in a sylvan setting, with low-rise schools and other institutional buildings between. The five fifteen-storey **towers**, clad in buff-coloured brick, were completed by 1965. The views from the upper floors must be spectacular, but seen from within the park they undermine the illusion of open countryside. Even in this stretch of Ullet Road some original houses survive, notably **Holt House**, 1874–8, a very large and rather austere classical building in red brick, for the cotton merchant and future Lord Mayor, Robert Durning Holt.

Directly opposite Holt House is the church of **St Agnes**, 1883–5, by *John Loughborough Pearson*. One of a cluster of ambitious religious buildings serving the new suburb. It cost £28,000 and was paid for by the stockbroker H. Douglas Horsfall (*see* topic box, p. 247). In 1969 Pevsner described it as 'by far the most beautiful Victorian church of Liverpool . . . an epitome of Late Victorian nobility in church design'. Externally it is of red pressed brick with red sandstone dressings, the same materials as the surrounding houses. The C13 style, combining

English and French elements, is typical of Pearson. It is a high, compact building, with aisles and clerestory, polygonal apse, and transepts at both the (ritual) E and W ends. The apse has blank arcading high up, and there are two turrets with short spires in the angles of the E transept and the chancel. No tower, but a lead-covered flèche marks the E crossing. Windows are lancets or have plate tracery, and those in the end walls of the transepts differ from each other. Two open, vaulted porches flank the short bay W of the W transept, and lead into a low, vaulted space below a gallery, which serves as a lobby. The visitor emerges from this shadowy area through a tripartite arcade into the soaring height of the W transept. The interior is ashlar-faced and stone-vaulted throughout with quadripartite rib vaults, and though not particularly large it conveys an impression of cathedral-like dignity [172]. The four-bay nave arcades have round piers with continuous balconies of trefoil-headed tracery above, and a clerestory of high lancets over all.

The E end is much richer, both in decoration and spatial complexity. A narrow ambulatory runs round the apse, divided from the sanctuary by an arcade with angel musicians in the spandrels. Above these is a continuous frieze in high relief representing the Adoration of the Lamb, and higher still, between the clerestory windows, statues of angels under canopies. All this **sculpture**, along with the **reredos**, dates from 1893–5 and was carried out to Pearson's designs by *Nathaniel Hitch*, who had worked for him on the reredos of Truro Cathedral. s of the chancel is the **Lady Chapel**, one bay long with aisles, the N aisle continuous with the ambulatory. The wooden **orchestra loft** was designed by Pearson in 1893. – Dividing chapel from transept, a wrought-iron **screen** of quatrefoil pattern, 1903; along with the **reredos** of 1904, designed by *G.F. Bodley* after Pearson's death. – The NE transept is completely filled by the **organ**, raised up high on an extraordinary polygonal platform, vaulted underneath and supported by a central column of black marble with ten more columns round the edges. The view of the chancel through this shadowy forest of columns is thrilling. (What was Pearson's inspiration for such a structure? In form, though not in style, it recalls the great pulpits by the Pisani in Siena, Pisa and Pistoia.) – Some playful **corbel heads** and grotesques in the transepts carved *c.* 1910 by a Mr *Thomson*, including a falling horse (a rebus for Horsfall) just to the left of the organ. – Several **stained glass** windows by *Kempe*, the latest in the SW transept commemorating the founder's mother (d. 1902). Two in the Lady Chapel by *Bryans*.

Just behind the church in Buckingham Avenue is the **vicarage**, 1885–7, by *Richard Norman Shaw*, paid for by Douglas Horsfall's mother. Red brick with stone dressings, the mullioned windows unmoulded and asymmetrically arranged, the general effect severe. On the street elevation the only projection is a shallow canted oriel with tracery, indicating the chapel on the first floor. Towards the church the composition is more complicated, with a pointed-arched doorway, the flat chimney-breast to the right, its left angle caught on a stone corbel, and canted oriels at each end, the one on the right running through both floors. Also by *Shaw* the simple **parish hall** behind.

Continue to the end of Buckingham Avenue and turn right into **Arundel Avenue**. Here, at the corner of York Avenue, is the church of **St Clare (R.C.)**, 1889–90 by *Leonard Stokes*. One of the most imaginative churches of its date in the country. It was paid for by the brothers Francis and James Reynolds, cotton brokers (Stokes was the godson of Francis Reynolds), and cost £7,834. The style is Gothic, but more loosely tied to historical precedent than Pearson's St Agnes of just four years earlier. Exterior of buff-coloured brick with stone dressings, the walls high and sheer, the window tracery late Decorated. No tower, only a turret with a spire in the angle of N transept and nave. The window in the cliff-like E wall is broad and high up and partly filled with blind tracery, and the hoodmould over it seems to hang down in a loop on either side – a foretaste of further unhistorical details within. Small statues of St Clare and St Francis in niches over N and W porches, possibly by *Frampton*. The interior [173] follows the example of Bodley's St Augustine, Pendlebury, 1874 (and ultimately of Albi, etc.) in having internal buttresses, or wall-piers. These are pierced to form narrow passage aisles, and linked by semicircular arches to create a low arcade

174. Ullet Road Unitarian Church, detail of Library ceiling, painted by Gerald Moira (completed 1902)

supporting a continuous balcony on each side of the nave. The bases of the piers are teardrop-shaped in plan – rounded towards the aisles and triangular towards the nave – and the front parts are carried up as triangular shafts till they meet a chamfered horizontal band at the top of the wall. The chamfering is exactly one side of the triangle, so each bay seems bordered left, right and top by a bevelled frame. Stokes wanted stone throughout, but unfortunately almost everything above the springing of the arches is painted plaster.

Furnishings. Over the high altar is the **reredos**, a large triptych combining painting and relief sculpture by *Robert Anning Bell* and *George Frampton*, 1890. It draws freely on Northern and Italian Renaissance sources, and provides a sumptuous focus for the whole interior. – Stokes's **pulpit** is remarkable: four sides of a hexagon, stone, with panels of openwork tracery, its sides sloping inwards towards the top. – **Font**, w end. Chalice-shaped, of gorgeous alabaster with a copper cover.

Hinges and other door furniture demonstrate Stokes's Arts and Crafts credentials. – Present **high altar** 1920s, **altar rails** 1933. – To the left a niche prettily painted in 1959 by an Italian Capuchin, *Fr Ugolino*, with angels drawing back curtains to reveal a view of Assisi.

The **presbytery**, attached to the NE corner and forming a single composition with the church, is simpler than Stokes intended. It should have had bay windows on the right, softening the junction. The hoodmould stops over the pointed-arched door incorporate the letters S and C, in a curvilinear style that strikingly anticipates Art Nouveau.

From the w end of St Clare return along York Avenue to Ullet Road. Here, between York Avenue and Cheltenham Avenue, is **Ullet Road Unitarian Church**, by *Thomas Worthington & Son* of Manchester (the influence of the son, *Percy Worthington*, may have been to the fore). The church, vestry and library (on the left as viewed from Ullet Road) date from 1896–9; the hall on the right and the linking cloister were added *c.* 1901. Unitarianism was a powerful force in C19 Liverpool, as such names as Roscoe, Rathbone, Holt, Booth, Brunner and Tate show. The congregation moved here from Renshaw Street in the city centre, and the ambitious new buildings demonstrate the wealth and confidence both of the Liverpool Unitarians and of the residential area around Sefton Park. The buildings, of red pressed brick with red sandstone dressings, are attractively grouped round three sides of a central garden, giving a collegiate feel. The **church** is Gothic, with Decorated window tracery. No tower, but the (ritual) w gable has a prominent squared-off projection with three arched openings, like a bellcote but without any bells. The statue of Christ in the gable niche is after Thorwaldsen. Three magnificent **doors** of beaten copper with Art Nouveau foliate designs, by *Richard Llewellyn Rathbone*, lead into the spacious lobby. The interior was also to have been of brick, but happily ashlar was used instead, paid for by Mrs George Holt. The arrangement is more church-like than early C19 Nonconformist chapels, with nave and aisles and a separate chancel. – **Choir stalls** by Messrs *Hatch* of Lancaster, the canopy above those on the right by *C.J. Allen*. – **Reredos**. Last Supper by *H.H. Martyn* of Cheltenham. – Good Art Nouveau light fittings by the *Artificers' Guild*, London. – **Font** of wood, 1906, designed by *Ronald P. Jones* and carved by *Allen*. – **Stained glass** mostly by *Morris & Co.*, after designs by *Edward Burne-Jones*, that in the chancel dating from the opening of the church and better than the later windows. – The **vestry**, right of the chancel, has **paintings** by *Gerald Moira*, completed in 1902. Four roundels on the ceiling represent Justice, Prudence, Temperance and Charity. Above the fireplace, a shallow-relief panel in painted plaster of the rising sun, a powerful Symbolist work.

Adjoining the vestry is the **library**, with even more splendid painted decoration of the same date by *Moira* on the vaulted ceiling [174]. The subject is the Triumph of Truth. A winged figure representing Time raises the victorious youthful female figure of Truth who scatters her

175. Gledhill, Mossley Hill Drive, by James F. Doyle (1881)

enemies, Envy, Calumny, Intolerance and Ignorance. She is accompanied by artists, scientists, religious leaders and other seekers after truth, ancient and modern, ranging from Moses to Newton. The figures are linked by serpentine golden rays, issuing from the lamp held by Truth.

The **hall** and **cloister** were given by Sir John Brunner and Henry Tate. The exterior of the hall is picturesquely composed, with a canted bay window to Ullet Road, a smaller semicircular bay to York Avenue, and a little roof lantern with an ogee cupola. Inside, it has an impressive open timber roof, an aisle down one side, and an attractively contrived inglenook with the arms of the donors above. In the cloister are two recessed bays with **monuments** from the earlier chapel in Renshaw Street. These include: a bust of William Roscoe, by *John Gibson*; Edward Roscoe d. 1834, by *Gibson*, an angel in profile looking up, representing Hope; William Rathbone d. 1868, by *J.H. Foley*, 1874, a large relief with the deceased on a sarcophagus and groups of mourners left and right; Charles Beard d. 1888, with profile-portrait medallion by *J.E. Boehm*; and William Rathbone d. 1902, with profile-portrait by *C.J. Allen*.

Leaving the church, continue E along Ullet Road. At the corner of Halkyn Avenue is the brick and terracotta **Mary Clark Home**, 1892, with prominent chimneystacks and a porch balcony with Renaissance ironwork. Designed by *Arthur P. Fry* as accommodation for elderly single ladies. A little further along on the opposite side is **Lathbury House**, 1965, an old people's home by *Bradshaw, Rowse & Harker*. Its most striking feature is a glazed-in concrete external stair, wrapped around a square central column which rises above the roof-line to support a cubic concrete water tank.

Ullet Road ends where it joins **Smithdown Road**. Here, on the corner of Greenbank Drive, is another picturesque **lodge** to Sefton

176. Palm House, Sefton Park, by Mackenzie & Moncur (opened 1896)

Park, 1878 by *Thomas Shelmerdine*. Just behind is the red brick tower of the former **St Columba's Presbyterian Church**, 1896–7 by *Woolfall & Eccles*. The part below the saddleback roof was formerly an almost transparent cage of terracotta tracery, but the openings have been filled in with louvres. The nave, etc., was replaced in the 1990s by an old people's home, the shape of which echoes the vanished building. A short way E along Smithdown Road is **The Brook House**, a lively, expansive pub of *c*. 1881 by *John Elliott Reeve*, with matching additions at each end, probably by *Walter W. Thomas*. Red brick and red sandstone (now painted) with timber-framed gables and mullioned windows.

From the opposite side of Smithdown Road there are buses back to the city centre. For a longer walk, and more of Sefton Park, return to the park lodge and turn s into **Greenbank Drive**. Immediately on the left is the **synagogue** of buff brick by *Alfred E. Shennan*, 1936–7, with faint echoes of Stockholm City Hall in the details. The galleried interior has Art Deco woodwork. After this come a few large houses of the 1880s, but for most of its length Greenbank Drive was never built up, and the SE side, intended for villas, is now allotments.

Greenbank Drive converges with Greenbank Lane, both roads ending at **Mossley Hill Drive**, which skirts the E and s sides of the park. On the corner of Greenbank Lane and Mossley Hill Drive is **Gledhill**, the best of the surviving C19 villas, designed in 1881 by *James F. Doyle* for the stockbroker R.W. Elliston [175]. Old English in the manner of Shaw: picturesque asymmetry in red brick and sandstone, with tile hanging, pargeting, half-timbered gables, mullioned windows and very tall chimneys. A succession of big detached and semi-detached houses put up in the 1880s, all in brick with dressings of terracotta or red sandstone, follows to the s. No. 2, 1883, for the cotton broker A.S. Hannay, is possibly by *H. & A.P. Fry*. No. 6, **Duffus**, is likely to be by *F. & G. Holme*, who were probably responsible for the showier **Bridge House**, next door, with dormer windows in elaborate Dutch gables. Round the corner in **Ibbotson's Lane** is **The Bridge**, similar in its details to Gledhill though smaller, and perhaps also by *Doyle*. These names are from the **cast-iron bridge** which carries Mossley Hill Drive over one of the streams feeding the Sefton Park lake. Leaving the drive and entering the park just before the bridge, a path immediately on the left leads down to the stream. This gives a view of the bridge from below – a workaday structure of lattice girders on octagonal columns – and also of a small rock-work **grotto**, one of several bordering the park's water features, created by *M. Combaz*, who had worked with Edouard André on the Paris parks.

Return to the main path and continue into the park. On the left is the **Palm House**, a splendid iron and glass conservatory by *Mackenzie & Moncur* of Glasgow, opened 1896 [176]. It was the gift of Henry Yates Thompson, whose great-uncle Richard Vaughan Yates created Prince's Park fifty years earlier. An octagonal domed structure on a plinth of polished red granite, which breaks forward at the angles to support eight statues (some marble, some bronze) by *Léon-Joseph Chavalliaud*. Their subjects were selected by Thompson to illustrate horticulture and exploration, ensuring in a thoroughly Victorian way that the Palm House would give instruction as well as pleasure. They represent Le Nôtre, James Cook, Mercator, Linnaeus, Darwin, Columbus, Henry the Navigator, and John Parkinson (Apothecary to James I). Inside are more marble sculptures: The Angel's Whisper, 1850s, by *Benjamin Edward Spence*; a version of the same artist's Highland Mary; Two Goats, by *Giovita Lombardi*; and a classical bench with an inscription commemorating Thompson's gift. In 2001 a full restoration of the Palm House and its sculptures was completed. Facilities that allow its use for functions and performances have been constructed below ground level.

Return to the main path and turn left, continuing into the park. (A detour left along the e side of the lake leads to a marble **statue** of the Liverpool merchant and philanthropist William Rathbone (d. 1868), unveiled 1877, begun by *J.H. Foley* and completed by *Thomas Brock*. Brock's reliefs on the base have been removed.) The path descends and crosses the second of the two streams which feed the lake. Just after this on the left is a vandalized and waterless **fountain**, a cast of the famous Shaftesbury Memorial in Piccadilly Circus, London, by *Alfred Gilbert*. Given by George Audley; unveiled 1932. The crowning aluminium figure of Eros has been removed to the Conservation Centre (*see* Walk 3, p. 191).

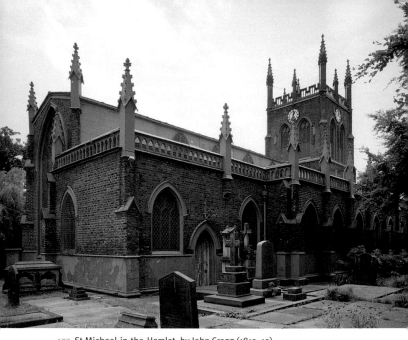

177. St Michael-in-the-Hamlet, by John Cragg (1813–15)

From the fountain, bear right and continue to the junction of Lark Lane and **Aigburth Drive**. Aigburth Drive forms the sw boundary of the park, and parallel to it, within the park, is a broad, level track originally intended for riding. At the corner of Lark Lane is the earliest example of demolition and rebuilding by the City Council on the periphery of the park: **Bloomfield Green**, a symmetrical group of two-storey Neo-Georgian flats for old people, opened 1958. They hark back to suburban municipal housing of the interwar years, and seem out of scale with their big Victorian neighbours and the tower blocks erected across the park a few years later.

Leave the park by the Gothic **gatepiers** at the end of **Lark Lane**, which, following the creation of Sefton Park, acquired a handful of interesting commercial and institutional buildings. At the corner of Sefton Grove is the former **police station** of 1885 by *F.U. Holme*, red brick and stone with Gothic details. The **Albert Hotel** at the corner of Pelham Grove is a large Gothic pub of 1873, an early demonstration of the architectural ambitions of Robert Cain, the brewer who later built the Philharmonic and the Vines (*see* Walk 3, p. 184 and Walk 6, p. 234). **Hadassah Grove**, the next turning on the left, is a delightful surprise: an L-shaped cul-de-sac lined with small but elegant houses, probably *c.* 1840, mostly brick, with stone dressings and classical doorcases. Further down Lark Lane on the right, opposite the end of Hesketh Street, is the former **Christ Church Institute**, 1884, with a gabled and half-timbered upper storey, the central part jettied out. Bickerton Street leads se from Lark Lane to **Newland Court**, *c.* 1984, terraced houses round a quadrangle, designed by *Innes Wilkin Ainsley Gommon* for the Hesketh Street Co-operative, one of the earliest co-operative housing schemes in the city (*see* topic box, p. 272).

Continue down Lark Lane until it ends at **Aigburth Road**, then turn left. **Sefton Park Library**, on the left, was opened in 1911, the last of the branch libraries designed by the Corporation Surveyor, *Thomas Shelmerdine*. Ashlar and roughcast on the ground floor with half-timbering above, and tall, diagonally set brick chimneys – like a Neo-Tudor village hall. In the entrance porch, a repoussé copper panel commemorating the opening by Andrew Carnegie, Celtic Art Nouveau style, by *J.A. Hodel*.

Cross Aigburth Road and continue a little further SE to glance at **St Charles Borromeo (R.C.)**, 1899–1900 by *Pugin & Pugin* (i.e. *Peter Paul Pugin*). Dec Gothic in yellow rock-faced stone with red ashlar dressings. (Ritual) W tower with statues in niches.

Return along Aigburth Road and turn SW into **St Michael's Road**, leading to **St Michael's Hamlet**. This was the creation of *John Cragg*, proprietor of the Mersey Iron Foundry, and originally comprised the church of St Michael-in-the-Hamlet, 1813–15, and five villas. This little cluster made up a secluded semi-rural settlement near the river, just the sort of man-made incident in the landscape admired by writers on the Picturesque. From *c.* 1840 further villas were added, then in the 1880s a tide of terraced houses engulfed the Hamlet, changing its character completely.

Cragg was a fanatic of cast-iron for all purposes, and used it very extensively here. Like his earlier St George, Everton (Walk 8, p. 264), the **church** in St Michael's Church Road may reflect the involvement of *J.M. Gandy*, and especially *Thomas Rickman*. Many cast-iron components used at St George recur, but at St Michael iron is also used for parapets, battlements, pinnacles, hoodmoulds and other details of the brick exterior [177]. As at St George, ceiling and roof are of slate slabs held in a cast-iron framework. Cragg's new method for cladding the exteriors of brick churches with iron and slate, patented 1813, is used for the dado (except on the rebuilt N side); the slate was originally 'sanded' to resemble stone. The clerestory walls consist of a slim core of brickwork sandwiched between slate slabs: Rickman complained of the 'extreme thinness'. The church has a W tower, six-bay nave with clerestory and aisles, and chancel. In 1900 the N aisle was seamlessly doubled in width, bearing out Cragg's claim that his modular, prefabricated buildings could easily be enlarged. The internal structure is entirely cast-iron, the nave arcade consisting of slender clustered shafts supporting spandrels of openwork tracery. The windows are cast-iron too, the tracery of the E window being identical with that of St George. According to Goodhart-Rendel, St Michael was restored in 1875 by *W. & G. Audsley*. The marble **font** is presumably theirs. – The E window has strongly coloured **stained glass**, 1858 or after, with biblical scenes in quatrefoils against vine scrolls and flowers. Lady Chapel E window, 1916 by *Shrigley & Hunt*; **First World War memorial** window in the porch by *Gustave Hiller*. – Well-preserved **churchyard** with many c19 monuments. Near the NE corner of the chancel is that of the Herculaneum Pottery Benefit Society, 1824, a simple slab with an appealing inscription:

> Here peaceful rest the POTTERS turn'd to Clay
> Tir'd with their lab'ring life's long tedious day
> Surviving friends their Clay to earth consign
> To be re-moulded by a Hand Divine!

The Herculaneum Pottery was on the Mersey shore, NW of the Hamlet (*See* Walk 1, p. 119).

Cragg's five **villas** are all stuccoed and painted, with Tudor Gothic details, and cast-iron windows, hoodmoulds and internal features. **Glebelands** stands immediately S of the church, with **The Hermitage** opposite (it has a pretty cast-iron veranda). **Hollybank** adjoins the churchyard on the E, and has good openwork cast-iron gatepiers. The round building in the garden was originally a summerhouse. **Carfax** is at the corner of St Michael's Road and St Michael's Church Road. **The Cloisters**, further SW along St Michael's Road, has a veranda at the back, and an elliptical cast-iron stair inside.

Opposite The Cloisters turn right into Melly Road, then left into Southwood Road to reach **St Michael's Station**, 1864. Beyond the railway was the site of the 1984 **Liverpool International Garden Festival**, the first of several held in the UK to bring about urban regeneration. The Liverpool project involved the reclamation and landscaping of 130 acres (53 hectares) of derelict and polluted industrial land. Houses have been built on part of the site, as was always the intention, but much of the remainder has reverted to wilderness. The **Festival Hall** survives, a serenely elegant structure by *Arup Associates*, won in competition in 1982. A gently curving vault with slightly lower semi-domes at each end, tied together by a lantern along the crest of the vault: the form is reminiscent of the Palm House at Kew. The steel framework of the central section has a skin of polycarbonate sheeting, while the ends are sleekly clad in ribbed aluminium. Column-free interior, designed for possible conversion to a sports and leisure centre after the Festival.

From St Michael's Station regular trains run to Liverpool Central, where Walk 4 begins.

Excursions

Speke Hall, Airport and Housing Development

by Richard Pollard

Speke is now a suburb of Liverpool, on the A561 7 m. (11.3 km.) SE of the city centre, from where there are frequent buses.

On the banks of the Mersey on the very edge of the city huddles **Speke Hall**, an extremely picturesque house and one of the finest timber-framed buildings in the North West. Almost all of what we see was begun by Sir William Norris in *c.* 1530 and finished by his son Henry about seventy years later. This is a quadrangle laid out around an intimate shady courtyard and surrounded on three sides by a now dry moat. On top of the red sandstone plinth the framing is dense with herringbone and quatrefoil panelling, and the roofline is broken by many finialled gables and massive stone chimneystacks. The apparent uniformity of the elevations, particularly around the courtyard, disguises a complex building history that is still not fully understood. The two best rooms both date from the early 1530s: Sir William's **Great Hall**, with all sorts of panelling and a spectacular embattled and pinnacled overmantel, and the **Great Parlour**, which has an excellent plaster ceiling with vine-trails, etc., inserted *c.* 1612, and another ambitious overmantel. Pevsner described its figurative carving as 'ludicrous'; 'naïve' might be kinder. The Norrises, like so much of the Lancastrian gentry, were recusant Catholics, and the house has an extensive network of hiding-places and spy-holes, including an original 'eavesdrop' over the courtyard entrance to the screens. Speke Hall is owned and opened by the National Trust.

Pevsner mourned the loss of the house's Arcadian **setting**: 'the trees between the house and the river have given way to a runway of Speke Airport, and the *Hinterland* has become all industry'. This began after Liverpool Corporation acquired 1,800 acres of the Speke estate in 1928 with the intention of emulating Manchester's Trafford Park or the Slough Trading Estate in order to alleviate unemployment in the city. But the first land to be developed, immediately w of the Hall, became an airport.

Liverpool Speke Airport was the city's most forward-looking inter-war civic project, the action of a great port striving to remain at the forefront of transport developments by establishing itself as the premier 'air-junction' in the North of England. It opened in 1933 with a farm serving as temporary terminal and hangars, but in 1935–40 a suite of

178. Former Liverpool Speke Airport, terminal and control tower, by Edward
Bloomfield (1937–9)

new buildings was erected which embodied the most advanced thinking of the time. The architect was *Edward Bloomfield*, working under the City Surveyor, *Albert D. Jenkins*. The plan is closely based on the Fuhlsbüttel airport at Hamburg (1929): matching hangars flanking a gently curving **terminal**, with tiered observation decks and central control tower. The integrated plan reflected current European developments, and the diluted brick Modernism shows the influence of Dudok, already apparent in Corporation housing schemes (*see* Walk 5, p. 227). But the monumentalism, particularly of the octagonal control tower [178], owes more to contemporary American airport architecture. References to flight abound e.g. in the glazing of the w hangar, which evokes the form of aircraft wings and airships.

A replacement terminal was opened E of Speke Hall in 1967 (now Liverpool John Lennon Airport) and in 1998–2001 the original buildings were converted to new uses by *Falconer Chester Architects*. The terminal is now extended as a hotel and the w hangar has been imaginatively turned into a leisure and fitness centre. The airfield itself will be built over as a business park. Nevertheless, Speke is still the most coherent example of the first generation of purpose-built airports remaining in Europe.

Housing was always a part of the Corporation's intentions for Speke. Its first plan projected a population of 55,000, reduced to 20,000 in the adopted scheme of 1936 drawn up by *Sir Lancelot Keay*, the Director of Housing. Styled a 'Self-contained Community Unit', this was conceived as a sort of proto-New Town in the manner of Manchester's Wythenshawe scheme, though in execution it was little more than a large, remote housing estate (now a severely deprived one). Planned community facilities, and the middle classes, were either slow to arrive or never did. Keay's response to the featureless site was a very formal grid plan structured around broad avenues. Construction of the houses, designed in the hipped-roofed, lightly Neo-Georgian style common to most of his suburban schemes, began in 1938 on Speke Church Road (beside *J.L. Pearson*'s **All Saints** church of 1872–5), and continued into the 1960s. The best building is **St Ambrose (R.C.)** on Heathgate Avenue, by *Weightman & Bullen*, 1959–61. Disciplined, with an elegant campanile and a broad, lofty interior bound by an ambulatory on three sides.

Further Reading

For a full description of Speke Hall *see* the National Trust *Guide Book* (latest edition 1994). The architecture and planning of the airport and its sources are put in an international context in Roger Bowdler et al., *Berlin Templehof – Liverpool Speke – Paris le Bourget: Airport Architecture in the Thirties*, 2000. *See* the forthcoming *Buildings of England, Lancashire: Liverpool and the South West* for a more detailed account of the housing estate and its churches.

Port Sunlight

The model settlement of Port Sunlight lies on the Cheshire bank of the Mersey. It can be reached in about fifteen minutes by underground train from James Street, Moorfields, Lime Street or Central.

The manufacturer William Hesketh Lever (1851–1925, later 1st Viscount Leverhulme) began his factory here in 1888. Alongside he built model housing for his workers, naming the new settlement Port Sunlight after his product, Sunlight Soap. Port Sunlight differs from earlier factory villages provided by benevolent industrialists (e.g. Saltaire, near Bradford). Its layout is leafy and spacious in the tradition of C19

179. Park Road, Port Sunlight, with houses of 1892 by Douglas & Fordham in the foreground

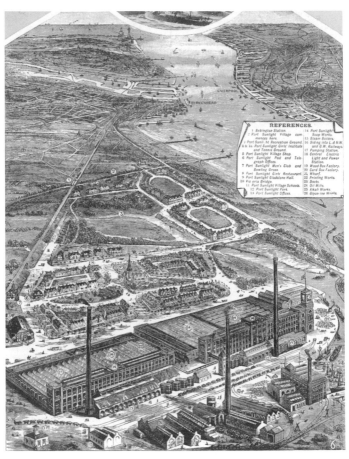

REFERENCES.

1 Bebington Station
2 Port Sunlight Village com-
mences here.
3 4 4a Port Sanit. M Recreation Ground.
4 & 4a Port Sunlight Girls' Institute
and Tennis Ground.
6 Port Sunlight Village Shop.
6 Port Sunlight Post and Tele-
graph Offices.
7 Port Sunlight Men's Club and
Bowling Green.
9 Port Sunlight Gladstone Hall.
10 Victoria Bridge.
11 Port Sunlight Village Schools.
12 Port Sunlight Park.
13 Port Sunlight Offices.

14 Port Sunlight
Soap Works.
15 Steam Boilers.
16 Siding into L.& N.W.
and G.W. Railways.
17 Pumping Station.
18 Central Electric
Light and Power
Station.
19 Wood Box Factory.
20 Card Box Factory.
21 Wharf.
22 Printing Works.
23 Docks.
24 Oil Mills.
25 Alkali Works.
26 Glycerine Works.

180. Aerial view of Port Sunlight before completion, *Illustrated London News* (1898)

middle-class suburbs, and its housing is varied and inventive in design as well as costly in materials and workmanship [179]. Architecturally, it is the most ambitious model village in the country.

The **factory** and **offices** (stone entrance front 1895–6, by *William Owen*, with additions by *William & Segar Owen* and *James Lomax-Simpson*) are at the s end, close to the railway station. Nearby the earliest housing is grouped round the Dell, an irregular grassy hollow following the course of a tidal channel that originally crossed the site. In the more formal N part of the Village, the contours were levelled and overlaid with a competition-winning Beaux-Arts plan of 1910 by *Ernest Prestwich*. The Causeway and the Diamond form its principal axes.

There are two main **house types**: the 'kitchen cottage', with three first-floor bedrooms over a kitchen and scullery, and the 'parlour cottage', with an additional bedroom and front parlour. They are for the most part arranged in 'superblocks', each enclosing an area originally laid out in allotments but now given over to garages. Lever employed many different architects (mostly North Western practices) which helps give the Village its variety. The most prolific contributors up to 1910 were *W. & S. Owen, Douglas & Fordham, Grayson & Ould* and *Wilson & Talbot*; most housing after 1910 was designed by *Lomax-Simpson*. A few London architects were also employed, such as *Edwin Lutyens, Maurice B. Adams* and *Ernest Newton*. The Village is therefore a showcase for the best late c19–early c20 domestic architecture, drawing freely on historical examples and vernacular traditions to produce a style of picturesque informality. Materials include half-timbering, pargeting, render and tile-hanging. Somewhat harsh red pressed brick and terracotta are typical of the earlier houses, while the later ones use a softer, subtler palette. Each originally had a fenced front garden, replaced at an early date with grass verges.

Public buildings are numerous and contribute greatly to the character of the Village. They include the Jacobean-style **Lyceum** adjoining the Dell, 1894–6, by *Douglas & Fordham*, which served originally as schools and also for Sunday services; **Hulme Hall** in Bolton Road, 1900–1, by *W. & S. Owen*, built as a women's dining hall, with mullioned and transomed windows and half-timbered gables; and the **Bridge Inn**, also in Bolton Road, 1900, by *Grayson & Ould*, originally a temperance hotel. **Christ Church** in Church Drive, 1902–4 by *W. & S. Owen*, is a late Gothic Revival church of great richness. In a loggia at the w end are the tombs of Lever and his wife, with effigies by *William Goscombe John*. Also by *John* is the **war memorial** at the intersection of the Causeway and the Diamond, unveiled 1921. It is unusually dramatic, with naturalistic bronze figures that seem to be defending the Village from attack.

Closing the view N along the Diamond is the superb **Lady Lever Art Gallery**, 1913–22, by *W. & S. Owen*. In contrast with the rest of the Village, it is classical in style, of reinforced concrete faced with Portland stone, and clearly influenced by early c20 American museums. As well as outstanding paintings, sculpture and decorative arts, it contains period rooms illustrating interior design of various dates, furnished with original panelling and chimneypieces.

Further Reading

The Village is more fully described in E. Hubbard & M. Shippobottom, *A Guide to Port Sunlight Village*, revised edn. 1998, and N. Pevsner & E. Hubbard, *The Buildings of England, Cheshire*, 1971. There is further information in *Lord Leverhulme*, the catalogue of an exhibition held at the Royal Academy, 1980. The Port Sunlight Heritage Centre, opposite the railway station, displays material relating to the architectural history of the Village.

Hamilton Square, Birkenhead

On the Cheshire bank, almost facing the Pier Head, reached by underground train from James Street, Moorfields, Lime Street or Central.

At the start of the C19 Birkenhead consisted of a small group of houses and cottages and the ruins of a medieval Benedictine priory. Steamers appeared on the ferry route between Woodside and Liverpool in 1819, giving rise to further building. Then, in 1824, the Scot William Laird established a boiler factory – soon a shipbuilding yard – on the shore of Wallasey Pool, and in the same year employed the Edinburgh architect *James Gillespie Graham* to prepare a plan for a new town.* The resulting street grid, measuring 1 by 0.25 m. (1.6 by 0.4 km.), s of and parallel to Wallasey Pool, is one of the most ambitious C19 town plans in Britain. The entire town was to consist of stone-faced buildings of high quality. Construction began at the E end around Hamilton Square, but a mid-C19 depression halted work, and the long, straight streets to the w were eventually built up in an undistinguished fashion.

Hamilton Square itself is very grand indeed, more coherently planned and more substantially built than most comparable Liverpool housing. The earliest houses, of 1825 or after, are at the N end of the E side [181] (including Laird's own at No. 63) and those adjacent at the E end of the N side. By 1839 only the N side had been completed. The s and w sides were built in 1839–44; the E side was completed soon after, with a gap for the future Town Hall. The architecture is strongly reminiscent of the Moray estate in Edinburgh, designed by Graham in 1822, including cast-iron balconies of the same anthemion pattern. The houses have basements, three storeys to the main cornice, and one more above. The ground floor has channelled rustication. Terrace ends are treated as pavilions, with giant three-quarter unfluted Doric columns, and centres are emphasized by pilasters. No two sides are identical, but this is hardly noticed because of the square's great size.

The former **Town Hall** (now Wirral Museum) was built as late as 1883–7 on its reserved site, to a competition-winning design by *C.O.*

*As part of his new town, Laird also planned to create **docks** in Wallasey Pool, though construction (under *J.M. Rendel*) did not begin until 1844. Beset by structural and financial problems, they were taken over by Liverpool in 1855, and completed by *J.B. Hartley* and then *G.F. Lyster* for the Mersey Docks and Harbour Board.

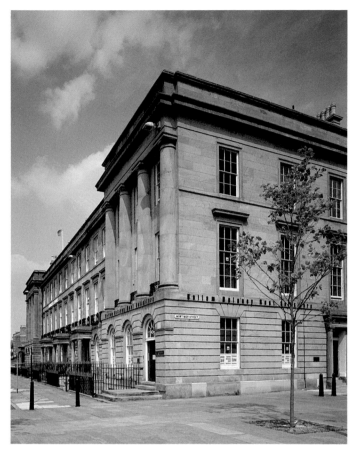

181. Hamilton Square, N end of E side, by James Gillespie Graham

Ellison & Son. Classical, with a portico and a domed clock tower, it derives from the town hall at Bolton, Lancs. The tower was partly rebuilt by *Henry Hartley* following a fire in 1901. Rich interior, with the former council chamber in front and assembly hall behind. Stained-glass window on the stairs, 1904, by *Gilbert P. Gamon*. Directly behind is the **Wirral Magistrates' Court**, 1884–7, by *T.D. Barry & Son*.

In the middle of the central garden is the unusual **Queen Victoria Monument**, 1905, by *Edmund Kirby*. A Gothic spire – a sort of Eleanor Cross – with two tiers of arches on free-standing granite shafts. On the w side a **statue** of John Laird, 1877, by *A. Bruce Joy*. On the E side, the restrainedly classical **war memorial**, 1925. It is by *Lionel B. Budden*, with sculpture by *H. Tyson Smith*, and is more conventional than the same pair's Liverpool Cenotaph (*see* Major Buildings, p. 59).

Further Reading

Among **general accounts** of Liverpool buildings, the classic work is J.A. Picton's two-volume *Memorials of Liverpool*, 1873 (revised eds 1875, 1903). The first volume covers political and economic history; the second is a street-by-street description, seen with an architect's eye. Also by Picton is *The Architectural History of Liverpool: a series of papers read before the Liverpool Architectural and Archaeological Society*, 1858. Thirteen articles by T. Mellard Reade, published as 'The Architecture of Liverpool' in the Liverpool journal *The Porcupine*, December 1865–March 1866, are bracingly forthright in their criticisms. C.H. Reilly, *Some Liverpool Streets and Buildings in 1921*, 1921, is entertaining and perceptive about buildings of all periods. The key C20 book is Quentin Hughes, *Seaport*, 1964. The outstanding black and white photographs in the original edition are marvellously evocative of the C19 port's rugged splendour, and in many cases form a poignant record of a now vanished scene. The same author's *Liverpool*, 1969, is strong on buildings of the 1950s and 60s; his *Liverpool: City of Architecture*, 1999, continues the story to the end of the C20. Also useful is *Buildings of Liverpool*, a guide issued by the Liverpool Heritage Bureau, 1978.

For the early C20, J. Sharples, A. Powers and M. Shippobottom, *Charles Reilly and the Liverpool School of Architecture 1904–1933*, 1996, looks at an important phase in the city's development, and has brief biographies of some leading architects. Postwar reconstruction is documented in *Liverpool Builds 1945–65*, issued by the city's Public Relations Office, 1967, and in the visionary *Liverpool City Centre Plan*, 1965, produced under the direction of W. Bor and G. Shankland. Lionel Esher, *A Broken Wave*, 1981, has an excellent chapter on Liverpool, reassessing the postwar era with the benefit of hindsight.

Among **major buildings**, there is no up-to-date scholarly account of the Town Hall, but for the furniture which is integral to its interior there is J. Dean, 'The Regency Furniture in Liverpool Town Hall', *Furniture History* 25, 1989. For St George's Hall, see the two very detailed and superbly illustrated articles by J. Olley in *Architect's Journal* 183, 18 and 25 June 1986; the *Victorian Society Annual*, 1992; and F. Salmon, *Building on Ruins: the rediscovery of Rome and English architecture*, 2000. For the Anglican Cathedral, the fullest account is V.E. Cotton, *The Book of Liverpool Cathedral*, 1964. J. Thomas,

'Building a Cathedral', in *RIBA Journal*, May 1983, focuses on the period after Scott's death, and P. Kennerley, *The Building of Liverpool Cathedral*, 2nd edn 2001, brings the story up to date. A full account of the Pier Head is given by P. de Figueiredo in 'Symbols of Empire: the buildings of the Liverpool waterfront', *Architectural History* 46, 2003. Lutyens's design for the Metropolitan Cathedral is analysed in an essay by John Summerson, reprinted in his *The Unromantic Castle*, 1990; Frederick Gibberd, *Metropolitan Cathedral of Christ the King, Liverpool*, 1968, is the essential account of the 1960s building, written by its architect.

The starting place for **dock architecture and engineering** is N. Ritchie-Noakes's indispensable *Liverpool's Historic Waterfront: the world's first mercantile dock system*, 1984. This, however, is limited to the docks s from the Pier Head. *Liverpool Central Docks 1799–1905*, by A. Jarvis, 1991, is an enlightening account of the docks N from Princes to Bramley-Moore Dock. Very little has been written about the most northerly docks. A. Jarvis and K. Smith (eds), *Albert Dock: trade and technology*, 1999, puts Hartley's masterpiece in context. For a fascinating elucidation of the whys and hows of dock design and construction see A. Jarvis, *The Liverpool Dock Engineers*, 1996. S. Mountfield, *Western Gateway*, 1964, is a thorough history of the Dock Board. F.E. Hyde, *Liverpool and the Mersey*, 1971, is the standard economic history of the port.

On **churches**, D. Lewis, *The Churches of Liverpool*, 2001, is valuable for illustrations, though the text is not always accurate. For **housing**, C.W. Chalklin, *The Provincial Towns of Georgian England*, 1974, has useful coverage of Liverpool. J. Longmore's unpublished Ph.D. thesis for the University of Reading, 'The Development of the Liverpool Corporation Estate 1760–1835', 1982, is extremely interesting. P. Mathias's unpublished M.A. thesis for the University of Liverpool, 'The Liverpool Corporate Estate: a study of the development of housing in the Moss Lake Fields of Liverpool 1800–1875', 1957, describes the eastward residential expansion of the town, while A. Allan, *The Building of Abercromby Square*, 1984, concentrates on one of the most prestigious early C19 developments in this area. I. C. Taylor, 'The Court and Cellar Dwelling: the Eighteenth Century Origin of the Liverpool Slum', in *Transactions of the Historic Society of Lancashire and Cheshire* 122, 1971, examines housing at the opposite end of the social spectrum. Alan McDonald, *The Weller Way: the story of the Weller Streets Housing Co-operative*, 1986, gives an insight into the first of Liverpool's new-build housing co-operatives. For **Warehouses** see C. Giles and R. Hawkins, *Storehouses of Empire: Liverpool's historic warehouses,* 2004. **Monuments** and **public sculpture** are dealt with in a comprehensive guide by T. Cavanagh, *Public Sculpture of Liverpool (Public Monuments and Sculpture Association)*, 1997, and a collection of essays edited by P. Curtis, *Patronage & Practice: sculpture on Merseyside*, 1989.

Among older **histories** there is Ramsay Muir, *A History of Liverpool*, 1907. J. Touzeau, *The Rise and Progress of Liverpool from 1551–1835*, 1910, contains interesting information relating to buildings, culled from municipal records. Other useful studies are G.H. Pumphrey, *The Story of Liverpool's Public Services*, 1940, with sections on transport, housing, water supply, etc., and B.D. White, *A History of the Corporation of Liverpool 1835–1914*, 1951. More recent publications include P. Aughton, *Liverpool: a people's history*, 2nd edn 2003, and Tony Lane, *Liverpool: city of the sea*, 1997, the latter a readable account focusing on the late C19 and C20 from a sociological viewpoint. Many articles on Liverpool have appeared in the annual *Transactions of the Historic Society of Lancashire and Cheshire*, a special volume of which in 2002 was devoted to a comprehensive Index. A huge amount of detailed information is contained in the 'Annals of Liverpool', a cumulative, chronological list of key events published annually in Gore's street directories from 1813 until 1940, and reissued as *An Illustrated Everyday History of Liverpool and Merseyside*, 1996, with an introduction by Fritz Spiegl.

Detailed **maps** begin with J. Chadwick's of 1725; other important C18 surveys are those by J. Eyes, 1765, and G. Perry, 1769. Three large-scale maps from the first half of the C19 show the ground plans of individual buildings, and are specially useful: R. Horwood's of 1803, M.A. Gage's of 1836, and the 5ft:1m Ordnance Survey begun in 1847. J. Bennison's map of 1835 covers the rural outskirts as well as the urban centre. For the development of the town before the publication of Chadwick's map, see Archaeological Survey of Merseyside, *The Changing Face of Liverpool 1207–1727*, 1981.

Among **unpublished sources**, two collections of **architects' papers** are of outstanding importance. Those of Edmund Kirby & Sons in the Liverpool Record Office not only document the activities of that prolific Liverpool firm from the 1860s to the 1960s, but occasionally shed light on the work of earlier architects; the Culshaw & Sumners papers in the Lancashire Record Office await cataloguing, but are potentially as rich for the 1840s–70s. The diaries of Thomas Rickman in the British Architectural Library provide a first-hand account of building activity in the second decade of the C19. Frustratingly, only very limited information about the City's historic architecture is to be had from **council records** relating to building control: no plans and almost no registers of plans appear to survive from before the early C20.

A fuller bibliography of general works, including much on individual architects and artists, can be found at the Reference section of the *Pevsner Architectural Guides'* website: *www.lookingatbuildings.org.uk.*

Glossary

Acanthus: *see* [2D].

Aedicule: architectural surround, usually a pediment on two columns or pilasters.

Ambulatory: aisle around the *sanctuary* of a church.

Anthemion: *see* [2D].

Apse: semicircular or polygonal end, especially in a church.

Arcade: series of arches supported by piers or columns (cf. *colonnade*).

Art Deco: a self-consciously up-to-date interwar style of bold simplified patterns, often derived from non-European art.

Ashlar: large rectangular masonry blocks wrought to even faces.

Atlantes: male figures supporting an *entablature.*

Atrium: a toplit covered court rising through several storeys.

Attic: small top storey within a roof. Also the storey above the main entablature of a classical façade.

Baldacchino: solid canopy, usually free-standing and over an altar.

Barrel vault: one with a simple arched profile.

Batter: intentional inward inclination of a wall face.

Beaux-Arts: a French-derived approach to classical design, at its peak in the later C19–early C20, marked by strong axial planning and the grandiose use of the *orders.*

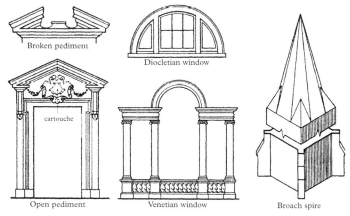

Broken pediment

Diocletian window

cartouche

Open pediment

Venetian window

Broach spire

1. Miscellaneous

2. Classical orders and enrichments

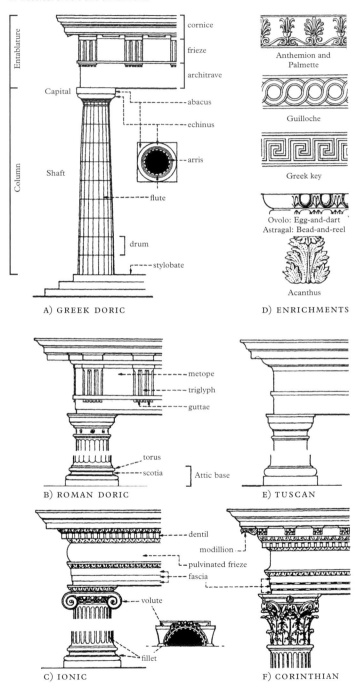

Entablature
- cornice
- frieze
- architrave

Column
- Capital
  - abacus
  - echinus
  - arris
- Shaft
  - flute
  - drum
  - stylobate

A) GREEK DORIC

D) ENRICHMENTS

Anthemion and Palmette

Guilloche

Greek key

Ovolo: Egg-and-dart
Astragal: Bead-and-reel

Acanthus

B) ROMAN DORIC
- metope
- triglyph
- guttae
- torus
- scotia] Attic base

E) TUSCAN

C) IONIC
- dentil
- volute
- fillet

F) CORINTHIAN
- modillion
- pulvinated frieze
- fascia

Broach spire: *see* [1].

Brutalist: used for later 1950s–70s Modernist architecture displaying rough or unfinished concrete, large massive forms, and abrupt juxtapositions.

Capital: head feature of a column or pilaster; for classical types *see* [2].

Cartouche: *see* [1].

Castellated: with battlements.

Chancel: the E part or end of a church, where the altar is placed.

Chapter house: place of assembly for the members of a monastery or cathedral.

Choir: the part of a great church where services are sung.

Clerestory: uppermost storey of an interior, pierced by windows.

Coade stone: ceramic artificial stone, made 1769–*c.* 1840 by Eleanor Coade and associates.

Coffering: decorative arrangement of sunken panels.

Colonnade: range of columns supporting a flat *lintel* or *entablature* (cf. *arcade*).

Corbel: projecting block supporting something above.

Composite: classical order with capitals combining Corinthian features (acanthus, *see* [2D]) with Ionic (volutes, *see* [2C]).

Corinthian; cornice: *see* [2A; 2F].

Cove: a broad concave moulding.

Crenellated: with battlements.

Cupola: a small dome used as a crowning feature.

Cyclopean: of masonry, with large irregular stones, smooth and finely jointed.

Dado: finishing of the lower part of an internal wall.

Decorated (Dec): English Gothic architecture, late C13 to late C14.

Diocletian window: *see* [1].

Doric: *see* [2A, 2B].

Drum: circular or polygonal stage supporting a dome.

Dutch or Flemish gable: *see* [3].

Early English (E.E.): English Gothic architecture, late C12 to late C13.

Embattled: with battlements.

Entablature: *see* [2A].

Faience: moulded *terracotta* that is glazed white or coloured.

Flying buttress: one transmitting thrust by means of an arch or half-arch.

Frieze: middle member of a classical *entablature*, *see* [2A, 2C]. Also a horizontal band of ornament.

Geometrical: of *tracery*, a mid-C13–C14 type formed of circles and part-circles.

Giant order: a classical *order* that is two or more storeys high.

Gothic: the style of the later Middle Ages, characterized by the pointed arch and *rib-vault* (*see* [5]).

Groin vault: one composed of intersecting *barrel vaults*.

Guilloche: *see* [2D].

Half-timbering: non-structural decorative timberwork.

Herm: head or bust on a pedestal.

Hipped roof: *see* [3].

Hoodmould: projecting moulding above an arch or *lintel* to throw off water.

Hyperbolic paraboloid: of a roof, built to a double-curved profile suitable for thin shell construction.

In antis: of columns, set in an opening (properly between simplified pilasters called *antae*).

Ionic: *see* [2C].

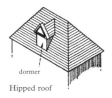

dormer

Hipped roof
Mansard roof
Flemish or Dutch gable

3. Roofs and gables

Italianate: a classical style derived from the palaces of Renaissance Italy.

Jack arches: shallow segmental vaults springing from iron or steel beams.

Jamb: one of the vertical sides of an opening.

Jettied: with a projecting upper storey, usually timber-framed.

Kingpost roof: one with vertical timbers set centrally on the tie-beams, supporting the ridge.

Lancet: slender, single-light pointed-arched window.

Lantern: a windowed turret crowning a roof, tower or dome.

Light: compartment of a window.

Lintel: horizontal beam or stone bridging an opening.

Loggia: open gallery with arches or columns.

Louvre: opening in a roof or wall to allow air to escape.

Lunette: semicircular window or panel.

Machicolation: openings between *corbels* that support a projecting parapet.

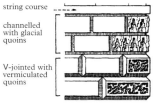

string course

channelled with glacial quoins

V-jointed with vermiculated quoins

4. Rustication

Mannerist: of classical architecture, with motifs used in deliberate disregard of original conventions or contexts.

Mansard roof: *see* [3].

Mezzanine: low storey between two higher ones.

Moulding: shaped ornamental strip of continuous section.

Mullion: vertical member between window lights.

Narthex: enclosed vestibule or porch at the main entrance to a church.

Newel: central or corner post of a staircase.

Norman: the C11–C12 English version of the *Romanesque* style.

Oculus: circular opening.

Ogee: of an arch, dome, etc., with double-curved pointed profile.

Orders (classical): for types *see* [2].

Oriel: window projecting above ground level.

Palladian: following the examples and classical principles of Andrea Palladio (1508–80).

Parapet: wall for protection of a sudden drop, e.g. on a bridge, or to conceal a roof.

Pargeting: exterior plaster decoration, either moulded in relief or incised.

Pavilion: ornamental building for occasional use; or a projecting subdivision of a larger building (hence *pavilion roof*).

Pediment: a formalized gable, derived from that of a classical temple; also used over doors, windows, etc. For types *see* [1].

Pendentive: part-hemispherical surface between arches that meet at an angle to support a drum, dome or vault.

Penthouse: a separately roofed structure on top of a multi-storey block of the C20 or later.

Perpendicular (Perp): English Gothic architecture from the late C14 to early C16.

Piano nobile (Italian): principal floor of a classical building, above a ground floor or basement and with a lesser storey overhead.

Pier: a large masonry or brick support, often for an arch.

Pilaster: flat representation of a classical column in shallow relief.

Piscina: basin in a church or chapel for washing mass vessels, usually wall-set.

Porte cochère (French): porch large enough to admit wheeled vehicles.

Portico: porch with roof and (frequently) *pediment* supported by a row of columns.

Portland stone: a hard, durable white limestone from the Isle of Portland in Dorset.

Presbytery: a priest's residence.

Prostyle: of a *portico*, with free-standing columns.

Pulvinated: of bulging profile; *see* [2c].

Quadripartite vault: *see* [5].

Quatrefoil: opening with four lobes or foils.

Queen Anne: the later Victorian revival of the mid-C17 domestic classical manner, usually in red brick or terracotta.

Quoins: dressed or otherwise emphasized stones at the angles of a building.

Rainwater head: container at a parapet into which rainwater runs from the gutters.

Render: a uniform covering for walls for protection from the weather, usually of cement or *stucco*.

Reredos: painted and/or sculpted screen behind and above an altar.

Rib-vault: *see* [5].

Rock-faced: masonry cleft to produce a natural, rugged appearance.

Romanesque: round-arched style of the C11 and C12.

Rood: crucifix flanked by the Virgin and St John, carved or painted.

Rostral column: triumphal column decorated with ships' prows.

Rubble: of masonry, with stones wholly or partly rough and unsquared.

Rustication: exaggerated treatment of masonry to give the effect of strength. For types *see* [4].

Sacristy: room in a church used for sacred vessels and vestments.

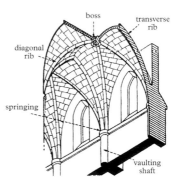

5. Rib-vault (quadripartite)

Saddleback roof: a pitched roof used on a tower.

Sanctuary: in a church, the area around the main altar.

Scagliola: composition imitating polished marble.

Sedilia: seats for the priests in the chancel wall of a church or chapel.

Sexfoil: a six-lobed opening.

Sgraffito (Italian): decoration scratched to reveal a pattern in another colour beneath.

Space frame: a three-dimensional framework in which all members are interconnected, designed to cover large areas.

Spandrel: space between an arch and its framing rectangle, or between adjacent arches.

Stack: used to identify an individual warehouse within a group.

Stanchion: upright structural member, of iron, steel or reinforced concrete.

Stele: an ancient Greek tomb marker like a headstone.

Stiff-leaf: carved decoration in the form of thick uncurling foliage; originally late C12–early C13.

Stoup: vessel for holy water.

Stucco: durable lime plaster, shaped into ornamental features or used externally as a protective coating.

System building: system of manufactured units assembled on site.

Terracotta: moulded and fired clay ornament or cladding (cf. *faience*).

Tie-beam: main horizontal transverse timber in a roof structure.

Tracery: openwork pattern of masonry or timber in the upper part of an opening.

Transept: transverse portion of a church.

Transom: horizontal member between window lights.

Travertine: a yellowish, open-textured Italian limestone.

Trefoil: with three lobes or foils.

Triforium: middle storey of a church interior treated as an arcaded wall passage or blind arcade.

Truss: braced framework, spanning between supports.

Tunnel vault: one with a simple elongated-arched profile.

Tuscan: *see* [2E].

Tympanum: the area enclosed by an arch or pediment.

Undercroft: room(s), usually vaulted, beneath the main space of a building.

Venetian window: *see* [1].

Volutes: spiral scrolls, especially on Ionic columns (*see* [2C]).

Weathering: inclined, projecting surface to keep water away from the wall below.

Index
of Architects, Artists, Patrons and Other Persons and Organisations Mentioned

The names of architects and craftsmen working in or near Liverpool are given in *italics*. Relevant illustrations are denoted by page numbers in *italics*.

Index

of Localities, Streets and Buildings

Illustrations are denoted by page numbers in *italics*. Principal descriptions are shown in **bold**.

Illustration Acknowledgements

Every effort has been made to contact or trace all copyright holders. The publishers will be glad to make good any errors or omissions brought to our attention in future editions. We are grateful to the following for permission to reproduce illustrative material:

Architectural Review: 83
Austin-Smith:Lord (Nick Kane): 139
Brock Carmichael Associates: 66
The Builder: 32
Edward Carter Preston Archive: 49
Martin Charles: 34, 35, 36, 64
Elsevier Press (Architectural Press): 54
English Heritage (NMR): 1, 2, 8, 11, 15, 16, 17, 18, 19, 20, 21, 23, 27, 30, 31, 37, 38, 39, 40, 41, 44, 45, 46, 47, 50, 51, 52, 55, 56, 67, 68, 72, 73, 74, 76, 78, 81, 85, 86, 87, 88, 89, 90, 91, 92, 93, 94, 97, 98, 99, 101, 102, 105, 106, 108, 109, 110, 111, 112, 113, 114, 117, 119, 120, 121, 122, 123, 124, 125, 127, 129, 130, 132, 133, 135, 137, 140, 141, 142, 143, 144, 145, 147, 149, 151, 152, 153, 154, 158, 159, 160, 161, 163, 164, 165, 168, 169, 170, 171, 172, 173, 174, 175, 176, 177, 178, 179, 181
Alan Fagan: 48
Illustrated London News: 180
Lancashire Record Office: 131
Ian Lawson: 26
Liverpool City Council: 9, 14, 61, 84, 155
Liverpool City Council/Liverpool City Centre Planning Group: 25
Liverpool Record Office: 5, 6, 12, 28, 29, 58, 60, 104, 107, 118, 131, 134, 138, 146, 167
National Museums Liverpool: 62
National Museums Liverpool (Merseyside Maritime Museum): 24, 70, 75, 100
National Museums Liverpool (Walker Art Gallery): 33, 57
Richard Pollard: 10, 42, 69
RIBA: 13, 43 (Concrete and Constructional Engineering)
Joseph Sharples: 96
Touchmedia: 3, 63, 71, 77, 79, 103, 115, 126, 128, 136, 150, 156, 162, 166
University of Liverpool: 116
University of Liverpool (Quentin Hughes): 22, 53
John Vaughan: 148
VIEW (Nick Hufton): 157
Guy Woodland: 4
Ken Worrall: 59, 65

A special debt of gratitude is owed to English Heritage and its photographers: to Tony Perry, who took the majority of the photographs for this volume, and to James O. Davies, Michael Hesketh-Roberts, Bob Skingle and Peter Williams, whose work we have also drawn on in quantity.